THE CHRONICLES OF A JOURNEY
And the Stories along the Way

THE CHRONICLES OF A JOURNEY
And the Stories along the Way

A memoir
by
RAY A. VINCENT

Adelaide Books
New York/Lisbon
2018

THE CHRONICLES OF A JOURNEY
And the Stories Along the Way

A memoir

By Ray A. Vincent

Copyright © by Ray A. Vincent

Cover design © 2018 Adelaide Books

Published by Adelaide Books, New York / Lisbon
adelaidebooks.org

Editor-in-Chief
Stevan V. Nikolic

All rights reserved. No part of this book may be reproduced in any manner whatsoever without written permission from the author except in the case of brief quotations embodied in critical articles and reviews.

For any information, please address Adelaide Books
at info@adelaidebooks.org
or write to:
Adelaide Books
244 Fifth Ave. Suite D27
New York, NY, 10001

ISBN-10: 1-949180-06-9
ISBN-13: 978-1-949180-06-0

Printed in the United States of America

To the memory of Mariannne Rosa Denomme, my mother, who launched me on my journey; and to my grandchildren, Noah, Severn, and Sloane, who are just beginning theirs.

Foreword

This is a true story. The names in the story and the places mentioned are real. The events occurred as related; although at times, tinged by the vagaries of memory and the colours of emotion. Therefore, a caveat: The story unfolds not only as memory recalls, but is also contaminated with a certain amount of bias and prejudices which, my points of views and personal interpretations contributed to.

    I am responsible for any errors, misinterpretations and false conclusions. When my heart spoke and debated with my mind, I tended to side with my heart. My hope is that after my children, my grandchildren, and my sisters have read this book—they will have gotten to know me a little better.

Prologue

This is not a novel, although, at times, it may read like one. The events and characters are real. The interpretation of events is related through the vantage point of my feelings and my emotions—from my point of view.

I have tried to capture the salient moments still hanging on—however precariously, at my age—in the dusty corners of my mind. This is the story of a journey. The journey crosses a tapestry of personal landscapes and experience. And the journey begins with family.

Large families are fine unless you are born into one and your parents are poor, ill-educated, and French Canadian; that will shape not only who you become; how you see the world around you; but also, how you define your goals and manage relationships.

You have no idea what the word "struggle" means unless you are born poor and raised in a family of twelve. Let me tell you, you do not ask for "seconds" at the dinner table too often. And you sleep wherever, and on whatever is made available to you. Two bedroom apartments can be somewhat crowded.

However, you knew, in my family, that once you walked inside the house, you were taken in; welcomed, and covered in the warmth of love and personal attention that only good parents can have for you. That's all they had to give us. And there was a lot of it, and it was unbounded, unconditional and selfless. And I came to realize later in life that, that was enough. As a matter of fact, being loved was the only thing that really mattered. Everything else, I have learned, is ephemeral, transient and illusory.

DAWN

Mud Lake

CHAPTER 1

A place called Mud Lake

I was born in Mud Lake. A place in the northwestern Quebec wilderness. When I pronounce the name today it still gives me a warm feeling. You will not find the name of Mud Lake on any Quebec map because it was the name the squatters on the south side of the lake gave it. The name became accepted, and folks in the county knew where you lived when you said, "Mud Lake". The mining company that owned the mining rights to the entire area within and without the lake, left well enough alone. "Mud Lake" became generally accepted. If the superintendent of McIntyre Gold Mines accepted the existence of Mud Lake, then, also did his general manager. McIntyre needed somewhere for its workforce to live and a place by any name would do. The mine was situated a short distance from the south shore of the lake.

The Quebec map; however, will show you where the town of Belleterre is. Belleterre exists now fully developed, adjacent two miles from Mud Lake. You locate Belleterre on the map; look a little bit northeast, and there you will see a nondescript little lake by the name of Lac Guillet—that, for all of us who lived there at one time—is Mud Lake—now enshrined with a modern new name. In the days of the early Mud Lake settlement, Belleterre only existed on provincial, municipal ministry planning papers. But, more about Belleterre and the effects of its intersection with my life, at a later time.

A year, or so, before the mine came into full production in 1940, Mud Lake had fifty to sixty families crowded on the rough and rugged shoreline, along with a few natives from Winneway and Long Point, who lived off-reserve. A one street settlement, a quarter mile long, made up of clapboard houses and log cabins.

I was born in one of the latter.

Mud Lake had no provincially recognized municipal organization; no town council; no mayor or reeve and, most significantly, no police force. Being situated a half mile from the mine and supplying a significant amount of its workforce, it became, by natural law, the adopted child of McIntyre's, and that strange symbiosis secured to the settlement the mine's supervision and responsibility.

The company cleared the settlement's one street in the winter with a heavy bulldozer, and it also cleared the main roadway leading to the settlement, towards the lake. In the summer, that same bulldozer pushed aside the brush and trees wanting to reclaim the roadway.

The company provided a building for a grade one-to-five schoolhouse, and it paid the salary of the school teacher. The mine also operated a water pump-house at the east end of the lake to supply water via a wooden pipeline; this provided the much-needed water for its mining and milling operation.

However, no running water was made available to the squatters. The lake and makeshift wells supplied household needs. Needless to say, chamber pots and outside privies looked after mother-nature. You disposed your household garbage on top of a pile behind the privy.

Those piles behind privies became veritable treasure chests of antique bottles and a miscellany of other old stuff, to my daughter Christine and her cousin Anne, when they went treasure hunting at Mud Lake in 1989; at that time they were in their early twenties. The settlement had disappeared; overtaken by trees and shrubbery—but I had told them—if you can find the semblance of a house foundation, look around for what looks like an earth mound—that would be that house's rubbish pile. They spent a whole afternoon of digging and scavenging. They came back to our fishing camp on Lac Simard later that day, dirty, laughing and giggling and, loaded with priceless memorabilia. I still have a lot of that stuff in boxes in my house.

The settlement as described was located on what folks called "lower" Mud Lake. About a hundred yards or so south of the street, a gentle rise occurred which turned into a steep hill, atop of which "upper" Mud Lake was to slowly take root. Most families with ambition and intentions to upward mobility aspired to one day being able to move "up the hill". Ours was one of them.

I am Born

I was told it was pouring rain that early morning hour of 3:25 a.m. when I was delivered. It was an unusual early February thaw that welcomed my arrival on February 5, 1946. Water was dripping in from different places in the ceiling of the four-room log cabin. My mom would relate later, how my aunts would be running around; from room to room; coal-oil lamps in hand, placing pails, and pots and pans all over the floors.

That is the welcome I received; it literally did rain on my parade.

My mother was a practical person; she had not one superstitious bone in her body. She did not for one moment take the weather conditions outside and the mess inside the cabin, as a nefarious harbinger of things which would attend to me later in life. She was happy that her eighth child and fifth boy, was kicking, screaming and healthy. And she loved me then and she would love me throughout my life; even on some of those dark days when even I, would not really love myself.

The mortality rates in those days and the environment we were born in, provided for very precarious birth outcomes. Therefore, I was baptized within forty-eight hours, my uncle Joe Vincent and my aunt Ida were my godparents; however, since they lived in Montreal, my uncle Alfred Denomme and my aunt Severia stood as proxy for them.

Ray A. Vincent

My Mother

Up to and including the day she died, I never heard my mother complain about any misfortune; disadvantages; or personal discomforts which have come her way. My sisters and brothers would support the veracity of that statement. My mother was courageous, compassionate and selfless. She is the greatest person I have ever known. My mother and sisters are probably the reasons I have always loved and had positive relationships with women throughout my life. I have never known a woman I did not like. In my mind; next to god, women are most important—first, they give life and, next, they make it worthwhile living it.

My mother, nee Marianne Rosa Denomme, was the only girl born amongst nine brothers. A lot of household work devolved to her, and my mom used to tell us that she had no time to worry and fret while growing up; she was simply too darn busy. What an apprenticeship that must have been, prior to moving on to marriage and motherhood—which she did at the tender age of sixteen.

My dad was twenty-three when the marriage occurred. We used to tell my dad later on, that he had robbed from the cradle. However, my mom was quick to defend him; she would rush to save him any embarrassment and emphatically assert that, "they were very much in love" and, that yes; he was a good dancer, and yes; he did indeed save her from the hard work demands of being in a family with nine brothers, but they had married for love.

My mother certainly debunked the theory prevalent in my first-year university biology course; that one could not get pregnant while breastfeeding an infant; that a lactating mother produced reproduction suppressing hormones which would inhibit ovulation—but my mother did just that—get pregnant—and often—while still suckling babies.

My mother was a good-looking woman: strong body frame, five feet six inches tall; ample hips and chest; long auburn to dark brown hair; with piercing dark brown eyes, and a disarming smile—little wonder our father raided the cradle.

Throughout her life, our mother made enormous sacrifices for her family; unfortunately, like most growing young adults, I realized this much too late. I had to become a parent myself before I fully realized what my parents went through for us. I should have told them how much I loved them, much more often than I did. I regret it; this thought saddens me to this day. It is too late now.

I was the second child born in the cabin; my sister Carmen, the third girl, had been born in what had been at the time, a brand new abode, two years and a half before me. I was the last born of my family in "lower" Mud Lake; my two younger sisters, Monique and Louise born in 1947 and 1949 respectively, had the pleasure of being born in an aseptic hospital room; which hospital was owned and staffed by the McIntyre Gold Mine and located at the mine site itself. The hospital was new and just recently opened. When my baby sisters came home from the hospital, they were received in the new house my father had built in "upper" Mud Lake.

Moving Up in the World

My father worked at the mine, but he had good carpentry skills; therefore, he and my uncle Alfred and some friends, got the necessary lumber and materials together and built the two-storey wood frame and brick paper clad house within eighteen months after my birth.

There were no legal documents as to title and ownership; no legally crafted demarcation lines as to lot enclosures and measured boundaries. No taxes. They cleared the ground, moved the materials up the hill and built. A well was sunk on lower ground; an outhouse was constructed; an area cleared for a large garden; and a pretty fenced area constructed for my mom's lovely flowers to grow in, at which location she would take many black and white Kodak pictures, of playing and laughing children, heads peeking through the flower beds—that was it—we had our house. We had left the post-war DP's (displaced persons) behind, on the lake shore. We had moved up in the world. Needless to say, other families followed us up the hill shortly after.

Don't misunderstand and misjudge me when I used the "DP" abbreviation; it was the word grownups used then to denote world-war two refugees, coming to settle those parts of Canada that were in great need of labourers. As a matter of fact, the word "Displaced Person" was an official nomenclature of the United Nations at that time. Some of my fondest childhood memories are those of the happy play times I had with my friends from Ukrainian, Croatian and Italian backgrounds. And here is the amazing thing: the Oleksiuk, the Oreskovich and the Carlusso kids of my age, all spoke the same French that I did when at play together; except that, once in contact with their parents they reverted back to their native tongue.

I and my older brothers kept in touch with many of them well into adulthood, and at locations all over the country. But more on that at a later time.

The New House

The new house was two-storied. My mother and father had their own bedroom on the main floor; ten children were accommodated in three bedrooms on the upper floor; three older girls in one room; me and two baby sisters in another room, and my four older brothers, in another.

I loved the new house. We had moved up the hill in early September. I have fond memories of my first spring in the fresh pine wood-scented house. I must have been three or four years old and the wonders of those early morning sights and sounds are indelibly etched in my memory. The memories of me lying on my back in bed, before anyone else would be stirring about, and staring at the ceiling and walls, are filled with wondrous imaginings. They are memories of peace, colours and enchanting sounds.

I would lie in bed and watch the slow rise of the sun's rays breaking through the openings in the curtains, and imprint all kinds of different shapes on the sloping roof, which made up the west interior wall facing me; and the light coming through the finely webbed muslin of the curtain would superimpose its own personal patterns, here and there. And add to this visual display, the early spring morning serenades of numerous songbirds and my morning risings into a wonder world was complete. Indeed, I was transported to some "Never Land" on those early sunny spring mornings; and the sprinkle of magic dust was all around me.

I have always attributed the fact that I became a happy, "morning person" to those early Mud Lake mornings.

My mother and sister Rose would be first up in the early morning hours. I would hear them rustling about in the kitchen downstairs, getting lunches and breakfast ready for my father, and my three older brothers; Louis, Pete, and Ivan. I would creep downstairs and join them. They would lay an extra plate for me and I would proudly join them around the table. My three brothers were old enough to work at the mine and they would walk the pipeline trail with my father, to work and back every day. I am glad that I took every opportunity to be around them; because it would not be long, before my older brothers would leave home to go work all over the country and the United States, for different mining contractors.

My Father

My father was well over six feet tall, square-shouldered and strong. He was light to fair skinned and he had very light brown hair, which, when seen in the sunlight would show tints of red. The grey-green specks in his hazel eyes would give his whole face a gentle, soft, and approachable appearance.

My father was a quiet man—so much so that he gave the impression of being shy. My father rarely initiated a conversation; he rarely spoke unless spoken to first. He was a very gentle man. My father's comments were considered, measured, slow and deliberate. I can count on the fingers of one hand, the occasions that I have seen him angry and lose his composure—and half of those occasions occurred when the Montreal Canadiens lost a hockey game.

My mother was the disciplinarian in the family, and because our dad was so quiet and gentle, when he did raise his voice about some of our misbehaviours, we would freeze and come to sudden attention.

We had become habituated to mom's tantrums; so our dad's intercessions were that much more effective—when my dad came into the picture you knew you were in some kind of serious trouble.

We learned early that you could not play one of our parents against the other. We were sure our parents had made a pact after the birth of their first child—in front of their children; they were to be united—an indivisible wall. My wife and I would adopt the same attitude when raising our children.

My father worked at the mine, but he was not an underground miner and that proved a very fortunate development for him and his family. My father died at the age of eighty-three and he outlived all my brothers by a large span. All of my brothers became underground miners and all died of lung diseases of one type or another. The youngest to die from work-related causes was my brother Ivan, who died at the age of forty-nine, from lung cancer.

Our father initially worked in the mill operations of the mine where through chemical and flotation processes gold would be separated from the ore. He transferred out of the mill when the sodium cyanide, and other chemicals they used, began to cause severe skin ulceration on his legs. By the end of the work day the legs of his pants, from the knees down, would be soaked with these poisons. He moved to the power and hydraulics plant and there, after a short apprenticeship, he became a Stationary Engineer 4th class; the lowest entry level grade—a fancy name given to a person whose job it was to watch dials and gauges, and, now and then make adjustments with levers and switches, whenever necessary. The job title gave the semblance of importance, but the hourly pay rate was not much more than what he had earned at the mill.

On pleasant summer days, my sister Carmen, who was all of nine years of age, would take me by the hand and we would walk up to the plant. I was four or five years old. I loved my dad's new job; he was usually alone and the place was so warm and dry and he seemed so important surrounded by all this sophisticated and strange equipment. That feeling was important to me—that my dad would seem important—not only had we stepped into another world but it was the world of my father. I was proud of him. He would let us open his lunch pail and after sharing some sandwiches we would bid him goodbye and make our way back home.

One day we met two bears on the trail when we were on our way to our dad's; a little one who climbed up a tree and a larger one who simply hung around not far away. We were so mesmerized by the small black spot in the tree that we paid little attention to the large one making snorting sounds and scratching and pawing the dirt. We did not say one word to each other and I don't believe we later told any of this to our parents. We turned around simultaneously, without one word spoken, with fear in our hearts and weakness in our legs. This was the end of our spontaneous visits to my dad's new job site.

Mom and Dad led by Example

Throughout the developmental periods of my life, my parents never limited or put restraints on my movements; they never questioned or said any discouraging comments about any of my goals and aspirations. Although my parents shied away from giving direct guidance, they certainly affected my moral outlook; and that outlook became critical in the kind of person I was later to become.

My parents guided by their examples and never by injunctions and decrees. They were not well educated—they never had the opportunity—but what they had, was more important than formal education: they were naturally intelligent and blessed with understanding, warmth, and compassion. As we grew up, we watched them. They let us explore, and if we stumbled—as we did on many occasions—they would lift us up, brush us off and push us on our way forward again. My parents had very little material stuff. They never owned a car in their entire life. After Mud Lake, they never owned a house ever again—there simply was no money—we were to become perennial renters. We got our first TV set in 1960, on monthly payments, when I was fourteen years old. But, the greatest gifts parents can ever give their children they gave to us every day:

love; a positive example; and most importantly—they gave us the freedom to breathe and wonder.

My friend Peter, and the Oleksiuks

He was my first friend. Peter Oleksiuk. He was about my height, but smaller framed and, my mother would say, of a sickly complexion—pale and sallow. He was one year older than me and for two years we were inseparable. His older siblings; Stanley, Olga, Johnny, and Annie were friends of my older siblings. Annie was twenty-two then, the age of my brother Louis; Olga was sixteen and beautiful; Johnny and Stanley about the same age as my brothers Pete and Ivan, twenty-one and nineteen respectively.

Peter's parents spoke very little French or English. They had left the Ukraine to escape the widespread famine and starvation brought about by the Stalinist regime in 1932-33. The forced seizure of their lands and livestock and the bullying of the Kulaks by the communists pushed a young farmer like Mr. Oleksiuk out of his homeland. The Oleksiuks; husband and wife to be, did not know each other prior to boarding the boat bound for Canada. They met aboard ship and were officially married by the vessel's captain. She came from the cosmopolitan city of Kiev and him from the golden wheat fields of the steppes. Unfortunately, the pretty city girl never would accommodate to the rigours of raising a family in the Quebec backwoods; and to the loneliness, and to the misery. Following her husband to Mud Lake would prove her undoing.

As I played with Peter I did not realize at that time that his dad was bedridden, slowly dying of cancer. Olga would talk about his last days; as he lay in bed writhing in terrible pain he would beseech his daughters to bring in the loaded 30-30 and lean it against the wall beside his bed. Of course, they would not acquiesce. The sisters kept those requests to themselves, and they hid the rifle lest one of the brothers broke down and felt duty bound to comply with their dad's wishes. After Peter's father died, Mrs. Oleksiuk could not cope and she deteriorated quickly.

The Oleksiuks lived down the hill by the lake shore. As five and six-year-olds we saw each other every day, either around his place or mine. We would take pot lids from my mom's kitchen and run around outside going through steering motions while making grunting noises of make-believe cars; and after receiving our favourite treat from my mom—a slice of homemade bread layered thick with pure lard and a generous amount of brown sugar, we would continue this imaginary car pantomime. We always played this game whenever we could get away with taking pot lids from my mom's or Peter's mom's kitchen, without being arrested at the door.

On the shoreline between the Oleksiuk's and the Hamelin's, a long wooden log dock jutted out onto the lake on which stood a twenty-foot diving platform. That diving board became the source of many panic attacks for me. I would watch with great anxiety, and with a rising wave of foreboding in my chest, as my brother Ivan, would climb the diving tower and dive through the water surface to disappear for what seemed to be an eternity. I was afraid that he was drowned, and that I would never see him again.

̰

A House of Ill Repute

The Hamelin's house was huge; two-storied, and with many rooms. It did not have a good reputation. Mothers tried pleadings and when that did not work, used threats to keep their sons away from Hamelin's. Mud Lake did not have a tavern or a hotel, but it had Hamelin's which happily filled the void. And my brothers later told me, when I was old enough not to be scandalized, that Hamelin's daughters were very friendly and of questionable virtue.

We had neither church nor chapel at Mud Lake; the Belleterre Catholic priest would travel the two-mile distance every second week, and minister to the souls of the faithful out of the grade school's one classroom. And from the stories I've heard, he would be seen on some occasions stopping by Hamelin's before heading back out to Belleterre—to cater to the lost sheep of his flock some said, or—to imbibe his soul others would suggest, or—to rejuvenate his body others would say. Those opinions were always lively subjects of debate in the settlement.

There were two houses out of bounds for young children: the Hamelin's and Mr. Rousseau's. Both were at opposite ends of the one street. One guarded the entrance and the other the exit; as if one didn't catch you, the other would.

Kids liked to go to the Hamelin's because there were children of our age there to play with, but we loved to go to Mr. Rousseau; the bachelor, because of the aura of magic and mystery we felt about him, and everything else about his house.

Mr. Rousseau lived right next to the pump-house and the mine had hired him to be the pump-house overseer and maintenance man. But Mr. Rousseau was much more than that to Peter and I; he was an entertainer, a conjurer, and a magician. We would only dare to enter his house if there were at least two or more of us. We would make our way to his kitchen where we would find him seated at his table, and there we would fall under his spell. The wondrous things he would do. No one else in the whole planet possessed such power, such magic.

He would take a deck of cards and with a brush of the hand, made cards disappear and reappear. He would pull coins from behind your ears, and after some quick and inaudible incantation, he would have you feel your shirt pockets to retrieve the same coins that had been magically pulled from your ears and deposited there. He would dice a potato into quarter inch squares, pop one at a time into his mouth; crunching, chewing and swallowing until he had eaten four pieces in this fashion, and then he would make regurgitating sounds and movements, and magically; one by one; out would pop four whole unblemished quarter inch potato squares.

But grownups did not like him. He had a debilitating speech problem. He spoke with a slur as if his tongue was glued to the bottom of his mouth. He was unmarried and he kept to himself. We were told to keep away from him as if from a person who carried a disease.

THE CHRONICLES OF A JOURNEY

I would learn later in life that if you display too much of your differences in public you must have the courage to meet and deal with the prejudices which they invite. And being different offers you an advantage in life; it allows you to come at the world from another angle. But Peter and I only saw what he was, nothing else: he was our magic man.

CHAPTER 2

Mr. Ayotte' store, Free Candy, and Rumours

We loved walking into Mr. Ayotte's grocery store after our visits with the magic man. Mr. Ayotte's store was located two houses away from Rousseau's, and right across from my uncle Alfred's, and we could count on some free candy from the jar on the counter. We felt special; no other kids got free candy.

And the store had a monopoly on the ice dispensing business. People had those metallic, ice boxes at home, with a compartment for holding a big block of ice, and these ice boxes would keep your perishable foods from spoiling. In the wintertime, huge blocks of ice would be cut out of the frozen lake, and he would then haul them up with the sleigh and horses, right up to his ice-house behind the store. We were not allowed to play in the ice-house as the door had to be constantly closed; it was a big log house with a sunken floor filled with layered blocks of ice reaching to the ceiling, and with each layer covered with massive amounts of insulating sawdust. You got to the ice blocks by digging through the sawdust, and applying big steel logging clamps to the blocks, and then you slid them out. And his system worked; he had ice for sale year round.

The store had huge metal signs on the outside, covering a good portion of the front of the building—the signs read, "Coca-Cola" and, "White Owl Cigars"—you could see them and read them as far away as Hamelin's. It was the greeting you got when you came in.

The first indication, I got, that all was not well for Mud Lake was at Mr. Ayotte's; folks would come in and talk about rumours circulating about; things they'd heard, coming out of Belleterre: plans were being made to phase out the settlement and relocate all the residents to the newly created town of Belleterre two miles away.

The town of Belleterre was a company town, but it had provincial support and direction. The town was properly planned; it had electricity, sidewalks, street lighting and it provided water and sewer services; a big new church, a grade one to eight, school; a big new hotel, and, believe it or not—it had, since the mine owners were Scots, a curling rink—of course with natural ice only, but a curling rink nonetheless.

However, for a lot of people, it was not happy news; it was not welcome news. It was unsettling news. There was the talk of organized resistance. Hard to imagine, but some folks were attached to Mud Lake. Uncertainties brought about anxiety and it started brewing slowly inside my small frame.

Hardship at the Oleksiuks, and a High-Grader to the Rescue

Rumours of the impending demise of Mud Lake notwithstanding, folks still carried on with their daily lives. But Peter's life took a dark turn that winter; his dad died in January. His sister Annie, the oldest at twenty-three, was leaving the family to join her husband-to-be in Pembroke; Johnny and Stanley, who brought in the only money in the house would soon move to go to work for mining-drilling contractors all over the country, so that left Peter alone at home with a teenaged sister; a mentally ill mother; and absolutely no source of income coming in. But Mr. Oreskovich saved the Oleksiuks from the pangs of hunger and the perils that a cold winter can bring.

Mr. Oreskovich and his wife saw to it that the Oleksiuks were supplied with an adequate supply of wood, and food to see them through the winter. Stan Oreskovich was a next-door neighbour, and he and his wife had had their share of hardships in their native Yugoslavia. Stan was the only person in Mud Lake who owned a chicken coop, and due to his handicap with the French language, he would pronounce the word "poule"—which in French means chicken—as "poupoule"—which, of course, we all thought very funny and "poupoule" became an attached and a very much used nickname, that everyone recognized as synonymous with Mr. Oreskovich. But Stan "poupoule" Oreskovich's chickens literally saved the Oleksiuks that winter.

Stan was a miner and my brothers said that he was suspected of high-grading: high-grading is the illegal practice of coming across a pure nugget of gold, and putting it in your lunch pail instead of the company ore bucket. The gold would be collected at home, and then sold on the black market at a propitious time. If Stan did high-grade, he was never caught; however, within a few years he had bought a new house in Belleterre, a brand new car, and later, sent his son Leonard to the best law school in Montreal so that he could be educated for the bar.

Our first Mining Fatality

An emotional shock wave went through the little community on February 8, 1950. At about 1:30 in the afternoon, three young men died in an underground mining accident. A "loose": a seismic event had occurred at the 2400 foot level and sent tons of rocks falling over them; killing them instantly. A tragedy of indescribable anguish and sorrow for the Labelle, the Bernard and the Matte families.

The Harmonium. And unhappy Developments

Spring brought with it, surprise and excitement; announcements of more bad news; and to my six-year-old mind—an unsettling and puzzling event involving my brother Louis.

My brother Ivan had bought a raffle ticket from some charity, and he came home one day from work with the happy news that he had won the first prize—a harmonium—and no one could play a note of music in the whole family. My mother was more puzzled than pleased, and the rest of us were simply bemused by this odd piece of furniture.

But we grew to like our harmonium. If you could not induce any music to come out, by running your fingers over the keyboard, after pressing the two-foot pedals which forced air through the reeds; you could always wind it up from a side crank mechanism; insert a selected music card, and beautiful sounds and melodies would be produced.

It sat there against the far wall of the sitting room, challenging any brave soul to experiment with it. Ivan would part the curtain which separated the kitchen from the sitting room and he would stand there in the dim light of the room, and spend a long time admiring his strange new possession. He would never touch it; he just stood there not knowing what to do next. It held him in a trance. My sisters and even my mother after a while had a great time with the cranked music as the harmonium came with a library of music cards.

And I heard many funny versions of the story of how the boys managed to haul that heavy music machine up the hill, and through the slippery springtime slush and snow.

My father came home after work one evening, and he brought the official news from the mine superintendent; all the workers had received the same information—the company would stop supporting the grade school effective September 1, 1952. The company was tightening the screws. It stood to gain favours from the provincial government if it acted the part of the heartless landlord. Closing the school would force families to relocate to Belleterre. Some families began the move to the new company town; but others, like ours, decided to resist and delay the inevitable.

Those who could would send their school-aged children to grade schools operating in the countryside, in farming communities where relatives lived; well away from Belleterre; and the adults would remain in Mud Lake and defy the authorities.

So in four months' time, my sisters Colette and Carmen would move away from the security of mother and family, and embark on an adventure which would take them to the farm of Uncle Adolphe Barrette and our aunt Marie-Rose, our dad's sister, in the village of Laverlochere twenty-five miles distant from Mud Lake. That was the plan waiting for execution. My sister Rose, and my three older brothers had stopped attending school some time ago; I was one year away from school admission age and Monique and Louise were too young.

The Provincial Police

One evening at the end of May, the provincial police were called in from Ville- Marie, a distance of forty-five miles. There had been a brawl at Hamelin's and knives had been drawn. No one was seriously injured. The police arrived in the early hours of the morning and my brother Louis was arrested, and taken into custody to Ville-Marie.

For the next few days, there was very little talk in our house. You moved about as in a funereal atmosphere. No one talked about much and certainly not about "the event". Louis was the last person in our family—and in all of Mud Lake for that matter—that one could imagine ever getting into trouble; let alone a fight. At age twenty-four he was the family's elder statesman and good-will ambassador.

One day went by and he did not show up and then two days went by and he still had not shown up; however, at noon of the third day he came in the house and started to pack his work clothes: he had a job with some diamond-drilling contractor, and he was leaving the same day. That was a sad day for my mother. From that day forward my mother began to change; she began to age. I learned much later that a mother is only as happy as her unhappiest child.

Some Native herbal Remedies

Peter and I were still playing together and exploring the world around us. One day in midsummer we were running between houses, and other grounds, some of which was covered with construction debris. I tripped and fell, and my open right hand struck a board on the ground through which a four-inch nail protruded. The nail went through the palm of my hand, and out through the back of it, so I could see the metal point. I had to place my two feet on the board to pry my hand free.

Within two days infection set in with pain shooting to my wrist and forearm. My mother consulted with some of the Long Point Algonquin people living off-reserve, down the hill, and she followed their advice: we went into the fields and collected plantain leaves and yarrow plants. She pounded the whole into a paste mixed with a small amount of lard, and this poultice she applied to both sides of my hand, which she covered with fresh plantain leaves; and bound the whole with clean cotton dressings. The infection subsided; the hand healed, and I was well on my way to playing outside again.

On another occasion in the fall, I had contracted a terrible flu. I was coughing, feverish, weak and confined to bed. My mom took the dried yarrow plants from the field; stalk, leaves and the flower heads gone to seed, and she pounded all that into a fine powder, which she stirred into hot water, adding some brown sugar. Needless to say this herbal decoction I drank without relish, but I must admit it did alleviate the symptoms.

More Oleksiuk Heartaches

But my friend Peter had much greater trouble facing him; events were fast developing that would change the course of his life forever. By late August, Mrs. Oleksiuk was in the throes of dementia. Peter would tell me how he walked in the house one day to find his mother covered in blood, from head to foot—she had taken all of her clothes off, and taking a fork she had punctured herself all over. She was becoming incomprehensible in speech and unaware of her surroundings. She could not be left alone; she could set fire to the house, and if she stepped outside she could drown accidentally.

Eventually, Olga had to contact the authorities. I saw what they sent to pick her up in. Peter and I had interrupted our card game and we had moved outside, watching. They did not send an ambulance—they sent a police car—as if she were a common criminal.

She followed the officers meekly, led by the hand like a child. She looked straight ahead of her; she never once looked at Peter.

When the car slowly pulled away, Peter began running after it, crying and screaming; bending down now and then, to pick up large stones which he would fling at the car through the rising dust.

Mrs. Oleksiuk would eventually be transferred to an asylum in Montreal, where she would spend the rest of her life.

Within a week of Mrs. Oleksiuk's removal to the hospital, Annie came to Mud Lake and took Peter away to live with her in Pembroke. Olga moved to Belleterre. Many years later Olga would tell me that the children did visit their mother at times at the hospital. She would never recognize any of them.

Colette and Carmen away from Home. And the loss of a Musical Instrument

The experiment of my sisters Colette and Carmen going to school in the country, and living on the farm with my uncle and aunt was not a success. It did not work out. The problem was Carmen.

Carmen was seven years old and Colette eleven. When my dad and mom accompanied the two girls to our uncle's place in September, Carmen was under the impression that they were going there for a happy weekend visit. She was in shock when she saw my parents leave to return home, leaving her behind; in her mind, she'd been abandoned.

My aunt told our mother later that for three whole weeks, Carmen would not speak. That she would hide and cry a lot. She followed her older sister, and did what her older sister did, but—she would not speak. In the classroom of the small country school, even though the teacher was her cousin Rose-Anna—still, she would not speak. Carmen told me years after when we were adults; that she was in shock, and traumatized from the abrupt parental separation—so much so, that the memory of those four months has been repressed to the point of remembering very little of that period in time. But Carmen did, eventually, although very slowly, come round.

THE CHRONICLES OF A JOURNEY

By the December Christmas school vacation break, the girls wanted home, and home wanted the girls. A difficult decision had been reached by our parents: we were moving. By this time most of the residents of the settlement had come to the same decision. This was a very difficult step for my father to take. He had built this house with his own hands, and within barely four years he was literally walking away from it. We did not hear him complain, but we knew he was hurting. Our mother told us to look on the positive side; we were going to electricity; inside plumbing; the telephone; central heating and—a curling rink.

I found out only later; when the boxes of clothes; the furniture; the steel-spring beds and the mattresses were being unloaded at the new place that something was missing: for the sake of space something had had to be sacrificed—our beloved harmonium had been left behind.

MORNING

Belleterre

CHAPTER 3

Belleterre: The big City and our First House

For the four youngest children in our family: that is, to those of us who had been born in Mud Lake, the move away from the hamlet of Mud Lake to the town of Belleterre, was like stepping out of the wilderness and into a whole new and brightly shining world.

We had moved out of a rough settlement of 350 people, to a modern town with a population in excess of 2,200 inhabitants. We were like kids stepping onto the main street at Disney World for the very first time, and gawking in awe at that lovely castle at the end of Main Street. And I quickly realized—and so did my siblings—that Belleterre was, indeed, what the name in French meant—a "Beautiful Land".

I and my four sisters stayed at our Uncle Fred's and aunt Severia's house on Second Avenue, while my sister Rose and my older brothers helped our parents unload, and unpack the household goods at our new place.

Well, it was not really a stand-alone house; it was a semi-detached dwelling, rented out to us by the McIntyre Mine Company. It was located on First Avenue; between a small credit union, used by the town folks and the miners for banking purposes, on our left; and a two-storied duplex, on the right. The exterior walls of the house were clad with white slate shingles, fashionable at the time.

Moving day was on a cold winter's day in mid-December. That first evening, the family had supper at Uncle Fred's, after which we all walked together to our new house. It was dark by then, but I enjoyed the four-minute walk and the novel experience of concrete sidewalks, and the street lighting reflecting on the fresh snow, and cars actually moving with some velocity on the well-maintained streets.

And there were so many cars that I could not keep count of them, even when I tried. We saw the rising smoke from the chimney. My dad and older brothers had made it a priority to warm up the house as soon as they had come in that afternoon.

The house had electricity for lighting purposes only, and that was it. Heat for the house was generated by a large wood stove in the kitchen, which also supplied heat for cooking and boiling water; and some heat also came from a big combination wood and coal burning cast iron furnace in the cellar-basement of the house. We seldom used coal because it was expensive; whereas wood was readily available and cheap. It did not take long for the younger children to move upstairs—not because we were sleepy—but because that was where the heat was—the doors had been kept open for long periods of time during the move, invading the whole place with cold. I learned first-hand the thermodynamic principle that heat rises when pressured by a cold mass.

There were only two rooms on the main floor: a very small sitting room to the right side of the front hallway entrance, and a fairly large kitchen area further down the hallway. In the hallway, and anchored to the wall; keeping guard and taking notice of everyone passing by; was our very first telephone set. It was an old-style instrument even for 1951 standards. You unhooked the black Bakelite earpiece tethered to the box by a two-foot cord and brought it to your ear; and you spoke in a black, adjustable wide-mouthed tube projecting out from the black lacquered box. It had a crank on the side wall of the box, to reach the operator, Mrs. Gaudet; you gave the crank two energetic turns; she answered and you placed your call. Ours was a party line shared with the tenant living in the other half of the semi-detached. You had to pay close attention and count the number of rings on incoming calls; three rings were ours, four rings the neighbour's. Many a time, either of the parties would accidentally eavesdrop on each other. A loud and irate voice at the other end quickly reminded you of your error.

Mrs. Gaudet, the operator, lived a few houses from us, and the switchboard was located in her home. The operator was on duty twenty four hours a day. I wondered often then, how she managed to work for so long without ever going to sleep.

The kitchen had a big wood burning "Belanger" stove, and oddly enough, the sink had a functional, manually operated water pump, even though it had a standard water faucet beside it—I guess if the piped water was interrupted you could revert to the well. Away from the stove, wedged in between the wood box and the wall, a tall icebox stood guard next to the back door.

A long and steep-angled stairway flanked to the left by a wall, led you upstairs. For some strange reason only known to the builder, the right side of the stairway, giving a full view of the kitchen as you walked upstairs, was left completely open—no bannister or railing—within two weeks I was to fall off from the top of those stairs, and strike the kitchen floor below because of that unprotected side, and knock myself unconscious in the bargain. I remember seeing blackness—if one can see blackness—and little stars and shiny crystals float before my eyes for a while.

Upon reaching the upper floor you faced the bathroom, and you saw the wonderful flush toilet staring at you, and beside it, a sink with a tap for cold running water. There was a bathtub, but hot water would have to be hauled up the stairs. The pleasure and convenience of hot running water would not be ours until the move to our second apartment. To the right of the bathroom was a long hallway, off of which two bedrooms branched to the left; one for my parents and one for the five girls; and, at the end of the same hallway, we found the other bedroom; fitted to accommodate four boys—the fifth; Louis, was working away from home. In the girls' room; Louise, the youngest, had to sleep at the foot of the bed while Carmen and Monique occupied the head. In the boys' room we slept two to a bed, and when Louis showed up—as he did on holidays—I migrated to the foot of the bed.

In the years to follow, we kept on moving to ever smaller apartments and because of that, I was not to have my own private bedroom with my own personal bed, until age sixteen.

Notwithstanding the crowded conditions, we were all so tired that everyone slept soundly that first night in Belleterre.

Ray A. Vincent

The First Morning—I put my Sisters in Jail

First thing in the morning, as our mom was busy preparing breakfast, my two younger sisters and I went reconnoitring about; I flicked the switch that turned on the one light bulb illuminating the entire cellar, and we went to the basement where the big furnace was located; and the wood in it was already crackling and spitting out heat.

We had come upon a most interesting place. We explored everything with trepidation and excitement. After a while, I came running upstairs, switched off the light, and closed the door behind me. Immediately, everybody in the kitchen could hear the blood-curdling screams coming from my sisters in the basement.

Since this had been a company town; the house had previously housed mine officials in charge of running and administering things; and, in the basement, in a poorly lit corner; an inviting doorway opened onto two jail cells. The town had had the need, now and then, of temporary holding cells in which to commit the drunks; the rowdies; and those prone to a variety of misbehaviours disturbing to the general peace of the good citizenry. The cells were now decommissioned, but they still had the iron bar cubicles with the iron-grilled doors, from which for reasons of safety and precautions, the locking mechanisms had been removed. And, after much coaxing, I had induced Monique and Louise to step inside one of the cells, and since the doors opened outwards, taking a heavy maple log meant for the furnace, I used it to block the door from opening; and had myself two terrified prisoners. My brothers thought the whole thing very funny; needless to say my sisters did not, and neither did my mother.

Summary Justice

Our mother was never the, "wait until I tell your father when he gets home," type. There was no backlog of cases in her courtroom. Hers was summary justice practiced in its most exquisite form. She heard from the complainant, and then she meted out a proportional and quick punishment—no hearings, no trial, no wasting of time on vapid explanations—and most times you got exactly what you deserved.

With a family of ten kids, order had to prevail—justice had to be seen to be done, and done in an expeditious manner. I got cuffed behind the head a couple of times and forbidden to leave the house for the rest of the day. The physical punishment did not bother me; however, not allowed to leave the house and play outside I viewed as cruel. But the punishment was highly effective. It was the last time I ever put my little sisters in jail, now knowing that the judge would not be on my side.

My mother was no pushover, and she was very clever. I remember many times when she would have the guilty party select his own instrument of punishment. One day when I deserved a punishment, she had me go outside and bring back a switch from a tree with which she designed to whip me—my mother knew: a) that I would pick the lightest and thinnest and, b) to further weaken the branch, that I would bend and twist it to create a notch that would ensure a break after the second or third stroke. We were both winners: she had made an example out of me, as my siblings looking on were terrified when they saw the branch break; so certain were they that the break came from the force of the blows—and I was pleased with myself, thinking that I had pulled a good one over her.

Belleterre and Friendships

Belleterre was built in a fairly rectangular shape. It was simple and attractive in its design. Four avenues of about the same length ran along the length of the rectangle in a west to east direction—the highway coming into town came from the west— and four streets of roughly the same length intersected the avenues at the rectangle's width in a north-south direction. There were narrow laneways in between each avenue, hugging each property lot line, but wide enough to allow the town truck to drive through and perform the weekly garbage pick-up—no more trash pile behind the houses. When I lived there we had no paved roads. The highway coming in was not paved and neither was the town.

Sand Lake stood about a quarter mile south of First Avenue; such a short walking distance from the town that most sunny summer days were spent there, playing at the lake with friends. It had clean, light brown-sugared sandy beaches all along its northern shoreline, and tall, lofty pine trees under which we gathered and threw our towels in their shade. It had swimwear changing-cubicles, and a town-provided lifeguard; swings; metal slides; picnic tables spread out, with some in the shade and some in the sun. I learned to swim there, and played in the bush trails, and climbed trees and mountains, and I picked blueberries there; I learned much about nature in the process, and I got to appreciate the benefits that peace and quiet have on the mind, and the love of a soft wind whispering through the pines. I grew and consolidated many friendships in the woods and the trails about Sand Lake.

To this day I am more in my element, and at peace with the world when I am on a quiet lake fishing or walking alone in the wilderness.

I made some good friends that first winter, spring, and summer of 1952—Remi Lacasse, Ronald Savard, Jean Lafontaine, Florian Labelle, and the Thibeault and Phillips brothers. I was to gather a few more friends around me when I started school in September, at six and a half years old.

These early friendships, very much like that with Peter at Mud Lake were friendships of a depth of feeling and sincerity of heart that only children can commit to, and be in a position to reciprocate. Strange to say, but I was more in love with my childhood friends than my siblings, or cousins. Childhood friendships are pure, and in mind at least—indissoluble. The bond is forged by unique shared experiences and emotions. Every day spent with a friend added a layer of growth to my identity and shaped somewhat, the person I was to become later on in life. Friends make us—for good or for bad—depending on what we absorb, or, reject from the relationship. Every friend I have made was equally important and was a friend for life. If I met someone, and we did not become friends; it was because we could share nothing of each other. And, if you cannot share each other, without conditions, you may as well never have known each other. Then you are a user, and the relationship is based on self-interest.

The Church, Social Life, and other Places

The town was dominated, as are most Quebec communities, by a large Catholic Church—St. Andre de Belleterre. The church was built on rising ground, its high, polished galvanized steel steeple, always followed the sun and reflected its rays in all directions.

Father Pelletier kept a strong hold on the flock, and come provincial or federal election time, he made no secret as to where God and the church stood: and God and the church always stood to the right of issues—never to the left—therefore; the Sunday sermons from the pulpit became unabashedly politicized by many, and not so subtle, references to the parishioners; that the colour blue was the colour of heaven, and the colour red was always used to depict hell. The Church got away with that medieval stuff in those days, but change was on the horizon—Quebec society and the Church's place in it would see dramatic shifts and changes in the early sixties.

Fifty yards to the east of the church stood the newly built school, which I would be attending that September. It was a modern red brick rectangular structure with four levels. The lower level accommodated the washrooms; the coal burning furnace room; the janitor's supply room, and a large open playroom area for the children to use on days of inclement weather, or to hold school plays, and school meetings in. The second level and ascending to the fourth were the lower grades, moving up in numerical order until you arrived at the last grades, seven and eight, on the fourth floor. The school was built with the future in mind—when I was admitted to grade one, it had an enrollment of 313 students and yet, only half of the classroom capacity of the school was being used.

The new hotel, the Chateau Belleterre—who came up with this presumptuous name I never knew—was located at the end of First Avenue, directly opposite the baseball field.

The hotel, although not a "Chateau", was impressive. It was new, modern, and solidly built. The bar and beer parlour was below ground and accessed from two side doors, each clearly demarcated in neon signage—"Men and Escort" and, "Women" respectively; unescorted women had no business mingling, unattached, with the men.

The main front entrance way and vestibule were built of construction grade glass blocks cemented together. That was innovative and cutting-edge construction material for those days. The floors of the main lobby and check-in areas were made of finely polished aggregate granite, which shone brightly under a layer of wax. It had thirty rooms and its own laundry facility. A large kitchen, catered to a well-appointed dining room. The lobby had large comfortable leather furnishings with low circular tables distributed here and there. Large, airy windows gave ample views of the outside—in short, it was the nicest, and the biggest hotel in all of Temiscaming County.

But, if the hotel was competing with Father Pelletier to become the social focus of the town, the church still held the field, and was; furthermore, the unrivaled cultural centre—that is, up until "The Star" movie theatre came upon the scene later on. But at that time the church held sway.

The church was reverenced. No female of any age would dare enter a church without being head-veiled. All schoolboys walking in front of the church had to remove, or at least, tip their hats—we were so enjoined to do by our teachers. Although our church did not have any signal exterior differences from other Catholic churches in the county, it's what it held in its basement that made me, between the ages of nine and thirteen, an ardent churchgoer.

I was in love with the church basement. Father Pelletier had turned the basement into a community centre, well before community centres had become fashionable across the country. The basement was accessible to all school-aged kids every day of the week; during school vacations; holidays and weekends. If the church was the cultural centre of town, then the basement was its repository. The basement also had a stage on which plays were performed, and it had a twelve- foot rolled-up cinema screen; ping pong tables, and long rectangular tables for the girls to do crafts on.

THE CHRONICLES OF A JOURNEY

A love of Reading and a Discovery in the Church Basement

By age eight or nine, I knew that I had inherited my mother's love of reading, and mine was, from an early age, of a voracious appetite. Therefore, the lodestone, the main attraction to me, were the books. There were shelves of books; books on the floor; books everywhere and of every description—fiction and nonfiction; animated books and magazines; and full-length novels. My head went dizzy when I came upon the complete 24 first edition collection of books of the animated "Adventures of Tin-Tin", by Herge—direct from France—the box buried under a pile of magazines.

At night, all the characters would appear and float in my mind: Tin-Tin, Snowy, Professor Calculus, and Captain Haddock, the silly twin detectives Thompson and Thompson, and Bianca Castafiore. I had the same excited feeling when at fifteen, I discovered the complete collection of Dickens in the Sudbury Public library. However, the church books were not allowed to be taken home; they had to be read on location—a condition easy for me to accept—since, with the exception of a few girls, none of my friends enjoyed the company of books.

Until the town built its own movie theatre in 1955, the church screened some movies, on Saturday nights; they were advertised the Sunday before from the pulpit; mostly to do with some scary and gruesome happenings in some saints' lives or other pious stories. But, on some occasions, Father would allow the showing of the odd Walt Disney animated releases, such as Bambi, Snow White, and Sleeping Beauty. Needless to say, those played to full houses. Father also allowed plays to be performed on the stage at certain times of the year, usually on Friday or Saturday evenings. I would get in either alone or accompanied by my older sister Rose. I loved the live performances; the booming voices coming from the stage; the interplay of the different intensity and shades of lights; some sudden scream from an actor. It was exhilarating to a twelve-year-old.

Ray A. Vincent

The Happy Times of Play and Discovery

That first winter was a time full of play and discovery. There was a big shed at the back of the house, with a very low hanging roof. Happy were those times when fighting with the buttons of my coat, I would run past the shed, usually early in the morning; turn sharply left, up the back lane, and not stop running until I got to my friend Ronald Savard's house, five backyards away.

In midwinter, we climbed on top of the drifted snow piled up against the shed and we hopped onto the roof, and then used the roof as a natural sliding slope. The shed had three partitioned enclosures or compartments: one, on the right side, was piled to the rafters with cords of stove and furnace firewood; the far left compartment was an empty garage; it had a fine sandy floor and a one-piece garage door which swung open through a cantilevered system of pulleys, steel cables, and weights.

One day my father came home with a baby fox, and he used the empty garage space as one big wildlife pen. Not a good idea. I think that even I, could have told him that it was not a good plan. Although the garage door closed tightly to the floor; one ought to have realized the fact that the floor was sand. The baby fox was put in the pen at two in the afternoon, with all the food and water to please the most demanding, and discriminating of foxes in the world. However, by supper, time the fox had vanished. We were saddened to have lost our pet, but—there it was, a deep hole dug under the door—and no sign of our fox to be seen. We took comfort in the fact that he left with a full belly—the food was all eaten. My father said, nonchalantly; as a distraction to the gloomy faces all round, that he didn't think he'd touched the water.

Company Space and the Mesmerizing Lamps

The middle enclosed section or compartment of the shed, accessed by a separate door, stored some mine equipment owned by the company—boxes of miners' helmets; cupboards of wrenches and hammers; shelves of rubber gloves and rubber boots tightly packed together, and this intriguing discovery: rows upon rows of carbide miners' lights which one could fasten to the front crown of a miner's helmet.

My parents had been told by the McIntyre official that no one—absolutely no one—was to access that padlocked part of the shed—it was company private property. The door was padlocked, and that made it only that much more enticing to me. From the privacy of the empty garage at the far left, I managed to pry a large board loose, pulled it forward and squeezed myself in with ease. After every visit to the forbidden cubicle, I would take care to replace the plank; making sure to put it in its exact location with the nails securely refastened.

The carbide miner's lamp fascinated me. I could not get enough of handling them and checking all the intricate construction details, from top to bottom. It did not take me long to figure out that the strange apparatus clipped onto the helmet. So I would put a helmet on my head, put on an oversized pair of boots on my feet; slip the big gloves over my hands; clip the lamp, and I was transported one thousand leagues away into some strange land, with all my friends from the worlds of Jules Verne.

The lamps as stored, could not be lit. They were empty of calcium carbide, and even if they had been filled, I had no knowledge of the method of igniting one. The lamp was a two-chambered metal flask with a burner disk fitted with a reflector, at which location the light was produced. The lamp, when operational, would have had calcium carbide crystals in the lower chamber, and water filled the upper chamber. A mechanism controlled the rate at which the water would be allowed to drip into the calcium carbide chamber. By controlling the rate of water flow the miner controlled the amount of acetylene gas produced. This, in turn, controlled the flow rate of the combustible gas and thereby the size of the flame at the burner, and thus the amount of light produced.

My Jules Verne universe would be fine as long as I was alone in it. But as soon as I began to introduce some of my friends to it—it came crashing down to an abrupt end. They were noisy and attracted unwanted attention. My sisters, alas, let the genie out; they complained to mother that the boys would not let them in the shed to play. Having to suffer the embarrassment of a public scolding, and the confinement to the house and bedroom for a few consecutive days, put a sudden end to my adventures in the middle shed.

Sears mail Order and my First Ice skates

By the end of January, the wonders of the Sears catalogue mail order system became convincingly evident to me. I got my first pairs of skates. The skating rink was on the same side of First Avenue, as the curling club was, not far from the Menard's. That first winter, my friends and I skated as much on the hard packed snow on the streets as we did at the rink. At times, I could see sparks coming off my friends' skates as the blades hit some uncovered stone.

At night, we would lie down behind a snow bank close to a street intersection at which there was a stop sign. As a car slowed down to a stop, we would spring to our feet, rush out and hang on to the rear bumper—sometimes with boots on—sometimes with skates—and hang on for dear life until we either lost hold, and stumbled, rolling forward or voluntarily let go, if we saw that the car was heading out of town.

The Announcement of a Marriage and my Brothers' Escapades

Springtime brought developments that affected my mother again. In March, Rose, the eldest remaining at home, announced her engagement to be married to Rosario, a miner who came from the farming community of Bearn. The wedding was to take place in August.

Then in early April, Pete and Ivan quit the local mine and left the house to join Louis, the senior sibling: Louis had gotten them jobs with the Eldorado Mining Company in Uranium City, Saskatchewan.

Eldorado Mining was a federal government enterprise. This was the period of post-war nuclear arsenal build-up. There was a lot of work and a lot of money to be made in Uranium City—particularly if you were a bonus miner. My brothers were excited and chomping at the bit to get going. There was no road access of any kind into Uranium City. They would fly out of North Bay to Toronto and then on to Uranium City. They were not to be alone—Louis had enticed quite a few other mining-experienced boys from Belleterre to head to northwestern Saskatchewan with my brothers.

The whole crew almost did not make it to their destination. When my brothers came home for the Christmas holidays, I overheard the stories of their traveling misadventures.

When they got to Toronto, the French-accented small-town boys from the Quebec backwoods, had a grand old time with drinking; partying; carousing and getting skunked drunk. No one could get up the next day. They all missed their connecting flight to Saskatchewan—and they would not leave the hotel—the venerable grand old King Edward; one of the best in those days. They were asked to leave. However, they were waiting to get on another flight and they refused to vacate the premises. The hotel management became insistent; the boys became intransigent—throughout the night of the third day, they commandeered the service elevator to the hotel basement; filling the elevator with coal and then dumping this coal into their rooms.

The morning maids came to the rooms to make the beds, and tidy up as usual: their screams could be heard two floors away; they were the screams of horror as in a murder scene. The big city police were called. We don't know if it's because the Toronto police had a generous sense of humour or if the hotel management had called the Eldorado Mining Company and they had agreed to cover the damages, but no one was charged. The boys were thrown into two cruisers; body and baggage and unceremoniously deposited at the front doors of the airport.

They got to Uranium City. My brother Louis, who had organized the trip, bought the tickets; and had seen to all the accommodations and food in transit, was not amused. But later on, when he would talk about the "disaster"—as he called it—he would laugh along with the boys.

Ray A. Vincent

Mother takes a Job and I Stumble on Money

As if she was not busy enough, my mother took a job—maybe to cover the cost of the impending wedding—maybe to add to the family income.

The little bank next door needed a cleaning lady and mother was hired. So, after supper she would go with Carmen to dust the counters; empty wastepaper baskets; sweep and mop the floors—Carmen's job was to empty the ashtrays.

In late spring I accidentally stumbled onto a little treasure. My mother was at her job and I hung around outside and played; one day I went to play underneath the wooden stairway leading to the front entrance of the bank. The snow was almost all gone. Now, customers leaving the bank on a cold and windy winters' day would sometimes accidentally drop coins out of their wallets or purses; those coins would end up under the stairs; to rest there, buried under the snow all winter long. Few, knowing they had dropped coins when faced with frigid weather conditions, would venture to crawl under the stairs to retrieve them.

How many five cents bags of chips? How many ten cents Pepsi bottles? How many Sweet Maries and how many Cherry Blossoms did my little treasure trove under the stairs deliver to me? Many—and, with what joy and relish they were consumed.

My brother Charley brought me a gift that summer of 1952. He came home one day with something bulging under his jacket; it was a little black puppy; "Ti-Pousse": literally translated, "Little-Thumb". We became inseparable. There was something important in the fact that I had become responsible for something alive, and feisty like me—and I felt that my puppy realized the special relationship. He did not act around others the way he acted with me; as if he understood some secret pact or agreement. He would not grow to be more than a foot and a half in length and a foot high; with a jet black coat with a distinctive white diamond on his chest. My little dog was to keep my spirits up when I was sad, or when I got sick. He would give me solace without asking for anything in return.

The Magical Antibiotic.

Mine was not a sickly constitution, but for the next two years, I would be sick with one thing or another. One day I developed scaly sores on my face; particularly, on my chin and forehead; on no other part of my body—only the face. The red sores were the size of dimes, not particularly itchy, but, and what concerned my mother—they had become leaky from under the scales. They were so awful and disfiguring that my friends started to stay away—their mothers would not let them come close to me. The injunction was understandable, but sad and frustrating to me since I was otherwise healthy, and without any decreased activity level. My mother went to my friend Remi's mom across the street and solicited advice. She came home with a jar of yellow powder. This yellow powder, I found out later, was pure sulphur, and when mixed with a little petroleum jelly, made an excellent ointment, and a very effective medicine.

It was a magical remedy; within a week the leaky, scaly sores had dried up; and the scales fell off to leave fresh pink skin underneath. I was back in circulation.

CHAPTER 4

A Marriage

Rose's wedding was upon us and grandmother Denomme would be our guest until the festivities were over. Her first name was soft to pronounce, just like she was—Emilia. Grandma Denomme was taller than my mom and thinner. But she had my mom's smile and her posture; she stood erect and dignified. I never saw her wearing any colour, but black. She wore long black dresses, covering her from chin to the edge of her shoes. She looked very stately to me; particularly when I would look at her coming slowly down the stairs; a slight smile on her lips, and her solid white hair smartly brushed and furled down at the nape of the neck into a bun.

One morning, she and I were the first ones about and alone in the kitchen. My dad had gotten up earlier, and he'd started the stove going. I accidentally burned a finger on the hot stove; I kept the pain to myself, biting my lip, but not saying a word; trying hard to show no distress—but grandma knew—how she had noticed, I don't know. She'd been quietly watching her grandchild. I guess it's a natural gift that mothers have—a gift my mother would get to display again, and again as I was growing up. Without saying a word, grandma put her hand behind my shoulders and led me to the sink; once there, she asked softly, "Which one hurts?" I produced the injured finger, and she ran ice cold water over it until the pain was reduced to a bearable level.

The wedding took place in the Moose Hall. I got to meet uncles, aunts and cousins I never knew existed. And, this was a special day indeed—you could drink all the sodas and eat all the deserts you wanted—without reprimands. The Cotes and the Vincents were a pretty quiet bunch, but not so the Denommes; they were the life of the party. They loved to drink, sing and dance; they were loud, and there were a lot of them. My mother's nine brothers were all there with their full families. By 7:00 p.m., the musicians let go with their violins, guitars, and accordion.

My mother said that my dad got tipsy as the evening progressed, but the only difference I noticed from his usual behaviour was that he became more talkative, and seemed –when I chanced to look his way, to be smiling and laughing an awful lot.

The marriage, unfortunately, proved to be not a happy one. Marriage is not an instrument one ought to resort to, in order to resolve personal problems. And Rosario had problems—debilitating jealousy and, drink. If a marriage begins with one party bringing in personal problems, the marriage will end up with two unhappy persons having problems.

Do not enter matrimony seeking out happiness, when you are unhappy while celibate. You should not enter marriage because you are lonely, feel unloved, or because all of your friends are getting married: that would be a lie to the foundation of a human relationship—you would be better advised to remain single. You should not enter marriage wanting something out of it—you enter marriage to contribute something positive, to it.

I could never understand why people get married without having committed to looking after each other's wellbeing. Do not get married if you are not ready to sacrifice yourself for your spouse—if you are not ready to be there when needed. Marriage is for selfless people.

Look closely at the habits and personality of the parents and siblings of your betroth; because what you will find in them—emotionally; socially; intellectually—you will find in your husband, or wife, later—and; in your children. Marriage is an institution for two happy and well-adjusted individuals— all others stay out—otherwise, step-in at your own risk, and under extreme caution.

Rosario was a handsome man. He was soft-spoken, quiet and intelligent; but he thought of himself before anyone else; he was selfish and he was jealous to a pathological degree. He later turned to alcohol and became physically abusive.

After the wedding, Rose and Rosario moved to an upstairs apartment close to the school. My sister had to tell her husband, prior to his going to work in the morning, what her itinerary for the day was going to be: where she was planning to go, and who she was planning to see that day.

One day, after a fresh morning snowfall, I walked to Rose's to have my school lunch with her, since she was so close to the school. Rose came home crying that night; her husband would not believe that the footprints in the snow on the stairs, were that of a grade two child. He was convinced and insisted they were those of a grown man. She went back to him that same night, but the flags were up; alerting of serious danger ahead.

A love of School, but a Reluctant Beginner

My introduction to school in September got off to a bumpy start. The weekend before school, I quietly began to have a change of mind. Saturday afternoon we got a heavy downpour of rain, and I figured that if I got sick with a cold, mom would keep me at home. The roof at the back of the house had a downspout missing; therefore, rainwater came cascading down in a torrent. I got underneath it and let the water pour over my head, drenching me from head to foot. After a while mother came looking for me. She was not sympathetic; she was angry and could not understand my foolishness. Stripped of clothes; a rub down with rough towels, and then fresh clothes, got me up and about again—not sick, but more hale and hearty than ever.

That Sunday night my mom made the usual busy preparations that mothers make the day before school opening— new pencils were sharpened; the scribblers, pencils, and erasers tucked in the school bag that still smelled of fresh leather. The new school clothes were checked again for neatness and put aside. You could feel the excitement. But, there was one problem—I had decided on Monday morning that school was not for me—I would not go. I was having a bad case of separation anxiety, very much akin to what my sister Carmen had gone through some years before.

With my new, stiff leather school bag strapped around my shoulders, mom took me by the hand and off we went. We made it only as far as the sidewalk. I tensed the muscles of my legs; I stiffened my whole body; in short, I anchored in. I cried, and I would not move any further. My mother was upset; she would encourage; she would admonish—there were very few times when my mother was at a loss as to what to do next—but this was one of those times.

Out of nowhere, we heard this gentle voice coming from behind us, "And what seems to be the problem?" the voice had asked. We saw a tall, lean man in his late thirties, standing there. He was dressed in a grey three-piece suit with a bow tie; pale complexioned; with a neat clean moustache on his upper lip; a dark fedora on his head, and a dark briefcase in his right hand. We were quickly introduced to Mr. Belanger; the new school principal. Mr. Belanger was one of those special persons that always carry a reassuring presence about them. He smiled, took my hand away from my mother, and we strolled; he and I, to school—as if we had done this every morning for many months—and we left my mother standing there on the sidewalk, pleasantly surprised.

I loved school—any school—from that day forward. The St. Andre de Belleterre elementary school was very well administered, and ahead of its time in terms of curriculum content and development. Because this was a new townsite, we were blessed not only with a new school building, but a new school staffed with young, energized, and enlightened teachers who came from the community. Our elementary school was exceptional for Quebec in those days, in that it had no religious order of nuns administering it, or, teaching in it. Our new principal was unmarried, and he had been educated in the classics at Laval.

Town folks found it interesting that he lived at the hotel; the school board paying his room and board. He had chosen this arrangement so as not to live with a family with school-aged children, and thereby face some possible conflict of interest issues. He was a good principal and a tactful manager of human relations.

Some of my biggest joys in first grade came, as would be expected, at recess time: playing with my established friends and making new ones. I made three new friends that year; one of the Lariviere family and two from the Boudrias—kids from First Nation families living off reserve.

I fell in love with my teacher; Miss Beauchemin. I would rush to the front of the classroom to be the first volunteer offering to clean the blackboard; and, how proud I was to be selected to go outside, and clap clean of chalk dust, all those blackboard erasers. After school, a group of us would escort Miss Beauchemin home— offering to carry her school work.

Upper grades got to enjoy special perks. I recall those warm and sunny June days, when outdoor class sessions would be held—one or two days only per calendar year—the janitor, teacher and the boys from grades seven or eight would move the classroom desks outside the school building. I loved those outdoor classes; with the fresh grass under your feet, surrounded by fresh air and the sound of nature. We were, indeed, an enlightened school—or maybe it all had to do with the new principal.

I particularly loved the Friday afternoons, grade eight literature class—the last class of the day. This routine would happen every Friday afternoon at the same time, from January to year end: the teacher would have everyone clear their desktops; load up their school bags with material necessary for weekend homework, and having put the schoolbags aside at our feet, ready to pick up when the dismissal bell rang— we were then exposed to the most innovative and rewarding way, to end the last forty-five minutes of the school week. She would have everyone bend forward and curl our arms on the top of our desk and then, lay our heads gently and comfortably in the crook of our arms. Then, we were told to close our eyes.

Seated at her desk, and in a clear and slow, cadenced voice, she would begin reading where she had left off the previous Friday—in serialized fashion—some story from adventure novels. We were introduced to "Don Quixote and the Man from La Mancha" adventures; to Jules Verne's many and exciting new worlds, and a variety of other experiences in story form very far from the reach of the kids from Belleterre—but, in those forty-five minutes at the end of the school week, we were transported away from the backwoods, and we floated away and lived in those experiences. Our minds and our imaginations were free to open up to possibilities; the shuttered dead ends were dispelled.

Bless the teachers who encourage the dreamers to dream. I did well in grade school; I was promoted directly to grade eight from grade six—I skipped grade seven altogether.

The Sales Pitch, and the WearEver man

As food is a proven quick way to a man's heart; the delay of it, when hungry, is a sure path to his sour temper. My dad came home from work every day at about 4:40 p.m.; before 5:15 p.m. supper was usually served, and we would be all seated and eating. One afternoon, at 4:30 p.m., a traveling salesman called at the house. The WearEver cookware man. He was selling every Belleterre housewife's dream—the "WearEver" line of pots and pans.

I was impressed with the middle-aged gentleman. He was well dressed, polite, courteous and very engaging. He was willing to take over the kitchen, and give an actual demonstration of his products. My mother was interested, and since she had already laid out vegetables and other things on the counter for supper, why not let him cook and see the outcome of his product.

He made numerous trips to his car and back; brought in half a dozen boxes and started to unpack. My mother had no idea how long his "demonstration" would take: she had not factored in the time of consuming sales pitches, singing the virtues of each pot, pan, and lid, as he would handle each item. I was intrigued—it was like watching a scientific experiment happening right before your eyes. Even today, I very much enjoy watching television cooking shows. I took a chair at the corner of the table, cupped my chin in my hands, and watched.

By this time, my father had come in some time before; he'd come in the kitchen and looked around; saw this activity; put down his lunch pail on the hallway floor; retreated to the small sitting room and put the radio on. By 5:00 p.m., our salesman was deep into the boiling of carrots, potatoes, and turnips. He was talking animatedly; he was in his element. My mother was entranced.

Out in the sitting room, my father was getting fidgety, and by 5:30 p.m. he was hungry and restless. He made a sortie out of the sitting room, a newspaper in one hand: it was now 5:35 p.m. He looked at my mom and coughed a few times to get her attention, and after catching her eye, he returned to the sitting room.

By the time 5:45 p.m. arrived, and with the smell of frying pork chops in the air, my father had had it. He reappeared in the kitchen, put his two hands on the back of my chair and then—he took command. He ordered all the "WearEver" pots and pans containing food to have their contents transferred to our own kitchenware; he asked that the salesman re-pack all his products in the boxes; and then, he politely told him to leave—after which, he announced that he was hungry, and that supper should be served.

He said all this calmly, in an even voice, only slightly higher than normal tone for him. And, within a few minutes, the WearEver set, and the WearEver-man were out of the house. And we got down to a great WearEver prepared meal.

We don't know how she did it. But she got it. Our mother got her complete WearEver cookware set. All six boxes of them. It may be that the quality of the prepared food impressed my father or, it could be some other wily tricks she used. The purchase was made on the monthly installment plan, of course; but by then she had her cleaning job at the bank.

The set was of high-quality anodized aluminum; a wartime innovative product—which she still had pieces of it in her cupboards when she died in 1988—along with her indestructible beige Melmac tableware.

First visit at the Hospital

My first experience with the mine funded hospital occurred because of the game of hockey. But, I was not a player on the ice; I was a spectator standing on the snowbank alongside the exterior of the boards—right behind the goaltender—not a clever place to stand. This was an adult men's game, and my cousin was the goaltender for the home team. I had decided to take a close-up view of his goaltending skills. My feet on the snow bank were at the same level as the top of the boards. A slap-shot from the blue line went flying over the goalie and hit me squarely over the left eye. I crumpled on the ice surface below. I recall coming to, lying on my back, on the table inside the rink shack, with my brother Charley pressing a towel to my forehead. Charley carried me home in his arms, and from home, we went by taxi to the hospital. Nine stitches later I was back home with a sore head. Sixty-three years later, the suture line and the scar tissues are still quite visible—a testament to poor surgical skills, or terrible technique—or, both.

The funeral of Aunt Eva and the Family Cat

In April, my father's fifty-four-year old sister died; my aunt Eva. She and my uncle Arthur were farmers. The farm was in lot number 8, concession number 9, in the small village of Guigues, in the general area of Laverlochere. It was my father's original homestead; he had been born and raised in that very house. When Grandfather Vincent had died in October of 1931, our aunt Eva and her husband, Arthur Cote (no relation to Rose's husband), had moved in to take care of my grandmother, Marcelline Turenne. The house and farm were eventually turned over to them. At that time, it caused some dissension and troubles between my dad and his sister and her husband, since my dad saw the family farm as his patrimony.

My mother always maintained that our father had been jilted out of his rightful inheritance. But, be that as it may, my father may have been hurt, but he was never a man to hold a grudge and openly show enmity toward anyone. And he loved his sister.

Aunt Eva was born in 1899 in St. Damien de Lotbiniere, in eastern Quebec—the birthplace of my paternal grandparents. She married our uncle Arthur when she was only fourteen years of age and she gave birth to ten children—four boys and six girls; one of the girls, Marie-Jeanne, entered the religious orders and became a nun.

The showing of the body and the family gathering was at the farmhouse. The coffin, three feet off the floor, was set up in the sombre, dimly lit living room. The family had had a large black shroud suspended from the ceiling, and this shroud covered almost all of the wall in front of which the coffin stood. Suspended in this manner, the back of the coffin was pressed so close against the wall that it came in contact with the cloth. The coffin was open, and the body exposed all day for viewing as was the fashion then.

Three things or events are, to this day, fresh and clear in my memory: the mounds of sandwiches and the smell of coffee; the cat incident, and the bright sunshine at the cemetery. I had never seen so many sandwiches collected in one place in all my life—sandwiches of all sizes and varieties; all using homemade bread.

When supper had been set on the large kitchen table and everyone called to dinner, the family closed the coffin and drew the heavy curtain separating the living room from the kitchen. The family, relatives, and friends got engaged in animated conversation over the course of their meal. I finished eating quickly and took the opportunity to wander around and explore. After looking at family photographs on the walls, and other curiosities about the house, I moved closer to the curtain. I parted the curtain and softly glided into the deserted room.

When I brought my eyes to focus in the vicinity of the coffin, a shiver went down my spine—first, the coffin moved—then, both, the coffin and the shroud behind it appeared to be in movement—any moment now, I expected my aunt Eva to flip the lid and sit up. I could not move, but I must have made some audible sound because, two older cousins came into the room, making a fuss as they flew by me, and charged behind the coffin; and after some shuffling about, they came out with the big grey house cat held by the scruff of the neck.

I do not recall much about the church ceremony the next day. But I remember vividly the bright sunshine at the graveside. I was not interested in the people sniffling and crying as the coffin went down;

my eyes were drawn to the bright reflection of the sun on the snow still on the ground, and playing against the high metallic steeple.

Uncle Alfred. The Uneducated man of Letters

For a man of little formal education, my uncle Fred was very intelligent. I liked to be around him. He, like his sister—my mom—was well read and naturally inquisitive. He had a clear, clean, direct way of speaking—very few pauses and hmm sounds in his speech—and, although he would look you straight in the eyes, it was not intimidating.

He loved to discourse. He had a habit of taking a hypothetical issue and debate it with the grownups around him. Given a chance at a formal education, he would have made a good lawyer or politician. Poverty has no bias, it disadvantages the precocious and the slow-witted equally.

One day I came home from school and my uncle Fred and my dad were talking about wildlife. I had to walk by them to hang up my coat on the nail in the basement stairway; I overheard my uncle say the French word for wolf cub, and the word he had chosen was incorrect; I stopped and told him that the right word was "louveteau"—and not, "petit loup", as he had said. My dad was upset with me. He said I was impertinent and impolite. But Uncle Fred came to my defence quickly; he told my dad that I was correct and that he should be proud of me, not only for my knowledge but also for the courage that I had shown in speaking out.

Second Visit at the Hospital, and I Meet a War Veteran

I was afflicted with many episodes of sore throats, and in those days the remedy of choice was a tonsillectomy. In late summer of 1953,

I had my second visit to the hospital. I stayed three to four days in the hospital, then I moved to a makeshift bedroom made for me in the sitting room. My throat was raw, but how could I complain about anything, with all these Popsicles and the tubs of ice-cream at my command.

Mrs. Gauthier had a peculiar tenant living in her basement apartment. I have forgotten his name. He lived alone and he seldom went about the town. He had one arm amputated at the elbow. He was a world war one veteran and he'd lost his arm at the front. Where he came from and why he picked our little town to live in, my parents, and as far as I know, nobody else knew.

My friends and I would go and visit with him, whenever we saw him sitting outside by the basement door. He would hold a lit cigarette on the good side, between yellow stained fingers; the loose and empty shirt sleeve on the other side was not left flapping about, but it was neatly tucked to his chest, in between the buttons of his shirt. He was a reluctant speaker, but we would insist, importunate, for war stories. His stories of war experiences were full of drama couched in the mystique of fear, violence, and adventure in strange lands. To our nine and ten year old minds, those were gripping hours we were allowed to spend with him. He had been in the trenches and he had lived the atrocities of war, the appreciation of which we could not fathom.

He left Belleterre as mysteriously as when he had arrived. One day we found out that he was gone; no one knew where.

CHAPTER 5

Our mother, The Story Teller

That summer of 1954, my mother began her neighbourhood community storytelling sessions—that is what my siblings and I called those fond memories, later on as adults, when we talked about them at family gatherings. She was to keep that up as long as she had children in elementary school—and as a matter of fact, as long as there were any children—and a few adults—interested.

As I said before, my mom was a great reader. She read novels of all kinds, but she had a love for the romance-adventure genre.

It started one summer evening after supper; after I, my sisters and our friends found ourselves bored with nothing to do; and it continued on Saturdays during school months—of course, not every Saturday, but with consistent regularity. It became an event that the neighbourhood kids very much anticipated, and they would enquire as to when the next story-time would take place.

It would take place after the dishes had been put away; after bath time; and, in pajamas—friends included in the routine. Later, we even had some adult pop in with their kids—and stay. My mother would literally relate the stories—in colourful descriptive details—with body language and sound effects—of the novels she had read. She would arrange us on the floor—her children and the neighbours'—in a large circle; and mother would then take centre stage—a straight-backed chair right in the middle of her rapt audience.

The "Three Musketeers" came alive in front of us—D'Artagnan, Athos, Aramis, and Porthos. We shared the fate and the hardships of the "Comte of Monte Cristo". We heard all of the Dumas's stories, and many other authors delivered in my mom's inimitable flair. Some stories were one-sitting affairs; the long ones were serialized; to be continued next time—to the chagrin of the disappointed faces turned up pleadingly toward her.

We went to bed filled with history, adventure, romance, knights, and kings and castles. And we slept well. No TV program would ever come close to giving us the same comfort, and peace of mind that my mom's stories did.

Mother Finds a Pen Pal

Where she found the time is difficult to figure out, but my mother had decided, going back to the Mud Lake days; that she had need of a long distance friend—a pen pal. And, not just any pen pal; it would have to be a French lady, from France.

She had made the initial contact through a newspaper advertisement. Mrs. Mermaz was a married lady from the south of France; the Cote D'Azur region. They exchanged personal and family photos; they wrote to each other regularly; they even mailed each other some foodstuffs—so much for the customs regulations of those days.

Like a lot of things my mom did; this also intrigued me; there was something exotic about the whole pen pal exercise. France was in war reconstruction mode at the time. One day my mother got a letter from Mrs. Mermaz; a letter of appreciation for the last package my mom had sent to France; in it were rave reviews for one particular item sent—a large container of "Magic Powder", a leavening baking powder. Shortly after, we received tubes (very much like toothpaste tubes), of genuine Dijon mustard; and, colour photos of her son in his officer's uniform; taken somewhere in Vietnam—the French were involved in their Indo-China war at that time.

Mrs. Mermaz had a six-year-old grandson. So the gift my mom sent to him, got talked about all over Mrs. Mermaz's town, we were told by return correspondence; and, therein enclosed were the smiling photos of the young cowboy. It was a complete cowboy outfit ordered from the Sears catalogue; it had the cowboy hat, vest and chaps, sheriff's badge, cowboy boots, and of course, the gun belt with the revolver and holster. In the days of the European craze with anything of an American western flavour, he must have been a very popular young boy with his friends, indeed.

I kept Mrs. Mermaz's address with me for many years; well into my adulthood—I thought, well, maybe one day—but unfortunately, I eventually lost track of it. My wife and I were to visit the south of France in 2011; Provence and the Cote D'Azur, as advertised, was beautiful.

I always wondered what had attracted the two pen pals of long ago—one, from the Canadian backwoods—the other, from the sophisticated south of France. I figured, it was what they did not have in common that attracted them to each other; their differences. Otherwise, they were of kindred spirits in many ways.

Saint-Jean de Baptiste Day

Saint-Jean de Baptiste day was an occasion of great fanfare and festivities back then, as it is today in the province, and as it has been, since the Nativity of St. John the Baptist was first celebrated on the banks of the Saint Lawrence River in 1636. The patron saint of French Canadians was celebrated in style not only in Belleterre but in all parishes having an active Catholic church. Every morning of a June 24th opened with an early morning mass, at which everyone was expected to be at; a procession headed by the clergy in full vestments, made its way up First Avenue, down Fourth, and wound its way back to the church.

Besides clergy, the procession was composed of gaudily furbished floats, depicting historical events of all kinds, and represented an array of organizations; from the Knights of Columbus to the 4H Club—and everything in between—and of course, every town had a float of its Little St. Jean—a curly-haired boy no more than seven years old, specially chosen, standing by the side of a real live baby lamb, both bedded down in two feet of dry hay.

Organizing committees had been hard at work for months. There were rows upon rows of kiosks set up many days before in which crafts were sold along with foods of all kinds. Saint-Jean de Baptiste day was in those days, a cultural event rolled into one large community fair. Unfortunately, during and immediately after the "Quiet Revolution"—a period I remember well—Saint-Jean Baptiste day became highly politicized with the rise of French Canadian nationalist sentiments. But in quieter times, the celebrations took many forms; we had live musical entertainment and a huge open-air evening dance.

Belleterre proposed to outdo all of its neighbours. The open-air dance was preceded by a communal dinner in the church basement. That year; however, the organizing committee added something extra: a huge outdoor bingo hall had been set up under canvas. There was to be only one bingo game, and that game was to take place before the open dance was to begin, so as not to compete with each other. The entry price was not cheap, it was relatively high—but, what a game—what a prize! —A brand new 1954, dark blue, Ford pickup truck.

The Winning prize.
And Rose's state of Marital Affairs

I was at home that night with my younger sisters; everyone else was at the fairgrounds when my sister Colette came in with the news that our brother-in-law had won the truck.

This event changed Rosario's career path. Shortly after the win, he left the mine, and he and Rose moved to his home farming village of Bearn. That small truck led to small jobs that led to bigger things. My brother-in-law always had good business acumen. He eventually became a successful trucking contractor with a fleet of vehicles.

However, it did not improve his marriage fortunes. Not many months after the move, Rose came home one day. The bus stopped in front of the house and deposited her, and two large pieces of luggage at our doorstep. With the exception of Charley and Colette, none of the other kids suspected the reason why she was home—we assumed she'd come for a visit. The real reason became clear after a week had gone by.

Rosario showed up at the house and he wanted Rose to return with him to Bearn. This occasion was one of the few in which I saw my father come out of his silence, and he did it aggressively; he was angry and he did not hide his emotion; he laid down the riot act. He, my mother, and Rosario were in conference in the sitting room; Rose was closeted upstairs. My father's voice was loud, but in control; he told Rosario that if he did not love his daughter—if he was not ready to care and look after her as a good husband should—she would remain with her family and he could go back to Bearn by himself, and do so immediately. We could barely hear our brother-in-law's voice. It was down to a whisper. He made apologies, tearful entreaties, and promises.

Later that afternoon, Rose and her luggage were in his car, bound for Bearn. A rocky start to a marriage. This was separation number two over a span of four years.

Rose became active with her local parish church; she joined every committee; she found solace in religion; pictures of saints adorned the walls of her house, and she subscribed to a variety of religious magazines coming out of Montreal. The church had become her surrogate family. Rose did not have children until after the ninth year of her marriage; she had need of a surgical procedure to correct a gynecological problem. After she underwent a successful surgery, she had four children within seven years. Although still involved with the church, her religious fervour cooled considerably; relegated to the background, but still there when she needed its support later in her life.

A School assignment with Serious Consequences

That fall, the grade three class was divided into groups and given different assignments. My assignment, with two other classmates, was to go out, and collect leaves from different species of trees; properly identify them as to the tree of origin; describe the colours and the reasons why leaves change colour; and finally, press them between the pages of a book, let them dry, then paste them onto binder sheets containing the descriptive text. The trio decided that our collection should contain a generous amount of maple leaves. After all, this was Quebec—the maple syrup capital of the whole world.

Maple trees grew in abundance about a half mile out of town, off the road leading towards the mine-site. We met at Lefebvre's Imperial Esso garage at 9:30 a.m., and we headed out to what was to become quite an adventure. When we reached a point on the road where we thought maple trees would be found, we left the main road and struck out into the bush. We found maple leaves; beautifully coloured and of all kinds of shapes and sizes. We pushed on, gathering other types of leaves, turning this way and that, moving forward and backward, focused on adding to our collection.

And all was fun until it was time to make our way back to the main road; the happy trio became very quiet, and looked at each other; the joyful feeling quickly dissipated: we had no idea where we were in relation to the road, and where we were in relation to the town—in short, we were completely disoriented—we were lost.

Panic did not set in right away—that was to come later, after we had crossed bogs and swamps with water up to our waist. Then one of our party lost his hat, tangled in the thick brush, someone else bruised a knee or scraped his hands moving branches away from his face. At this point, voices started to sound different, quavering, breaking and high pitched. I knew we were in trouble when the boy—the senior in our group—carrying the bagful of collected leaves, put it aside when we stopped for a rest, and when we got up to walk on, he did not retrieve it; and although we all saw the bag sitting on the ground—no one picked it up—our minds confused and preoccupied. Then, someone started to cry, bawling out, "Help"…"Help" at the top of his lungs in between a stutter of sobs.

By the time the sun was beginning its decline; we were wet, cold and shivering. We looked like little people from a wild, uncivilized country; our faces were streaked with tears, scuffed and dirty; we had nettles and pieces of small twigs stuck in our hair. When we reached the top of a high cliff we were exhausted from the climb, so we stopped and rested. From this high vantage point, we heard a low rumbling sound—the sweet sound of motor cars. I climbed a tall pine tree: although I could not see the cars I could clearly hear them, and I saw in the distance, the rising plumes of dust being kicked-up by the tires—the seven to four o'clock shift on their way home. We only had a ten to a fifteen-minute window of opportunity, in which to track and follow the sound before that last miner would be home.

We made it out; wet, cold and hungry. And, embarrassed. No one ever mentioned the bag of leaves left behind. I got home just in time for supper.

And the third Hospital Visit

But, that was not to be the end of that adventure for me. I had picked-up a viral infection. On the second night, I lay in between my mom and dad in their bed, battling a high fever. My mother told me later that when I became delirious she did not hesitate, she called Mr. Savard—our one and only taxicab operator—and had me brought to the hospital in the middle of the night. Admission number three—I have never been hospitalized since.

I was diagnosed with cerebral meningitis and remained in the hospital for almost a month. My mother's visits were memorable; she always managed to bring me something. For the first time in my life, I got to eat—and enjoy—the taste of red grapes. Upon discharge, I remember a general body weakness, particularly in the legs. I missed six weeks of school in total, but I recovered my health quite well and caught up with the school curriculum by the time Christmas rolled around. I and my two buddies got a passing—if sympathetic—grade on our leaf collecting assignment.

My father and the Montreal Canadiens

I have never seen my father play any sports or engage in anything coming close to a sporting activity. My father was no athlete. However, he was a hardcore Montreal Canadiens hockey fan. It became a passion—a personal thing. I have seen him not being able to sleep, so upset was he, that his beloved Canadiens had lost a game against Toronto. It was as if his honour and the fate of French Canada depended on how well the Montreal Canadiens did. Therefore, on March 13, 1955, he was beside himself.

He'd been listening to a game over the radio; Maurice Richard got a penalty and he was ejected from the game. The incident was reviewed in the next few days by the league president, Clarence Campbell and Richard was handed a suspension for the remainder of the regular season plus all of the playoffs. In my father's eyes, and those of French Quebec in general, the suspension was viewed as an injustice, an unfair punishment given to a Francophone hero by the Anglophone establishment. Riots broke out in the streets of Montreal; tear gas canisters were thrown about in the arena by the fans; Campbell's life was threatened and twenty thousand partisan fans ran amok outside. My father, ever the quiet reasonable man, applauded.

The team made the Stanley Cup finals but lost in the seventh and deciding game by one goal. The riots have taken on a mystical quality in the decades since, and is viewed by some as the precursor to Quebec's "Quiet Revolution".

In Love Again

In the spring of 1955, I was to fall in love again. My second love affair, after Miss Beauchemin—this one was a blond, blue-eyed Russian or Ukrainian beauty. She was eighteen or nineteen years old, and she could neither speak English nor French. One day she just appeared—and got quickly surrounded by children, like a queen amongst her subjects. Children have a way of knowing the heart of a person—if it is mean-spirited—or kind-hearted and welcoming—without the need for verbal communication. We were all seated around her in a field of tall, yellow waves of dandelions. She showed the older kids how to make dandelions wreaths and garlands by interweaving the long stems, leaving the yellow flower head showing their beauty on the exterior. She made wreaths for the girls and placed them on their heads; the boys got garlands put around their necks. Almost like a dream, a wisp of fog—within a few weeks, she would be gone. She'd been visiting a "DP" family in town.

The Savards. And Colette starts Dating

I practiced and perfected the timing of my arrivals at Ronald's house. They had their supper much later than us, so I would call on him when I knew he had just sat down to his meal. Mrs. Savard would ask me in to sit and wait—that was the cue I would be waiting for—I would proceed directly to the living room and go through the stacks of magazines she had stored there. She caught on; one day she had a box full of outdated publications for me to take home.

Ronald had an older brother, Roger, of the same age as my sister Colette. For whatever reason, my mother did not take kindly to him. One evening after supper, my mother gave me a very unpleasant task to do—I was to spy on her behalf—a task that I found distasteful, but I said I would do it. My assignment was to go about town and report back on Colette's movements, particularly if they were movements in concert with Roger.

Roger was seeing my sister; he had a car and they would drive around as young people are wont to do; going to the lake or hang around in Paquin's restaurant. Later that evening I tracked the car parked in the dark and deserted schoolyard; and I told my mother when I came in—probably the first time I had lied to her—that they'd stayed all night at Paquin's; having sodas and listening to the jukebox. The siblings had to stick together.

Charley and onset of Strange Behaviour

Late in the spring, Charley, who was then twenty, had left the house to take work out of town for a diamond drilling company. Charley was starting to act strangely. He had few friends, and he would disappear for entire days without telling anyone where he had been at. My parents showed no concern. No one could get hurt in Belleterre.

Ray A. Vincent

Pocket Money Activities

That left me the only boy remaining at home along with four girls. Around this time I started to get involved in activities that would bring me some money. I picked raspberries, selling them door-to-door; I attended the men's competitive baseball games, but not as a spectator; I would patrol the outside perimeter of the field and retrieve balls hit out of bounds, in the deep grass or the edges of the bush—baseballs were expensive—one would get ten cents for each ball returned to the home team officials.

One day, on a sunny Sunday afternoon—and, the only time in all of my life that I ever asked money from my father—I met him alone on the sidewalk coming from the ball field. I was with a friend who had money in his pocket, while I had none in mine. Shyly, I asked my dad if he would have ten cents to give me. Without hesitation, he reached in his pocket and produced a whole quarter. I looked up at him proudly and he beamed back a big tender smile. The meaning to me of such moments, I am unable to adequately describe.

Mother Takes Charge and Saves a Toddler

My mother's take-charge character and quick thinking were demonstrated again one day that summer. A young family lived in the upstairs apartment of the house next door. On that late, quiet Saturday afternoon, a piercing scream came out of the apartment. My mother and father went outside to see what was happening. A young woman was running down the exterior stairway holding a toddler in her arms.

The child had tipped a pot of boiling oil meant to cook french-fries, all over himself. The toddler was in shock; you could see the little chest heaving with every moan and whimper—the crisis was beyond the stages of crying. My mother took the child forcibly from the young woman's arms, and she ran to the restaurant thirty yards away. Once inside, she pulled Roger Savard away from his burger and said, "Hurry, get in your car, we're going to Ville Marie."—the only hospital with a burn unit in the area.

Later, whenever in my life I was to be faced with difficult decisions to make or had challenges to meet—I would think of that incident and say to myself—what would my mother do in this situation? That approach has helped me on many occasions.

My Friends in Bearn and my Dislike of Country Hygiene

Up until the day we left Belleterre, I would spend four weeks at Rose's out of my summer school vacations. I made good friends in Bearn; Ronald had an uncle there and I visited the Savard's on their farm almost every day. I liked the July hay harvesting time, bringing in the bails to the barn and driving the tractor. However, some of the farmers' habits did not sit well with me: the upstairs boys' beds had the smell of urine in them; and there was farmyard dirt all over the kitchen and living room floors; and then there were the flies, hundreds of them in the air; on the sticky paper bands hanging from the ceiling; and on the furniture and on the food.

One day I was asked to come and partake in a family delicacy—fresh picked field watermelon—I liked watermelons, but not when I had to fight the flies in order to hold on to my portion. For a long time afterward, the sight of cut watermelon slices would make my stomach nauseous.

A Growing Dislike

Rosario had a pulpwood lot in the vicinity of Lac D'Argent and a concession from the government to harvest for the local mills. I hated it when we went there. My sister was without children, so she would accompany him whenever he went out to work on his woodlot. He would cut down the tall poplars with a chainsaw, trim them and section them in four-foot pieces, and then he would haul truckloads with his big truck to the mill in Temiscaming. We stayed in the bush for entire weeks at a time; we would go out to the woodlot in the morning and come back home for supper time. We had to live in a primitive wood camp. I was twelve at the time and I hated it. I hated the smell of frying baloney in the air in the morning when I got up. This baloney was mixed in with yesterday's boiled potatoes and became part of our morning breakfast. I hated being alone with two adults and away from my friends. And, I started to hate my brother-in-law's consistently demeaning and abusive language toward my sister.

I was hurt and embarrassed by it. He was a master of sarcasm and humiliation. And his sadism loved an audience. I never heard him say anything loving or complimentary to his wife whenever I was around them. Thankfully, this work at the woodlot only lasted one summer vacation period.

Colette goes to Teacher's College

My sister Colette would start Teacher's College in the fall in Ville-Marie, at an all- girls' school run by the nuns. This was a two-year program. Colette was sixteen when she was admitted. To my mother's joy, admission to Teacher's College would see the end of her relationship with Roger Savard.

"Tell Your Parents: they Charge More than they Pay Down"

Mr. Riendeau was the grocer across the street; his son, Yvon, was the crying classmate (the senior) of the maple leaf collecting misadventure. We had a running account at his store. Only the poor have running accounts with unpaid balances at grocery stores. Every payday my mother would put money down on the account. One day

I went in to pick up some items of grocery; I was twelve- years-old; he told me—a twelve year old kid—to tell my parents that they were getting behind—that they bought more per week than they were paying down on—hence they were falling behind. He did not have the guts to say this to them directly—he used me.

On that day, walking home with a heavy heart, I realized for the first time that we were poor. People with money did not buy food on credit. I never told my parents of this conversation. As a matter of fact, I told this to my sisters only but recently.

The next occasion that the fact was brought to my attention that we were poor, was at Sheridan Technical School, my high school in Sudbury; Mr. Gowalko, my gym teacher, asked one day if, "Those were the only pairs of pants I had to wear?" since I wore them constantly. Without missing a beat, I told him that they were not—the other pair was reserved to go to church with. That's how my mother would have responded.

The Announcement of a New Apartment

The announcement came one evening after supper. We were moving. My mother was excited; my father, as usual, was quiet. The new apartment would be modern; central heating; hot running water; a propane gas kitchen range; a Frigidaire refrigerator. We all caught our mother's excitement—except for our father—who remained quiet. The move took place before the start of school; August 1955.

CHAPTER 6

The New Apartment and Improvements

The new apartment was also located on First Avenue, directly facing Paquin's restaurant. It was on the upper level of a large four-plex, square building. The right lower level was occupied by the Loyal Order of the Moose Lodge—the hall where Rose had had her wedding reception. On the left side of the Moose Hall was a Ladies Wear Shop run by a Jewish couple, Sam and Esther Silverstein. Our apartment was on top of the Moose Hall, and the Dhiel family was next to us, atop Sam and Esther's shop. You accessed each apartment from ground level through enclosed stairways, each located on opposite sides of the building.

Although small, our apartment was very nice; a great improvement over the previous address. The floors were hardwood-covered, with some areas clad with linoleum; off the entry, to the left, my parents had their bedroom; then, a living room leading to an outside covered balcony facing Paquin's; a dining room with a two-way swing door which lead to a small kitchen; and off of the dining room to the right, was a bedroom for my four sisters; and, from the kitchen you accessed a small bathroom.

The back of the apartment had a long wooden balcony shared with the two apartments; a long wood stairway connected in the middle and led down to the lane behind the building.

We loved our new place. We had the novel luxuries of hot running water; electricity coming out of wall outlets; central heating; a refrigerator and a gas-fired kitchen range. But, there was something missing—nowhere for me to sleep; and, that state of affairs would last for the next six years; four in Belleterre and two in Sudbury—I was to be relegated to a living room couch. In other words; for a very long time I would have no privacy, and I would not be able to get some sleep until the last person walking about had retired for the night.

Our neighbours, the Dhiels

Our neighbours, Mr. and Mrs. Dhiel were in worse financial shape than we were. Mrs. Dhiel had five small children to look after, and an alcoholic husband to endure. Mr. Dhiel was a bartender at the hotel and many a night he would come home using the privacy of the back laneway, swaying from side to side in his walk, and hanging on to the railing as he struggled with the back stairs. There were evenings when I would cover my ears, in order not to hear the shouts and arguments; the beating blows, the thumping against the walls and the crying. On many occasions, my mother would take in the Dhiel kids to eat with us, because there was no food in their house.

Sam and Esther

Sam and Esther's shop was an oddity in town, but it was a curiosity that attracted customers. It was the only store that catered exclusively to women, and it was the only commercial shop in town, whose owners barely spoke a word of French.

Why two Montreal Jews would set up shop in our little town is difficult to understand. Sam and Esther were in their early fifties and childless. Sam was short and rotund, with a thin crown of hair on an otherwise balding head, and he had a permanent cigarette attached to his lips. He drove a massive-sized brown car. Esther was a study in contrast; she was tall, much taller than Sam, and skinny with a pale wrinkled face; she had long, dry and wiry yellow blond hair; and she carried the constant odour of garlic about her. Sam spoke more, but not much better French than her, and Esther spoke it with a heavy German-sounding accent.

Sam would be on the road often; so most of the customer contacts were with Esther. Because of his many absences, we suspected that Sam had other stores around the province. Sam rode this big car, and every second week he would roll up to the front of the store with the front and back seats loaded to the ceiling with ladies' garments. Colette and Carmen complained that the stock was dated and out of style—some unsalable stuff Sam had picked up in Montreal at rock bottom prices—however, people would flock over and go through it.

The Movie House

The "Star Theatre" was attached to our building, separated by a concrete block wall. It had just recently been completed, and it effectively ran Father Pelletier and his church basement operation, out of the movie business. The new movie house had a big front stage and accommodated four hundred seats spread over five thousand square feet. I saw The Ten Commandments, Ben-Hur and Elvis' Love Me Tender and Jailhouse Rock, there.

In 1956, I saw John Diefenbaker in person on the stage when he was touring the country; building the Quebec wing of his party, prior to his election win in 1957, as Prime Minister of the country. He spoke such horrible French I could not make out one word he said. But I enjoyed the fiery oratory and the theatrics of the aspiring Quebec politicians with him. The speeches had capped the carnival atmosphere of the day; bright placards were nailed to lamp posts, and at noon, a car had gone up and down the streets, loudly proclaiming through loudspeakers attached to the roof, the virtues of the evening's political rally.

Some Forewarnings of Things to come

I was to learn later, when I returned to school the next month, the probable cause of my father's silence over supper at the old house, when my mother had made the announcement of our impending move to the new place. My school friends openly talked about what they had overheard at home—the rumours that McIntyre may be closing down the mine in the near future.

Stand by my Friend and a Fight with the school Bully

Amongst my circle of friends, I became attached to Florian Labelle and made a new friendship with Roger Paquette. Florian and I were together one day after school, and we made our way to the ice-rink now located between the post-office and Father Pelletier's presbytery.

The shack was closed so a group of us played on and around the rink. The school bully for our age group, Maurice Marleau, was running after Florian, tripping him and pushing him into the snow. Florian had blond hair and clear blue eyes; he was soft spoken, and frail for a twelve-year-old, but he was gentle and very intelligent. He usually stayed away from the rough and tumble ways of my other friends. He owned a bicycle; a complete metal "Meccano" set—something to die for in those days—and boxes and boxes of comic books.

We knew that Florian carried a deep pain in his heart—his father had been one of the young miners killed in the mine accident, in February 1950. Maurice kept on pushing Florian down, every time he made an attempt to get up. So, I walked up to Maurice and challenged him to a fight—and no sooner had I thrown the glove down—I regretted my foolishness—I was sure I would get killed. But there was no way to back down now, and live to speak to my friends again.

We squared off on the slippery foot-path leading to the shack, with a ring of excited boys around us, some looking away, fearing the disaster about to happen. Not only was Maurice bigger and taller than any of us; he was also at least a year older—he had been held back two years in the same grade due to poor marks.

In size, he towered over me. He was big, but he was also clumsy; I had to trust to my agility. He moved his arm all the way back and swung forward with a mighty swing—I ducked—and he slipped, losing his balance in the forward momentum. He lost his footing on the icy surface of the footpath and he fell down face forward; I quickly jumped on top, covering him with my body. In an instant, both of us stood up, and he put out his hand to me to shake on—an understood token of truce. He wiped his face, and noticing the blood coming from his nose, he ran home, leaving me in complete command of the field. My friends were in awe as the circle closed in around me—I never told them that he had lost his balance and crushed his nose when he hit the frozen ground—I never laid a hand on him.

And next day the story circulated in the schoolyard—how I had beaten Maurice to a pulp—and they'd been witnesses to it.

A Spring Time money making Activity

The new ice-rink was open seven nights a week and all day Saturdays and Sundays. I spent all my winter outdoor time there, helping to the extent I could, Mr. Berube the caretaker; with ice cleanups; flooding and bringing in the firewood to feed the red-hot pot belly stove. Springtime came and I got myself involved in a new money making activity—for money was needed to catch the movies playing at the Star.

Every Saturday morning, beginning in mid-April, and continuing as long as the snow melt was happening along the ditches of the road leading to town—I would go out bottle scavenging. A friend would take one side and I would take the other; a fifty-pound empty potato bag slung over our shoulders; we would rake in a small fortune.

In those days, everyone drank, and drank in their cars—throwing empties out the window and onto the snow banks—beer and pop bottles appeared everywhere through the melting snow. We came back loaded—sometimes hitching a ride back because of the heavy load. We made straight for Mr. Latraverse's store to convert our loot into cash. The morning's work got us a movie ticket plus a soda and chips, and the odd Cherry Blossom, or Sweet Marie.

The Art and Science of eating Chocolate Bars

One of the things I learned at the time was that one ought not to eat Cherry Blossoms in the darkness of a theatre—not only because they have to be seen to be appreciated—but because they could turn into a sticky, messy disaster. They had to be eaten outside, in broad daylight. A scientific approach was required to properly eat, and more importantly—appreciate and enjoy—a Cherry Blossom or a Sweet Marie. I got to figure out the best angle of attack; that is, not to assume a precipitate and aggressive attitude—a certain amount of foreplay would conduce to a better outcome—therefore the best way was by slow, considered movements. The Cherry Blossom has to be coaxed and nibbled at one corner first, enjoying and savouring the chocolaty-nutty flavour; then, one sucks at the sweet, thick and slowly dripping liquid oozing out; and then slowly you eat your way to the cherry hidden inside.

Now, a Sweet Marie needed a different process, although the underlying principle was the same, that is—take your time. After gently unwrapping Sweet Marie, you ate around the soft caramel core, concentrating on eating the chocolaty peanuts first; once the caramel core was stripped naked, then—and only then—did you dive in and finish the job.

My First Fish and Summer Play with Friends

A few days into summer vacations I came across a spool of fishing line; actually, a heavy green fibre line used for winter ice fishing. I went to Mr. Desjardins, our local butcher, and got a chunk of fat with a little meat on it, and proceeded to a small bay behind the presbytery. I tied the line to the hook, secured the chunk of fat to it, and swung the whole into the shallow water. I attached the free end to some brush and went to play with my friends.

Late in the afternoon, when I remembered my line I went back to it. And there it was—my first fish ever—a pike thrashing in the water, well hooked to the line. My father cleaned it and we had it for supper the next day. I caught a few more fish that summer—catfish—which no one wanted to handle. I would clean them myself, starting with gutting them out and then using pliers to pull off the smooth skin. And then no one would eat them—but I did—nicely fried whole in butter they made an excellent meal.

One day Florian, Gaston, Ronald and I, found a canoe on the shoreline. We took it out on the water and headed toward an island some four hundred yards away. By the time we reached the halfway point, we realized why the canoe had been abandoned—it was leaking like a sieve. There was a bailing bucket inside, and we paddled and bailed the water out as if the devil was on our tail. We made it safely back to shore, but with water over our ankles.

That same summer, the four of us headed out to the town's garbage dump located behind the mine site. A lot of bottles could be found there, and other valuable junk that could be converted to usable things; parts of old bicycles, parts of old appliances—they could all be rehabilitated, one way or another. We took a path cutting through a wooded area. This was a shortcut, but we needed to make our way across a narrow, but deep ravine. Two large logs were set side by side, with planks laid diagonally across them. I volunteered to cross first, and I realized after two steps forward that the boards were not nailed down. One log moved; the planks slid off, and I found myself hanging on for dear life between the two parted pieces of timber. As a large board slid off to crash on the rocky bottom fifty feet below, it hit me in the thigh and the side of the knee. With my friends holding onto the loose logs, I crept back, hand over hand until they were within reach and pulled me to safety. Another promising adventure had to be aborted.

A Murder in the Neighbourhood

In July 1956, I was walking toward home when I got the sense that something out of the ordinary had happened. A crowd had gathered in front of Paquin's; other folks were coming out of the group and beckoning to other people—we had our first murder ever recorded.

In the small hamlet of Gainsmore, a few miles from us, someone had been shot dead.

Gainsmore had a population of approximately one hundred and fifty persons. A married man had befriended a widow living alone with her fifteen-year-old daughter. The court evidence at trial revealed that the man was sexually abusing the young girl. Mother and daughter decided to take the law into their own hands.

The man had the habit of sitting on the widow's verandah with his back to the front screen door. Being in the middle of the hot July season, the main door was left open during the day. While the man was not around, the mother went inside and figured out where the middle of his back would be; she then cut out a one inch hole at that location, and told her daughter that was where the muzzle of the hunting rifle should be pushed through, before she was to pull the trigger. That fateful day, the high-powered rifle had been loaded in the morning and the hammer fully cocked. When the man came calling he was entertained as usual by the girl's mother, and he was seated in his favourite chair—what followed went exactly according to plan.

At the conclusion of the trial, the mother was sent to prison and the daughter went to a reformatory.

Early migrations to Sudbury and Belleterre under Assault

Sometime in August, Colette left to go to work in Sudbury, Ontario. Charley, now married, already lived in Sudbury, and Pete also newly married, lived in Chelmsford, a small town in close proximity of Sudbury. Colette had gained her teacher's certificate. She could teach the elementary grades, but she opted for a change in vocation. Once in Sudbury, she took employment in office-clerical work at the Sudbury St. Joseph Hospital.

May 19, 1957, saw Belleterre under assault, an advancing threat was moving ever closer to town. By May 20, the citizens were put on standby to evacuate; an out of control forest fire was slowly creeping towards town. You could see, hear and smell the fire. From our rooftop vantage point, we could see the tongues of fire shoot up in the sky, and hop from tree to tree. The front of the fire was about four hundred yards away; every able-bodied man was mobilized to firefight.

By May 21, the wind shifted when the flames were within one hundred feet from the closest house at the edge of town. That wind shift turned the tide and saved the town. Folks started to unpack luggage and boxes. The fire had come in from the northeast end of town, so the exit to the west was always clear and safe. Some cottages by the lake were destroyed and the entire cemetery was surrounded by burnt forest.

A Lesson in Free Enterprise and the Reward System of Production

One day I got a lesson on the free enterprise system and the method of pay commensurate with production. Mr. Fillion lived in a big house behind us across the lane. He had a large mound of split furnace wood in his driveway and needed to move it to the basement. He had heart problems, so he asked five of us to help him out. He removed a basement window and he showed us where we were to neatly stack the wood against a concrete wall.

I organized the crew—two in the basement; one to receive and one to stack—three outside; one to fill the wheelbarrow, one to push it, and one at the window to pass the firewood on toward the receiver. I was in the basement neatly cording the wood against the wall. When I found the flow slowing down I would go to the window and exhort more speed. If anyone slacked off I would tell him to pick it up; if a dispute developed I was the arbitrator. Mr. Fillion was the overseer.

We got the job done and now it was payday time. He had a little office in the basement. He took us down there and lined us up, and pulled a small metal cash box out of a drawer. Everyone got twenty-five cents—except me—I got forty cents.

He gave a short lecture on the economic principles behind the production and reward system: he who produces more, either by his efforts or his methods, had earned the right to a higher level of reward. I don't believe the explanation impressed my friends.

I am not anti-union—unions have been instrumental in bringing about positive improvements in wages, and health and safety in the workplace—but what I disagree with are unions' efforts to bring production activity down to an average of the membership or, at worst, down to the lowest common denominator—down to the slowest producer. I remember once, working as a summer student at the Falconbridge Nickel Mines smelter in Sudbury, and being approached by the union steward, who tapped me gently on the shoulder, took me aside and said, "Slow down young man, we don't work like this around here"—that was my introduction to the union-shop mentality. What he was saying, in effect was: don't embarrass us, blend in, lower your activity level to that of the average in this workplace.

Throughout my life, my work ethic has always been to do whatever I am asked to do, as well as I can do it, and work at it as hard as I can. I never held the attitude that someone owed me a living—I never thought that my employer was there for me—I always understood the relationship to be the other way around.

The Lady on the Blacklist

In the province of Quebec you can walk into any grocery store and come out with your loaf of bread, and if you wish it, a bottle of wine and a case of beer.

Coming home from school, I would take shortcuts in between houses, and I had a favourite route. One day, going by the last house before I entered my lane, a lady's voice came out through a screened window and asked me to come over to the door. She handed me fifty cents, and she asked me to go to Latraverse's and pick up a quart of beer for her—in those days you could buy those large-sized bottles which sold individually. And she said that there would be ten cents in it for me—a twenty percent commission.

The regulations were not what they are now, and anyhow, merchants in town knew all the families, and all the children on a first-name basis. I brought back the beer to the lady and got my reward. The next afternoon, the same trip to the store was repeated and with the same outcome. However, on the third afternoon, Mr. Latraverse asked me who the beer was meant for—he'd assumed it was for my father—and I told him it was the lady's. He took the bottle back and put the money in my hand, telling me to return it to her; he could not sell her beer or wine—she'd been "blacklisted" by her husband some months before.

My mother explained to me what the husband had done, and she said that all husbands had the right to do so—however, wives could not return the same favours to their husbands. I do not think this practice would sit well with the women's liberation movement of today—or with the courts.

My Friends Laurent and Roger

The Paul family lived on Fourth Avenue. Mr. Paul had a stable behind his house and he kept a team of pulling horses. He would hire them out to whoever needed to get wood out of the bush, or for other similar tasks. His son Laurent, was a friend of mine and in the winter when his dad was not around, Laurent would harness one of the horses to a big sleigh, and we would carouse up and down the laneways picking up kids along the way. Mothers today would not tolerate this unsupervised freedom and it's actually amazing that no one ever got hurt—but we had great fun—you blend parents in and the fun ceases.

Roger Paquette and I decided one winter to build an ice-rink behind his house. This got us in some deep trouble with his mom and dad. His parents had gone away for the weekend, leaving an older sister to watch over the house and the kids. We got our ice pad going, flooding every hour on the first day; it was wide and long—too long—it reached up to and underneath the back stairs. A three-inch layer of ice proved very difficult to remove, in minus fifteen degree Celsius that Sunday afternoon, after his mom and dad had reviewed our project.

CHAPTER 7

Hermille: Our first Millionaire

A year or so after we had moved away, Belleterre celebrated the appearance of its first millionaire. Hermille—"Mi-mille" for us—Lambert. Hermille had been the butt of jokes and pranks as he grew up, not mean or vicious, but still; at his expense.

He was physically handicapped but he was accepted as a friend and he attended the same school and the same classes as any other kid in town. He walked dragging one foot, and he had tremors in his left arm and wrist. He was physically disabled, but intellectually very normal. Although we made the odd jokes, everyone in town had a special place in his heart for Hermille—after all, he was one of our own.

One day Hermille won the one million dollar Montreal Olympics lottery jackpot. Hermille and his family remained in Belleterre—it was home—where he was known and accepted.

My friend Florian. A Tragedy

When Florian died the whole town stood still. It was a major tragedy; it involved two close-knit families; the Labelles and the Savards. The families knew each other very well; the children always played together, and practically shared the same households; and I was both, Florian's and Ronald's best friend.

To make matters worse, Mrs. Labelle had lost her husband in the mine accident of February 1950; and now she was losing her thirteen-year-old son. She was left alone with Ginette.

Mr. Savard had left the taxi business, and he was trying to get a fledgling car repair garage up and running. One day in July 1957, he was busy cleaning the carburetor of a pickup truck; the hood was open and the engine was running; Mr. Savard was stretched out and bent over the engine, a large container of cleaning solvent—gasoline—resting at his elbow.

With the roar of the engine in his ears, he never heard Florian creep up behind him, moving closer to his right shoulder, curious to see what he was doing. A spark was produced from the open carburetor, igniting the vapours and the gasoline container burst into flames. Mr. Savard's instinctive reaction was to eject the flaming container over his right shoulder, and behind him, away from the engine. Florian got the flaming liquid poured all over himself. He died in hospital three days later. He was buried in the Laverlochere cemetery alongside his father. I was one of the pallbearers—along with our other friends.

Mr. Savard went through a very difficult period, but he remained in Belleterre with his family by his side, and with the community to support him.

Mrs. Labelle broke under the mental strain of the two losses; she would later join some religious sect, and she and her daughter moved to the group's headquarters in Florida—this I was told years later when I visited Belleterre as a young man and made enquiries of my friend's mother.

A Short-lived BB-Gun Owner

I became the proud owner of a BB gun—every twelve-year old's dream—however, after I started shooting down skylarks off of the clothesline, and taking pot shots at the open street lamps—my mother made the dream one of very short duration; she returned it to the store.

Unknown to me, Esther happened to be a great lover of anything with wings or that which went about on four legs. When she was looking out her back door one day and saw birds falling dead from the sky, she quickly lodged a complaint with my mother. And, so did Mr. Paquin later, after he had seen me hanging around the lamp post by the restaurant, and by nighttime, he noticed that the bulb was out. Two strikes and I was out—the BB gun disappeared.

Town Scandals

Two scandals occurred one week after the other. Father Pelletier was a great believer in Divine Retribution, but alas, he viewed himself as one of its agents.

One Sunday, as I was kneeling at the communion-rail, along with a row of parish communicants humbly awaiting the host; hands covered by the veil—why we had to cover our hands no one could ever tell me—the lady kneeling down next to me was skipped—Father did not give her communion. He obviously had some unpleasant information about her, but he had forgotten his "Luke, 7:37", where Jesus pardoned and gave his blessing to the woman, "Who lived a sinful life". And I was not the only person who noticed. Within an hour after mass, the whole town was talking about it.

And then, within a few weeks of the communion incident, the president of the Loyal Order of the Moose was charged with embezzling Lodge funds. The charges proceeded to trial and he was convicted. He was the father of twelve children and he lived on Fourth Avenue.

The church and the Lodge incident had no connection, of course—one party was suspected of lascivious behaviour and the other criminally convicted of greed. Unfortunately, in the eyes of public opinion, the former was demeaned, and treated with scorn as long as she lived in town; whereas, the latter was accepted back into the fold without much concern, or comments raised about his past activity. One was stigmatized and talked about behind her back, on the basis of unproven rumours; while the other enjoyed a certain amount of status and notoriety, even though blemished in reputation and character by a criminal record of actual facts.

THE CHRONICLES OF A JOURNEY

The Miners' bus and the Paroxysms of early morning Coughs

The mine supplied a bus on which the workers would hop on at 6:30 in the morning. The pickup point was at Paquin's, right in front of our place. Every time we heard the early morning paroxysm of death rattling coughs, my mother would remind us that; if we kept swallowing that hated spoonful of cod liver oil that she produced every lunchtime—and if we never smoked—we would not cough like these men did.

The group would build up slowly. They came shuffling in through the early morning mist, in twos and threes; drop their lunch pails at their feet, and light up. The conversations would be short, quiet and soft, they knew there were people still sleeping. As if on cue, one would start and then another, coughing themselves red in the face; some bent double at the waist, hands resting on their knees; they would heave hard, spitting on the ground, and remain bent over, out of breath, exhausted by the effort. Mr. Fleury would have turned purple in the face by this time. When some stopped and stood up others would begin the painful morning ritual all over again.

Smoking was bad enough, but smoking and inhaling the heavy dust at the workplace was a morbid combination. The bus would sidle up to the curb and the men get in. You could still hear some muffled coughs as the vehicle pulled away.

Colette Brings a Boyfriend Home

One weekend Colette came back for a visit—with a male companion—her boyfriend, Roger Lalonde. Colette was changed, she had taken on the look of the big city girl—in dress and manners. She was sophisticated and spoke with the assurance and confidence of maturity. Roger was a dispatcher and telegraph operator with the Canadian National Railway.

Frail and pale looking; he did not impress my father. They had no sooner left to return to Sudbury than my father turned to our mother, and said, shaking his head, "Did you look at the scrawny arms? Did you see the delicate white hands and slender fingers? This man couldn't do a full day's work if his life depended on it."

Our first Policeman: Joe Lariviere, the Policeman without a Gun

In 1957, the town hired a policeman. We had no police chief. We had no police car; but we had a newly passed town bylaw that said that as of this moment in time, we had a policeman—we had Joe Lariviere—the mayor, Ken Godin, personally hired him.

We had no police department, but Joe would work out of his house. And in order to give Joe some semblance of official authority, the town issued Joe a policeman's cap—a nice, deep blue cap, with a wide shiny black visor. It had an impressive gold badge with the Quebec Fleurs de Lis emblem embossed on it, sitting solidly atop the visor.

Joe loved his new job and he took to it with some energy. The cap made up for the little money he was getting paid. He would carefully place it on his head at a jaunty, if not cocky, angle. When a call came, Joe would run for the hat, and with all the dignity he could muster, jump in his pickup truck.

People did not take exception when Joe was hired for the job—Joe was a native Indian living off-reserve—he was married and had four children. He had lived in Belleterre for many years. He was one of us. Joe was lean, tall and good looking. He seldom smiled and the quietness about him made people pay attention. However, if Joe proudly wore the symbol of authority on his head, he lacked that most important piece of policeman-hood—Joe was not allowed to carry a firearm on his person or, in his pickup truck for that matter.

Folks around town joked and laughed; they called Joe a school truant officer at worst or a town by-law enforcement officer at best.

But, Joe took his job seriously and he did a good job; he issued tickets to poachers during the walleye spawning season; he stopped the odd fight at the hotel or at the hockey games; he put a stop to drag-racing on the Avenues; and he enforced the town curfew—any kid on the streets after sunset was terrified when he saw Joe's pickup turn a street corner—Ronald peed his pants one night, when Joe met him coming out of Latraverse's with a bag of chips in his hand—Ronald said Joe had fooled him by creeping up behind him with his headlights shut off. And Ronald wanted some revenge, something had to be done to regain some of his lost dignity—he would squeal on Marie—Joe's sixteen-year-old daughter.

Late one evening that summer, Ronald had caught Marie and Fernand Ayotte "fooling around" in a darkened change-room kiosk by the lakeside. When Ronald threw rocks at the wooden kiosk, Fern and Marie had come rushing out—her, brushing down her skirt, and him zipping up his pants. He would tell Joe what kind of a daughter he had.

When I reminded Ronald that Fern was nineteen and that he was twelve; and that Fern was big and strong and could easily break his nose and give him two black eyes—he abandoned the vendetta.

Then, the day arrived when Joe came into his full glory. That long-awaited seat of prestige and recognition was finally pushed towards him—and that—because the Russians were coming after us.

He was put in charge of the sirens. Two were installed; not to warn the citizenry of impending forest fires and other natural disasters, or, the commencement of the curfew hour: not at all; they were installed to warn us of an incoming nuclear attack. Now, who in their right mind would want to attack Belleterre, situated as we were, in the deep bush, and in the middle of nowhere? Well, Mayor Godin and Joe Lariviere told us who would—the Russians—that's who.

They'd come back from a meeting held in Rouyn, where everyone had been told to go home and inform their people to be prepared. Grownups laughed, of course. But Father Pelletier did not, and neither did the children; the children because they were scared, and Father Pelletier because people had been told that; if they were on the streets when the sirens went off, to run to the church basement—that would save them—because of the thickness of the poured concrete? —Or because the church was the repository of the blessed host? —became a subject of much debate.

The mine ownership did not put up a fuss about interruptions to production that the drills would cause—Ken Godin saw to that—he was the mine superintendent. One siren was secured to the light post in front of the church and close to the school. The other was in the centre of town, on a post not far from Paquin's, and close enough to my house that we could throw stones at it—and we did—to see who had the "better arm".

There had been heated arguments between the elected officials of Ville-Marie, and those of Belleterre, as to who should get the sirens. Belleterre had won out because it had no cows or sheep about the town—after all, it had been officially designated a "city" by the provincial government when it was incorporated—whereas, Ville-Marie, with the same population, was a farming community, and really, of what import were all those dairy cows and those sheep, to the Russians?

Joe had found a new purpose in life—he would save Belleterre from nuclear annihilation. And so, for the first six months following the installations, he had everyone going crazy with his practice drills. He was in full charge and control; at the pull of a switch, he made people move as he wished. And it had to be seen to be so, to consolidate a sense of importance in the whole exercise. And in Joe's mind; in order for the drills to be effective, they had to be brought about unannounced—meaning, at his whim.

First, you had the slow and low whirring sound, like that of the tubes the kids would whirl in a circular motion over their heads at the beach; and then, it moved on to the fast, and the loud siren screaming frenzy of fear it was meant to be.

After six months, people would methodically go through the motions and say—there goes Joe, playing with his new toys again. And, after a year and a half, drills were seldom held. And, after two years, Joe told the mayor that maybe the Russians wouldn't come after all; which was hoped for—because, by that time, the sirens had broken down; they'd become the victims of rust, sub-zero winter temperatures and the lack of any regular maintenance; and no amount of coaxing by Joe, would make them obey his commands to wail away.

St. Jean de Baptiste day in Rose's Village

That June 24th, 1958, the celebration of Saint-Jean de Baptiste day in my sister's village, became a very important event when it was announced that the internationally celebrated French Canadian folk singer, Jacques Labrecque, was to give a live stage performance to close off the Saturday night.

Our school provided free bus transportation for anyone interested in attending his concert, and since my sister lived there I convinced my parents to let me go.

There was an added bonus for me, which I was not aware of at the time. Labrecque loved fishing. So it came about that, besides getting paid for his performance, at the last moment Labrecque asked if someone could take him out on a fishing trip to any local lake. An expedition to be paid for by the committee. The request was agreed to, and my brother-in-law who had a cottage on Lac D'Argent was chosen as the guide.

At that time Labrecque was a big recording artist in the province, with international appearances in France and England—he was the Gordon Lightfoot of Quebec. He was big and tall, somewhat balding at the top of his head, and he had a well-trimmed narrow moustache on an otherwise round face. He had a crystal clear tenor voice.

We went fishing, the four of us, Rose and her husband, Labrecque, and I. We got to the lake late, and very early the next morning I saw him standing outside enshrouded in the lifting fog. He was picking up a fishing rod and tackle box. Obviously, the man did love his fishing. My sister and Rosario were still sleeping, so he asked me if I wanted to walk with him to a waterfall we'd seen coming in the day before. I jumped at the invitation.

After a few casts, he looked around and asked me if I knew how—in the old days—all this wood got to the lumber mills—I said

I did not—and out came the booming voice and, "Les Raftsmen" went echoing all over the lake. The memorable refrain—"Bing sur la Ring, Bing sur la Ring Bing-Bing"—still plays on my mind today. He followed this with—"au Bois du rossignolet"—before we were interrupted by my brother-in-law coming up the path. I had an unforgettable weekend.

A Thief in the Presbytery

Later that summer, one of our friends became suddenly rich, and he loved to display his new found wealth. He had pockets full of silver—they bulged—I had never seen so many dimes and nickels in my life. We were treated to colas, chips, and movies for two weeks running. His circle of friends doubled in no time at all.

Difficult to keep a secret when you have so many friends. Adrien was an altar boy and he was privy to some information none of us knew. Adrien knew where in the presbytery, Father kept the week's church collection. No one locked their doors in Belleterre and while Father was at the church some two hundred yards away, Adrien was busy filling up his pockets. Adrien lived on Second Avenue and his father was an electrician at the mine. When the secret became public, and restitution made to the church, we did not see Adrien about town for quite a while—neither at his duties at church, nor on the street—his sister told us he could not sit down for the pain for a whole week.

An Annual summer Invasion. American Fishermen

Many American fishermen from Ohio, Michigan and New York State, came to Belleterre for the summer fishing season. Some came with their families or fathers came with their teenage sons, and they would find accommodations and meals at the "Chateau". A lot made the fishing trip an annual affair. At the end of August, they would get ready to return home for school start-up.

By this time my friends and I had gotten the timing right; when we saw activity around the big station-wagons we would mill around like fish in a fish-farm at feeding time. They would give us boxes and armloads of clothes of all kinds, jeans and white T-shirts; in those days you recognized an American—he was the guy with the white T-shirt on. The only time in Belleterre I got to wear a pair of jeans or a white T-shirt is when I received them from our American visitors' families returning home. I am sure they thought they were helping out some third-world kids.

I love Americans—I have nothing bad to say about them. Someone asked me one day; if I was stranded on a deserted island who would I want with me—without hesitation—I would pick an American. They are a practical, courageous and resourceful people.

Olga and her Husband strike it Rich

When Olga Oleksiuk left Mud Lake in 1950 with only the clothes she had on her back, to marry O' Brien Rivard, they had settled in Belleterre and raised their family there. They also lived on First Avenue, and I recall babysitting their first born—"quat-toast"—a purposely misspelled nickname in French slang, meaning ('four toast") because that was the three-year-old's favourite breakfast.

O'Brien worked at the mine and he had a passionate hobby—he was an amateur geologist and an avid part-time mining prospector. He wandered all over the unchartered bushlands, bringing back rock samples from interesting geologic formations; had them analyzed at the assay laboratories in Rouyn, and then registered and staked his claims in legal form. He kept doing this for years. It was a hobby which got him out of the house but brought absolutely no financial rewards. People would laugh at him—until one day—at the age of thirty-five, O'Brien struck it rich.

Overnight, O'Brien and Olga became Belleterre's second millionaires—a true "rags-to-riches" story. He had come upon a rich copper-nickel ore body. The deposit laid fairly close to the surface some fifteen miles west of Belleterre. McIntyre purchased the mining rights from him for $1.2 million dollars—a considerable sum at that time—plus, production royalties for the lifetime of the mine. The Lorraine mine opened in 1963 and closed in 1968. It made the Rivard's a lot of money. They did not move away, but added to the tapestry of the town; barreling up and down the dirt and dust covered streets with their latest Cadillac.

The mine Closes and Tearful Goodbyes

The sad news came to town on February 5, 1959—on my birthday— the gold mine was to close by August of that year. Everyone knew that when a mine opens it is an announcement that it will close someday, but that realization did not make it less hurtful to the men, nor less devastating to their families. The gold reserves were exhausted. The mine had produced 960,000 ounces of gold in the course of its existence—1937-1959—. The first two months following the announcement were a mixture of sadness and anxiety for me. However, as springtime turned to Summer I became reconciled to the idea that we would leave. I would lose my friends—a very difficult experience for a thirteen-year-old— I would lose my playground as I knew it; that is, my lake, my forest, my familiar streets, and laneways, in short—a big part of myself. But, I was also excited about the unknown, what was to come; I was indeed looking forward, although with trepidation, to a future with new experiences. But—heart of heart—how I had deluded myself. I was to be six months into our new world, and I would be literally crying to go back to the embraces of my old friends. How I missed Belleterre that winter of 1960.

My parents had no time to waste on emotional drama. They accepted the fact that we had to move and set to plan for the future. I had two brothers, Pete and Ivan, working and living in Elliot Lake, Ontario. Both were married and raising families in what was at the time, the boom-town of northeastern Ontario. Uranium mines were in full production. My brothers secured a job for my dad at the mine they worked at. My father would relocate the family to Sudbury, a two-hour drive east and he would commute every weekend to be with us.

In July every worker got a severance pay based on years of service. Our father got nine-hundred dollars. I remember the day well: all the money laid on the table after mother had counted it twice—I thought we were rich. In early July, Rosario loaded our furniture, boxes, and belongings onto his big truck and we were off to Sudbury—on another adventure.

NOON

Sudbury: The Flour Mill

CHAPTER 8

My New Home—Bare Hills and Black Rocks

By the time we came within view of Wahnapitae, I felt that something did not look quite right. And, when we went through Coniston a few minutes later, something was definitely awry—it was the landscape—or, the literal lack of any!

What a welcoming mat for a fourteen-year-old used to green forested hills; peaceful lakes and tall whispering pines dotting sandy beaches. The scorched earth and scrubland in front of me were to be my new home: the Sudbury of the 1950's and 60's.

I had been uprooted from as idyllic a country a boy can wish to grow in, and thrown into some kind of barren moonscape, dominated by two smokestacks constantly belching out caustic sulphur fumes in the air; I had been moved away from an environment where the air was clean and wholesome, to one where the blue sulphuric haze emanating from the smelting process, stayed stuck at ground level, and never left your nostrils; your mouth and your throat. I had been moved from a place where everyone spoke French, to a French Canadian enclave of Sudbury where none of my new friends could speak a full sentence, in a French-language idiom that was easily understood.

The Sudbury Francophones spoke what we called where I came from—"fran-glais": that is; a smorgasbord of "francais" and "anglais"; an odd mixture of bastardized French slang, alongside a mediocre English vocabulary.

Ray A. Vincent

The Worst year of my Life

That first year in Sudbury proved to be the worst year of my life. I was terribly unhappy and I made everyone in my family feel my unhappiness. And it showed in my behaviour. I disturbed our family life—and at times I was mean and cruel—and it did not help that my new friends preferred staying indoors, watching TV instead of coming outside to socialize and play.

We did not own a television set until two months later. And when we finally did; gazing at that stoic Indian face on the 'Test Pattern', waiting for CKSO's Basil Scully and Trudy Manchester to make their appearance, became one of the day's highlights. However, television and to some extent, the local Sudbury Star newspaper became valuable English language learning tools for me at that time.

Our Apartment on Queen Street—A Step Backward

The new apartment at 190 Queen Street (Queen Street was renamed Nolin Street in the 1990's) was a step backward from the place we had vacated in Belleterre.

The building was a triplex, with two apartments side by side on the first level, and a third apartment on the upper level. The building sat on a very narrow lot. Two tall maple trees stood guard between the front of the house and the sidewalk. To the right, between us and the Quesnel's fence; a narrow gravel driveway led to a wood framed garage at the back. The left side almost touched the other neighbour, Mr. Desormeaux. Our apartment was on the right, at ground level, with a front and a side entrance. The front entrance opened to a small living room which connected to a small kitchen; at the far end of which was my parents' bedroom. Next to my parents, on the left, was the four girls' bedroom—two bedrooms for seven grown-up persons! A short hallway connected the bedrooms, at the end of which was a very small bathroom. All the floors were covered with a dingy linoleum, cracked at the centre and curling at the edges.

My bed—a couch—was located in the kitchen since my parents had decided on purchasing a TV set (on payments), and the living room would, therefore, be a busy place most evenings—not conducive to a restful sleep—the fact that there was no door between the living room and the kitchen was dismissed as a small inconvenience. My siblings or my parents moving about in the kitchen early in the morning, became my natural alarm clock. My sleeping couch was squeezed between a wall and the kitchen table.

The side entrance led straight ahead to the kitchen area; however, if you turned left before ascending the stairs leading to the kitchen, you descended to the basement where you met a laundry area and the furnace room; there was also a small private room at the far end. Our landlord, Mr. Laframboise, had built himself this small private room—always under lock and key—to be used by him when he came in town to collect his rents or, run some errands which may keep him in the city overnight. He came and went unannounced and at his convenience, all the while infringing on our privacy. He lived in Warren, forty miles east of Sudbury.

Making Plans to Return to Belleterre. Unhappy and Acting Out

Within a week, I was making plans to return to Belleterre. No sooner arrived, I was planning my departure. I was a teenager now, and I would make my own decisions. I would go to high school in September, see myself through to springtime, and when school vacations arrived I would pack it in. I would move back—to my uncle Fred, or—my sister's in Bearn. How I longed for every face, then; and for any sight or sound that reminded me of Belleterre.

I am now ashamed when I think back on my behaviour in those first few months. I became mean and difficult with my sisters, and rebellious with my mother. I am mortified now when I recall one day making my mother cry—I forget the reason—but it would be the first time I ever saw my mother cry—and I had been the cause of her grief.

There would be another occasion not long after that when I made her cry again—but I vowed then, that I would become the best son a mother could ever wish for.

She was the last person on earth that deserved to be hurt. Mother was alone with us all week, and even though she had her hands full at home, she would scour the newspaper every evening looking for a job she could do.

Father came home late Friday evenings and got picked up by his ride for the return journey to Elliot Lake by mid-Sunday afternoons. This was new for us; we were used to having a full-time father around, and now we had him barely two days out of seven. My father was very quiet at the best of times and hardly noticed in the house, but my sisters and I missed his presence terribly. And so did my mother—it was hard on her—but she did not complain.

As a matter of fact, mother loved the big city. She saw and understood the potential for growth; the opportunities that would one day open up for her children—even for her rebellious son.

The Flour Mill

The area of Sudbury we lived in was one of the oldest parts of the city—the Flour Mill—so denominated, because it had once been the location of a flour depot; the flour contained within six massive concrete silos—still standing on location today, alongside railway tracks and Junction Creek, but barricaded and empty. The silos, now home to pigeons and rats.

It was a predominantly French Canadian working-class section of the city, with the workers and their families living in crowded, rented tenement housing, with some living in private dwellings. The Flour Mill and the Borgia Street area was where the poor of the city lived. There were other sections of the city where working people clustered in concentrated ethnic groupings—the Donovan, for the Poles, Ukrainians and the Finns—Gatchell and Copper Cliff, for people of Italian descent.

The City of Sudbury. My new home

The city we had moved to, numbered approximately 80,000 inhabitants at that time, 35 percent of which were francophone. The main employer was the International Nickel Company (INCO), extracting nickel and copper from the world's largest known reserve deposits. The number two nickel mining company in Sudbury was Falconbridge Nickel Mines.

Sudbury's lifeblood during the sixties was the mining industry. When world demand for nickel rose, economic activity in Sudbury increased; when the market for nickel was sluggish, the mining companies decreased production and laid off workers. The demand for nickel rose dramatically during the decade that we moved to the city; partly because of a great demand for stainless steel in home appliances and automobiles, but also because of the war in Vietnam, especially after 1965, which saw the full-scale participation of the United States in that conflict.

I Make New Friends and get reacquainted with Old Ones—Books

And I started to make friends. And I discovered the Sudbury Public Library. And I brought books home by the armfuls—English language books—the Public Library became my unofficial English tutor.

A fourteen-year-old makes friends quickly. Living across from us was the Chamberland family; Roger became my best friend. Norman Quesnel and Gordon Valiquette also lived on my street and we became good and long-lasting friends.

Gordon and I had probably watched too many western movies—we decided to become blood-brothers—literally—one day we made cuts to our forearms, and mixed our blood together like we had seen the Indians and white men do in the westerns. Gordon and I were to attend the same high school and many years later the "blood-brothers" were to cross paths again—this time professionally—as City of Sudbury civil servants. Gordon was to become the manager of the Sudbury Transit System while I was to become the manager of the City of Sudbury's Social Services Employment Support Division.

Louise in trouble In the Waters of Ramsey Lake

Our apartment on Queen Street was four houses removed from a dead end at its western part. The end of the street faced squarely onto the foot of a steep black mountainside. So, when I wanted to play outside, the choices were narrowed to three—the street, the rocky mountaintop, or Roger's yard. I could always go to O'Connor playground—but that was way over on Dell Street.

Of course, in summer there was always Lake Ramsey, by Bell Park. Louise almost drowned there that first summer. Monique and I could swim, but Louise could not. Monique and I were jumping off a cliff and into the deep water of some ten to fifteen feet, and Louise not being aware of the depth, followed us. I knew she was in trouble immediately. She was screaming and going under. I ran back to the top of the cliff and dove in under her, making sure to come up behind her so that she would not grab me, and put us both in danger of drowning. From behind I kept her propped up, and by forward pushes managed to get her to shallow water, where she walked out on her own.

My Friend Roger Chamberland and the fine Art of Counterfeiting

Roger Chamberland and I became best friends notwithstanding the fact that you would be hard put to find two individuals so unlike each other. He was six months older than me, of the same height, but frail in body build and strength. I loved books; Roger did not. I was athletic and loved sports; Roger was no athlete, he was a spectator. I loved school; Roger did not. I dressed conservatively; while Roger was the spitting image of TV's "The Fonz," in "Happy Days". He wore his black hair heavily greased in "Brylcreem", ducktail fashion. His comb was always kept busy, and when not in use you saw it sticking out of his back pocket. I did not smoke; Roger did. I was indifferent to girls, while Roger knew every pubescent girl in the Flour Mill.

Opposites must attract; Roger and I became fast friends and inseparable. He was fun to have at your side; Roger always seemed happy. He never planned a day—he just got up and lived what the moment brought him—totally different from the way I went about my daily routine.

He wore glasses with thick bottle-end lenses. He had a way of looking at you square in the face while speaking, and then, he would cock his head ever so slightly to the side. He did this all the time. One day, his older brother told me—Roger had an eyesight, problem—cocking his head was compensatory—his way of bringing the images in his eyesight into proper focus.

He was constantly coming across the street to our house—my mother had it figured out pretty quickly—I had three eligible sisters—Carmen, Monique, and Louise.

Roger lived in a family of five children; three boys and two sisters. He was the middle boy. Of the sisters, one was a toddler and the other seven years old. In my eyes the family was well-to-do—they owned their own house, and they owned a car—and his father was a tradesman; a full-time employed carpenter. They lived in a two storey detached, imitation brick-clad house, fenced-in by a low white picket fence at the front, and tall dense lilac trees on both the left and the right side. The house was on a big lot with plenty of play area. The back of the house had a big garage where Mr. Chamberland kept his Station-Wagon. The garage was accessed by a rear laneway.

We seldom saw Mr. Chamberland; he left for work early in the morning and returned home late; sometimes he would be gone for weeks when the construction project was out of town. Roger's dad owned something quite unusual in those days—an 8mm home-movie camera.

The Chamberlands took summer vacations—another sign of wealth, in my eyes—and they'd come back with all those boring movies

I'd be forced to watch. In my first winter, Mr. Chamberland put up an ice rink on the front lawn, and did movies of our hockey games, and captured all of our animated arguments over contested goals, and assorted infractions. Those so-called boring movies became precious, treasured archives for me, when Roger played some of them at my house on Haig Street, at a time when we were well over sixty years of age.

And Roger was very creative. One day he introduced me to the fine art of counterfeiting. Two weeks after my arrival and shortly after my first meeting him—Roger felt the need to impress his new-found friend—so he took me to his father's garage where, he said, he could change a penny into a ten cent piece in no time at all—and, if I vowed to keep the method secret—he would teach me.

He would juxtapose a penny and a dime together, clamp the pair snugly in the vice at his dad's workbench, and with a fine-meshed file, bring the penny down to the exact diameter of the dime; and then, with fine finishing strokes and sandpaper, he got the burrs off the edges of the penny. The end product: you had a shiny silver dime in one hand, and a black-brown dime look-a-like in the other—eleven cents had been converted into twenty cents. You repeated this process until you ran out of pennies.

And then, off we would go to the Laundromat on King Street. With no customers about the place, I would stand guard by the door while Roger would set about filling the pop machine with our newly minted ten cent pieces. We would come out awkwardly, lumbering from side to side like inexperienced cowboys off the saddle; our front and our back pockets stuffed full of cold Cokes and Ginger ales. It did not take long for the jig to be up; a few weeks after, a full-time attendant was seated comfortably, reading his newspapers. We then shifted our field of operation to the unsuspecting Donovan area.

Mrs. Chamberland

Now, Mrs. Chamberland was everything that my mother was not—she was the complete opposite. She was slovenly and an awful housekeeper. Her house was always in shambles. She was dark complexioned, short and obese; and had the constant appendage of a lit cigarette dangling from her lips. Most times I walked in her house, she was lying horizontal on the couch. Her housekeeping reflected the person in minute detail. Her short cotton dresses were always bespattered with all sorts of food stains. She wore her unkempt black hair shoulder length. She reminded me later, about one of Macbeth's three witches around the cauldron—except for the missing warts on the nose and chin. She seemed always to be out of breath and was one of those mothers who addressed every required disciplinary action with the, "Wait till your father gets home" threat; which of course never worked toward any of its intended effects. When Mr. Chamberland was not home—which was often—the kids ran the household.

The Challenges of the English Language

The main challenge that my siblings and I faced, had to do with the English language. Strange to say, but television helped and of course reading helped a great deal, and so did living in a predominantly francophone neighbourhood. My sisters and I—with the exception of Colette—could barely put an English sentence together. We could pronounce but the most rudimentary words—I often pronounced the word "knife" with an audible "k"—which of course made all my friends laugh.

Monique and Louise Introduced to the Separate School System

Monique and Louise, twelve and ten years of age respectively, were to attend Nolin French Elementary Separate School in the fall. This Catholic elementary school was located a four minutes' walk from our house. However; because they had absolutely no knowledge of the English language, the school principal (a nun), decided in her wisdom—and without parental consultation—to send our baby sister and Monique, to an English language introductory program being run at St. David elementary school, in the Donovan. This was an egregious injustice perpetrated on young, vulnerable children, who had no one to advocate on their behalf—my parents were new to Sudbury; they were too timid and they did not know the system.

So my sisters, who could not speak a word of English, were made to take two bus transfers to get to St. David's—a school already bursting at the seams, beyond full enrollment.

Louise's English class was perched on the stage of the school auditorium since no other appropriate school room was available, (the "Portable" had not yet been discovered); one day a child fell off the stage with his desk on top of him.

Louise and Monique were sent home with lines to learn by heart, and if they could not recite them without errors the next day, Miss Blake (sister to Toe Blake, coach of Montreal fame), would have them put out their hands to feel the pinch of the leather strap—Miss Blake would be charged with a criminal offence in today's world—and be dismissed from her employment to boot!

Young children coming from the province of Quebec were treated in a despicable manner by the French Catholic Separate School Board. Shame on the Sisters and the Board to have let this go on for so long, unchecked. They were pedagogic dictatorial bullies, in whose hands children were systematically and psychologically, abused.

Our Mother ahead of the Curve. Mother Goes to Night School

And the time came quickly for my parents to enrol me for my first year of high school. And my mother had not wasted her time either. She was working two part-time jobs; housecleaning for Dr. and Mrs. Desmarais, and babysitting for Mr. and Mrs. Pezet. For her time, my mother was way ahead of the curve. She was also a model Canadian citizen. And, unusual as it may seem, very "liberated" for a woman who raised ten children. Mom always lead by example—she shocked us one day—we learned that she had enrolled in night school at Sudbury High. She was going to learn English. Our mother always led by example.

Carmen becomes a Secretary

Carmen was enrolled in the Commercial Institute of Sudbury, which provided a French-speaking section. In 1968, she would become secretary to the Director of the French Catholic School Board.

Upon graduating from the Institute at the age of seventeen, she was offered employment by the Jesuit Fathers at College Sacre Coeur (Sacred Heart College), on Notre Dame Avenue, as a secretary to the Principal of the school. After three months with the College, she was offered employment with the fledgling new University—Laurentian University—then located in temporary quarters on Elgin Street, between the Empire Theatre and the Plaza Theatre.

There were three floors accommodating different classes, and Carmen was secretary to one of the Francophone Deans. Later on, when it was ready to receive students, she would move to the main campus on Ramsey Lake Road.

Our sister came home one day and related the story of the Sudbury "Keystone Cops" Fire Department. The temporary campus on Elgin Street was three doors away from the Fire Station, then located at the corners of Elgin and Beech Streets. Dr. Tombalakian, a chemistry professor had carried out some experiments the day before. In the afternoon of the day after, while the room was empty of students, smoke was seen billowing from under his classroom door. No one dared to open the door. And Carmen called the fire hall, situated not more than two hundred feet away; and she told them, "We have a fire at Laurentian University". Six fire engines came bolting out of the station—sirens blazing—and all of them screamed right past the Elgin Street campus—and a bewildered Carmen—they were heading out at full speed to Ramsey Lake Road, where the new campus was still in the process of being built. She called the station back and asked, with some sarcasm, "Can you please send us just one fireman, with one extinguisher, at the Elgin Street university campus?"

They responded, and put out the combustion caused by the chemical interactions of the garbage leftovers of the chemistry experiment. There was smoke damage to the classroom, but no physical injuries to persons in the building.

In 1968, Carmen went to work for the French Separate School Board, as secretary to the Director of Education. Carmen worked uninterruptedly—except for periods of maternity leaves—until retirement. Carmen capitalized on her Quebec grounded education; as French-speaking—and trained—secretaries and teachers, were very much sought after in those days.

Off to High School. Sheridan Tech— Sudbury's little "United Nations"

For that September, the logical high school for me to attend—a five-minute walk from our crowded apartment, would have been the French-speaking College Sacre Coeur run by the Jesuits; located at the corner of Notre Dame and Kathleen. But mother would have none of it. "We now live in Ontario", she'd said—end of discussion—an English public high school it was to be.

I thoroughly enjoyed my five years at the Sudbury Sheridan Technical School and the good friends I made there. At that time, Sheridan Tech was Sudbury's veritable little "United Nations", due to the various ethnic backgrounds of its student body. To this day I am forever grateful to my mother for her foresight and wisdom. The best friends of my high school years were of Finnish and Ukrainian descent.

The Disappearance of a Friend

One day, a week before the start of school, my little dog "Ti-pousse" disappeared. He was properly tagged and registered. We searched the neighbourhood and visited the pound to no avail. Many following nights I would lay awake in anticipation of a scratch or a whimper at the door. My dog was either stolen or run over by a car. It was the beginning; there would be other disappointments and sorrows to visit me in that first year.

Registered in the wrong Program

Roger, Gordon and I, had been to school the week before school-start, to register, and pick our programs. I needed someone to shepherd me along this process. Roger was of no use to me in that department, so Gordon was my interpreter and my guide and we got everything settled in no time.

I was given my homeroom number, the name of the homeroom teacher, my locker number, and my combination lock—I didn't know I needed money for the lock—so Gordon lent me two dollars.

I was impressed with my new school. It had a sparkling new wing still attached to the old section, and you could communicate between both of them. The new section had the latest of educational supplies and equipment, particularly the science classrooms—it was ultra-modern for its time—and it had a great new double gymnasium. The new addition had given the school extra classroom space, science laboratories, enlarged shops, and a big bright lunchroom. We walked up and down the hallways and took to the stairs to investigate the different levels, both, in the old, and the new sections of the building.

I realized and appreciated at that moment, why our mother was so enthusiastic about our move to Sudbury.

A slight problem came to the surface on my very first day at school. Mr. Miller, my homeroom teacher, circulated a form to each student which asked us to identify our "shop" preferences; and I then realized—I was in the wrong program. My friend Gordon, who had done my footwork, had myself registered in his program—the Technical Program. I had intended to register in the General Course program, which was the program stream which led to University admission.

Mr. Miller told me to fill the shop preference form and not to worry, that it would all be rectified—and it was—but only after four years of dogged insistence on my part, did Mr. McDorman, our school principal, with great reluctance and debate, grant me the transfer.

I was struggling with the language, and had to go through some embarrassing moments: standing up in class when it came to my turn to recite a reading from the Shakespearean play of the term, or address the whole class and explain—in English—the solution to a math problem—however, I enjoyed my classmates notwithstanding. And furthermore, I got involved in extra-curricular school activities—the cross-country running team; the track and field team; and later on, the school hockey team.

At the time, the school year was divided into three terms: the fall term (Christmas); the winter term (Easter); and the June finals. Your final mark on each subject was arrived at by averaging your mark achievements over the three terms. By Christmas, I was barely keeping my head above water. But by Easter, I had passing grades in all subjects, and in my June finals, I was well on my way—I stood in the 85th percentile of my class. Not bad for a kid from Mud Lake.

CHAPTER 9

Problems of Adjustment. Poverty

Unfortunately, as good as things were turning out to be at school, they were not so good at home. I knew I was not the only adolescent in Canada growing up without a private place of his own; without privacy within his own home. But that knowledge was no solace to me; it provided no solution for me.

Me was not some hypothetical somebody else. I had no quiet place to retreat to when I wanted some quiet time; no wall to hang-up a picture that meant something to me; no private drawer to fold my clothes into, except a cardboard box in my parents' room; no place to study and do homework, except the hustle and bustle, the noise, the comings and goings, around the kitchen table. I never enjoyed the luxury of privacy. I became ever more difficult around my family, more worrisome, and an increasing source of grief to my mother.

I may have had good Sudbury friends, but they were not like my Belleterre friends. We had moved when I was fourteen; when young persons are at a critical stage in their emotional and social development. Had our move occurred when I was ten or eighteen, I don't think I would have gone through such a difficult transition.

And being poor did not help. I know, and I appreciate the old saying that says, "Money does not buy you happiness" but, believe me, you would much rather be unhappy and well-to-do, than unhappy and poor—the unhappy and poor are doubly unhappy. I saw how we were. We had little money for the basics, let alone for extra things. I came to detest powdered milk or mixing Carnation Condensed milk, 50-50 with water. I hated "boudin" (blood sausage) fried in margarine for supper. My canvas running shoes smelt from over-use and were breaking up at the seams. I wore the same black jeans at school so often that my gym teacher, Mr. Gowalko, asked me good naturedly one day if those were the only pants I had.

When my wife and I looked back some time ago at my grade nine and grade ten school yearbooks—she picked out the fact that I was wearing the same shirt in both pictures, two years consecutively. Poverty may shape and mold you into a better person later on in life; however, on the immediate scene, it certainly made me appreciate the value of money. There is not much difference between the concept of poverty and that of slavery. Conversely; money is the doorway to freedom. The comment of Mr. Riendeau, our Belleterre grocer, forever haunts me, "Tell your parents; they are falling behind; they charge more on the account than they pay down on it".

I became frustrated and I sought attention—and I began to act out. And then began my times of "troubles".

Times of Troubles

At one time, while still in Belleterre, one of my brothers had bought a 22 calibre semi-automatic rifle, and it was kept with my parents for storage. It shot 18 long range and 20 short range bullets. The rifle and bullets were stored in the basement of our new place.

One day I upset Mr. Laframboise. The house was empty, so out of sheer boredom, I decided to go in the basement and do some target shooting with the 22. I took a Hollywood magazine featuring a full-size picture of the face of Elizabeth Taylor on its front cover page. I tore the cover page and pinned it to the door of Mr. Laframboise's little room. And from twenty-five paces, I took two shots—both perfectly placed—between the eyes. After admiring my marksmanship I took the picture down and put away the rifle.

The next week, Mr. Laframboise happened to come around to collect his rents. He showed my mother the two bullet holes, and the lead slugs embedded in a cupboard, at the far end of his small room. He was not impressed.

One weekend at supper time; when dad was at home, I refused to eat the fried liver and "boudin" my mother had prepared—the cheapest foods you could buy. He asked me to eat what had been served; that he'd worked hard to put that food on the table. I replied sarcastically to the effect that; what was the difference?—in the garbage can—or in my stomach—the "boudin" and liver would ultimately find their way, either in the city sewer system, or at the landfill site. I said that with all the bitterness and venom I could garner. He stood up, came over to me and landed a sharp slap across my face.

Of my dad's ten children, I was probably the first one he had ever hit. My dad was gentle. I was taken aback, but in some perverse way, I was also happy—my father, whom I loved very much, was finally paying attention to me.

The following Monday morning, when I walked into my homeroom, Mr. Miller took a note from his desk and handed it to me. I was to report to the vice principal's office—Mr. Thomson. Now, no one was sent to the vice principal's office unless a disciplinary matter was to be dealt with. I had no clue why I was going to see Mr. Thomson, but I was soon to find out.

My mother had called. How she had made herself understood is amazing in itself, but given the heavy ethnic concentration at our school, I'm sure that this was not the first call put to Mr. Thomson from a parent who could barely speak the language.

Mr. George Thomson was a good man, and he took the parents' concerns seriously. He was good looking, brown to reddish hair, and very tall; at least six foot four, and slender. He had a rich baritone voice and he spoke in crisp, short sentences; but the voice was soft and pleasing to the ear. When he stood up he towered over you; he stood straight like a soldier standing at attention.

He said that my mother had called and had expressed concerns over my behaviour at home, and she'd wanted to know if that had anything to do with what may be happening to me at school. I told him that school was fine and I enjoyed being here. Then he told me he was aware that I was trying out for the junior football team. I said, yes; I was. He asked if I found the tryouts hard. I said, yes; they were.

And he asked, how were they hard? I told him I went home with cuts and bruises, and I woke up sore and bruised in the morning—I gave him honest answers. I was too innocent to figure out the line of questioning and where this was leading to.

He then said that I just met with the end of my scholastic football career and dismissed me. I went back to my homeroom somewhat puzzled. When Gordon asked in between classes, why the heck I had been sent to Thomson—I told him—my mother had just gotten me kicked off the junior football team. And I warned him: if he ever played any school sports, to never display or admit of carrying any bruises.

I was not upset or angry at my mother for having called the school. I had my hands full with other sports; hockey, track and long distance running. I never mentioned my meeting with Mr. Thomson. He had probably called her already anyhow. Sadly, things did not improve at home. I went through a short-lived episode of adolescent-paranoia.

On two consecutive evenings, I surrounded the floor around my sleeping couch with thumbtacks, and I slid sharp knives, cutting edges facing out and hemmed-in between the cushions and mattress. I was barricading myself behind this infantile protective moat.

Why this anger and this withdrawal? A cry for attention, no doubt. I was not psychotic. I knew full well what I was doing, and more importantly, why I was doing it. And it was not a generalized aberrant behaviour exhibited throughout all of my relationships—it was directed only and solely towards home. And that caused my mother to cry for the second time.

Brother Pete Administers Discipline

She did not say a word to me, but since my father was away working at Elliot Lake, she called my brother Pete who lived a half hour driving distance from us. In between her sobs, I heard my name being mentioned a few times.

The phone call had been put before breakfast, and when I came home after school, my brother Pete's car was at the front of the house. My mother and sisters were nowhere to be found. They had vanished.

I was fifteen; Pete was thirty, six feet two; at least two hundred pounds and muscular. I got the beating of my life. He would throw me and bounce me from wall to wall, and only stop to ask if I wanted more. I am surprised that the neighbours did not call the police. The harder he would hit me, the more determined I was to stand my ground and challenge him; and the louder I would scream out invective, and blasphemous words at him. With a cut and bleeding lip; two black eyes and two lower back, broken ribs on my body; my brother Pete stopped and left the house—visibly shaken.

I also left the house. I crept up the mountain and remained in seclusion, huddled amongst the black rocks until well after sunset. Stiff and in pain—particularly when I took in a breath—I made it back down and went home.

There were no questions asked, and few words said that night. My mother made me supper, and then we all went to bed.

I knew I was loved, unconditionally. I made a vow that night that I would strive to be a model son. I kept that promise as best I could throughout the remainder of my mother's life. My body may have been in pain for some time thereafter, but my mind was at peace. When we next met, my brother and I behaved with each other as if this event had never occurred.

In time, we became the best of friends, and went out together often, on fishing and hunting trips. When I turned sixty he was seventy-five by then. I came close on many quiet occasions—in the boat or alone by the campfire—to open up and thank him for having stepped-in that fateful afternoon and pounded some sense into my head. Shyness and reticence would get the better of me. I missed the opportunities to say, "Thank you", or as my wife would put it, I did not—"grab the moment".

It is those of us who always wait for that perfect moment who always end up missing out, because we miss the simple signal, and thereby fail—to grab the moment. He died four years later, at the age of seventy-nine.

Ray A. Vincent

Colette Gets Married

Colette got married to Roger Lalonde, in November, and that created a little bit more breathing room for the girls; instead of four to a room, they'd be three. But it reduced some of the family income since she had been contributing financially and now that would be gone.

The discovery of Mr. Universe and the World of Dynamic Tension

One day, I was in the basement shooting pucks at targets I had propped-up against the cement wall. I had set up an old mattress and put clothes baskets on their sides, and I would take wrist-shots from varying distances. Done as a daily routine, I improved my shooting skills and accuracy tremendously.

One puck rolled right across the other end of the room and came resting underneath the washing machine. When I finally found it, behind the machine and resting amongst a group of boxes, one box, in particular, got my attention; it was that of a muscular man in swim trunks, expanding a massive chest and flexing his biceps. I laid my hockey stick aside, retrieved the box and opened it.

The contents of that box turned my little world upside down; it brought rays of sunshine into an otherwise dreary sky. I had come upon Charles Atlas—Mr. Universe—and the world of "The Dynamic Tension" method of bodybuilding.

Ivan had bought the complete program years before, and he had never had the opportunity to peruse its contents because of work absences. When I opened the box, a colourful fly-leaf with three glowing quotes stared at me—"Step by Step and the Thing Is Done"—"Nobody picks on a Strong Man"—and, the now world-famous advertisement slogan—"Are you Tired of sand being Kicked in Your Face? I Promise New Muscles in days!"

It was complete; the charts; the exotic Latin names of all the muscle groups in the human body, and their locations fully displayed on glossy colour pictures; diagrams of all the exercise positions and equipment necessary; booklets on the training program; the number of repetitions on each exercise; when to move on to the next level; a book lecturing on general behaviour and the achievement of a positive mental attitude to living, and a book on a wholesome diet. In short, a fully charted pathway to living healthy and well.

The "Dynamic Tension" program consisted of twelve lessons filled with diverse exercises and one final perpetual "maintenance" lesson. And it worked—I added tone and muscles to my body and a peaceful mindfulness to my daily life. Charles Atlas became my Guru. My life took on three divisions—school, sports and "Dynamic Tension". The results spoke for themselves. I gained confidence, and became more self-reliant, and focused on the positive aspects of life. I shied away from negative influences. If anything did not improve my mind and body, I would have nothing to do with it.

I Register with Sudbury Minor Hockey

I was a decent hockey player, and the Sudbury Minor Hockey League offered a more competitive hockey program than the high school system did. My friend Claude Laporte and I went to De-Marco Brothers sports shop and registered. We went to the tryouts held at the Sudbury Arena and made the cuts for the Midget Triple A division. The highest level you could aspire to. By chance, we both ended up on the same team—the Kinsmen. Claude was a goaltender, I played right wing.

The games were played at 7:00 a.m. in the morning and on weekends. I was up at six and Claude's father would drive us downtown. If he was not available, we would take the bus and hope to get to the game on time. After the game or practice, we walked our way to school in freezing temperatures.

My parents did not own a car; therefore, for them to get me around town was not possible; and they provided no encouragement whatsoever in my pursuit of any sports activity. I played two years in the city league and my parents, and my sisters along with my brother Charley came to only one of my games—a big provincial tournament being hosted by Sudbury. They did not mind my being involved in sports, they simply did not have the time to be there by my side. I understood that, and I also benefited from it. When I got involved in any sport, it was because I enjoyed it—I did it for myself and my teammates—not for my parents. No coercion or pressures were ever put on me. They did not enquire about the results—I showed it to them the next day out of The Sudbury Star's sports pages.

Today, minor sports involvement seems to be more for the sake of adults than it is for children. And it is so expensive as to be out of the reach of many children. The vicarious enjoyment of minor sports by parents, poisons the games children play. It perverts the basic tenets and foundation of sporting activities for youth; which are meant for the healthy development of children and young adults. It is not meant to be a venue through which parents relive their youth, or modify their own failed aspirations. I played two years in the city league and then I played the last three years with my high school team—the Sheridan Tech Blue Devils.

The SMHA Annual Banquet and an Eye Opener

In our last year of city hockey, Claude and I decided to attend the year-end Sudbury Minor hockey banquet being held at the Kinsmen club at the far end of the Kingsway. We were told by our coach, Mr. Patten (the Sudbury Star's sports editor) that there would be awards handed out and that Claude and I were to be recipients of some of those awards. Claude's brother would drive us there and our coach would provide the ride back to the Flour Mill. We had a great time; there was a banquet; speeches and awards followed. Claude won the league's 'best goaltender' award, and I won the league's 'most gentlemanly' award. The evening concluded with the showing of a Walt Disney movie, and then everyone made their way outside to pick up their rides home.

We looked everywhere for Mr. Patten, but to no avail, we could not find him. We decided to go back in, sit down in the hall and await his return—we had no options—the distance from the outer limits of the Kingsway and the Flour Mill was way too far to walk. We decided to wait a while, and if he did not show up we'd ask some of the men still around to give us a lift back to town.

Suddenly, the lights went out in the hall. Claude and I rose to leave, thinking they were shutting down completely; but we sat down again when the hum of the movie projector could be heard, and lights flickered on the screen in front of us. We were in luck, we said to each other, another Disney movie was in the offing.

It was a movie alright—but not of the Disney variety—she came, without introduction and unannounced on the screen; a beautiful, big-chested redhead was gyrating to a drum beat, slowly and seductively removing her bikini top: then some man's voice yelled out, "TURN ON THE LIGHTS—WE HAVE KIDS OUT THERE!" And sure enough the lights came back on, the movie stopped—but not before Claude and I had gotten a full look at what was underneath that bikini top.

We were told that Mr. Patten had left the hall right after the awards presentation, and after what had just happened we were too shy to ask for a ride home. And we walked, and walked, all the way home. But strangely; the memory of those large naked breasts with the pink nipples; swaying gently to the rhythm of the music, made the distance seem so much shorter.

Brothers Leave Canada and Father begins Chronic Unemployment

In early spring, Pete took my dad to the provincial government, Labour Ministry office on Pine Street. My father was applying for his Ontario ticket as a 4th class Stationary Engineer. His Quebec license was not recognized in Ontario. Since my father could not read English, let alone write it, Pete was allowed to sit-in by his side and act as interpreter and scribe.

I do not know the outcome of the test—I suspect he did not pass—I don't recall my dad getting any documents in the mail informing of his success; I would have known since I would have been made to read it to him.

Trying to get his Ontario license and certification, was motivated in great part by recent developments in Elliot Lake. Demand for uranium was plummeting worldwide and therefore production was being cut back—the boom-bust economic cycles of the mining sector. My brothers, Pete and Ivan had found jobs in New Mexico, USA, with Red Path Mining and Tunneling. They would leave Canada at the end of July. My father was to be laid off at the end of May—one of many layoffs to happen to him in the next seven years. A sadness and general depression settled over the household. The main source of income would be stopped, and the return of meagre payments from Unemployment Insurance was to begin again. My dad was fifty-nine years old at the time, and not many employers would offer a job to someone on the verge of turning sixty when there were so many young men around. There were still young children at home, Louise was only twelve, Monique was fourteen, I was sixteen, and Carmen was eighteen.

A visit to Bearn and Unhappy Times

Early that summer my sister Rose and her husband Rosario came for a visit. They invited me to return with them to Bearn for a two week holiday. I jumped at the invite.

For the first few days, everything was fine, my brother-in-law was on his best behaviour. But it did not take long before he started to get nasty. He would berate and demean my sister. Nothing she did was good enough; he would name women they both knew and say that they were much better wives to their husbands; much better housekeepers, and so on. It became so embarrassing for me that I spent most of my daytime hours at the Savard's farm, with Michel and Gabriel.

One morning, as I lay in bed, I heard him say to Rose that I was using too much hot water. She explained, with that plaintive voice she used when talking to him—which I detested and found humiliating—and I would squirm, when she called him "dad"—that, coming home after playing all day at the farm, I had to take a bath. He replied that if she did not speak to me about it, he would, and then he left to go to work. By the time I had gotten up and got dressed, I had made up my mind. I was leaving that day. I was very upset. I had lunch, went outside and started to walk. I said nothing to Rose. I had no money. I would hitchhike back to Sudbury.

After walking two hours or so I reached the junction of Ville-Marie and Fabre. The traffic flow on those country roads is very light in daytime and practically non-existent at nighttime. My first destination was Temiscaming, and then North Bay and from there; Sudbury. I got a ride to Fabre, and by this time night was coming on. After walking some distance out of Fabre I got another ride which took me some five miles away from Laniel. By the time I walked into the village of Laniel, it was past midnight and I was dead tired and still forty miles away from Temiscaming.

Laniel is a one street village. The odd dog was barking, but otherwise, everything was eerie quiet. I got scared by the night's hallucinatory play of lights and darkness, which produced moving shapes in front of me that did not really exist. I jumped onto the flatbed of a truck and slept there as best I could. When dawn broke, I got back on the road, tired and hungry, and started to hitchhike again—but this time—back to Bearn.

I said nothing to Rose, she thought I had been at the Savard's house overnight. But I told her I wanted to return home, and return immediately, and that I had no money. She called mom, who wired the bus fare to the local Credit Union, and I was back in Sudbury the next afternoon.

My next return to Bearn was to attend my brother-in-law's funeral, twenty-five years later.

CHAPTER 10

Problems with Charley

It did not only rain, but it started to pour. One day in August, before the start of school, my nephew Michel and my niece Claudia came running to our place and told my mom that their dad was angry, and he was breaking things in the house. Michel was ten and Claudia was eight; they lived in St. Georges Street. She told the kids to stay with my sisters, and mom and I made our way to Charley's.

When we got there he was standing alone in the kitchen, his hands in the cupboards and laughing like a madman. He saw us, but that did not deter him. He would pick up individual pieces of china plates and fling them against the walls; then he would pick up glassware and throw them in the sink where they would shatter to pieces. My sister-in-law, Margo, had taken refuge in the bedroom and she came out when she heard mother's voice.

Oddly enough, I did not find the whole mess and ugly scene, a traumatic one. My mind took on an objective and analytical stance—the whole apartment was filled with sadness, despair, and selfishness. Where had love and compassion gone to? There are tragedies that need never to have happened. What was happening here was purposely hurtful. It was beyond explanations. I'll take a wise man before an intelligent man any day.

When Margo had come out he'd stopped and walked out. She told us he had been drinking. I did not believe her—there was not any evidence of liquor anywhere in the house. My brother Charley had a history of depressive illnesses going back to his teen years.

When my brother went out, my mother took a broom and began cleaning up, moving about like a robot; and she said nothing. I went home alone, disgusted. My nephew and niece stayed with us for two days before returning home again.

Starting with the evening of that incident, I began a practice that I would follow well into mature age; that is, catalogue everything that I witnessed and experienced in daily life (as a matter of fact, I started a daily diary); I would adopt and model what is good and uplifting from those experiences; reject what is negative and evil—that maxim has never let me down.

Escape into Books and Long Distance Running

I became more reclusive. And, I threw myself more and more into books and sports. As books became my intimate friends, I slowly distanced myself from the Flour Mill gang.

Spring at Sheridan Tech meant not only the coming on of midterm exams, but it also heralded the long distance running and the track-and-field tryouts season. With the winding down of hockey and basketball, the cross-country team was being selected.

The announcement came over the P.A., system that morning, asking any boy—from grades nine to thirteen—interested in cross-country running, to assemble at the MacKenzie Street entrance at 3:30 p.m., appropriately dressed in running shoes and gym trunks. The running coach, Mr. Pajala, our history teacher, would address the group with more information, the announcement had said.

Gordon asked me to join him and try out. Gordon was ready to try and take anything on. He even joined the school Debating Team—and made it—how a French Canadian kid had the guts to stand up on a stage and debate in English was a marvelous thing. Gordon was short, redheaded and fiery, and let's not forget—he was my blood-brother. There were to be two tryout sessions, a week apart; and the top seven runners would be selected for the team. Four of last year's team members were there, and over fifty boys from all grades.

Lower grade runners like me and Gordon were never given a chance to make the team. Grades nine and ten were usually there to gain experience for future year's tryouts.

This was a three-mile course, starting at the MacKenzie Street school entrance and ending at the opposite entrance on College Street. The course went north on MacKenzie to Kathleen Street; then Kathleen west over the railway tracks to Regent Street South; up the heartbreak CKSO hill, and from there south to Elm Street; from Elm we proceeded east to Lorne Street at which intersection we made a left turn to the underpass, taking us to College Street, and on to the finish line awaiting us at the school.

Gordon and I were together for the first quarter mile, and then he faded back. By the railway tracks, where Kathleen joins Regent I had caught up to the lead pack. By the top of heartbreak hill, I was in the lead, last year's top runner Jim McBride, in second place. Coming down Elm, we were shoulder to shoulder, but as we turned left at Lorne, making our way through the underpass and within sight of the school, he increased the pace, moved ahead and finished first.

Quiet and shy Mr. Pajala took me aside and congratulated me on my first tryout performance, and he took pains to talk to me every day until the next week's tryout session. I finished first in the second tryout and our school team went on to win the Sudbury District High School cross-country championship that year. Our team placed second in the Northern-Ontario NOSSA meet, held a few weeks later.

In intra-school competitions, I never lost a race at a mile and over distances, during my entire stay at Sheridan Tech. I earned my sports letters and a school jacket.

Charles Atlas could be retired to the background: now my new heroes were Bruce Kidd, Bill Crothers, and Glenn Cunningham. And I read the biographies of Roger Bannister and Paavo Nurmi—the flying Finn. In citywide high school long distance races, my main competition came from Real Bisson of Sacre Coeur and in my last year, Terry Mckinty, from Lockerby High.

I have to thank Gordon for my introduction to running which started on that fateful spring tryout. I continued running well into my fifties and ran many marathons including the flagship marathon of the world—the Boston marathon—in 1999. Sports; hockey and definitely long distance running, started to trump everything else in my life. It provided the antidote to the sense of inadequacy brought about by poverty. I was looked-up to in the school hallways. I was bringing the school some trophies and earning it a running reputation.

Mr. Gowalko convinced me to leave the city hockey league (rules did not allow you to play both leagues simultaneously), and join the school team. Claude and I left the city and joined the school team. Scholastically, I was doing reasonably well, but sports and a training regimen gave me a clear identity and a sense of self-worth which nothing could replace. I started more and more to stay away from Roger, he was becoming a distraction. And he was to quit school shortly. I began to spend more time with my Finnish friends from school; Osmo Timonen, Tim Myllymaki, Erki Erkilla and Arvo Liinamaa—all from the Donovan.

Carry-out Boy at the IGA

Another big step in my movement toward purpose, and establishing that sense of calm and maturity that I could feel building within, came on my first summer school vacation—I got a job—a defining event for me. I then put aside forever my plan to move back to Belleterre.

A large food chain store—IGA—was opening up on the east side of Notre Dame Avenue. Roger had seen a newspaper advertisement inviting applications for a variety of positions; full time and part-time work, one of which was for baggers and carry-out boys. A carry-out boy bagged your grocery order; put the bags in a cart; the cart was then pushed to your car and the contents unloaded in the trunk or the back seat. You got paid an hourly wage, plus you got tips, and last but not least, the opportunity to flirt with mothers' pretty daughters. A dream job for a high school student at that time.

Applications were received and a summary interview given at the same time. The applications were filed and the interviews took place at the Kingsway Hotel. Roger and I went, filled our applications and got our interviews. I got a call early the next week—I was hired. I rushed across the street to Roger's with the news, confident that we would be working together after school and on weekends.

Roger had not received his call yet. After a week went by with no call, Roger was resigned to the fact that he had not been selected. I was probably more disappointed and saddened than he was because I knew how he had set his heart on getting this job. However, in his usual cavalier way, he made light of it and said he would get something better through his father. He did get work on a construction site with his father—but it was short-lived—he could not tolerate his father's constant criticisms.

The job, along with being recognized at school, gave me a heightened sense of purpose and importance. I was floating on air. My first two paycheques went towards purchasing an assortment of clothes. Shortly after, I bought real track shoes at DeMarco's—the ones with removable spikes. Next came a new pair of skates and then; taking out the girl next door, to a movie at the Regent—in that order. Neither long distance running nor, Charles Atlas' "Dynamic Tension" exercises, managed to suppress the surging blood-testosterone levels in a healthy sixteen-year-old body.

Introduction to Sex at the S.S Kresge Store

My first encounter with sex happened at the S.S. Kresge department store. Sheridan Tech, being a "downtown" school, Gordon and I would sometimes take our lunch bags and walk the ten minutes to S. S. Kresge's on Elm Street—Zellers next door was not as accommodating to students, they'd see our lunch bags and kick us out right away.

So, we'd go to Kresge's; move up to the long counter facing Elm; order a pop or a tea; open our lunch bags and eat, chattering away—that went on for a while until one day, a staff person came over and told us—we could order lunch and eat it there—but we could not bring in our lunch from outside.

I loved Kresge's—it was a 5-and-10 cents type of store. It had everything poverty could buy you. And, it had a large and well-stocked newspaper and magazine display rack—which did not escape my attention. The colourful "Playboy" was there on full display—no brown paper sheet nor sealed plastic cover in those days—and, black and white copies of the "Nudist Adventures". Such temptations were difficult to walk away from. Those tantalizing Vargas Pin-Up girls in "Playboy" were what a boys dreams were made of. At that time, all below-the-waist anatomical features were airbrushed out—which for me, only added to the intrigue and mystery of the female anatomy.

How nonchalant I tried to appear in front of that stand; how many innocuous periodical and magazine I leafed through before getting the courage to plunge ahead to the main target. Sweaty hands and gawky-eyed, I would flip through the erotic magazines. I would lose track of time. And, how concentrated my mind became so as not to lose the meaning of a suggestive pose or of any heretofore unknown revelation.

Some days I would walk out red-cheeked, with "Playboy" firmly secured and squeezed into a damp armpit underneath my jacket, stolen from the stand. It would end up in Roger's garage, high up in the roof rafters, to be rediscovered anew at a later time.

Susan, the Next Door Neighbour

Susan was a pretty seventeen-year-old girl. She had moved to Sudbury from Cache Bay and had moved in with her aunt in the apartment next door. She had come to the big city to find employment. She was a redhead and being seventeen, slightly taller than me. We would sit on the front porch in the coolness of the evenings and talk for hours about a host of things. My first bold step was to ask her to walk with me to the corner of Notre Dame and Queen where there was a restaurant. I felt her reticence—she was older and taller than me—but she agreed. The Cache Bay girl just loved country music.

I'd put coins in the jukebox and after a Coke, and listening to Ray Charles and Patsy Cline, over and over, we would return home—by this time—holding hands.

Roger was beside himself; he said I had all the luck—I had the job, and now, I had the girl. We went to a movie or two, walking downtown and back. The possibilities that money opened up was amazing. But the relationship was completely platonic and it was destined to remain so. An incident involving Roger, Susan and I made sure of that.

Roger Highjacks his Father's Car

One evening, after his father and mother had gone to bed and were asleep, Roger came across the street to our porch, where Susan and I were sitting. Roger cocked his head, and asked me matter-of-factly to go with him, and help him get his dad's car out of the back lane garage. We would then come around, pick up Susan, and go to the A&W on Notre Dame.

He opened the garage door quietly, put the big Station-Wagon in neutral, and we pushed it into the lane. He put the key in the ignition and fired-up the engine. We drove around the corner to my place, picked up Susan, and we were off. Susan assumed he had permission—I knew he did not. We went north, down Notre Dame to Lasalle Boulevard, then we came back up Notre Dame and stopped at the A&W burger stand, radio blasting and having a grand old time.

Attendants on roller skates came to Roger's window, took our order, and skated it back to us in no time. We had a great time, radio on, sipping on the frosty cool root beer, chatting away. We were in the process of returning the car when Roger made a drive-past and noticed his house still in full darkness.

And then he made the fatal mistake—he pushed his luck.

Probably to impress Susan; he suggested we go view the "slag-dump" off of highway 144, just beyond the city limits. And why not? It was a beautiful evening and everyone was asleep. So, down Kathleen west, we go and we turn left onto College, and we come to a red light at Lorne and Elm Street. We come to a full stop. Our next move is to turn right onto Elm and head west and thence to the "slag-dump".

Just as we were all enjoying the good life, a police cruiser had moved ever so gracefully right behind us, and—Roger panics. When the light turns green, if he keeps his cool and proceeds right or, failing that, if he keeps on driving straight ahead on Lorne Street heading south—we are all safe from the long arm of the law. However, in his panic, Roger makes an illegal left turn, in order to hightail out of there and take the closest route back home.

Then, all hell broke loose; cars started honking their horns, in the back seat Susan was screaming, and of course, right on our heels—the police car is on our bumper—red lights flashing. We were pulled into the Edwards Grain parking lot and Roger was asked to follow the officer back to the cruiser. Roger, of course, was not licensed, and he admitted having taken the car without the owner's consent. He faced some heavy fines, and he still had to face his parents.

The police department must have called ahead because when we pulled in front of Roger's house, it was all lit up and we had a welcoming party waiting. The flashing police lights had drawn half the street to their windows and their front porch—including Susan's aunt.

That was to be the end of my budding romance. After the police escort, Susan was forbidden to have anything to do with me, or with Roger. Roger quit school midway through grade ten and moved to Ottawa to be with his brother. Roger was to seek me out forty-nine years later, at age sixty-five, and I was overjoyed at the reunion. And so was my wife—she'd heard a lot about this person in my life. Roger, Emily and I, spent many happy times together, particularly, at his favourite place—the Sudbury Slots. He died of cancer ten months later. He always knew, but he kept it a secret from us until the last six weeks.

"Snorky" The Sophisticated Russian

Alex Sedunow, the sophisticated Russian, had also been a friend of mine. Alex was the kind of student everyone wanted to be friends with. Even the teachers liked him. He had a way of ingratiating himself into any group—he was always accepted. He was opinionated and forceful, but not the way a bully would be. He convinced you. And, if you were not convinced, the very fact that he had swayed the group—you happily joined in—before you knew what the heck had happened.

He was of average height and stocky to almost overweight, and he had a swarthy complexion. Average looks—no Rock Hudson. He spoke with a slow, soft voice—almost a whisper. And he would not let you go until he was sure you had understood his point. If there was a deal to be made, Alex worked it out. And he had a nickname—"Snorky"—where he got it from I have no idea. But he was quite comfortable with it. He was big, and he acted big. His dad was a businessman in town. Snorky came to school, driving big shiny convertibles. The girls loved him—and they filled his car. He talked to the teachers as if they were his personal friends. And he talked to any girl in the hallways that took his fancy. Alex had a following—an entourage—and, whatever you wanted, Alex could get it for you—for a price. He was not a mean person; however, he was persuasive and most importunate, if he wanted something.

We had many debates at that time, on the issue of Quebec separatist sentiments then making front page news stories. I said, we (French-Canada), could bankrupt the country if we decided to block the St. Lawrence Seaway—you'd have no entry to the Atlantic, I said. Snorky then took me aside, away from anyone's hearing, and with his face, an inch from mine, said in his soft, persuasive manner, "Ray, you ever heard about something called "NATO"? The US Marines would walk right in and kick all your Quebecers asses in". I didn`t want to start an international incident—I offered no rebuttal.

Alex went on to become the City Clerk of Walden; a municipality at that time, situated on the western outskirts of Sudbury. His position was next in command, after the CEO. But unfortunately, Snorky's wheeling and dealings eventually caught up to him. Alex was running cheap US booze across to Canada. One day, Customs Officers from both countries set him up. He crossed into the US at Sault-St. Marie; as he would do at least once a month, and on the return journey they inspected him. His car was full of undeclared liquor, destined to be sold to his contacts in Sudbury.

Alex lost his job and his reputation. All of a sudden, all those hangers-on, and supposed dear friends he had —they all disappeared. My colourful friend died suddenly in 2003, at the age of fifty-nine.

Osmo my Friend from Finland and the Sauna Party

Osmo Timonen, my Finnish friend, was also one of my best friends in high school. We both came from working-class neighbourhoods, Osmo in the Donovan and me, in the Flour Mill. Like me, Osmo was shy, and what made matters worse for him, he spoke English with a heavy accent. He was born in Tampere, Finland. Except in the winter time, Osmo always went about with leather sandals on his feet.

Blue-eyed and blond hair, he was short and a bit on the heavy side. An excellent skier; but that was the extent of his sporting activities. He was strong in math, electronics and the sciences. He was a member of the school Science Club. He was very intelligent and inquisitive.

We would go duck hunting in the fall behind Black Lake; using his uncles' shotguns—Osmo had lots of uncles—and, being the taller, I would strip down to my underpants and wade in the cold water; chest-high, to retrieve the ducks that my mother would have nothing to do with.

Osmo had the strangest living arrangements. He had no siblings and was being raised alone by his mother. He had no one around, he called father, but he had an awful lot of "uncles" around the house. I never got to know if his mom was a divorcee, or if his father was dead. He would not want to talk about it.

The big building they lived in on Antwerp Street was a few houses down from Sampo Hall. The big square building had many apartments, mostly tenanted by Finnish people. I was there often and their apartment was always full of men: "uncles". None spoke

English. They could not all be his "uncles". I suspected his mom was running a bootlegging joint to make ends meet. And something odd I would notice; although not employed, Osmo had a car.

One day, he organized an end of school year "sauna party", at one of his ubiquitous "uncles" camp. He knew this "easy" Finnish girl who had an "easy" girlfriend. What a better way to celebrate the start of summer vacation than with the loss of our virginity, he said. I swallowed hard and said, "Oh yeah, for sure".

The fact that my two younger sisters were to attend this party put a bit of a damper on my libidinal urges. Nevertheless, the plan was as follows: when all the guests had gone home, we and the "easy" girls would stay behind and engage in never-ending orgies of "easy" sex. Problem was, the "easy" girls had not been consulted about our end of year sexual intentions. And we had no booze left to soften-up the field—the guests had gone home with what they had brought in. And, what made matters worse—the "easy" girls proved to be anything, but easy. They were finicky, not in the mood and definitely, not amorous.

More experienced hands would have found ways to take control and save what was becoming a very precarious, and embarrassing situation. While I was on the couch, making small talk with the "easy" girlfriend about subjects totally removed from sex, we could overhear Osmo's pleading conversation coming from the adjoining bedroom. He kept reassuring his consort that we had a whole box of condoms—which was news to me. He kept mentioning the condoms as if that knowledge should fill her with wild unbridled passion. But to no avail. She kept insisting that she much preferred another hot sauna and a jump in the cold lake—spoken like a true Finn. She would have made her mom proud. And this entertaining conversation went on for some time until Osmo finally threw in the towel and admitted defeat. He came rushing out of the bedroom and told the "easy" girls to pack-up, he was driving them home.

So much for the hot sex. But it had been entertaining.

After we drove the girls home, we drove around downtown for a while, but all he kept on talking about, was on how much money he had spent on the condoms; and to show me how prepared he'd been, he pulled a packet out of the box—the top had been torn away, ready for action—had the "easy" girls been more cooperative.

Osmo and I go To the Drive-In

A year after the "sauna party", he arranged a blind date for me with a Finnish girl, and to return the politeness, I convinced my sister Louise to be his date. A safe, no fooling around double-date. We were going to the Lasalle Drive-In. As usual, a double feature was playing.

Halfway through the second movie, we were all tired and wanted to be driven home—all of us that is, except Osmo. He wanted to continue the evening at a restaurant, or at A&W.

In those days, when you went to an outdoor Drive-In, in order to get audio, you lowered a window and hooked a speaker box on the inner side of the window. My date and I were in the back seat and the speaker was attached to my window. When Osmo realized we really wanted the evening to end and to be driven home; he became agitated and upset. He threw his popcorn out, you could tell he was not happy. He started the engine and revved it up, put on the headlights, and before I could say or do anything, he angrily pressed on the accelerator and headed towards the exit.

We were already moving along on Lasalle going west, when he finally made out what I was shouting at him—my window had popped-out of its rubber grooves; dangling and still attached somehow to it was the metal speaker box, with five feet of cable trailing outside. He was good at electronics; he told me later that he wired the speaker box to his car radio—now he said, he had a stereophonic audio system.

A Sad Ending

Things started well but eventually did not work out for Osmo. After graduation, he enrolled at the Kirkland Lake Institute of Technology and graduated with high standings. He got his Electronics Technician certification. Osmo could have done anything and achieve great things in that field. But fate would have it otherwise. Back in Sudbury, Osmo got great jobs, but for some reason, success drove him sideways. Osmo was still searching. What I had found in sports, books and good parents, Osmo found illusive or without significance. He got involved with the biker gang culture and drugs. One day I read in the local paper, how a man in his thirties had taken his motorcycle onto the railway tracks, and challenged an incoming diesel engine head-on. Osmo had died instantly.

Books and the Public Library

More and more, books became a powerful influence in my life; they became a place of refuge as well as a source of knowledge. In books—all sorts of books—fiction and non-fiction alike, I found peace and order. I became a secret lover of the English language. I purposely read slowly, so that I could savour the essence and feel the texture of every word and sentence. By nineteen, I had read most of the classics, and I started to build up a modest personal library. I spent hours at the McKenzie Street library, and unbeknownst to me, my future wife was there all the time. Is it possible that some force—beyond that of books and logic—kept drawing me towards the library? Emily worked throughout grades nine to thirteen, as a student, at the main branch—we must have crossed paths.

An Application for a Rent-Geared-To-Income Unit

Sometime in the spring of 1961, my sister Colette, now married and living on Ash Street, had filed an application on behalf of our parents, with the Sudbury Housing Authority. Colette had found the apartment on Queen for us two years previous. Sudbury Housing, as we got to call the agency, provided public, rent-geared-to-income houses and apartments for those on low annual incomes. The rental housing vacancy rate index in Sudbury was extremely low—demand very high and supply scarce.

The Sudbury Housing Authority agency was new in town, and therefore, its inventory of rental units was very small. Securing a unit was based on scoring high on a points system. And even though my dad was now laid off again, my parents never thought we would get a call. But a call we did get. We were to move to our new house on Cabot Street—not to an apartment—but to a house—at the end of October. Colette had come through again. We were leaving the Flour Mill and moving into a new subdivision—the Northern Heights.

THE NORTHERN HEIGHTS

CHAPTER 11

Not in their Backyards

We moved on a weekend, in the middle of October 1961. The housing project had opened for occupancy in August, and we were one of its first tenants. Every unit was brand new.

It was a project built amongst well established middle-class subdivisions. It was a social experiment—the blending of private ownership and public rental houses—that was not, initially, well received. The city Housing Authority had fought long and hard to gain admission, and to be welcomed, to the Northern Heights. It had met with stubborn resistance from established homeowners. The petitions had been canvassed and presented, and debates had gone on in the council chambers for the past year and a half—no one wanted public housing in their backyards. The rumours circulating was that public housing tenants were welfare recipients; sole-support mothers; social misfits and rabble-rousers of all descriptions. There were impassioned delegations sent to address city council; all armed with petitions and all had council chambers packed with their vocal supporters. Basically, what the objections centred upon, boiled down to this main point: why allow the riff-raff to come in and alter the character of our neighbourhoods—and, reduce property values.

The Selkirk subdivision of Northern Heights was particularly aggressive in its objections. Strange things happen; ironically, a few years later, I got involved in a committee that was instrumental in bringing in a city-funded greenbelt, and a playground field in the Selkirk Street area.

However, to his credit, Mayor Max Silverman stuck to his guns and, with the support of council, the Cabot and Hearn Street public housing project saw the light of day.

The Subdivision

The subdivision was in an enclave, nestled between Burton Avenue and Frood Road, and consisted of two streets—Cabot and Hearn. Cabot Street ran north-south and was intersected at its midpoint by Hearn Street, which ran east-west. Our semi-detached was at 20 Cabot.

Beginning at the entrance off of Burton, at the north end, Cabot had rows of family semi-detached homes; seven to each side of the street, making fourteen dwellings in total on that street, all with private asphalted paved driveways. At the south end; or the opposite end of the street, stood two large multi-apartment buildings meant for the elderly; or single mothers with one dependent. Hearn Street had twelve semi-detached; six to a side. A small children's park or play area was located where Hearn intersected Cabot. The subdivision was well planned and located at the top of a mountain, it provided a nice view of New Sudbury to the northeast; particularly from the vantage point of one's bedroom window.

The Benefits of Public Housing Rules and Joyful Tenants

My parents were not aware of the rules and province-wide regulations, pertinent to public housing. That had never been an area of interest to them; for that matter, they did not know that any rules existed—they had not the slightest idea about the "living accommodation codes"; and family, "mandatory square footage allocations" per household members—they were just happy to have been given a place to park the family. They knew that the monthly rent would be related somehow to the family's monthly income, and since dad was unemployed at the time and the only income was unemployment insurance and my mother's small wages; the monthly rent had been set at forty-seven dollars. My part-time student job earnings did not factor in since I was a high school student.

The rent was now less than half what we had paid on Queen Street. But, as I said earlier, my parents were not aware, and neither was anyone in the family—including Colette—of the regulations governing mandatory square footage allocations of living space—in accordance with the number of persons in the household.

So, we arrived at the house and opened the door to a pleasant surprise awaiting us. Compared to Queen Street, 20 Cabot was palatial in size, and in looks. It was sparkling new—never been lived in. All was wood-floored, except the entry vestibule and kitchen, which were covered in heavy felt-backed linoleum.

You walked into a vestibule with a clothes closet; to the right was a large living room, a wood stairway between the living room and the kitchen led to the bedrooms and the bathroom upstairs. The living room was connected by two hallways, which made their way, front and back of the stairway, to an average size kitchen where the back door was located. Off of the right hallway, was a door leading to the laundry room area and, in the middle of the floor, was a trap door with a short stairway going down to the earthen floor of a dry-cellar. Upstairs were four bedrooms—yes, four!—two large rooms on the west side, facing the front of the house; and two smaller rooms on the east side, facing the back. To the right of the stairway landing was my parents' bedroom, and beside theirs was my two younger sisters' room. To the immediate left of the landing and opposite the hall was a bedroom for Carmen, and opposite Carmen's room was —finally—my very own private room, with a clothes closet and a built-in bookshelf on top. And, between Carmen's room and mine was located a large bathroom with a bathtub—and a shower—the first shower fixture and facility we had ever had.

We had come in before the moving truck had arrived. We went all over, up and down the stairs many times, no one speaking a word until the silence could no longer be contained; the dam burst and we all started to speak at the same time.

My sisters and I had the same initial impression—we thought we had died and gone straight to heaven. I cannot overstate the importance of adequate housing in a family member's sense of well-being; on a family who has lived in overcrowded conditions; particularly, its impact on the family as a whole. Carmen; at eighteen, now had her own bedroom, and at sixteen; I now had my first private bedroom—ever—this was a first time event for us; it was as if we had had a door open up, inviting us to walk through, and as we did, a new-found mantle of dignity and confidence had been wrapped around us.

We gradually started to take ownership of the new place. And in the spring, my mother and father cut away a slice of grass at the front, underneath the picture window, and turned the ground over; they planted flowers—dahlias and other perennials.

We planted four small elm trees at the back and there are four big elm trees standing there today, as a testament to our having lived there. They are still there.

Long Distance Runs

My old neighbourhood in the Flour Mill was a twenty-five-minute walk away. But I was closer to the Donovan area and to my friends that lived there. My walks to school took me through the Donovan by way of Burton, Snowdon and Melvin streets.

Cabot Street was a perfect location for my running training sessions; the terrain was hilly, windy and challenging. My long training runs took me up the long and steep Frood Road, heading north, onto Turner Avenue east; then south on Notre Dame to Dell Street and through the Flour Mill towards the Snowdon hill; and then Burton, and back to Cabot Street. An eight-mile distance. The run, being atop of the heights, provided a great view of the northeast part of the city.

Long distance running became a quasi-religious, trance-like activity, and it became part of my daily life. I found a peacefulness in the rhythmic cadence of the strides, arms and the body movements;

a peace and a total calm difficult to find anywhere else. I gave myself up to the moment; to my body, and to the rhythm of my breathing. I moved out of my body, and I watched. The long run became my Buddhist meditation session. I started to run because it was a school sport, a competitive activity that I was good at, and I continued running well into advanced age because I enjoyed it—running became a way of life. A way to get in touch with my emotions and put personal problems into perspective, allowing for sensible resolution.

Not only did running become a passion, it became a means of expression. That problem I was wrestling with while putting on my shoes, became a problem solved at the end of the long run. The unhappiness I felt before the run, was gone by the time I got home. The endorphin-carrying-hormones released through the bloodstream by long distance-running does affect mental perception, but they are positive effects leading to positive mental states. And, on the physiological side, the benefits of running on the body's cardiovascular system are immeasurable.

New Neighbourhood. New friends

I was told that our houses were probably built on the city's old landfill site, but that did not deter me from enjoying the view from my upstairs bedroom window the less. I enjoyed the evenings; with the bedroom window wide open, looking up at the night sky, and thinking of the big, wide world out there calling me to move forward.

New families kept on moving in throughout the fall, and up to the end of the following summer when the units became fully occupied.

Diane Martin lived alone with her grandmother, in one of the apartment buildings at the end of Cabot. She was most peculiar. She would only speak to me from her second-floor balcony. And she could speak for hours. She would never come down and go for a walk, and most disconcertingly, when she met me on the street or on the bus, she would completely ignore me, as if she had no idea who I was.

I met and became friends with Guy Lavalle, Rob Traynor, and the two St. Georges brothers, all of them living on Hearn Street. Unfortunately, we attended different high schools and therefore only got together on weekends and the odd evenings. Rob was not inclined to sports unless it was of the female kind, but Guy and I played hockey and tennis together quite often, and the St. Georges boys were more interested in the ladies than hanging around with the guys that much.

Guy had an unusual skin condition. He had an inordinate amount of sweat coming off his hands; at all times; and it had nothing to do with stress. The palms of his hands were constantly drenched, and I teased him about it, I called him "faucet". He didn't mind the teasing, he knew it was meant in good fun. He simply could not control the hand sweating. He did not have this problem of excessive sweats with any other part of his body—only the hands. He would bring a towel with him whenever we went to the tennis courts so that he could wipe off the racquet handle. When you shook his hand it was like squeezing on a sponge full of water.

There was a family on Hearn Street whose circumstances reminded me very much of our neighbours in Belleterre; Mr. and Mrs. Dhiel.

The Frasers were a family of six, the father was a bartender at the National Tavern, and he also was, like Mr. Dhiel, an inveterate alcoholic. He had a daughter my age, and I visited and watched TV in their house. We talked a lot and enjoyed each other's company. My sisters would also be with us on many occasions. She had three brothers, all younger than her. I wondered at times why she would always stay up late and seemed not to want to go to bed. She told me that she would never go to sleep until her father had gotten home, and she would go to bed only after she knew he had fallen asleep.

I only understood the meaning of her words; what she was really trying to tell me after I had started my profession as a social worker. Bartenders never come home until well after midnight, and their wives are usually asleep by then.

We were standing in the vestibule, close to each other one night. Everything was quiet and dark; you could just make out the sound of our own breathing. We heard the car pull up and she became very agitated.

He fumbled with the doorknob and came in. He was drunk. It took him a while, in the darkness, to realize that I was standing four feet away from him, but when he did; he got angry. He felt for the wall and turned the light on. There was saliva dribbling from his lips and he steadied himself with one hand against the door as he kept on asking her, in a drunken slur, if; "I was the reason?" She moved away and disappeared into the darkness of the house. When he moved forward and let go of the door, I slipped away behind him.

But my mind kept on holding on to his voice. I met her again often and we talked a lot—but that night was never mentioned.

The Woodwork Shop and my Difficulties with Curves

At the end of the school year, I brought home a completed project from my woodworking class. I was very proud of it. It was a useful piece of furniture that my parents got to use and enjoy. It was a coffee-table; well shellacked and made of solid oak, and it had side wooden pockets to store magazines and newspapers in. The four legs were curved and attractive. The whole was true and well squared. The table top was two and a half feet, by one and a half, and with the slanted side pockets at each end, it was perfect for the end of our living room couch. Everyone at home liked it, and it stayed with my parents many years after I had left the house.

But for all my troubles in bringing this woodwork project to light, I thought I should have received more adulations.

First of all, I had great difficulty in bringing to life the gracefulness of the curves in the legs. I ruined so many pieces of oak on the big upright band-saw, that I was told I was wasting a lot of expensive school supplies; so many pieces of oak were ending up in the waste bin.

Finally, Mr. Heuman lost his patience. Mr. Heuman was born and raised in Germany; he was tall, big and muscular. He talked with the accent of one just off the boat. He had a round florid face and he was completely bald. He was popular amongst some of the boys; he was the teacher in charge of, and the leader of the school's weightlifting and bodybuilding club.

After having come to my workbench many times with fresh advice, only to return to his desk, shaking his head; he walked to the front of the class, and told everyone to stop what they were doing—he'd had enough. He asked me to take my four table legs and join him at the front. Then, he proceeded to tell the whole class—in a thick German accent—that my legs were a perfect example of how not to curve wood at the band-saw. So far, I could take this. After all, he was right. But then came the thunderclap; he said, "Mr. Vincent, have you never noticed the lovely curves in a woman's body"—and he made up and down, curving and undulating motions with his hands as he said this. And, of course, as expected—the whole class burst out laughing—even Osmo; my bosom friend. And I became very red in the face. I went back to my bench swearing that if ever I had the chance, I would put Mr. Heuman's head through that damned ban-saw.

I was upset and angry, and therefore, when John Yalacha, the big Slav, came around with a grin on his face, making vertical undulating motions in the air, I lost it. I took a handful of sawdust and threw it right in his face. He had sawdust in his hair; in his mouth; in his nostrils and in his eyes. The way John acted up, you would think he'd been mortally wounded; he flapped his arms about and wiped his mouth, and he kept on saying that he was going blind. John was on the senior football team; he could have turned my body into a pretzel if he'd wanted to, but by this time he had gotten the attention of Mr. Heuman.

Mr. Heuman wanted absolutely nothing to do with our impassioned explanations; he told us to go and explain directly to the vice principal.

This would be my second encounter with Thomson and, what would he do to me now—kick me off the running team? But to John, that was going to be another one of many face-to-face meetings with the vice principal. By the time we were ready to go up to the second floor, John looked clean and composed; and he told me that the last thing he wanted, was another visit with Mr. Thomson. His football could well be on the line this time. Both of us stood to lose a lot.

But the big Serbian has a plan.

We walked into the vice principal's office almost holding hands, looking every part the best of friends. We were to tell Thomson, apologetically; that we were equally to blame for the sawdust mess. And, we were to apologize for having disturbed the class, and right there in front of him, shake hands with each other with all the sincerity that deceit could muster.

One cannot beat the wisdom of experience—it worked perfectly. We were dismissed with some undeserved accolades from Mr. Thomson: he was so pleased and gratified to have witnessed Tech students demonstrate such levels of mature responsibility; indeed for him, it was a testament to the high-quality faculty, he and Mr. McDorman supervised, or, some such words to that effect.

John and I put this behind us, but I was still left with the problem of the legs without graceful curves. Osmo came to the rescue; he said that by now he had seen lots of female curves—without clothes—and he would transfer this valuable knowledge to my legs. And, he did a good job.

Some Contacts with Roger

By this time I saw very little of Roger, and I had only occasional meetings with Gordon since he reported to a different homeroom. However, one day Roger shows up to my house with his girlfriend, and he is carrying a duffle bag slung over his shoulder. He wants to meet away from my parents, so we go to my room for privacy. He opens up the bag and produces a fairly new short-barreled 22 calibre rifle. He needs money badly. He tells me nothing about its origin, but for ten bucks I can have it. And that is how I came to own that rifle at age seventeen.

Later, my son Christopher and I hacksawed the barrel shorter still, so we could put it in a backpack and take it with us canoeing in the provincial parks—in case we met with bears.

The only other time, and the last time I was to see Roger—that is before we were to reunite in our sixties before he died—was at my last high school track meet, at the Sacre Coeur field. I didn't know he was there—he had quit school for some time by then—but, he was there, and he had made his way to trackside. Into the bell lap of the four-lap mile race, I was in second place, four yards behind Real Bisson of Sacre Coeur College, with two hundred yards to go I hear the familiar voice, yelling "Go get him, old man", I kicked and won the race.

Cathy O'Neil and the Church of the Latter Day Saints

My new friend from Hearn Street, Rob Traynor, had a girlfriend from Sudbury High School, she was in grade ten. And she had a girlfriend, Cathy O'Neil, who lived across the street from Rob, right beside Guy's house and three houses away from me. There was no father in Cathy's house; she lived with her mom and an older sister and two older brothers. The only income in the family was the monthly provincial welfare cheque, known as Mothers' Allowance. I was to become familiar later, with all those income support and social services programs, when I became a social worker for the city of Sudbury.

Rob and his girlfriend would go for walks and one day Cathy is with them. They ask me to join them for the walk to the Victory park playground and back. Victory is on Frood Road and that would make it a forty minute walk, there and back. By the time we got there it had started to rain, so we took shelter underneath the long overhanging roof soffit. It was damp and cool, so we huddled close together.

Cathy was short, brown haired and blue eyed; and then her head bent back, and those blue eyes looked at me. And that is when, and where, my lips first touched the lips of a girl.

I met her mother once, but she would not say a word to me. One of her brothers was a few years older than me, and out of high school; the younger one, Michael, later became a great quarterback for Sheridan Tech and led the school to two city championships. Her sister was a year older than me, and I know she resented someone my age and attending grade eleven, having anything to do with her younger sister, in grade nine.

The O'Neil's belonged to the congregation of the Church of Latter Day Saints, and they were strong practicing Mormons. This may have been a reason why Cathy's mother would not say a word to me, a French Canadian Catholic.

The Mormons are a very nice and fairly gregarious folk, but when it comes to matters of outside relationships—they close ranks and circle the wagons—which is perfectly understandable.

I was to see that behaviour later in my father's reaction when Louise started to date an East-Indian man. I was never solicited for membership in their church. No nice, clean-cut young men; with short haircuts, and white shirts; ties and black blazers, ever came to my house, offering to share a bible reading. I would have talked to them, and if it had been wintertime, I would have taken them out of the cold. I talk to any religious groups that come knocking at my door. Jehovah Witnesses and anything else in between. And why not? Hearing someone else's version of life and how they interpret the divine, can never harm you. It could probably enrich you.

I saw Cathy on a few occasions during that first summer. Anytime I would go to her door, I got the same answer—she was out "babysitting". The relationship died away with the passing of time.

CHAPTER 12

Hank and Keith and the Army Cadets

But I was getting more involved with other activities. Besides school and sports, and my part-time work, I now decided to join the Army Cadet Corps. Drills and exercises took place every second Thursday night at the Riverside Drive Armouries. A running team friend, Hank Richer, and a classmate, Keith Ferris were in the Cadets.

Hank lived right downtown, at the corner of Cedar and Elgin Streets, in a big apartment block beside the liquor store. They rented a place on the first floor. I was there a few times. What struck me was how the rooms were partitioned; there were no wooden doors anywhere; the kitchen was separated from the sitting room by a heavy curtain, and the two bedrooms off a hallway were similarly separated by heavy curtains.

Hank was very nice and a good friend. Anyone who looked at him probably suppressed a smile. He was of average height, and his hair was cut "brush-cut" fashion and it stood high on his head; and, he had huge ears pushed outward which gave him a comical look. And to add to the odd picture; when Hank walked, he carried the palms of his hands facing completely to the rear so that if you walked behind him, you could not help but stare at the two big palms, the protruding ears and Hank, moving about monkey-like.

Keith had been involved with the Cadets since elementary school. He had told me some time before that his plan was to go to university after graduation through a full sponsorship by the Canadian Army's Regular Officer Training Plan (ROTP). If accepted, the army would enrol you in a university of your choice or, you could attend Royal Military Colleges in Kingston, Royal Roads in British Columbia, or the French language military college in St. Jean, Quebec. That bit of information on free post-secondary education registered clearly in my mind.

I had stumbled upon a pathway to university without cost to me or my parents. There is absolutely no way I could otherwise afford the cost of post-secondary education—those were the pre OSAP days.

The Hidden Secrets of Jennifer Munro

In the fall, Claude Laporte, of my city midget Kinsmen hockey club days, and I, resumed our friendship at school. He introduced me to a cousin of his, Jennifer Munro. Jennifer and her family had moved to Sudbury from Blind River prior to the start of school. Her dad had seasonal labour work on construction sites, and he was hoping to get on with Inco. In the years spanning 1960 to the mid-70's, to secure adequate housing in Sudbury was very difficult for a single person; and extremely difficult for a family. The vacancy rates were almost at zero. Inco and Falconbridge were hiring out of town workers and bringing them in by the busloads. Urban Renewal construction projects were all over the downtown. Sudbury was in its boom cycle.

Some new hires coming into town had to resort to sleeping in their cars until an apartment or a room would turn up. People would line up at the Sudbury Star publishing building, wanting to be first to grab a freshly printed paper, and scour the "apartment for rent" want ads section.

Jennifer's family was crowded in an upstairs apartment behind "Maria's Cozy Restaurant", at the corner of King and Notre Dame. The place was meant for two persons, but the family of five crowded in together as best they could. Jennifer was seventeen and the oldest.

The first time I met her, over coffee with Claude at the corner restaurant, I thought she had come out of the hospital or was just recovering from some illness. She was pretty, tall and thin; but what struck you was that overwhelming listlessness and the sadness which she carried about her. She was extremely pale and had shoulder length, blond, dry and stringy hair, and soft grey eyes.

But she talked about anything you wanted to talk about; she was engaging enough, but her smile was quiet and unrevealing—you seldom heard Jennifer laugh. After a long walk alone together, we would stand by her door for a long time, barely speaking. She loved to press against my chest and just lay there in my arms and sway from side to side, imperceptibly. She was very gentle and kind. We went out to the movies and for coffee, and I brought her home to meet my sisters and my mother. They all like her.

Her living conditions in the upstairs apartment were much worse than mine had been on Queen Street. I went in once and could barely find space to sit down. When we came back to her place, we stayed on the hard ground at the bottom of the stairs, embracing and swaying from side to side. One day before Christmas, she said she was going away to live with her aunt and uncle in Vancouver. We had known each other since early September. She moved away without explanation. It's almost like she'd been a mirage, and the last three months had been nothing but a dream.

I was sad. I had lost something that had become dear to me. In my innocence, I had become attached and I found the severance difficult.

Ten months later, Claude called me. He said that she was back in town, but that I should stay away—that she had changed—that's all he said.

I called her house and I was told that she was out with her sister, somewhere on Whissell Street. I got the address; it was across Junction Creek, on the east side of Notre Dame Avenue. I walked over, intending to take her out for a walk and a coffee.

I found the house. Her sister was babysitting and the baby was asleep. Jennifer was there, but she would not look at me, nor would she talk much. She walked about, but her movements were zombie-like. I tried to communicate but to no avail. When she left the room temporarily, her sister told me it had nothing to do with me, that it was just the way she had become. I could not believe it. Someone does not just "become"; there has to be a cause to initiate a change.

Experience affects who we are and how we see and understand the world around us. Jennifer had been damaged—either before she left Sudbury or, while in Vancouver. I tried the old embraces and cuddles. There was nothing there. A cold void and some spasmodic trembling were all I could elicit. A total emptiness of feelings and warmth. No reactions to my approaches. A catatonic person in my arms. I could as well have hugged a block of granite.

I walked back home in a light drizzle, sad and confused. It reminded me of the feeling I had in my heart when I had walked home from Charley's house that night of the breaking of the dishes.

Something very bad had happened to Jennifer. She had withdrawn from the world. I never saw her again, but at times I have seen her pale face surface in my dreams. I tried Claude, but he could never give me any satisfactory answers. He was evasive.

My Father and the Cycles of Unemployment Continue

My father went through the last period of his work life—from 1962 to 1968—working at part-time jobs. He took any job that came his way; one of those was as a night-watchman for Laberge Lumber on Dell Street, and then he worked as a seasonal groundskeeper at the Sudbury Idylwylde Golf and Country Club—any work where he could contribute into the 'unemployment insurance' program was a blessing.

He would bring home bags full of golf balls he'd find in the out-of-bounds area of the golf course, and proudly hand them over to me. I would end up passing them on to my friends—golf was not a sport I could afford to play.

And winter time would be Unemployment Insurance (EI) time for dad. It became a well-rehearsed routine. He would gather his contribution stamps book and he and I would go to the insurance office on Pine Street. I would sit at the table and fill the forms for him while he went up to the employment officer, and had his name entered in the log book and registered for employment. He had to report in person to an officer on a regular basis. We were there so often we got to know the regulars, and they got to know my dad. I figured that at that time, the family's annual disposable income was much less than what it had been when we lived in Mud Lake, or Belleterre. Thank God for Sudbury Housing and the virtues of public housing's rent-geared-to-income scheme.

The Double Jeopardy of Sickness to the Poor

In the spring of 1963, my dad took to bed. He was very sick with gallbladder attacks. He needed to be hospitalized and undergo surgery. This could not have come at a worst time. His EI claim had just expired and he was due to report to work at the Idylwylde within the week. Now he was without income, either from unemployment insurance or from his seasonal job. And there was no guarantee that the golf course would take him on when he was healthy again; a sixty-plus- year-old man is not a great asset in a labour intensive work environment.

In those days, gallbladder surgery was a big deal; they opened you up—no arthroscopic procedures then. He was scheduled to be in the hospital for three weeks, but then he developed an infection which delayed his discharge by another week. I visited with him daily, since St. Joseph hospital was a ten minute walk from school.

Traumatized

I remember coming home after visiting him one day, and I was so completely down and depressed that I broke down. The first time in my life that I cried out of despair. I closed the door of my bedroom and sat down on the edge of the bed and, holding my face in my hands, I wept quietly for a while. That was out of character, and I surprised myself. And, then and there, I made myself a solemn promise—I was not ever, to become a poor man.

I became composed and focused and felt much better. A psychiatrist would probably have had a field day with me—I had become traumatized by the consequences of poverty.

The Fear of Indebtedness

To this day, debt has always terrified me. I cannot tolerate the idea of owing money to anyone, at any time; owing money keeps me awake at night. I was probably the last man in Sudbury to apply for a credit card. My motto became: distinguish between your wants and your needs; and, if you cannot pay for it now, and with cash; you cannot afford it—with the exception of homes, for which we would take out a mortgage.

My wife and I have been married forty-nine years and throughout our work life, we made it a commitment—from our first year of marriage onward—to live only on one income. Hers was put away in savings and investments. We could not have done this without sticking fast to my motto—if you can't afford it; you don't need it. We raised two children and that policy has not always been easy to follow; we cheated and strayed at times when vacation and holiday trips came along. But, at the end of the day, it's not the amount of money you earn that matters—it's what you've been able to put aside and squirrel away.

Colette gets Mom Hired

One door closes and another opens. Colette, who worked in the office at St. Joseph hospital told our mother of an opening coming up in the laundry department. This was a union job and the posting had just come up, so mom filed an application. St. Joseph hospital was Sudbury's first and its biggest hospital. It was administered by the order of the Grey Nuns, and it had a mandate to operate as a bilingual hospital throughout its departments. There was a significant French- language presence in its administration, nursing and support staff. Colette took the application directly to the head of personnel—a Sister.

The Sister said to Colette, "Well if the daughter is any indication of the mother's abilities—the mother must be a pretty good worker". And my mother was hired that very day, without an interview or any contact with personnel. And with this development, some sense of financial stability returned. This was full-time permanent employment, with benefits. Colette had come through for the third time.

Living in the "Projects" and Social Perceptions

We had a Sudbury Transit bus route stop, very close to the house, at the corner of Cabot and Burton. On a cold winter day, Monique walked into the house and I noticed that she was red-faced and she had tears down her cheeks, and she was trying to avert her face as best she could.

She had been walking home and because of the bitter cold, she boarded the bus on Kathleen Street. Realizing she was short of money for the fare, she told the driver that her destination was only two stops away and would he take her on for what she had, and she would make up the difference later. Other riders were listening in to the conversation. He mumbled something and told her to get on. He got into a conversation with people around him and she overheard him say something to the effect that—"What else can you expect from people living on welfare and in low rental housing."

I wanted to pick up the next bus and go and punch him out, but my mother intervened and I calmed down.

I became more conscious of where we lived. Although I liked the location in the heights atop the hills, when someone asked me where I lived I quickly replied the 'Northern Heights', and only when pressed for more specifics would I say Cabot Street. And that was fine because most of the time people did not know about the public housing project located there. It's only when I was offered a ride home—many knew the family did not own a car—by friends, and once by my boss at IGA, and by my school coach, Mr. Gowalko; that I would wince and try to convince them that I did not mind walking. But I did accept some rides home and I would notice—and I swear it was not my imagination—the conversation slowed down when the driver realized where he was taking me to.

Daryl Sutton, the darling of Sheridan Tech once offered me a ride home after school and I refused her in front of her friends. My buddies thought I had suddenly gone insane. Guys were dying to get a smile or a glancing look of recognition from Daryl.

I had the overarching pride of the person who has not much else about him to hang onto; my self-esteem became precious beyond reason.

Sad News

Two sad events affected me the fall of 1963. That fateful day, November 22, 1963, I had heard at work about the shooting in Dallas, Texas. When I left work and walked home he was being attended to in hospital, and by the time I walked in the house, the news was all over the TV, that president John F. Kennedy had died by the hands of an assassin. We were saddened by the news and almost incredulous that this could have happened. For me, John Kennedy represented youth and vigour, hope and the way forward to social justice—the new and the enlightened American Way.

That same weekend, a car accident took place at the intersections of Elm Street and Lisgar Street downtown. My friend, Susan from Cache Bay, was instantly killed, along with her boyfriend. Their car had been struck broadside by a transport truck coming down Elm Street. They were engaged to be married in the spring. It was all over the news. Roger called me and we commiserated, but unfortunately, it was not possible for us to attend the funeral which was being held in Sturgeon Falls.

Ray A. Vincent

Community Involvement— Being Part of the Solution

With the exception of Victory playground in the Donovan and O'Connor playground in the Flour Mill, children living in the Burton Street and Selkirk subdivision areas—including our own—had no organized play areas in which to play. Cabot Street had a small play area for pre-school children; that was it, nothing for older children or teenagers. Mr. Kennedy, the manager of Sudbury Housing, sent a letter to all the tenants and the neighbouring private homeowners, inviting anyone interested to show up at an open meeting to discuss the possibility of creating a community playground area for the neighbourhoods.

The first order of business would be the creation of a Playground Association Working Committee and its executive. I was one of three from the public housing area to show up. The meeting took place in the social activity room of a Sudbury Housing high rise apartment building on Humber Court. We had a good turn out from the private owners; they showed interest and they got involved. A playground Association was created that day and I ended up as a member on the board of directors—someone had to represent the housing project, and of the three of us, no one else had shown interest to sit on the committee—I did not have to contest an election. An appointment may not be an ego-boosting accomplishment, but I was happy to be involved in some small way to improve the environment where we lived. And it was a good learning experience for a seventeen-year-old.

I had gone to the meeting and I had volunteered because I believed it important for children and young adults to be as physically active as possible. And furthermore, talking about physical and mental health was not enough; adequate facilities and sound adult guidance was necessary. I have to commend Mr. Kennedy for his foresight and leadership. Although there were to be personal problems, involving Mr. Kennedy and the Housing Authority later on in his career, I always liked and respected him.

When I left Cabot Street to be married in 1968, we had; with funding from the city's Park and Recreation Department, set up a baseball diamond and swings; a place for children to play on different slides and jungle-gym equipment; a green area with walk paths for adults and, in the winter, a skating rink was set up.

I personally learned a lot—how to plan, organize and cooperate with others in order to get things done. The playground still sits there today, at the corner of Selkirk and Burton.

An Unexpected Apparition

I had fifteen minutes left to the end of my shift when I looked up towards the door. I almost dropped the bag I was going to place in the cart. There was no mistaking the apparition walking through the door.

Standing there with a shy smile on his face was Peter Oleksiuk. Peter had gone to my parents first and dropped his luggage there. He'd gotten our address from his brother Stanley, who kept in touch with my brothers. We walked back together and he told me why he was in Sudbury. Peter lived in Toronto and he worked in a food products factory. He'd fallen in love and gotten engaged—going on nineteen—the relationship had recently broken up, and his girlfriend had gone home to North Bay.

Peter had taken the Greyhound bus to North Bay to talk to her and her parents, and hopefully, mend things over. On his way back to Toronto he'd decided on dropping in on us. Not surprisingly, he was somewhat depressed and in very low spirits. He wasn't sure if there would be a reconciliation. He only stayed with us that night. He liked the big city of Toronto, he could not see himself living anywhere else. I saw him off at the bus station the next day. I have always disliked bus stations. They are such lonely places.

One day; twenty-one years later, I was attending a work-related conference in Toronto—at the Royal York—I opened the phone book in my room; found a Peter Oleksiuk and called. There was no mistaking the sound of the voice at the other end—he even threw in a few French swear words of exclamation. We met for lunch the next day.

He got to meet my wife, and we went over a lot of history. He was happy. He had married Louise—the North Bay girl. And, like Emily and me, they had a girl and a boy.

Advantages of Being the only Boy at Home. Recipient of Match Making

My sisters Monique and Louise had girlfriends and although they would not force dates on me, they tried to match me on a few occasions—but these kinds of dates do not usually work out—it's almost like having your sister tag along—it felt too incestuous; like you were going out with your own sister.

One girl, in particular, was interested in me; but then she proceeded to mention one day, that she had felt so depressed the previous week, that she had come under the influence of some irresistible force, pressing her to go in the middle of Elm Street, and let herself be run over by a bus or a transport truck. Well, I had my own problems; and needless to say, the last thing I needed was to be an escort to a girl waiting for an opportunity to commit suicide. Mentioning to a prospective partner that you have suicidal tendencies does not do much to crank up a romantic atmosphere.

Now there was a girl; Jeannine Cholette, that I was interested in. She was Monique's friend. She was short, with a dark complexion and some freckles, deep brown eyes and a cute snub nose. I think she had native Indian blood in her. She had been adopted as a child. She was very quiet, and I was too shy to make the first move and ask for a date. I was very much interested, but nothing happened. She was at our house constantly. She graduated from Sudbury's French Teachers College along with Monique; and when Monique went to teach out of town, contacts between the two came to an end. Carmen's girlfriends were somewhat out of reach since they were two to three years older than me.

There were definite advantages being the only boy—a teenager—amongst three girls close to his own age—besides the opportunity of being set up with dates. I must admit that my sisters spoiled me; they would wash my hair; comment on and critique my wardrobe—whatever there was to critique—and at times they would iron my shirts and pants. I have been blessed with having great and beautiful sisters, but like it happens so often things get taken for granted, and it is with a sense of my deep chagrin that I did not tell them how much they mattered to me; when it mattered most for them to be told so. I realized later, as I realize now, what beautiful sisters, they were to me.

Why do we appreciate something, only after it starts to slowly move away from us? My sisters loved me and I knew it. Sadly, I don't believe I ever told them how much I appreciated them.

CHAPTER 13

A Young Man Full of Pride and Anger

And then, there was the second proposal from Daryl Sutton—and again, I refused her. I don't know why. I was angry and bitter, but I couldn't say why and at whom. I felt inadequate in many ways.

Daryl was pretty, gentle and a very nice person. Light brown hair and grey eyes. She did not have one ounce of affectation about her. In the fall, in October I believe, most high schools held a "Sadie Hawkins" dance in the school gymnasium. It had become an annual ritual—the girls asked the boys of their choice to go to the dance with them. I don't know how the custom of this dance and its gender reversal on partner requests came about, but it was a dance that most guys looked forward to. In those days girls were not as forward and bold as high school girls are today.

If a girl had the courage to take the risk of rejection and ask someone to go out to the dance with her, it meant one obvious thing—she was interested in you. Daryl sat behind me in grade thirteen English class. Daryl participated in a variety of school activities, and she was good at them all: she was a member of the school swim team; the girls' basketball team; the badminton team; the volleyball team and, a boy's heartbreak—she was a school cheerleader!

And Daryl asked me to be her "Sadie Hawkins" escort—and I had the temerity to say no. It is difficult to explain why I refused the invitation.

In retrospect, the best answer I can give is that it was an act of overt protest. I had had not one moment of hesitation and I even got a perverse sense of satisfaction in the refusal. She was without a doubt, the nicest and the most gentle of girls in all of Sheridan Tech—and the most sought after.

It could be what she stood for outside of school that irritated me to anger—from a psychoanalytic point of view, mine would make for an interesting case study. She was the girl raised with a silver spoon. She had all the advantages and the social graces that well-to-do parents can impart. She was composed and at ease with anyone at any time. She had the best of clothes and manners. I was convinced that Daryl had never had one difficult day in her life—she'd never boarded a city bus, and if she had, I was sure that, unlike Monique, she had plenty of money for the fare. And she lived in a house so far distanced from the closest Sudbury Housing project that she probably had no idea what public housing was. She represented everything that I was not. The refusal hinged on more than the fact that I had not the proper dress clothes to go to the dance.

Quebec separatist-revolutionary sentiments were all over the newspapers at that time, and it affected me in some way. I was angry at the world; at my socioeconomic status; at my backwardness—and I took it out on Daryl.

The Request for a Program Transfer

Mr. McDorman was not a man easily convinced. Our principal was a short, stocky man with a florid face, and he kept his flat dark brown hair greased and combed slickly back from the front of his forehead to the nape of his head. For a man in a position of responsibility and approaching sixty, he did not have any streak of grey hair. He wore his reading glasses at the tip of his nose when he needed them, otherwise, they hung loosely on a lanyard around his neck.

In May of 1963, I went to his office to discuss my transfer to the fifth year, grade thirteen general program. This was to be done now, before the start of the new school year in September. I had been forewarned that he detested these requests for program transfers; so I was somewhat prepared for the rough reception I was to receive.

My opening line was to remind him of Mr. Miller's, my grade nine homeroom teacher's previous assurances, on my registering by error in the Technical program, that a transfer could easily be done at any time. I don't think Mr. McDorman even heard what I said; his mind had been made up before I had sat down in front of him. But I would not be deterred, and I became importunate. The more obvious his resistance to accede, the more persistent I became. I told him of my desire to enrol in the army's Regular Officer Training Program (ROTP), and that I needed grade thirteen for admission. He explained the low success rates experienced on those transfers; from the Technical to the five year Academic Program, and then he shared a little bit of inside information with me.

Based on province-wide grade thirteen academic exam results of the past three years—Sheridan Tech had an extremely poor track record—one of the lowest rankings in the whole province. It became then obvious to me what his real concerns were—he did not want transfers like mine to further negatively skew the statistics.

The long distance runner's personality came through; I would not let go; I would not quit. Mr. McDorman became another challenge to overcome, another challenge on my way to the finish line. I brought my grades eleven and twelve marks to his attention—he knew, he had them on his desk—they were excellent. I told him of my career plans and that ROTP was my only means of entry to university. He would look down now and then at my school marks on his desk, and every time he did so his head would shake from side to side, as if in a debate with himself. He looked at me, pushed the papers away and walked over to a filing cabinet. He came back with a thin file in his hands, sat down again and opened it.

The previous year, all grades eleven students in every high school in the province had had to write a province-wide, mandatory, standardized test of aptitude and scholastic ability—an IQ test by any other name. I remembered well sitting in the large, hushed lunchroom, with hundreds of other students, pencil in hand and pouring over thick legal size pages after thick legal size pages of questions.

No student or parent ever got to see the results. This would not be acceptable today. Mr. McDorman had my test results in his hands, his glasses perched at the tip of his nose and carefully going over the record, flipping through the pages and giving me sidelong glances. He pushed aside the file, took a note paper and scratched things on it; looked up at me and said, "Ok, this is what we'll do. Here are the courses you need to take to meet the requirements of grade thirteen; you're in, but" he said, looking straight in my eyes, "you're on probation; you're failing by Christmas—you must drop out." I left the interview happy. I don't think Mr. McDorman was—his province-wide ranking status was on his mind.

The Adventures of a Door-To-Door Subscription Salesman

The very first week into the school vacation period, I began to look for a full- time summer job. IGA had cut back my hours by half. Opening up the Sudbury Star's employment want-ads section, I saw an advertisement soliciting applications from students; grades 12 to 13—and specifically male students—to do door-to-door canvassing in the Timmins area. Interested students were to present themselves at the downtown Holiday Inn; five positions were to be filled.

When the appointed time came, I got dressed in my best interview outfit and presented myself. So did twenty or so, other young men; I knew two of them, Fred DeLuca from St. Charles College, and Bernie Trudeau, from Tech.

After filling an application and handing it in, we waited for the interview. Two men in their mid-thirties, and with an obvious American New York city-like accent, sat behind a desk, a haze of cigarette smoke over their heads; carrying out the interviews—Fred told me; two Jewish guys from the Bronx. They talked fast, smoked a lot and they seemed agitated—today, I would make them out as shysters and con-artists.

The interview was short and peculiar; they gave me a thorough up and down look—it seemed like a physical examination—and they asked two basic questions: one, would I consider myself a shy person, and two; did I want to make a lot of money! And the guy stretched the word and raised his voice at the word "lots". I lied to the first question: I answered, "No"; and to the second question, of course, I answered, "Yes".

I found out later that we were all asked those same two questions. The interviewers spent additional time explaining what they, and the successful lucky applicants, were to do in Timmins.

We were to sell magazine subscriptions—door-to-door—and pose as struggling students working our way through university—which was a bold and an outright lie. We even had a written script, which we were to memorize and deliver, word for word, to unsuspecting aproned housewives, and beer slugging men who chanced to open their doors to us. We were told to practice the script on each other in the car on our way to Timmins, and throughout that first night in the motel room.

They told us that the Timmins gold fields were booming—and, at that time Timmins, indeed, was in a boom cycle; and these guys had heard about it—and they were determined to get a piece of the action: and that's exactly how they talked. And after Timmins was canvassed, we would move on to another northeastern Ontario town.

And lucky me; I got hired, and so did Fred DeLuca. I talked to the manager at the IGA store and I asked for a month off; I said I was taking a holiday. It was granted. I was covering my behind.

We left Sudbury, Timmins bound, early the next Sunday morning. And we were to start hitting the streets first thing Monday morning. The entire party consisted of the five newly hired employees; our two employer bosses; and a female 'clerical assistant'—a more flimsily dressed, gum-chewing-slutty-looking 'clerical assistant' you could not have found anywhere else on the planet.

The two Americans drove big, six-seating sedans; a big Buick and an even bigger Cadillac. We were four to a car and Fred and I stuck together.

Here was the deal: our accommodations were paid—in a flea motel—and two meals per day; breakfast and supper, otherwise we were on our own dime. At the end of the week, we were to be paid a commission based on the amount's worth of subscriptions sold. And there was a "sunset clause" in our verbal, unwritten contract: if, after two weeks of door-to-door work, we wanted to quit—they promised to get us back home; and that promise, I committed carefully to memory.

To their credit, there was nothing fraudulent about what we were selling; they were indeed real, legitimate subscriptions to first class magazines—MacLean's, Fish and Game, Good Housekeeping, Chatelaine, Popular Mechanics, Readers Digest, etc.,

We were each given a city map with a delineated block of streets as our day's assignment; driven by car and dropped off in our zone.

Timmins is very much a landlocked city, surrounded by miles upon mile of bush and, consequently; it can be a very hot place to be in, in mid-July—particularly for hot asphalted, street walking and financially struggling university students trying to earn a little bit of door-to-door money.

Timmins is a hard-working, blue-collar town, full of good people; but people not necessarily high on the literary scale. I think we would have been more successful in selling comic books, or cheap romance novels. The only people I found at home in the middle of the weekday, were unemployed people or women alone with a bunch of small children tugging impatiently at their skirts—not the type of people interested in a magazine, or, the plight of the poor struggling university student.

By Thursday, four days into the job, Fred and I had not been able to sell one single subscription; and our supply of pocket money was running critically low. Only one of us out of five had been successful in producing a few sales.

Our two American bosses were getting frustrated, and at a loss to explain why we were not cashing in on all that Timmins gold. They held numerous sales motivation meetings in their room, and at each new meeting, the pitch of their voices got increasingly higher.

Finally, at the fourth such meeting, on Thursday after supper, the big sales incentives were laid out for all to hear and for all to have a fair and even crack at: tomorrow, Friday, whoever brought in five subscriptions would get his commission doubled; and now—the mother of all incentives—whoever brought in ten subscriptions would get his commission doubled—and get to sleep with the 'clerical assistant'.

The room was quiet but for one person; the 'clerical assistant' lounging on one of the beds, was chewing gum and making giggling sounds, looking around the room and winking at the dispirited and tired sales staff.

We filed out of the bosses room quiet and at a loss for words.

The incentives did not help Fred and me; however, word went round that someone had won the big whammy! Someone had sold ten subscriptions and was to have a good time over the weekend. What Fred said was probably true, "Ray," he said, "that son-of-a-bitch probably paid out of his own pocket for those subscriptions—meaning to cancel them after he gets laid." And we laughed the harder to make up for our jealousy.

After two weeks and still magazine-sales-virgins, Fred and I decided to pack it in—we asked to be sent home. I still had my part-time job at IGA waiting for me.

We thought they'd buy us bus tickets; but no, gas was cheaper. One of the American guys put us in his big Caddy and drove us all the way home to Sudbury.

And, Fred was probably right again; "He's dumping us off the creep, and I bet you, he's picking up two or three more struggling university students, to bring back up with him to Timmins."

A Return to Belleterre

In August, after a four-year absence, my sisters Monique, Louise and I, made a short visit back to Belleterre. We stayed at our Uncle Alfred's place. The revisit to our old hometown failed to impress my sisters with any significant amount of emotion, but it proved beneficial and cathartic to me. It smoothed out the attachments of old memories and sifted out the fantasies, and brought those memories under focus and into the clear light of present-day reality.

In four years the town had changed considerably. Following the mine closure of 1959, many of my friends and their families had done exactly what ours had done; they had moved away to start all over again somewhere else.

When we left Belleterre, the town population hovered at about nineteen hundred, and four years later it counted no more than eight hundred souls. The company town had been decimated, and at the time of our visit there was talk of the possibility of a pulp mill setting up shop with the help of government loans; however, at the time when we were there, there were absolutely no employers in town.

Ronald Savard, Gaston Lefebvre, and Roger Paquette were still there, but they, like me, had changed. We looked at each other and saw seventeen and eighteen- year-olds, and we tried to resurrect the thirteen and fourteen-year-old that had once been in us—and it couldn't be done. We felt like impostors. We were physically and mentally not the same persons our memories had impressed us with. They, who had stayed behind, still had a kinship of sorts and a bond amongst each other; that had slowly slipped away from me. In retrospect, it was foolish on my part to have thought that I could simply pick up the threads of my relationships where I had left them, in June of 1959. My life experiences and points of view had taken on new perspectives and were different from my old friends'.

They were finished with school. They were looking for any work they could get their hands on, in mining, forestry or the big city factories. They were resigned to leave what had been their home since birth. I was still in school and planning for many more years of it.

It was one thing to see the town visibly economically depressed, but it was heartbreaking to see the citizenry psychically affected also. A large percentage of the population was living on, and dependent on, provincial government welfare support programs. Many small businesses had moved away, and along all the four Avenues some houses were empty, and some windows shuttered. The houses that were occupied stood there as if frozen in time; showing signs of neglect and lack of proper maintenance. With the exit of more than half of its regular population, native Indians from surrounding reserves were drifting in and picking up what cheap housing was available. The once booming and forward marching company town was on its last gasp.

On the first night of our arrival, my uncle took me aside and asked me if I would be interested in teaching elementary school English. He could arrange a meeting with Mr. Lafond, the chairman of the school commission, who could if I was interested, assist me in getting a position as a teacher of English in one of the schools in the district. English language instruction at the elementary school level had become a high priority with the ministry of education—English instructional classes had been practically non-existent in my time. This was quite an opportunity since formal teacher certification would be waived if I had an Ontario grade thirteen diploma.

My uncle made a phone call, and I met with Mr. Lafond the next day in the living room of his house. We had a good conversation. His nephew was a family physician in Sudbury. He was to become our family doctor later on; his office was on Dell Street, in the Flour Mill. Mr. Lafond gave me a blank contract to bring home with me, read over and, if interested send it back to him, signed. He so much as guaranteed me a position.

Roger and the "Retreat" in the Bush

I slept at Roger's one night and it was not the merrymaking night of twelve-year- olds, and it proved as long a stay as I could tolerate. I had been asked to stay the whole week with them. The whole family atmosphere, once so exuberant and happy, was now too bleak and depressing to stay around for an extended period.

The next day he conducted me and Ronald and the two girls next door—cousins visiting each other—to a bush shack he had built himself. He called it his retreat camp. A trail behind his house led to it, a half mile into the woods. He told no one but he was setting this up as a sex tryst, which reminded me afterward of my friend Osmo Timonen's misadventures in that very same quagmire. Roger's efforts ended up pretty well with the same results.

The "retreat" had a hinged door, the interior was floored with wood planks covering an area eight feet by six, it had a potbellied stove in the middle of the floor with benches at two opposite ends, and the walls were papered with coloured, and black and white glossy magazine pages of naked women.

One of the cousins—the one from Belleterre—could not be enticed to enter the shack, but the other, having less of a reputation to expose to public scrutiny being from out of town, did. I stayed outside with the reluctant cousin who was not interested in conversation but only in getting her cousin out of that house of sin. After repeated calls and entreaties made to her cousin inside, she started to violently knock on the locked door.

Finally, her pretty, more mature and physically endowed cousin came out, red-cheeked, and readjusting her clothing. Roger and Ronald followed, and Roger showed all signs of not being happy with me—and with Ronald for that matter. All the way down the trail back to town, he kept at it.

My job, he said, with irritation mounting in his voice, had been to lead my companion away from the shack—at the very least away from the damn door. And then he turned to Ronald and admonished him with fumbling, he said, "Like a moron", at the girl's jean buttons. "Damn it," he said, "I had finally got her bra undone, and that took some work, and there you were sweating and still fumbling with the first button on her jeans". Ronald complained softly that he couldn't help it, it was so very hot and stuffy in there, and he was nervous, he said.

And then Roger turned to me again, "And you," he said, "the guy from the big city. How could you allow all that racket and knocking to go on outside? That," he said, "threw everything off; it scared Ronald into moving away to the other end of the floor, and she started to pull down her blouse. And," he continued with disgust, "she was so, so willing," and he stayed on the o and trailed it for quite a while. The look Ronald gave me convinced me that she may not have been as willing as Roger wanted us to believe.

So ended another frustrating sexual experiment that the vigours of virginity could not carry out to a successful conclusion. On our last day in Belleterre, my sisters and I went to the Friday night teen dance held at the "Chateau". Two of my Savard friends from Bearn owned the band and played music around the district. Saturday morning we were on the bus back to Sudbury.

That visit got my heart and mind closer to Sudbury and further away from Belleterre. I got to meet my friend Roger once more some years after this, but on that occasion, it was much closer to home.

A Meeting at the Hotel Royale with Roger and his Brother

Some late evening in the early seventies I got a call from Roger Paquette. He'd picked up my number from the phone book. He and his younger brother Alain were lodged at the Garson Hotel Royale—a fancy sounding name, but a dive by any other name is still a dive. They were in town looking for work in the local mines. I told my wife about my old buddies and I got dressed and went out to meet them.

Garson was a twenty-minute drive away. It was a happy reunion and some interesting stories were told over a few beers. His most recent stories kept me laughing all the way back home. Good old Roger would never change. The most recent episode had just happened the night before. As a preamble; he mentioned how stupid his brother had always been, and that no amount of life experience would ever change him. A yokel from the Quebec backwoods, he said, he would always remain. Alain just sat there sipping his beer and smiled.

There had been two hookers in the bar the previous evening, and they were looking for business. Alain had done the sociable thing and bought the ladies drinks, and with his heavy French accent contracted a deal; the ladies agreed to meet the boys in the brothers' room within a half hour. So the boys rushed to their room to make themselves as sex ready as possible. The agreed half hour went by and no girls. Then forty-five minutes go by; and still no girls. Alain, with some of his sexual ardour waning fast by then, turns to Roger and says, "By the way, you owe me fifty dollars"—he had paid the ladies one hundred bucks—in advance.

The other story that followed this one had taken place the previous year, in Rouyn-Noranda—why the brothers did their sexual escapades in tandem—as a team—I could not figure out. They had picked up these two girls and they were having a good time, again in a hotel room. While Alain was huffing and puffing and making the mattress squeal; Roger was behind the action, snapping coloured photos with his new instant Polaroid camera.

After a month at the work camp, they go home for a week's time off, and as usual, Mrs. Paquette gets busy with the boys' laundry. And of course, as luck would have it; there, stuffed amongst the dirty clothes are the glossy coloured pictures of Alain doing his impersonation of a porn star—all from a rear view angle. You can see the girl's face, but not Alain's. An upset mother Paquette confronts the boys with the incriminating evidence, and the brothers stolidly deny any ownership of the naked male body. Undeterred, the angry mother says, tapping an accusing finger on the butt of the porn star, "I know this is not you Roger, but it's Alain, I've wiped and washed that behind often enough—I'd recognize that ass anywhere." That was the last I ever saw of Roger Paquette.

Mr. McDorman and the Grade Thirteen Ultimatum

We were two weeks into the new school year when the principal calls for a meeting of all grade thirteen students, along with faculty. The meeting was held in the library. We were all seated around the library tables, the teachers were standing along the perimeter of the room, leaning against the walls, shuffling awkwardly and talking with soft voices to each other. We were quiet. The whole scene had the appearance of a game being set up and shortly someone would emerge, step forward and explain the rules. With the lengthening delay of the principal's appearance, even the teachers stopped their murmurings and an air of suspense took over the room.

We heard him walking up the hallway. Mr. McDorman came in, glasses swinging and bopping on his chest, and he turned around and locked the door behind him. He was the only one who spoke and no questions were taken nor any solicited. The speech was short and to the point. Sheridan Tech was getting hammered on province-wide grade thirteen departmental exams. We were ranked at the bottom 20th percentile; the Board of trustees and the Director of Education were asking for improvements and looking for McDorman to deliver. He was on the hot seat and he did not like it at all. So the ultimatum came down—the same line I had heard in May—you produce passing grades at the Christmas term, you stay in; you show failing grades, you're out. After a few words addressed to the staff, he unlocked the door and walked out.

I felt I had just witnessed something akin to a sense of justice having been meted out. I had felt singled out with that threat put over my head back in May—now I had a heck of a lot of company with me.

I struggled with chemistry and geometry, but I brushed aside my pride and sought out some peer tutoring from Tim Bischoff, the class whiz. This helped a great deal, and by doubling the study time on each, I passed all subjects at the Christmas exams.

An Application to the ROTP Program

In November I filled my application for admission to the Canadian Army ROTP program and submitted it along with a strong letter of support and recommendation from Mr. Bob Tyler, my science teacher. I was a cadet with the Sudbury 2nd Battalion Irish Regiment of Canada. Not only was Mr. Tyler one of my favourite teacher, he happened to be an Army Reserve Major that I got to see and talk with regularly at the Riverside Drive Armouries.

A week before my eighteenth birthday, I received an officious looking brown envelope, with the government of Canada crest on it. I opened it; with my mother looking over my shoulder. The letter had the Canadian Army insignia at the very centre and it said what I had hoped it would—my application had been accepted at stage one of the recruitment process—it went on to explain that there would be two other stages, the next involving intensive tests and interviews. I was to await further notifications. The language was terse, direct and to the point—no gushing, welcoming preamble and no congratulatory words—very army-like. Needless to say, I was overjoyed. I was moving forward.

CHAPTER 14

Off to the Recruitment Centre

In early March I received a large envelope personally couriered right to my door. In it were Canadian Pacific rail transportation vouchers, taking me from the Sudbury downtown station to the Toronto Union Station on Front Street. And there was a letter of further instructions, to do with my designated pick-up point at Union Station, at which point I would be taken to the recruiting depot in North York.

When I got to Toronto the following week, brown army vans were waiting for us—Keith Ferris, myself and others from different parts of Ontario, and Eastern Canada boarded the vans.

When we got to the Recruitment Centre we were shown our sleeping quarters—the barracks located on-site—and the mess hall where we were to take our meals while at the base. We were given a brochure describing the next day's activities and a detailed, timed agenda—a full day of written tests, the whole gamut—aptitude, intellectual, and batteries of personality and psychological inventories. The remainder of our arrival day was left to us to do what we wanted to do with it—as long as we were back by the 11 p.m., curfew time.

Keith and I walked off base down the hill past Sunnybrook Hospital and took a Transit bus to downtown. Downtown to us meant, but one thing—the glitzy neon lights of Yonge Street. I had some money in my pocket since I still held my job at the IGA. The army would reimburse our meal expenditures once the session was over—nothing in advance, except travel tickets—but the meals on base were very good and without cost.

This was my first time in the big city; I thought I had been dropped in the middle of a big, glittering amusement park. I was like a kid left alone in the candy store. Keith; however, was not new to downtown Toronto, and I followed him like one of Karl Lorenz's newly imprinted chicks. The new sights and sounds were mesmerizing—the seductive video arcades; the flashing neon signs; the noisy traffic; and posters all over, advertising The Beatles concert coming up in September—all new stuff to me. And Keith had an amazing knowledge of everything important in Toronto, particularly that which existed south of Gerrard Street—the Strip Joints—and the jewel of them all; at the northeast corner of Spadina and Dundas Street West, in the centre of today's Chinatown—the Victory Burlesque Theatre.

And for the Victory, we set our bearings and we charged straight ahead. Total nudity was not permitted in those days, but that made the performances all that more tantalizing—teasing our frail imaginations and leading us right into censored territory.

Stepping out of the Victory we walked and took in all the sights until we were dead tired. And Keith kept on forever asking, on the ride back to the Depot—"Ray, how is that possible; one tassel rotating clockwise, while simultaneously, the other tassel is rotating counter-clockwise?" he would ask, incredulous and flushed in the face, "that defies the laws of physics," he kept on repeating. And I heard that question on and on again until we finally got back to the Depot, to a good meal and a good sleep—at least, a good sleep for me—I suspected that Keith was still wrestling with his conundrum.

I wondered why the media would call it Toronto "The Good." It appeared to me, as I was getting ready for bed at the end of my first day in the big city that I had just stepped away from a den of iniquity.

Testing began at 10 a.m., and went on until 5 p.m., with a forty-five-minute lunch break. The tests were conducted over two separate locations. We started at one building in the morning and moved on to a different building after lunch. Fifty candidates from across Ontario and other regions of eastern Canada were being tested; ten finalists would be selected after phase two of testing, and the interviews that came with it. Phase two would take place at a later time. Western Canada was going through a similar recruitment process. We were told at the end of the day that those of us continuing on in the selection process, would be informed later by telegram. Phase two would be composed of more testing and intensive interviews in front high ranking officer panels. Phase one would reduce the number of candidates and only those moving on to phase two would be invited back.

Before making my way to Union Station to return home, I stopped at a second-hand bookstore close by, and picked up some books, one of which was an original 1882 copy of Lord Alfred Tennyson's complete works of poetry—which I managed to lose in our move to our new house in 2013—my only consolation was that the volume was not in great condition. I then stopped at a flea market and bought Monique and Louise, each a piece of jewellery. I then boarded the train feeling more self-assured and confident than I had felt in a long time. I felt good in the knowledge that I could make my way with some success in the world of mature men. I felt I could take on anything I set my mind to.

At the end of April, I received a telegram informing me that I would be proceeding to phase two of the selection process.

Phase Two and Keith's Important Geography Lesson

A few days following the telegram, my travel documents, and information itinerary came in. Keith had also made the first cut and again we were travelling companions. He told me something on board the train that I committed to memory.

The war in Vietnam was then picking up momentum, with the Americans making some serious commitments in troops and material. The conflict became daily front page news story. Keith was thinking ahead; he was thinking about the interviews awaiting us with the panel of officers. If he got some inside information he never told me. He was studying an Atlas of the world on his knees; he turned to me and giving me the book he pointed to Southeast Asia and he said, pointing to Vietnam, "This is where Vietnam is located in relation to China, Cambodia, and Laos. Remember this," he said, tapping the page, "I'm positive this is a question we'll be asked; they'll want to know our knowledge of current world affairs." And he handed me the map to study, and then he laid back and stretched his long thin body in the coach seat. This proved to be a critical piece of advice.

The original group of fifty was down to twenty, and that number was to be further reduced down to the final ten, by the end of the day. Again, the testing sessions began at 10 a.m., but this time the entire morning session was confined to batteries of personality-character inventories—nothing on aptitude or intelligence testing. At 1 p.m., the group was divided into two groups; one group was individually interviewed by a panel of officers and the other group by a second, different panel; and later on we switched.

The process was very formal and impressive. Strangely enough, unlike many of my colleagues—including Keith—I was not overly nervous or intimidated; I was simply thoroughly excited and fascinated by everything happening around me. You were called; you went in front of a closed door; you opened it and you walked in; alone—and if you had never felt alone before—you certainly did then.

You walked into a large room which looked and even smelt important; the central wall was adorned with a huge picture of the Queen, and on the other walls hung pictures of high ranking officers and historical military events. At the end of the room, below the Queen, was a massive rectangular desk behind which sat six sober-faced officers—all ranked from Major-General to Colonel—after all, if we were to join the club; the higher ranking brass should have the final say.

Closing the Deal

They already knew who I was, they had all my documents and test results in front of them. They introduced themselves and tried to make me feel as comfortable as the occasion could allow. I took notice that one officer was a French Canadian and I recognized the famous Royal 22nd Regiment insignia—the beaver with the royal crown on its back and the words "Je Me Souviens", inscribed underneath. They asked a variety of questions and one in particular, toward the end of the session, brought some chuckles from the panel and a broad warm smile on the face of my French Canadian compatriot. The question had been something along the line of, "Why did I want to join the army and what branch, if selected, would I want to be deployed to?" My answer, without hesitation, was, "To serve my country by becoming an infantry officer in the Royal 22nd Regiment—the Van Doos." I think that clinched that first-panel interview. If anything, I was assured of one solid vote.

The Geography Lesson Pays Dividend

With only a ten minute respite, I went down a hallway and into another room to face the second panel—a different room and different officers. This panel was also made up of high ranking officers, and after the usual introductions, the general line of questions centred around my family, my opinions on certain subjects; where sports stood in my life and my interests in general. And after some further talk and discussion, an officer asked; how up to date was I on current world events? I answered that I considered myself fairly up to date and that I followed the news and world developments with interest.

And then it came—and I could have kissed Keith at that very moment; a tall, thin officer stood up to his full height; walked to a large map on the wall; picked up a long pointer stick and invited me to come forward and join him. He handed me the pointer and directing his eyes to the map, he said, "See that map, I would like you to move closer to it, and make a circle with the pointer, indicating where the country called Vietnam is located."

I took the stick from his hands and walked over to the map and put a big circle around Vietnam. "And," I said, "Vietnam is in Southeast Asia, bordered to the north by China, to the southwest by Cambodia, to the northwest by Laos and to the east by the South China Sea." I think that clinched the second interview in my favour.

THE CHRONICLES OF A JOURNEY

Do Not Upset the Commanding Officer

It was getting late in the afternoon and I was afraid of missing the train bound for home. I got really concerned when I was called and told to stay in the barracks; there was to be another interview—this time with the base Commanding Officer. Now I was doubly concerned; I was sure I would miss my train departure, and the CO would probably thank me very much for my interest, and inform me that, unfortunately, the army had no interest in me.

I walked into this huge room; it was not well lit and the waning daylight outside made things worse. I could just make out the large shape behind the desk. However, as I got closer everything came into better light and clear focus. After shaking hands, I was instructed to sit down on the chair directly facing him. He was a big man, with a deep bass voice. He took his time and looked at me for a while like he was sizing me up for some mission. Then he thanked me for my time and my interest in the ROTP program. He said that after lunch the group had been narrowed to fifteen candidates and that the fifteen would be notified within four weeks, informing on the results of the final selection. He made small talk—and by this time I was really getting tired and losing concentration, and I was hungry. I could not understand the purpose of this casual conversation. Towards what, I sensed was the conclusion of the interview, he asked me nonchalantly, "Are you returning home today?" By this time my mind was in a fog and I just wanted to get up, shake hands with him and take my leave. "I'm not sure" I responded, "I guess so."

All hell broke loose, then; he turned red in the face and looked straight at me, and he yelled in a booming voice, "What do you mean 'you're not sure?' and, you 'guess so?' You either know or you don't know. There are no in-betweens in the army. The army is not a place for 'guesses.'"

And as quickly as the thunder had come, the clouds parted a little and the sun came out again; and in a conciliatory tone of voice he asked again, "Are you returning home tonight?" I replied in as clear and controlled a voice I could muster, "Yes, sir, I am going home tonight, sir." And, with this he gave me his hand, I shook it warmly, saluted, turned around and left.

If I had clinched the previous two interviews I had certainly screwed up this one. Honesty sometimes does not work to your advantage.

The Day I Blew a job Interview with the Province

I recall one day being interviewed for a welfare caseworker position, with the provincial Ministry of Community and Social Services. The interviewer remarked that the welfare job I had with the municipality had pretty much the same duties as the duties listed in the provincial job document; so, he asked; why did I want to work at the provincial office?; and I responded with honest and innocent candour—that the pay scale was higher with the province—needless to say, I did not get the job.

The Decision Arrives and I make Travel Plans

In early June, a couriered hand-delivered letter came in from the Recruitment Depot. I was being congratulated and informed that I had been accepted as an Officer Cadet. I was to report at the end of August for basic training and that further instructions would be forthcoming.

Strangely enough, although this news brought some amount of joy and happiness, it also brought with it a considerable amount of anxiety. I was going to leave my loved ones and I was going to be on my own for the first time—and alone.

I decided I needed some time to relax and decompress and therefore I planned for a long trip—a long bus trip—before August arrived. A bus trip all the way to New-Mexico. I said goodbye to my job at IGA. I was going to visit my brothers, Pete and Ivan.

My mother was actually happy about my decision; I could see the joy on her face. She had not seen her older boys in three years.

A part of her would be travelling with me, and I would be bringing back a part of the boys with me upon my return to Sudbury.

A Long bus Trip and a Visit to New Mexico

The Greyhound bus terminal was located at the corner of Elm and Paris Streets—what is now the home of the downtown Liquor Store. Mr. Barbeau was behind the counter and I went up to him and asked if it was possible to buy return tickets, Sudbury to Grants, New Mexico; he looked at me with a quizzical expression, and then he asked me to wait while he went to check the route connections. He came back and said yes, it was possible; but it would be a long trip: I would cross six states before reaching my destination—Michigan, Indiana, Illinois, Missouri, Oklahoma and northern Texas—and I would experience over fourteen stops and numerous bus transfers before finally arriving in Grants, New Mexico.

The cost, return-fare, was ninety-eight dollars Canadian currency. I produced the money and he started to print the tickets—all of them attached. He came back with them and before folding them, he smiled and held them up way over his head; holding up the first ticket—Sudbury to Toronto—as high as he could raise his arm—and they being all attached, the last ticket being the return—Toronto to Sudbury—was trailing behind him on the floor. He was still smiling at me as he folded them neatly and stuffed the whole into an envelope.

I went home and pulled the same trick with my family, standing on a kitchen chair the last ticket was brushing the floor. I separated the bundle into two manageable packets, one enveloped for the outward, and one envelope for the homeward journey.

I was leaving Sudbury in the first week of July, in nice warm weather, and oblivious to me was the fact that the average temperature in Grants in July was 35 degrees Celsius and days of 42 degrees Celsius were not unusual. I packed what I thought would be adequate clothing for a three-week vacation, and I made lots of room for an assortment of reading material. In my quick decision to travel, and in my inexperience, I had made no arrangements to secure a Canadian passport, nor had I gotten any US denominated currency. Passports in those days for Canadians travelling to the United States was not the big deal that it is today; as long as you had your official Canadian birth certificate with you. However, not having US dollars proved a vexing problem on more than one occasion on my trip.

I had eighty Canadian dollars with me and the further southwest I travelled, the more puzzling; odd looking and funny my Canadian dollars were to become to my American waiters and waitresses, and the more reluctant they would be to accept them. In my innocent enthusiasm, I had totally forgotten that even though they spoke English in the United States, the US greenback was supreme around the world at that time; and my currency looked like one coming from a third world country to them. And, another thing of no small importance which I had omitted to do, was to inform my brothers of my travel intentions—I almost gave them a heart attack when I presented myself at their doorstep.

Travel Impressions along Interstates 45, 44 and 40

The trip proved to be an endurance test. Thank God that I was young and healthy, because four days and four nights of around the clock travelling, interspersed with short stops to switch buses, at which time you ate a quick meal as best you could and boarded a new bus; four nights of interrupted sleep in a stuffy, crowded bus; four days of increasing heat and humidity as we headed in a southwesterly direction, took its toll—I got fatigued and mind-muddled. Our fourteen stops ranged between one hour and a half to fifteen minutes in duration. The longer ones were for bus transfers.

The first leg of the trip, Sudbury to Toronto proved uneventful enough. However, in Detroit, we had a long bus transfer stop, so I decided to step across the street from the terminal and made my way to a restaurant for something to eat. Being so close to Windsor, my Canadian money was accepted without raising any questions. The place was not overly busy; a young man with long curly hair was seated on a stool at the lunch counter, strumming his guitar and singing a soft folksy melody, his guitar case open at his feet ready to accept any donation.

Years later, when Don McLean became famous with songs like, "Castles in the Air," "And I Love You So" and, "American Pie," I could swear that it was he who had serenaded me and a scanty, indifferent and uninterested audience, that early evening in July of 1964.

My Canadian currency had been accepted almost at par in both, Detroit and Chicago, but that was to be the last of my easy transactions with my "funny" money.

The industrial aspects of Detroit and Chicago were impressive. With every passing factory, auto plant and steel mill you sensed the economic powerhouse of the United States—and the interstate, and the window seat of the coach drove me right through the heart of it. The journey through Illinois and Indiana showed the other side of the colossus; the agricultural muscles of the giant, with great open fields of livestock, and miles after miles of never-ending corn fields and a variety of other ripe grain crops. The efficiently coordinated transportation systems of trucks and trains moving all over this large country reminded one of a well-directed orchestra. The bus ride gave me a great vantage point from which to appreciate the vibrant power that the US was at that time in its history.

Canada Advertised in the U.S

In St. Louis I got my first indication that Canada did indeed exist after all in the eyes of Americans—large colour posters advertising the upcoming 1967 Montreal World Exhibition were plastered all over the bus terminal interior walls. It made me feel good and patriotic.

But the posters did not shield me from the beginning of my Canadian money woes.

Ray A. Vincent

Apple Pie and Canadian Currency Don't mix Together

After ordering tea and apple pie, and consuming them with delight, I presented a five dollar bill: the waitress looked at the tendered money and she was genuinely puzzled and hesitant; she didn't even want to touch it—like it was going to harm her. I said I was Canadian and I motioned towards the posters; I lied and said I was from Montreal and showed her my Quebec, birth certificate—to no avail—she called the manager. He came over and flipped the bill from side to side a few times, bringing it close to his eyes, and then holding it at arms-length. By this time, other patrons were showing signs of interest and crowded around to have a better look at the funny money. The manager had withdrawn to his office with my money, and any moment now I expected the FBI to come charging in. But he reappeared saying, yes, the bank had said they could take it. But the exchange rate, which I presumed he made on the spot, was atrocious. From the little change I got back, I had paid three times what the tea and pie ought to have cost me. And this was just the beginning; the more we moved southwesterly, the more foreign and alien the money in my pocket looked to anybody it was presented to.

St. Louis and Springfield, Missouri, introduced me to the fact that there were a lot of people of colour in the United States of America. It seemed to me as if the black people of America had converged on those two cities to make them their home and city of choice. Of course, I had never seen so many black people gathered in one location in my life—to be honest—I had not seen many black people in my life, ever—except for the few I had come across in Toronto. And it got me frustrated and confused. It was obvious that they were the product of poverty, and yet, it was difficult for me to imagine poverty existing in such a rich and powerful country.

More puzzling to me was that they did not appear to mind their lot; although I felt sorry for them they seemed happy enough. Every bus terminal was provided with black baggage handlers and I wasn't familiar with that kind of service. I could not understand why someone was needed to carry anyone else's bag or suitcase. I insisted on carrying my own—I even volunteered to help a poor and what seemed to me, overworked porter, at the Springfield bus transfer.

He was not amused nor was he grateful, even though I am sure he realized I was only trying to be kind; he tried an unconvincing smile as the flashing white teeth and glossy black arm gently pushed me out of the way.

I Meet with a Travelling Companion

At the St. Louis terminal, a well-dressed young man of about my age had boarded the bus. He appeared gentle and well educated. The first thing he did upon reaching the landing beside the driver's seat was to scan slowly up and down the aisle-way to find a seat—or a face—to his liking. Our eyes met and like kindred spirits, we communicated without a spoken word. He came over and took the empty seat beside me. I was glad because by this time I was somewhat melancholy, and his company would provide a welcomed distraction. Finally, I had someone to converse with.

He was on his way home to San Francisco, his family was awaiting him. He had spent six months crisscrossing continental Europe, and he was now returning home to attend the University of California, at Berkeley, in the upcoming fall term. He explained that he had flown as far west as his money would allow him—St. Louis—what money he had left was on the bus ticket taking him home.

On our way to Tulsa, we were entertained with an amazing show taking place on the far horizons all around the bus. A lightning display was taking place all over the wide open plains of the farm country. I told my companion that the bus was taking us right through an artillery barrage. He did not seem to understand the metaphor.

The late afternoon sky was covered by a massive canopy of dark storm clouds. My friend said we were crossing hurricane country; it was five o'clock, but it looked like it could be ten o'clock it was so dark outside. The pulsating and zigzagging veins of orange lightning happening at long distances, and diffusing in the darkness without the audible attendant peals of thunder, enveloped the landscape ahead of us with the magical powers of nature. The lulling drone of the engine carried us through with marked indifference to whatever was happening outside. There was an uneasy quiet inside the coach, everyone wrapped around their own dream world of confused hopes and desires.

A Companion Too Close for Comfort

My travelling companion proved gregarious and friendly—maybe too friendly for my liking. He had annoying habits—he was a "Cuddler"—and a "Toucher"—unwittingly or purposeful I do not know, but it made me uncomfortable. When I turned myself toward the window and fell asleep—or, made believe I was asleep—he would also turn in his seat, but in my direction, as if he also was about to try and get some sleep. His head would end up on my shoulder, his arms would find their way to my chest and neck, and in a short time, he was all over me. By the time we got into Tulsa, I was looking for another seat, which proved more difficult than I thought since the bus was full. Halfway between Oklahoma City and Amarillo, Texas, he started his cuddling maneuvers again, but this time I turned squarely to face him and told him to keep his hands to himself.

To my surprise, he seemed genuinely hurt by my comments, and he kept quiet and aloof for the balance of our journey together.

Tea Should Be Served Hot

In Amarillo, we had a half hour lunch, and a rest and stretch period; I ordered a cup of tea and the waitress brings me a tall, frosty glass of ice-tea. I brought the error to her attention and reminded her that I had ordered a cup of tea—not iced-tea—but, hot tea. She looked at me as if I had two heads. Incredulous that someone would want to drink hot tea when the temperature outside was 39 degrees Celsius.

No one in this part of the world, it seemed, ever ordered hot tea—let alone ever drank any. My companion explained to her that I really meant, and wanted; and that I would only drink hot tea, not cold. She replied that it could not be had but she had hot coffee if I wanted any. And coffee—hot coffee—I had. When I came to pay she was further taken aback by the colour of my currency; and by this time she was convinced that we had been setting her up all along, just to make fun of her. My touchy companion came to my rescue and paid the twenty-five cents.

In Albuquerque, my travelling friend and I parted ways. He was transferred to another bus, taking him to the west coast, and I was continuing a further seventy-five miles northeast, to Grants.

It was already fairly late in the evening. We had a forty-five-minute rest and transfer stop, and as I proceeded to the washroom area my companion followed me. Now, probably as a goodwill farewell gesture and to show how well he thought of me, once inside, he comes close and says in a soft voice, "Do you want any Mary Jane?" Now to be honest, at that time, I did not have a clue as to what he was referring to. I could not recall him or I having made the acquaintance of a Mary Jane at any time since we had left St. Louis. He quickly realized what a babe in the woods, he was dealing with, and he came a bit closer, and said in a softer tone of voice; "You want any marijuana?" I politely declined, and with a smile and a handshake, we parted ways.

CHAPTER 15

First Day in Grants, New Mexico

It was Saturday when the bus rolled into Grants and it was well past midnight. We came in through Interstate 40, the old Route 66, which passes right through Grants—at that time a city street; Santa Fe Avenue. I asked the bus driver to let me off at a motel—any motel—which he did. I walked in tired and drowsy. I registered and paid—in advance—with my Canadian money. She took my money but still hung on to the keys; she looked me up and down for a while and examined the twenty dollars in her hand, and then she checked the registration card closely. The fact that I had just stepped off of a Greyhound bus, and I had a suitcase at my feet clearly bespoke the fact that I was, indeed, a traveller—a serial killer or a bank robber was left to her imagination. She surrendered the keys and told me that checkout was at 10:00 a.m. Later, I realized that the reason for her mistrust was understandable.

The small conservative town of Grants had exploded from a population of 2,200 persons in 1950 to 12,600 people at the time of my visit. The population boom had all to do with the accidental discovery of uranium oxide in the late fifties, and this had sparked the opening up of a number of producing mines in the area. So the hotel and motel owners had seen a lot of riff-raff and adventurers of all kinds come and go—and create a lot of mayhem amongst the good law abiding town folks.

In my room, I retrieved my brothers' telephone numbers from my wallet and I made a quick inventory of what money I had left. With the cut-throat exchange rates I'd been getting in the restaurants and coffee bars, plus my room cost, I was down to twenty dollars Canadian of my original eighty dollars. And I had to pay for a taxi to Ivan's house.

Early the next morning I woke up to a beautiful, bright sunshiny day. As I walked across the already hot asphalted courtyard, I was not aware that during my sound and peaceful sleep, my landlady, the motel owner, had made a few phone calls after we had parted the previous night. Again, when I thought about it later, I could understand it in a better light; this was a small western town full of early western American history; self-sufficient, conservative in attitudes and always on their guard.

In the daytime light, everything about the motel looked different. I walked into the office and she was standing behind the counter. She was waiting for me, and she had some company with her. Settled deep into a large armchair, off behind the door so that I could not see him when I walked in, was the Sheriff of Grants County. His arms, bent at the elbows, rested fully extended on the armrests of the chair; while his big body covered all that there was of the chair. I took a quick glance at the big man in a brown uniform, broad-brimmed hat pushed to the back of the head, and the big gold badge shining on the left breast of his jacket. I thought he was asleep, he looked so like a man at peace with the world; he was so quiet and gentle looking. I turned my back to him and went to the counter to hand over the key, and I asked the owner if she could exchange my twenty Canadian dollars into US currency.

And that's when the big body came alive. The voice of the Sheriff rang out loud and clear behind me, "Where you heading to, boy?" it asked. That ringing word, "boy," with the heavy western accent, and the emphasis put on the interrogation question mark brought to mind all the Western movies I had ever seen. I had just been about to ask the lady if I could use the motel telephone when the booming voice had come out. I turned around and faced him. He had not changed his position in any way and he still carried the same peaceful, stolid attitude.

I told him where I was from and that I was in town to visit my brothers, Pete and Ivan Vincent. At the mention of my brothers' names he moved his big body forward and his whole demeanour changed. He became active in his chair, slowly getting up and rising to his feet; and he now had a broad smile on his face.

He knew Pete and Ivan, he knew Pete particularly well—Pete was a mine superintendent working for Red Path Mining and Tunneling—and he was well known in Grants. I was to learn later that he and Pete often went deer hunting in the mountains outside of Grants. When I reached for the phone to call a cab, he offered to drive me to my brother's doorstep.

I thanked him, but refused the kind offer—I was going to give my brothers enough shock simply by making my appearance at their doorsteps—the last thing I needed was a police escort.

My Brothers Elated but Shocked with Surprise

I directed the taxi to Ivan's since he was the closest to the motel. When I walked in at about eight-thirty, the family was at breakfast. Mark, the oldest child at ten years of age opened the door, but he did not recognize me immediately, but when he finally did; he ran to the kitchen to inform his mom and dad. Ivan walked toward me in stunned silence, with Berthe following with her hands clasping her face.

The first words I heard from Ivan were exclamatory French swear words, and then he embraced me in his arms. Robert, the eight-year-old, would not let go of my hand and he led me all over the house. Ivan and Berthe introduced me to their adopted daughter, Diana. She was American born and they had adopted her the year previous when she was four years of age. I had some breakfast and then Ivan called our brother Pete, he said, "Get over here as soon as you can, you have to meet someone we both know very well," and, he added, "bring Claire and Terry along."

Pete did not hurry, after all, it was his weekend off to enjoy with his family. Sometime after eleven, he drove up the driveway. Claire was first to walk in, and when she saw me she let out a scream, and then Terry, the eleven-year-old, followed shortly behind her, with Pete, trailing not far behind. Needless to say, he was speechless; and then the French exclamations came out—pretty well those that Ivan had chosen.

They were all very happy to see me, but I received some strong admonishments and criticisms on the fact that I had not prepared them in advance; either from a phone call from Sudbury prior to my departure or by not sending a letter by normal post. The scolding notwithstanding, I was hugged and embraced warmly by everyone, and they enquired; about home and our parents. I gave them the latest news, including my admission to the Officer Training Plan.

They were not pleased with my army plans, and Pete told me he could get me an office job with the mining company immediately—in the personnel office. They told me later that when they first saw me, they had assumed that, now that I had graduated from high school, I had come to them seeking employment.

Because Pete had more available space, it was decided that I would be using his house as my vacation headquarters and they—my brothers and their wives—would organize a vacation itinerary to fill my two weeks stay with them.

It is hard for me now to easily recall or understand the dreams, while awake or asleep that filled my mind that first evening I was with them. And when I do recall them, I can hardly believe they were mine, so strange, so unreal were they.

Grants—Hot Days, Cold Nights

When I got up in the middle of the night, it was cold in the house, even though the air conditioner had been shut off at bedtime. The town of Grants is tucked away, fairly high, to the northwest of New Mexico, eighty miles from the Arizona border to the West and two hundred miles from the Mexican border to the South. It is rich in early American Wild West history, with both, Navajo and Mexican cultural influences. And being situated a mile and a quarter above sea level, it experiences wide-ranging temperatures between night and day. The summer average daytime temperature hovers around 34 degrees to 40 degrees Celsius, however, because of the elevation, nighttime average temperatures are anywhere between 12 degrees and 15 degrees Celsius. You fry during the day and you shiver at night.

Grants had been one of the reasons that saw the mines in Elliot Lake close down. In the mid-1950`s, a Navajo sheepherder found an interesting piece of yellow rock on Haystack Mountain, ten miles west of Grants. Uranium had been discovered. When the US Atomic Energy Commission put out contracts for extraction and milling of the ore, it created a mining boom in Grants. The deposit turned out to be one of the largest uranium reserves in the world—little wonder that Elliot Lake uranium mining gradually phased out. Grants proved a lucrative destination for Pete and Ivan—both were making six- figure annual incomes—small fortunes in those days.

Pete held one of the highest paying jobs, he was the mine superintendent; he knew as much about mining as any mine engineer would—back in the fifties, the company had enrolled him in courses at Ryerson, Toronto. Ivan was an hourly-paid bonus-system production miner. My four brothers always made very good annual incomes. They had small families—Louis was childless—they all drove the latest model and the most expensive cars on the market (except for Charley, who did not drive), and they spent lots of money on themselves—and not a penny was passed on to our parents. But more on that subject at a later time.

On my first day in Grants we went to church, after which Ivan's family joined us at Pete's for the weekly barbeque get together. The church had no central air, only large ceiling fans and by ten-thirty it was already 28 degrees outside. But the air was dry, which proved of some small comfort to the hot temperatures. The church congregation was interesting, composed of no more than thirty percent white Americans with the balance made up of people of Mexican-Hispanic, and native Indian descent.

The Local Native Indian Population

I had occasion to interact with, and observe the local native Indian of the area; and their dealings with white Americans around

Grants—in shopping malls, gas stations, and grocery stores. They appeared more self-confident and outgoing than our own native populations. They appeared much more American than ours appear Canadian. I was struck by the language and articulation differences between the two countries' native peoples. Our Canadian native Indians speak with a pronounced nasal, choppy and hesitant phonetics, whereas the native Indians around Grants—the Navajos, the Apaches, and the Pueblo Indians, tended to speak a much smoother and clearer form of phonetic English. There was little difference between the language sounds of a white American in a grocery store in Grants, and that of a Navajo walking in and asking to buy a loaf of bread.

There would have been a marked difference in language sounds, between a salesperson at S. S. Kresge, in Sudbury, transacting business with a native person from one of the Manitoulin Island reserves. It seemed to me that American Indians identified with American culture and values, to a much greater extent, than our own Canadian Indians did with Canada's. The contrast between gradual assimilation and hanging on to antiquated cultural vestiges was noticeable, if not striking.

A Casual Walk at 40 Degrees Celsius

On Monday, my brothers being at work, I took a walk to the indoor swimming pool; about a twenty-minute walk. This was close to the noon-hour; the streets were deserted and the houses' window curtains tightly closed against the blazing sun. But I had the feeling that I was being watched—and I was—every now and then, the corner of my eye caught the furtive parting and the fluttering of a curtain, here and there. My sister-in-law, Claire, later told me that no one—absolutely no one—ever walked about the streets under a midday July sun. The sheltered folks must have thought I was a burglar, under the influence of drugs, or mentally deranged—little did they know I was a harmless, innocent Canadian.

Ray A. Vincent

My Three Little Friends

My three little nephews took a lot of pride in parading me around, amongst their neighbourhood friends; and of course, the fact that I was to be an army officer in the near future, monopolized the talk of all introductions. But the friends seemed to be more interested in my intriguing—to them—accent and my odd habit of wanting to stay out under the hot midday sun.

They also thought that I was fearless; I ventured in the tall grasses and shrubbery around the baseball field and happily retrieved their errant baseballs—an activity they were very loth to do.

Mark and Terry told me over supper that the tall grasses were full of rattlesnakes hiding away from the hot sun—and one bite, they nodded in unison, would kill a horse. That was the last I ever went to their playing fields.

A Full Day Outing with Claire

Before the end of my first week, Claire had arranged for a full-day trek to visit the historical-sights within a hundred mile or so radius of Grants. Heading west to Arizona we visited the nearby Acono and Navajo Indian reservations, and we stopped to look at the Pueblo Indian original craft ware on display. Claire added to her significant collection of Turquoise Jewellery; by buying more pieces from the ladies in the Pueblo village markets.

Before midday, we headed to the Petrified Forest National Park and the Painted Desert; a three-hour drive west of Grants, in the middle of Navajo and Apache counties. This area was in the north-eastern part of Arizona, twenty-eight miles from Holbrook.

Holbrook had had a reputation in the days of the "wild west" for Sheriff gun-battles with cattle rustlers, and a sign still stood outside the town which announced that it had once been a town, "Too tough for women or churches." The problem of doing the tourist exercise of sightseeing in the month of July, in Arizona or New Mexico, is the unrelenting blistering heat following you whenever you step into the open air. Thank goodness for big cars with well-functioning air conditioning systems, and Pete's big Cadillac was comfortable and cool.

I felt sorry for Terry; he felt the ill effects of 40 degrees Celsius temperatures more than Claire or myself, and for that reason, he remained in air-conditioned environments—car and restaurants—as much as we could let him while we moved about outside.

The crushing heat notwithstanding, I took lots of pictures of all the unusual things coming my way. The petroglyphs, the images, the symbols and designs carved and incised on rock surfaces, were captured by the lens of my camera. And with some US money put into my hands by Claire, I bought souvenirs to bring back home with me.

I enjoyed the day trip with Claire; I got to see how different and yet, how beautiful our planet could be seen from anywhere around all its cardinal points. And the different cultures and races mixed onto the already colourful canvas enhanced and enriched the view.

My Sister-in-Law Claire

I also got to know my sister-in-law a little better. She tried hard to put a good face on it, but she seemed a lonely and unhappy woman to me. She was timid and lacked self-confidence. She spoke in a soft, plaintive voice and most of her comments seemed to end on a question mark as if she wanted you to confirm her point of view. She was short and thin, with brittle bleach-blond hair. She always dressed very well and for the occasion, and she loved to wear her turquoise jewellery whenever she could.

I remember when Pete and Claire came to our house on Queen Street, to bid their goodbyes the day before they were to leave for New Mexico—Claire was crying as she kissed us all. She was leaving her parents in Chelmsford and her in-laws in Sudbury. And I wondered now, as we were driving back to Grants in the late afternoon if her crying had had to do with the fact that she was going to miss us, or, if it had to do more with the fact that now she had become my brother's prisoner.

Ray A. Vincent

Time with my Brothers

My brothers took vacation time off work and we spent two days together, camping, and horseback riding the mountain trails, and fishing around Bluewater and Ramak lakes.

Strange thing I found about horseback riding is that as soon as I mounted the horse, instinctively, he knew I was a neophyte at this game. He took control of me—not the other way around—and totally ignored my commands. The guide had to take the reins to get me through the excursion.

My Brother Pete—The Outdoorsman who Hates Mexicans

My brother Pete hated Mexicans and he made no apologies about the fact. My brother was not liberal in his politics, nor was he in his social views of the world about him. He was a hard-nosed, gun-packing conservative. He was a manager; used to giving directions and expecting that things would get done. He told me once that if he had five labour jobs open, and ten, sober Mexicans applied, and five drunken Irishmen; he would give the jobs to the Irishmen—that's how much he disliked Mexicans. He saw the Mexicans as lazy, indolent and plain unreliable—and as to native Indians—he placed them not far behind the Mexicans. Whenever he had need of a large number of experienced miners, he would hold job fairs in a conference room at the Sudbury Holiday Inn, and hire as many Canadian miners as he could.

Pete was tough, fearless and a great outdoorsman. He would have been in his element as an early western frontiersman. Ivan told me that in the fall of the previous year, the two brothers were fishing on this same lake when a boat full of Mexicans, drifting in with the wind, kept on coming closer to Pete and Ivan's fishing spot. Pete shouted out to them to keep their distance, that they were encroaching on their spot; and when the Mexicans ignored two further warnings and kept on coming closer; Pete reached into his backpack; brought out his pistol—a 48—and fired two shots within ten feet of their bow.

Pete was listening to Ivan's telling of the story—he just laughed, and after spitting out a mouthful of tobacco juice, he said, "Well, didn't that get their attention? Didn't they get the fuck out of here in a hurry?" And Ivan said, "Yes, it did, but you were lucky to get back to shore and find your truck still in one piece." Pete just smiled and kept on casting.

Of the five boys in the family, Pete loved the outdoors the most—I probably took second place—and he dressed the part—casual and western style, with denim and knee-high cowboy boots, and a plug of chewing tobacco tucked in his cheek. He was licensed to carry a concealed handgun and he always had his forty-eight fully loaded, tucked away neatly under the seat of his car or his pickup truck. He loved country and western music, but when I was with him driving around Grants in his Caddy, he would play the Rolling Stones', "I Can't Get No Satisfaction," ad nauseam.

That song was indicative of more than a passing fancy; it was a barometer predicting stormy marital weather ahead; a harbinger of things to come. He and Claire were to divorce some years later.

Another Attempt to Set Me Up

In the middle of my last week, Claire tried to set me up with a date—over the disapproval of my two brothers. The prospective date would be Claire's lady friend's daughter.

This daughter was twenty-one years old, and Claire insisted that this was a very nice young woman who had no steady boyfriend at the time. Claire asked her over—mom and daughter—for a barbecue, and we got to meet each other.

There was no mistake that she was twenty-one, as clear as there was no mistaking my eighteen and a half years of age. She wore a low cut mini-dress, fashionable at that time; and she was well endowed—and she knew it. She displayed her charms with a skill and effectiveness, which belied a high degree of experience. She was pretty, short, blond and blue-eyed.

I was mystified—why would a girl like that, not have a boyfriend was difficult to understand. We were to go to a movie that Friday, and I was leaving to go back home the next day, Saturday—exactly two weeks since my arrival. Now, my brothers were no simpletons, they knew a set-up when they saw one. They took Claire aside that evening of the barbeque and they had a talk with her. I don't know the details of the cancellation, but the date did not happen. A missed opportunity that I did not even have a clue had been in the making.

My Departure

When I went to the bus terminal at 7:30 p.m., my two brothers were with me. Shortly before boarding Ivan asked me how much money I had on me, he then consulted with Pete, and they came to me and gave me twenty dollars each, shook my hand, and hugged me goodbye.

I was to see Ivan again four years later when he stood as my best man at my wedding—Pete did not show up.

My Brothers—Selfish and Uncaring

My four brothers never had a day of unemployment in their entire working lives. They made good money and had small families—Louis was childless—and drove the latest model of the biggest cars on the market. Yet, my brothers never gave one penny to our parents—ever—at any time.

It was unfortunate that they left the family at an early age, and became independent so quickly. It was as if our parents had had two families: the first five, Rose and the four boys; and then myself and the four girls. Charley became the separation point between the first and the second phase of the family, as there were about five years separating Charley from Colette—the beginning of the second phase. So with that kind of family dynamics, what my parents experienced with the younger five children, my older siblings were oblivious to, and not personally acquainted with. And they made no effort to acquaint themselves with the hardships our parents were to face.

But they ought to have bothered themselves and enquired. That is what caring children do. When we had barely enough to pay the rent and clothe ourselves, my six-figure income brothers were living the good life.

I never once in my life begrudged my brothers for anything they had and which I did not have; for anything that could have made my way through life easier.

On the contrary, I was proud of their achievements; and as a matter of fact, I sincerely believe that I became a better person, a better husband, and a better father because I was left alone to make my own way in the world. Whatever I ever accomplished I achieved by myself. I made a point of learning from the mistakes and successes of others around me.

However, our parents deserved better from their eldest sons; they deserved more care and respect; they were not loved as they deserved to be loved by their eldest sons; as beautiful and as selfless as our parents were, that could not be said of my brothers—and that certainly was not for lack of parental example.

My older brothers would come home, having been away working for contractors; and bring mom duffle bags full of dirty clothes to wash for them, and they would not as much as buy a box of laundry soap. They expected to be cleaned and fed; and to their shame, they also expected our mom and dad to feed the friends they brought over to the house; who stayed with us for weeks at a time until they returned to work.

They bought their beer and whisky enough—they were the only ones drinking any, our dad never drank—but they would not buy one item of groceries; when they ought to have known that the bill at Riendeau's was getting ever higher and that my dad's meagre pay could not keep up with the weekly food expense—groceries on credit because the boys were in town, and Riendeau would remind us—we were getting behind. What a disgrace! That is not what loving children put their poor parents through. That is not loving; that is not being mindful and caring—those are signs of selfishness—the actions of users.

If they were not aware of the financial difficulties our parents were going through, that does not absolve them—it makes the matter worse. When they should have looked at us, they chose to look away. When our mother had her coat repossessed by AVCO Finance because she could no longer afford the monthly payments, my brothers were not there for her.

My parents never deserved to be treated that way, they deserved better. My parents never cried out for help, they simply gave until there was no more left to give. And, shameful to say, nothing was ever given them in return.

There is an old saying that goes something like: You hurt a good friend; you are a fool. You hurt good parents; you are damned.

Back Home

I got home very tired, which is an indication of how difficult four to five days of round the clock travelling can be—and I was young and in excellent physical shape. My mother, of course, wanted to get a full debriefing of my entire trip—and especially, she wanted news about her sons and grandchildren.

I learned from mom that Carmen, now twenty-one, was seeing a young man and that things were serious—an engagement was in the offing.

CHAPTER 16

Preparations to Leave and Trepidations

I would be leaving in three weeks for two months of basic training at Camp Borden, then I would be off to Kingston. I found the three weeks at home very difficult and a strain on the family. I began to have serious doubts about my future and the military's place in it. I asked myself if I had been too precipitous and impulsive in my decisions to pursue the ROTP program. I was not sure in my mind and I became anxious and uncertain—it was almost as if I was hitting the depressive stage of the manic-depressive personality syndrome.

At home, no one would talk about my impending departure, no one asked me what this new adventure of mine was all about—what the military program was all about. I realized, that this was not an unusual thing with us—the family never talked about family problems or issues—certainly, never about money—this was beneath us and; furthermore, if you kept quiet, it may all disappear on its own.

No one knew or ever got to know how scared I was at that time. My sisters took me to a house party at the Kingsley's on St. George Street. The Beatles were the rage at the time, and Lucy Kingsley went out of her way to get my attention, but my mind was preoccupied and miles away from the Beatles and the party.

I Hurt my Sisters and I Hurt Myself

The week I was to leave my sisters bought me a going away present—a beautiful sweater. That did little to alter my mood; a few days later we got into some argument over a matter which I cannot recall; and later that same day, when they were in the living room watching TV, I went upstairs and came down with the sweater and threw it at their feet.

I went out and walked for a long time. It was dark outside and late into the evening when I made my way up Notre Dame Avenue north; I turned left on Kathleen and continued on Burton toward home. Everyone had gone to bed by the time I walked in. The sweater was still lying on the floor, at the same place it had landed, untouched. I went to bed feeling miserable.

Camp Borden and Basic Training

My mother was packing my clothes into a large travelling trunk we had picked up at Eaton's; she would do a little packing each day as more of my good clothes became available from the laundry. And I noticed the afternoon following my outburst, that the sweater was neatly folded in the trunk. I was leaving the next day, and my sisters were still not talking to me. I had hurt them and I felt terrible about it. The day before departure, I bid goodbye to my buddies on Hearn Street. The next day at 1:30 p.m., I hugged my parents and took a cab to the downtown Canadian Pacific train station. No one was at the station to see me off.

From Toronto Union Station, I was conveyed to Borden in the usual military van, where after entry documentation and a briefing, I was conducted to Officer Cadets' training barracks, my arms full of bed linen. We were expected to make our own beds; we had left our mothers behind.

The first order of the day after breakfast was to report for a haircut—a crew-cut, down to the scalp—the mandatory everyone-look-a-like haircut of the army; after which we proceeded to the quartermaster's stores for clothes and officer-cadet uniform fitting—by mid-November I had to return for a refitting; in two and a half months, my one-hundred and fifty pounds had put on an additional eighteen. The outdoor activities were conducive to a good appetite—and we were very well fed.

THE CHRONICLES OF A JOURNEY

When I returned to barracks shortly before lunch, there was a note awaiting me, folded in half and tucked into the message bin by the door of the bedroom. It asked me to report to the CO's office—the captain of the Francophone squad wanted a word with me. We had a total group of sixty officer-cadets at the base, forty from English speaking Canada and right up to the east-coast, and twenty from the province of Quebec. I wondered why the captain of the French section would want to speak to me. It became clear as soon as I had saluted and sat down. He came to the point immediately—military fashion—he told me that given my language and cultural background, I ought to be in his unit, and therefore, would I agree to transfer to the Quebec group; he went on to explain that this would probably be more fitting for me, and it would bolster the number of his group and mitigate against the normally expected attrition of numbers. He wanted a decision on the spot—again, the military way—no mulling-over time. And neither did I hesitate with my response. I told him that I preferred to stay where I was, with my English speaking cohort, and that my hometown friend Keith, was already in my barrack, and we got along very well together. He looked at me hard for a few seconds, but he remained stoic, showing no overt reaction of displeasure at my response to the request.

Our home for the duration of basic training was an imposing concrete structure, with two large symmetrical cement pillars standing guard at the entrance. The four entrance doors were eight feet in height, of thick and heavy polished oak with a large brass plates in the middle, top and bottom; the middle plate told everyone in big capital letters where they were—BLOCK B—and each door was fitted with large brass handlebars. You needed two arms to swing those doors open—and we were strong young men. You walked onto a mixture of polished concrete and ceramic-plated floors throughout—the hallways; the bedrooms; the washrooms and the laundry room areas—all solid stone flooring, hygienic standouts and spotlessly clean at all times.

The building had two wings, and we slept two to a room. Each room was inspected by a sergeant every morning at seven—he inspected the uniformed cadet standing at attention by the side of his made up bed—and he meticulously inspected the bed, expecting it to be made in accordance with code and specifications. And, he would note down in his pocket notebook any inspection deficiencies—deficiencies that were not to show up again at the next day's inspection. If inspection deficiencies appeared more than once you were punished—the dreaded 5:00 a.m. morning parade square report—you were made to show up on the parade square, at five in the morning, regardless of outside weather conditions, in full battle dress, walk smartly up to the drill sergeant waiting for you, snap a crisp salute within four feet of his nose and shout out for the entire base to hear, why you were to report—what deficiency you were guilty of. And no sooner done, you were sent back to barracks as if nothing had happened.

I know the routine well, I got put on parade report twice. The barracks were our home for the purposes of rest, fraternization and sleep; our meals were taken at the officers' mess hall, a three minutes' walk away.

Our two drill sergeants could not have been more dissimilar; sergeant Richards was always choleric, to the point of turning purple in the face when he screamed his orders, and he was drenched in strong cologne or aftershave lotion; whereas sergeant Dixon was also loud, but never lost his composure and what is strange in a sergeant, he gave the impression that he was shy most of the time.

Officer-Cadets and Protocol

The regular enlisted men and women, and the non-commissioned officers who served in the armed forces, took their meals in the enlisted men's common mess hall; with the same type of eating arrangement that all officers-cadets had gone through months before at the Toronto Recruitment Depot—you queued up with your tray in hand, buffet style; and walked up and down and served yourself.

However; we, as officer-cadets, carried the rank-designating pips (a crown) on our shoulders and therefore, as second-lieutenants, we did not eat with the enlisted men—we ate, as officers, with all the other officers—rubbing shoulders with all commissioned ranks; from the full lieutenant, to the base Commanding Officer.

The dining room was very formal; white tablecloth, silverware and candelabra on the table; and once we were seated—we were served by attending waiters; which, needless to say, I enjoyed that novel experience, but it took me some time getting used to.

And the food was excellent; I gained weight, the hard training, and physical exercises notwithstanding. The officers' mess hall had a well-appointed bar, and once you registered your cadet number you were allowed a bar-chit which entitled you to order any alcoholic beverage; the cost being deleted from your monthly training allowance. I was not, and never have been, a big drinker—I think I only used the privilege of my "chit" but on two occasions, during my stay at Camp Borden.

We were quickly introduced to the army's saluting protocol. All inferior ranks, in their walkabout around the base or meetings, initiate the right arm salute, and the salute is returned or reciprocated by the higher ranked officer. This takes some getting used to and, a good eye to pick off the rank at a distance. At eighteen years of age, I was not used to seeing thirty or forty-year-old men assume a rigid neck, and vigorously raise their right arm and salute me as we passed each other. As second-lieutenants, officer-cadets received salutes from all enlisted men and non-commissioned officers. In turn, all officer-cadets saluted all those officers above the rank of second-lieutenants.

There were odd moments for us when the saluting protocol was somewhat altered to meet training needs. The sergeant (lower ranked) that you showed great respect and deference to, while on the parade square, or while he yelled at you during morning inspections and during training sessions: that same sergeant would initiate a brisk salute when he met a cadet on his way to the officers' mess—and he would call you sir, while you called him, sergeant.

The Dawn of Rising Doubts

Within a few days, Keith and I had toured the base grounds. A big World War 2 vintage Sherman tank stood by in a memorial park not far from the barracks. There was a small shopping mall at the far south end with a convenience store, a clothing store and other small commercial outlets, similar to those that you may find in any small town—some officers and enlisted men had their families with them on base. There was also a theatre and a small community hall where dances were held on weekends.

But what drew my attention, not far from the mall, alongside the base gymnasium, was a beautifully maintained 440-yard cinder running track. I had brought my running spikes with me, and I spent many hours on that track, running out my stress and frustrations. I had started to wrestle with self-doubts and I began to second guess my decisions in regards to the army as a career. However, for the time being, the daily drills and the training program went on.

I was treated very well, yet, I was unhappy. The physical training I could handle easily enough, but the classroom sessions I found dull and without challenge. And I was so uninterested in school work that I found myself satisfied with barely passing grades—with only getting by. For whatever reason, I was losing the motivation and drive that had been my mainstay over the last few years. I started to dislike the regimented life. From sunrise to sunset my life was organized and planned out for me. Keith had no problems with it, but I had. When I confided in him, he could not understand me. There was no room for individual initiative—actually, it was frowned upon. I felt stifled; you dressed the same way; you walked the same way; you ate the same way and we even started to talk the same way.

Keith scolded me when I started to talk and complain like that; he said I drove him crazy. One day we were walking together, he stopped me in my tracks when he saw where I was taking our conversation, he stopped, looked at me hard and said, "Ray, what did you think you were joining? —A Hippie commune?" And he was absolutely right.

I had had reason to be anxious in the weeks before leaving home. I had felt then, that I had not thought through my application to the program well enough. Maybe I had not been honest with myself. I had used the army as a way of getting something and I was still searching for what that something was. Originally, I had seen the officer training program as a conduit for free, post-secondary education, but now, even that held little interest for me.

But be that as it may, whatever angst, I may have laboured under at the time, life still went on and I was still in the program, and I was determined to see myself through. And there were plenty of activities and training maneuvers to keep me occupied.

A Night Exercise—Leadership Training

One evening we had a night exercise scheduled at about midnight. We were driven ten miles out by truck into the deep woods of Camp Borden. We were then divided into groups of three, given a terrain contour map, a compass, and a flashlight; and each group was dropped with a half-mile separation from each other.

We were to make our way across unmarked territory through the forest and get to a predetermined rendezvous point within a predetermined time allowance.

It was pitch dark. After much-contradicting comments as to the proper approach to moving forward, with the aid of our flashlight we decided to fix our compass direction onto the nearest visible tree, advance to it and then fix on another one dead ahead, always keeping the compass needle on the proper bearing. This worked out pretty well, and we made good progress until we came upon large open fields—no trees.

And this was where a natural leader popped-up—and it wasn't me—one of our trios said, "Ray, you move on ahead until I tell you to stop, we'll make you our next tree." By adjustments of my body to the right or left, we got accurate bearings, and we did this in stages until we got to the opposite end of the fields.

We walked out about two hours after having been dropped off by the truck at the side of the road. Some of us had our face or hands scratched; I had lost my Tuque in the thickets, but aside from that we were in good spirits. Out of twenty trios, we came out third.

A big mobile canteen truck was waiting for us at the rendezvous point, serving hot coffee and thickly buttered bread; and there were large open canisters of strawberry jam, from which we scooped the delicious stuff. The air was cool and crisp at that time of night and this was the best snack I had ever had.

The Ten Mile Run and the French Captain Celebrates

On an early Saturday morning a few weeks later, all cadets had to participate in a ten-mile run. This was mandatory; no exceptions made. Again, we were driven by truck to the starting point ten miles out; the finish line was the base gymnasium entrance gate. I took care to take my track shoes with me. It was a clear sunny morning in mid-October. There were young men lined up across the dirt road displaying all shapes and sizes; the big guys were already sweating from anxiety and stress, and the race had not yet begun. When the signal to start the race came, some, as expected, sped away much too fast. I stayed in the middle of the pack for two miles or so, then I moved up. At the halfway mark, on a long straight stretch of road, I looked back and I could not see anyone behind me. I got in first, had time to shower and get dressed before the runner in second place came in.

At dinner that night, the French Canadian captain gave me a congratulatory shake of the hand, and he mentioned that in all the years he'd been on the base, no Francophone had ever won the ten-mile endurance run. He treated me to a beer and, moving slightly away from the bar, he brought the conversation again around the subject of a transfer to the Quebec squad. When I mentioned Kingston he said that would be no problem, he'd have me admitted to the College Royale Militaire de Saint-Jean—the Quebec equivalent to the Kingston Royal Military College.

I thanked him, but I refused his second request. I did not understand his persistence—I certainly was not a special cadet on the base, I had not shown any extraordinary officer-cadet talents or skills. The only conclusion I could draw was that of cultural bias—he was adamant that Francophones should stick together.

THE CHRONICLES OF A JOURNEY

Starting in November our weekends were free time for us to use as we saw fit. I had made plans with Keith, to take the bus to Toronto and see a Maple Leaf vs Montreal hockey game. At the last minute Keith backed out, he said he had found a girlfriend on base—which was easy enough; there were lots of available girls on base. You could meet them all at the Saturday night dance.

But, I suspected a different reason; he was getting tired of my whining and complaining—he'd told me so—I was probably starting to drag him down with me.

I very much wanted to see the Montreal Canadiens and my hero, Jean Beliveau, so I kept to my plan and I went alone. And even though I saw my hero score a goal, the quick trip to Toronto ended up being the loneliest two days of my young life.

I checked into a cheap and sleazy hotel on Jarvis Street. As I checked in and registered, a young girl not much older than me was pacing the lobby. I took to the stairway with my small handbag and made my way to my floor. And there she was. She had taken the elevator. She just stood there swaying slightly from side to side without saying one word; not twenty feet from my door, with an engaging smile on her face. I thought she was a very friendly Toronto girl—it did not clue into me until years after—what her profession had been. She must have gotten my room number from the desk clerk—her employer—and took the elevator to get to my floor ahead of me.

I bought a standing-room-only ticket for the game at The Gardens. I was amazed at the speed and the passing accuracy of the game. Beliveau scored and Montreal won, but that was not enough to lift the heavy melancholy hanging over me as I made my way back to Jarvis Street.

When I returned back to base the next day, it did not feel like I was returning home; I felt cold and so detached that I had difficulty concentrating on the moment at hand; I had difficulty getting in touch with myself. My emotions were dulled and my heart was lifeless. I had determined before I stepped out of the bus, that I would stick it out until the Christmas break; go home for the vacations; admit defeat, and not return.

I kept the decision to myself, but I informed the CO's office of my intention to leave the program in mid-December. He asked me to reflect on it for a few days, and get back to him if I still held to my decision. Well before Christmas, I reconfirmed my intent to leave, and then things moved very fast.

The army does not like to keep quitters hanging around those still on active duty—it's bad for morale. Until such a time as my decommissioning and transport arrangements could be finalized—which took three days—I was removed from my room—and relocated to a separate area reserved for those leaving the program. I was excised and in effect, put in segregation. To my surprise, I was not alone; there were about six of us not returning after Christmas, four from the French group—a disparate ratio given that there were only twenty of them, to begin with.

This could have explained the earlier pressure put on me to transfer. And as a further sign that we were now branded as outcasts—we were told to take our daily meals at the enlisted men's mess hall—an immediate demotion; no more white tablecloth; no more silverware; no more personal dining room service for us.

Up until that time, I had taken pride that my life had been moving forward, but when I left the army—the week following my decision—it struck me hard that I was now moving backward, and everything ahead was uncertain. It was a long and depressing bus ride back home.

W.H Auden's poem, "The Average" kept surfacing and repeating its apocalyptic message in my mind:

> 'So here he was, without maps or supplies
> A hundred miles from any decent town;
> The desert glared into his bloodshot eyes;
> The silence roared displeasure: looking down,
> He saw the shadow of an Average Man
> Attempting the Exceptional, and ran.'

That's what it felt like; that I had run away at the sight of my own shadow—the spectre brought about by the distress caused by my own dishonesty.

THE CHRONICLES OF A JOURNEY

I have nothing bad to say about the military or the military lifestyle; it simply was not meant for me. And I was fortunate to realize this when I was still young and just about to turn nineteen; with still a lot of roadway ahead of me on my journey forward.

TRANSITIONS

CHAPTER 17

Home is a Place Where They Take You In

As they have always done, my parents and my sisters received me back home with open arms, love, and happiness. My parents' house was always a haven for me. My sisters were very happy to see me, and I walked in wearing the going away sweater they had given me.

My father never said much; however, over breakfast a few days after my return home, when we were all seated around the table; he said, looking around and making eye contact with everyone, "No one should be concerned or worried about Ray; he can accomplish anything he sets his mind to."

I got up from my chair, walked up to him and I kissed him on both cheeks—the first kiss I had ever given my dad—what a selfish person I had been all this time. If ever I had need of an encouraging word or a token of love, it was at that time—and somehow my father had been aware of it.

Embracing the World of Work and Opportunities

And now began a period of quick job successions that would not have happened if Sudbury had not been in an economic boom cycle; and with it, jobs were going begging for takers.

I was always a planner and well organized; I went to visit my teacher of Electricity; Mr. Liinaama, at Tech, and received a letter of recommendation signed by him, drafted on school letterhead. That letter did wonders for me. I should have gone back later in my life and thanked him for this letter. It was another opportunity lost—I should have grabbed the moment—there are not many given us over our lifetime.

I filled an application for employment with Inco, to work in the electrical department. This was in early January and I was interviewed in the second week of the month. The next day, I walked over to Elgin Street and filed an application with Falconbridge Nickel Mines for employment, again, in the electrical department. After reviewing my application on site, the Falconbridge hiring officer sent me immediately to the Levack office to speak to Mr. Novak, the head of Electrical—I was hired on the spot. This was a Thursday, I was to start work on Monday next.

I was to be an electrician apprentice and I was assigned to the Fecunis Lake mine site, six miles northeast of Levack and thirty plus miles north of Sudbury. An apprentice was a good position, the base level of a good trade, and in five years I would be a full-fledged mine electrician earning a good hourly wage. However, on Friday, an Inco personnel officer called the house congratulating me on my being hired by them. I thanked him, but I refused the offer of employment, explaining I was already hired by their rival, Falconbridge.

In retrospect, I made a mistake. I should have cancelled Falconbridge and taken Inco's offer.

Fecunis Lake Mine and the Early Morning Rise from Bed

To report to work for seven-thirty a.m., at Fecunis Lake mine, I had to get up at five-thirty, walk in the frigid January temperatures to the Frood hotel on Kathleen Street to pick up my ride.

Our driver, Billy McDonald, was a simple and very good-natured single guy from Corner Brook, Newfoundland—we all loved his accent and in no time it became a contest as to who could imitate him best. Billy lived on Montague Street, around the corner from the pick-up point. He drove an old van with all the rear seats taken out, and wood benches laid out lengthwise alongside both sides of the vehicle—this way, Billy could accommodate more paying customers.

Half the riders were asleep by the time we reached Azilda. Billy's droning voice was one of the few sounds heard throughout the morning drive, and it centred on two main topics; the previous night's hockey game, or, if there had not been any games; the hot Indian woman he had picked up at the bar of the Frood, or the International—and he would proceed in minute, and highly descriptive details to describe his amorous adventures.

On the way back, everyone being fully awake, more people would join in the conversation, but Billy's themes did not vary; it was either the games coming on that night or the next barroom conquest he was planning for.

The return ride brought me home between five-thirty and six o'clock p.m. This meant that for thirteen hours of the winter time; from Monday to Friday, I never saw daylight. I went to work in the darkness; my workday was in the darkness of the mine's underground where nothing ever sees the light of day, and my return ride home was in darkness. The job at Inco—if I had taken the offer—would have been based at the Copper Cliff Mechanical shop, a twenty-minute drive from Cabot Street.

My Partner. The Elusive Dick Daggett

At Fecunis, I was assigned to work with Dick Daggett, a first-class electrician, and a nice man. Dick was to be my mentor; I was to follow him and he would teach me all there was to know about underground electrical maintenance work—there was only one problem—Dick was not the most ambitious person in the world; he disliked working, and he would rather spend energy finding ways to catch-up on his sleeps—and he had this down to a science. Dick's job was to service any and all electrical pieces of machinery used for work underground, mostly on location; from level number 1, at the top, down to the very bottom of the mine, at level number 6.

He had developed creative ways of passing on to the next incoming shift, any work that had any signs of complexity to it; and he had got this down to an art form.

Throughout all six underground levels, Dick had built up resting stations; little nooks and dens in the most out of sight and uncanny places, and to these, he would repair to catch up, on a half to a full hour of sleep. They were ingenious little retreats, only of a size large enough to admit his small frame; padded with comfy stuff he'd brought from home—old sofa seats, old and torn winter jackets, anything easily stuffed in a bag and conducive to a good snooze. And those were inconspicuously spread and difficult to detect unless you knew what you were looking for—atop large ventilation pipes; between the big electric transformers and a rock face; behind broken and abandoned pieces of equipment; and on benches in the refuge station. All these places had to meet three criteria—isolation; warmth, and dryness. He had at least one such hideaway place at each level. And while he sent me climbing the wet and slimy ladders which connected each level (the emergency and shaft inspection routes), changing burnt-out light bulbs; Dick would snooze.

He wore the dirtiest and greasiest clothes you could imagine, even his face was grimy. I could not for the life of me, figure out how he managed to get his face dirty. I figured that it was his way of giving the impression that he worked a great amount of time on the machines.

And he had this disconcerting habit; whenever we walked along he'd grab at his belt, wrench it upward, while pulling and itching up his pants, all in the same motion.

The Search for God in the Depths of the Fecunis Lake Underground

One day, something happened that spooked Dick into spending less of his time alone in the hideaways, and more time with me around machinery. We actually started to take motors apart and began real work; like rewinding armatures.

We went down the cage that morning as we did routinely every morning, but this time we went down to the bottom of the shaft to inspect the sump pumps. This was as far down as you could get—bottom of level number 6. After sounding off the appropriate numbers of horn signals, giving the all-clear message to the hoistman on the surface, we opened the cage gates.

I was bent over, picking up my work belt and tool bag when I heard Dick let out a gasp and a muffled exclamation.

The words literally jumped off of the face of the stone wall: it announced; in bright, blazing white paint and in two-foot sized lettering—"GOD DOES NOT EXIST!" Now, to anyone almost a full mile down in the dark subterranean world, this is a bit of a wake-up call, particularly so early in the morning. We inspected the sumps and greased the contacts against the dank moisture, and Dick kept on looking over his shoulder all the while. We made our way slowly back up to the surface, stopping at each level to perform necessary, light maintenance work.

Each level entrance had a white painted message. Level 5 cried out as you stepped off the cage, "I CANNOT FIND YOU, GOD!" all in the same large lettering. The 4th level said, "YOU ARE NOT HERE, GOD!" The 3rd level asked, "ARE YOU HERE, GOD?" The 2nd level said, "WHY HIDE FROM ME, GOD?" While the 1st level shouted-out plaintively, "WHERE ARE YOU, GOD?"

Now anyone coming to work and proceeding from level 1 to level 6, read a sequential message that had some order to it, and made some logical sense—from asking where God was, to an assertion that since no evidence of His existence could be found; therefore, the conclusion that He did not exist.

Dick was not impressed with my observations, neither was he interested in the subtleties of the semantics—he was freaked out of his mind and he just wanted up to the surface as fast as we could get there—he said it was time for lunch.

Ray A. Vincent

Dick's Explanation

When we got down to lunch, Dick didn't eat much and he was not himself all afternoon. Dick was very superstitious; he'd put his lunch-pail aside, stretched himself on the bench and explained that his eldest son had quit school, checked-out of mainstream life, and had gone out to California to join some Hippie commune. Dick had disowned this son and turned his back on him. As far as Dick was concerned; his son had come back to haunt him.

And the Real Origin of the Subterranean Searches after the Truth

But, as we found out later that day, there was a more benign explanation to the cryptic writings on the walls. A crew of long-hole drillers had on their roster some long-haired, and long-bearded post-graduate philosophy student, out on a one- year university leave, doing some thesis research. He was a driller's helper earning some money to cover his doctoral year expenses. Some of the guys in our van knew him; he was harmless but some thought he was a bit off his rocker. Ever since he'd been around Fecunis he kept on pulling one stunt after another.

Before coming off shift the previous night, he had gone from one level to the next, paint can in one hand; brush in the other; philosophizing to his heart's content. He was fun to be around according to his work buddies, and he could pull his weight, he was no slouch. But if he came suddenly upon you, at some turn in the drift, the long beard and the long hair could run up a little chill up your spine.

He may have been amusing and entertaining to his buddies, but Dick was not amused in the least. Dick filed a complaint with the shift-boss.

I learned absolutely nothing "electrical" at Falconbridge's Fecunis Lake mine. The days were very long, the travelling horrendous and the hourly wage of an apprentice electrician, not much more than a labourer's. I asked out of the apprenticeship program, and for a transfer, and I got it—to the Falconbridge smelter. Closer to home, but another kettle of fish—out of the frying pan and into the fire.

The Graveyard Shift—Where Life on Earth Ends

My job title at the smelter did not bother me the least, "Process Labourer"; work was work and I had never been afraid of work at any time in my life.

However; the hours of work were quite another matter. From my very first week, they put me on the night shift, midnight to eight a.m.—"the graveyard shift". Now I got to understand the meaning of that designation; I got to appreciate why they called it "the graveyard shift," that's exactly where it sent you—to the graveyard.

Working from midnight to eight a.m. was never meant to be done by anyone who calls himself a human being. There is nothing as gut-wrenching as watching the sun rise outside as you stand there, rod in hand, helping with the tapping of a blast furnace, or moving a wheelbarrow from one place to another on the floor of the hot, sulphur-fogged, smelter environment.

My body had difficulty adjusting to being awake at a time when, for the past nineteen years, it had been asleep. Every cell in me was in revolt. I was awake when most honest folks were asleep, and asleep when those same folks were going about leading their normal lives. My stomach was upset and the food actually tasted different. The graveyard shift made me feel sickly; that I really was sick or not, was irrelevant—I felt sick. I knew that working the floor in the direct heat of the blast furnace was to be temporary; until people ahead of me retired or quit, and then I would move to other more challenging, if not interesting duties; and I knew that the graveyard shift would also be temporary. But that was like telling the prisoner not to worry—he would be put "to the rack" only one more time!

Another week of "graveyard" was one too much for me. So at the end of March 1965, I said goodbye to Falconbridge.

Ray A. Vincent

No Shortage of Work. Moving on to Other Jobs

The mid-1960's in Sudbury was a young job seeker's paradise. Certainly, if you were male. It never failed to amaze my father-in-law later on, when I would relate the many and varied work experiences I had accumulated—and all that, before the age of twenty! He would smile that disarming smile of his; chuckle softly as he shook his head from side to side—in disbelief, more than likely.

You could go from job to job. You could literally quit a job on Friday, and start another one on Monday—most definitely, if you had a high school graduation diploma in your hand. I had three things going for me; I had my high school diploma; I also had a technical education background with a letter of recommendation—very important around Sudbury—and I had been in the officer-cadet program—just the fact that I had been there was noted. And there were more jobs in Sudbury than there were job-ready people available to take them.

So, the following week I was knocking on the doors of Inco. The Inco employment centre on Frood Road gave me a sealed envelope and sent me to the Copper Cliff engineering office with it.

Hired on by Inco. The Process and the Physical

The preliminary hiring protocol was interesting, to say the least. Hiring was done only on designated days of the week. Job seekers walked up to the second floor of the large, rectangular, grey concrete building at the corner of Frood Road and Beech Street. You walked into a wide open floor area where rows of chairs were lined up against three walls, in which all prospective applicants were seated; awaiting their names to be called—for whatever position applied for and with whatever qualifications endowed. Written applications had been filled earlier and deposited with a personnel staff member seated behind a partly enclosed office space.

My name was called; I was asked what job I was applying for and if I, or any of my relatives, had ever worked for Inco before;

and my responses noted down—I told him my interest was with the Electrical department, and that my brother Charley worked as a miner with the company. I was asked about my last grade achieved at school and I produced my high school diploma; my letter of employment 'recommendation', from my technical school program electricity teacher, and those were taken from me and deposited into a folder; I also submitted, although unsolicited; my ROTP program admission letter and that raised an eyebrow and that piece of additional information was also placed in the folder.

I was then asked to go to a cubicle in the back and provide a urine sample in a glass bottle; which upon returning, the bottle was labelled and identified, and I was then told to sit down and wait to be called in to see the company doctor.

The doctor called me in; he had me strip down naked, took my blood pressure and heart rate and had me step onto a weigh scale—162 pounds—I had lost weight since Camp Borden. Then he had me bend forward and touch my toes, and while bent down like that, he ran his fingers slowly up and down my spine—you needed a good back for mining work. He then had me stand straight in front of him; he reached down and put three fingers on the left side underneath my scrotum, and he asked me to turn my head to the right side, and cough hard; he then applied the same finger pressure to the right side and he had me repeat that same cough again, this time turning the head to the left side—I figured Inco needed employees with good backs and without hernias. He gave me a requisition to present at the Cedar Street Public Health laboratory—for a chest X-ray—which I did the next day.

That was the routine Inco pre-employment physical examination at that time, which anyone with intentions to work at Inco, had to undergo.

The good doctor then sent me back, fully clothed, to the personnel officer, who gave me an employee identification number (my badge number); which I would later receive incised on a copper disk the size of a dollar coin. Every employee had to faithfully and visibly display this badge whenever on company premises or face company sanctions.

He jotted something down on paper—he told me of the contents, but I did not understand—he put the note in an envelope and told me to proceed to the Copper Cliff Engineering office. The name of the person the envelope was destined to, was written longhand on the front cover.

I was impressed with the whole hiring process; it was well orchestrated, it was fast and efficient with very little time wasted.

Applied for Electrical but Sent to the Machine Shop

The office in Copper Cliff was a busy place, but without the noise and bustle of Frood Road. Here, everyone moved from room to room with stealth and in silence; went from desk to desk, padding quietly on the carpeted floors.

I was led to the north wing; the engineering section with rows of draughtsmen bent over their elevated tables; pouring over blueprints, slide rule in hand. The person I was to see made himself available soon enough, he poured over the note, jerked his head up and said, "You gotta go see Bill Armstrong at the Copper Refinery. You've been hired on as an apprentice machinist." News to me, but I didn't mind—a job is a job. He gave me directions to get there—he assumed I had a car. I walked the forty-five minutes down Power Street, and across highway 17 to finally arrive and present myself at the Refinery.

I had applied for the Electrical department, but I was being assigned to the machine shop—that had probably been what the hiring clerk at the Frood office had said to me before sealing the envelope—and I had not heard properly—maybe still too distracted by the memory of the medical fingers dancing underneath my scrotum.

The Copper Cliff Refinery Machine Shop

The Copper Refinery machine shop general manager was operating under a great deal of stress. The machine shop was a critical operation. I was very inexperienced, yet I could sense the anxiety and mental agitation in his body movements; the pallor of his face; the moisture on his upper lip and the tremor in his voice.

The shop was large and noisy with machine noises of all kinds, and the clanking of steel on steel all over the floor. It was a place full of action, where important things happened—and you could feel it. The machine shop was a critical component of the entire mining operation at Inco. If a mechanical part could not be repaired or remanufactured from scratch in-house; to exact specifications and tolerances; then production literally could come to a sudden halt until such time as an outside order, placed in the US; overseas; or somewhere else in Canada could come in. Amidst all this hustle and bustle Bill's little office stood, not more than fifty feet away.

My Interview with the General Manager

He was a tall and a big man; about fifty years of age. He was busy on the telephone, talking animatedly when I walked into his office. He waved his hand and motioned for me to take a chair and sit down, while he wrapped up his conversation. He put the phone down with some energy; he barely looked at the papers I handed him; he looked at me and said, "Ever done machine shop work at Tech?" I said, yes, I had. "Taken any trigonometry?" he enquired, and I replied that yes, I had, up to grade thirteen. "The problem here," he continued, "is that too many of the older guys are weak in that area." Then he stood up, shook my hand and said, "You start Monday morning, I'll introduce you now to the shop foreman, and he'll tell you who you'll be assigned to work with." He shook hands again and led me to the shop floor.

His hand was clammy and beads of sweat were resting on his forehead, and some were rolling down the side of his face below his sideburns. "I'll say this though," he said as if wanting to convince himself, "we have damn good craftsmen here, but unfortunately, only a few have any formal mathematics."

He introduced me to Al Lalonde—one of the nicest gentleman I ever had the pleasure of working for—and Al told me I would be teamed-up with Art Noble.

Ray A. Vincent

My Shop Foreman

Al Lalonde was everything that Bill Armstrong was not; Al was always cool, calm and collected. He spoke in a measured voice and nothing ever fazed him. He was a tall man, handsome and square-shouldered; he had what people would call an athletic build. Later, when I assumed management positions with the City, I remembered how Al Lalonde treated employees and I modelled some of my supervisory approaches after big Al.

He was soft-spoken, and he had a habit of looking you straight in the eyes while he put a reassuring hand gently over your shoulders and explained the details of a blueprint, the specifications, and tolerances of the job to be executed. No anxiety in his voice, no affectation, no hurry; explanations were clear and given in a calm, even voice. He inspired confidence. If I had any doubts about my skill and ability to properly do certain jobs—and not spoil expensive material in the process—when Al turned away and left, I knew I could do it. He made you believe in yourself.

And I copied his habit of sending birthday cards to each and every one of his staff on their birthdays. It was very unusual, given the industrial setting, for hurly-burly blue-collar workers to receive a birthday card through the post from their shop boss.

But Al Lalonde did it. And I introduced the practice within the white collared bureaucracy.

I Discover a Natural Ability. I Am Becoming a Machinist

The apprentice rotated to different partners every three months; this way, you got to work on different pieces of machinery, since each first-class machinist worked at a different machine. You picked up different skills and honed others as you went along. The apprenticeship program at the machine shop ran along the same lines as that in place in the electrical department—five years. I loved the machine shop from the very first day I set my foot on the floor, and I realized immediately what an important part of the entire production process we were. I was in a busy hive of activity and I loved it. There was talk around the shop at that time of the impending introduction of computer programmed and driven machines, and how it would impact the trade and the hands-on work machinists did, but at the time that did not concern me. I lived in the moment.

A Good Man, Art Noble. And My Love for the Machine Shop Continues

When I reported to Art Noble that Monday morning, and after Al had introduced us, Art took me around the floor to meet the other first-class machinists, and introduced me to them; and he explained briefly what type of machines they operated, and their functions. It was a big shop and we had two other apprentices on the floor.

Art operated a lathe and even before switching on the machine, while it was still quiet in our work area, he takes me aside and says, confidentially, "Listen, just do as I say: we're too busy here to start running around repairing mistakes. But please," he continued "ask any and every question you can possibly think of during the day; I'll be more than happy to answer them and if I don`t have a ready answer, I'll try to find it, and;" he says with a wink, "we'll get along just fine." And we did—we got along very well—and I learned a lot from Art.

Art was five years away from retirement. At first impression, he came across as grumpy and aloof, but if you accepted him as he was those small character traits soon disappeared.

And when he turned the lathe on, and I thought we were about to start the job called for by the blueprint on his desk, he said, "Well, let's not hurry just yet; you have to know what those lathes work with. Potters and sculptors work with lumps of clay, and there are many different types of clay;" he said, "and we're the same; except that we work not with lumps, but with rods of steel; many different types of steel—each type used for a specific purpose," he concluded, with his engaging wink.

So we went to the far end of a long wall, and there lay all of our raw un-sculpted materials—of different lengths, different diameters and of different internal molecular structural compositions—hot rolled steel; cold rolled steel; bronze; copper and stainless steel. He explained the different aspects, qualities, and uses of each metal.

When we got back to the workbench, he quickly peeked at the work order and the blueprint and he says, "Go over and get us a three foot long, three and a half inch diameter piece of cold rolled steel, centre it, and set it up in the chuck for us."

How happy I was! I was doing something practical; something useful; something that had a consequence and a purpose, a link in a chain with other useful things. And, it was something I enjoyed doing, and that I had some natural talent for.

I cut the piece; scribed concentric circles to locate each centre; punched the centre guiding holes and then drilled the two small centre holes at each end, and placed the piece in the lathe and secured it up to the chuck.

Here was a job I loved doing; machinists indeed were artists and sculptors; makers of useful things—and they got paid for it.

My Partner is a Special Man

I was asked at lunchtime by the other apprentices, what my impressions of Art were. I was honest and I talked in positive terms about my tutor. I found out that not everyone liked Art; he tended to be a bit sour and taciturn at times, he was a man of few words; he was not a great conversationalist but for that matter, few machinists were. His free time was always occupied in reading.

Art had a habit which annoyed his colleagues; his coffee breaks and lunch times were spent at his workstation, comfortably settled in a padded rocking chair, reading. This reclusive habit was not appreciated in the shop. Art may have kept to himself and did not socialize with the boys, but he had a big trump card—he was one of the best machinists Inco had—and his colleagues acknowledge the fact.

Art was above average height, strongly built and of average weight; he sported a brush cut hairstyle and he had chewing gum forever in his mouth; he wore his safety glasses perched at the tip of his nose, and when he chewed gum the glasses bobbed up and down.

I loved working with Art and I learned a lot from him, and not only from a professional point of view. Art was a good man, in his head and in his heart. It is strange how things sometimes work out in life; I was to cross path with Art again, four years after I had left Inco.

When I got married, my wife and I moved to an apartment on Eyre Street, the West End of town—Art was our backyard neighbour across the laneway; he lived on Whittaker Street. And we were destined to cross path again in 1980 when he was to support my admission into the Mysteries and Privileges of the ancient brotherhood of Freemasonry.

You learn fairly quickly if you enjoy the subject at hand, and I progressed well through the more difficult stages of my early apprenticeship. I moved on to other machines well before the three months allocated for each. Within six weeks the foreman would come to me in mid-afternoon, asking if I wanted to pick up some overtime work.

I never refused overtime—it was easy money—and you got time-and-a-half pay, sometimes double-time—and the company provided a free hot supper catered from outside, and more importantly for me—on those occasions—I felt needed and appreciated. Overtime work was offered to everyone starting with the most senior man—the union shop method—who would have first right-of-refusal if he did not accept, the overtime was then offered to the next most senior person and so on down the line.

The morning following the overtime work, the senior machinists would come around to see what kind of quality and volume I had produced. I received some accolades and some positive criticisms from different quarters, but the only thing that mattered to me was what my foreman had to say.

The only problem overtime work created for me—and it was no small problem—was the issue of transportation back home. My regular ride was with the boring mill machinist Kirk, who lived in my neighbourhood. One night, I was the only one left working in the shop, I found myself without a ride and had to resort to walking all the way back, at midnight, from Copper Cliff to Northern Heights. I had counted on hitchhiking a ride into town—and it never happened. I ended up working a double shift and then spending two and a half hours walking home.

Kirk and I Share a Common Bond

Kirk, my regular driver had served in the German army during world war two. He had been in a tank battalion that saw action on the Eastern front. Kirk was missing the sight of his left eye—actually, more than that—Kirk had lost the entire left eye; he wore a black patch over the cavity. A war injury. The injury had also affected the angle of his jaw so that when he spoke in his deep guttural German accent, saliva would dribble to his chin. What with the patch; the malformed jaw; the deep accent and the wet chin; and being tall and big, Kirk presented an ominous and imposing figure.

But Kirk fooled everyone's first impression; he was really the most gentle and helpful person you could ever wish to meet. He was an indefatigable worker and he had an obsession with accuracy.

Kirk and I had an affiliation of sorts—although not one of a happy nature. Kirk's son had been a student at Sheridan Tech; we had been in grade twelve in the same year but not in the same class. Kirk's son was a good athlete, a star on the senior basketball team. I remembered well the news of his accidental death, by drowning, two years previous. Once Kirk realized that I had personally known his son, I became his special friend—who knows; maybe he saw a little of his son in me.

Father Is Pleased with Me

My father was very pleased when he fully appreciated the nature of my work at the Refinery. He knew all about machinists' work, the craft, and the trade; and he would remind me on more than one occasion, that being a machinist was a rewarding trade, and that I should count myself very fortunate.

Yearning for Something Better.
The Self-Consciousness of the Labourer

However, inasmuch as I loved my job and the people I worked with, there was an irrepressible force; an increasing pressure, pushing me to look over and beyond the labour work horizons. Maybe it was too much bookishness, too much reading; maybe it was an unconscious, but strong desire to break the mould, the yet unarticulated wish to move away from the manual work of my father, and of my brothers—the desire to throw away the blue-collar forever and move to a more genteel work environment. In effect, I had always wanted a job where working with ideas meant as much as working with hard material. Where you worked; wearing a shirt and tie; where you worked behind a desk with clean hands and without grime accumulating underneath your fingernails; where you started work at nine a.m. and you went home at four-thirty; where there was no graveyard shift to put up with; an office job with an hour for lunch and where you were paid an annual salary, and not an hourly wage, is what I yearned for. But most of all, I wanted a work life, unlike my father's, a work life where I could go on working forever if I wanted to—where I could draw a pension at retirement, and where I would never, ever, have to line up and apply for unemployment insurance.

I was nineteen years old; brimming with self-confidence; with a good command of the English language and a swelling rise of ambition growing within. I went searching for an opportunity.

CHAPTER 18

An Opportunity Taken

By mid-June, there was some serious talk on the shop floor about a potential impending general strike by our union, the United Steelworkers of America. If a strike occurred, it would involve all the production and maintenance workers; from underground miners to all surface operations having hourly paid union members.

I saw these developments as a timely opportunity to make my move. I called my uncle in Belleterre and enquired about the elementary school teaching job. He informed me that the staffing complement was completed and that no vacancies now existed at the small school. However, he said that the town of Senneterre, way up to the northeast was looking for a high school English language teacher.

Now, Senneterre was way up there in the cold country, it was in the tertiary line of defence in the US-Canada Distant Early Warning Line (the DEW line). He gave me the name and telephone number of the director of education for that district.

I called him and he gave me an appointment date. I took a week off work and made my way to Rouyn-Noranda to meet the director.

I changed into my good meeting clothes—white shirt and tie—in the bus terminal washroom when I got there. The director was genial and showed interest in hiring me, but he was reluctant to make the decision by himself since I had no teaching experience whatsoever; no professional certification and my age was not a factor tending to promote an offer of employment—I was barely older than the kids I would be teaching. So, he did the proper administrative, and the astute political thing—he let somebody else make the decision—he looked at me and before shaking my hand and sending me home, he said, "Wait for a second, I'll make a phone call to the principal in Senneterre." He spent a few minutes on the phone and after hanging up, he looks up to me and he says, "Go and talk to him, if he wants you, I have no objections."

The Affable Jesuit

By this time I had missed my bus connection to Senneterre, so I took a taxi and within an hour I was presenting myself at the office of the high school principal.

He was a Jesuit, but dressed in full regular lay person's clothes; you would never have guessed he was from a religious order. He was short, corpulent and he chuckled a lot; you got the immediate impression of a man at ease with himself and the whole world around him. He looked at the credentials I had with me and he would test my English by switching from French to English, now and again.

He was a typical Jesuit; errant knights of the Catholic Church—modern, forward- looking and loud-mouthed extroverts. He was very affable and comfortable to talk to; a man obviously well-travelled who had seen a lot of the world—not your closeted parish priest. His conversation had a smooth, easy flow, he was never hesitant or provocative; his whole demeanour communicated peace and acceptance, it seemed to say to me, "I'm on your side".

He knew Sudbury well, he'd been there and he knew many of the Jesuit faculty at College du Sacre Coeur on Notre Dame Avenue. He made no secret that they were in dire need of an English language teacher, and he made passing comments about the difficulty that geographic isolation played in young teacher retention—or the lack thereof.

He shook my hand and gave me a contract to take with me and to return to him, signed.

And that is how I became a high school teacher of English up in Senneterre.

Making my way toward the bus station I felt that I had gotten this job under duress; that it was late in the hiring season and; therefore, I had had the principal at a disadvantage, and that the job offer was a last grasp at a floating log from a man drowning at sea. I knew that if I had had competition from a duly qualified teacher, I would not have had the job offered me.

My Father's Reaction

On hearing the news, my father was very unhappy with me personally, and with my decision to leave Inco specifically, but in his usual manner of handling disappointments, he kept his discontent and anger to himself. But I knew how he felt. He would barely look at me, nor would he talk to me.

Carmen Gets Married

On the seventh of August, my sister Carmen got married to Normand Larocque. At that time I was making preparations to head to my teaching job—the travelling trunk was pulled out—and my poor mother set to the task again of neatly folding my things in it.

Preparations to Leave—Again

I had accumulated close to two-thousand dollars of savings from my work at both, Falconbridge and Inco—I was not a big spender. I withdrew all the money and closed the account, and sometime in mid-August, I took my mom to the kitchen table and counted out eight-hundred dollars, which I laid out in front of her. She gathered the crisp twenty dollar bills and tucked them away in her apron, and she got up and gave me a hug.

I had picked the timing, this was a transaction done in private between her and me. The balance was to see me through my new adventure and get myself fitted for two, tailor-made suits. And I also knew that, with Monique starting her program at the Sudbury French Teacher's College that coming September, and my dad unemployed; the money given her would come in at a very opportune time.

Senneterre

Senneterre was somewhat insulated from the outside world. It was not warm and welcoming to strangers. Located three-hundred and fifty miles northeast of Sudbury, somewhere about the 52nd parallel; equidistant from Sudbury and James Bay. It had taken this name in honour of Captain Senneterre of the Languedoc Regiment that fought the British under Montcalm. This little jewel of information was proudly displayed in a document on the wall, well encased in a glass enclosure; so located for all to read as you walked into the foyer of the high school.

Senneterre had a Canadian Air Force base—part of the federal government's contribution to the DEW line—some twenty miles north of the town, on which American jets and airmen were also deployed. Canada had a twenty-four aircraft squadron and Radar Warning System installed there as part of the tertiary "Pine Tree Line", which had been set up as a US-Canada initiative to detect incoming Soviet bombers during the cold war period. It was an active base when I was there, as we were in the middle of the cold war. The population of the town was close to four thousand—the highest number it would ever reach—and the closest town was Amos, some twenty-five miles northwest.

Although the town's commercial sector and employment numbers benefitted from the air force base nearby, its generally older population did not welcome the intrusion of all kinds of newcomers at street level; nor the screaming of jet aircrafts above.

The town fell back to its accustomed rhythm; and its reliance on the lumber industry regained its prominence, when the Air Base was decommissioned in the mid-80's and, as foreseen; it lost half of its population in the process.

Ray A. Vincent

My Arrival and my Landlords. The Perrin's

I arrived in town by bus on a Friday afternoon and took a cab to the address given to me by the principal—Mr., and Mrs. Perrin would provide me with room and board at fifty dollars a week—a little less than half of my weekly salary. I had no choice, the town was a going concern at the time and there were very few other accommodations available. It was to remind me later of Sudbury's housing crisis situation of the late 60's and the early 70's.

The Perrin's were expecting me. Mr. and Mrs. Perrin were nice but cold and very business-like. He was short and overweight, and he was balding and hanging on to a thin crown of hair more prominent at the back than at the front where he had none; he spoke seldom but smoked incessantly. She offered the opposite picture; she was thin and tall and carried the majority of the conversation. She talked in short, clipped sentences, like someone who does not want any misunderstandings, and who does not like to repeat twice what can be clearly understood once—she reminded me of my sergeants at Camp Borden. She gave me a tour of the house.

I was shown my upstairs bedroom and given the meal schedule, and the TV viewing time schedule—I would eat what the family ate and would watch what the family watched—and that was fine with me.

Then I was introduced to their two younger sons and to Valerie, their seventeen-year-old daughter—and that was not so fine with me. I was to be her nineteen-year-old English teacher and I was not comfortable with the idea.

And I was to live in my student's house. It did not conduce to an ideal teacher-student objective and impersonal relationship. I had not gone to teachers' college, but I could detect shoals ahead in the waters when I saw them. Even the family meals together were uncomfortable but I got used to that.

However, my first day in town kept me busy, I had other things to be concerned with and to prepare for. After hauling the big trunk upstairs to my room, I sorted out and put away my clothes, lined up my books on the dresser top, and took out Monday's written itinerary to review. Monday afternoon at one p.m., was our first scheduled organizational staff meeting, in preparation for the school opening day; the next Monday week.

My room was not a sitting room; it was a small bedroom, a room vacated by Valerie's older brother working in Rouyn. It was Spartan—a single bed; a closet; one dresser with yellow plastic flowers in a pot on top; a small wobbly table by the window sill with two steel folding chairs closed and leaning against it. That was it. I picked up a book, threw myself on the bed and felt like crying.

I skipped the family supper that first night. The sun was sinking fast and it was getting chilly in the twilight of early September. I walked the town streets and watched a men's softball game being played under the lights at the local ball field; munching on hot dogs and gulping down cokes. I looked around at the crowd. It was hard to accept the fact that everyone around me was happy and laughing and shared the laughter and happiness with friends and loved ones; oblivious of me in my loneliness. And I was very aware that they were all around me, while I doubted if anyone in that crowd was aware of my presence—seemed to me then that no one in the entire world knew of my existence.

First Staff Meeting and Impressions Thereon

If first impressions are meant to impress, I am not sure that I impressed any of my new colleagues—at least not in a positive light—but I drew a lot of attention—the sort of attention a unicorn would draw walking in the middle of main street. I was way over-dressed and I was blushing way overmuch. I had had two tailor-made three-piece suits made out for me by a tailor on Cedar Street—a grey suit and a deep royal blue suit—after all; I figured a teacher had to be well dressed—or so I thought. I had on my blue suit together with matching vest, while of the dozen or so staff assembled in the school conference room, no one was dressed the way I thought a teacher ought to be dressed, all—male and female staff alike—were as casually dressed as they possibly could be. You would think that they had just come in from grocery shopping—some probably did—or had come directly from the cottage to attend this meeting—and some actually had.

And I looked like the baby-faced rookie that I was; lost amongst grown-ups—and the more I realized this—the more I felt out of place and blushed. But our principal—God bless the Jesuits—the man of the world that he was, came to my rescue.

The first thing he did was to make straight for me, put his arm around my shoulder and in a deliberate and patriarchal manner, took me under his wing. He introduced me to everyone, and—I had an urge to hug him for this—told everyone that I was new to the profession; that I had had no formal training, and that therefore, he charged them all to look after me—the school, he announced, finally had its teacher of English. Then he carried on with the remainder of the agenda.

I was to teach all four grades, nine to twelve—Quebec never had a grade thirteen in its high schools. Grade nine would be an introductory class; and for grades ten to twelve I was left to develop the instructional content, after finding out from my students at what level of proficiency they were at—in effect, what they knew or did not know, coming in. This seemed a logical and convenient approach to me—but it proved to be anything but. I found out soon enough that you cannot tailor individual learning programs for ninety some students. And to add to the challenges; the ministry curriculum guidelines were vague and non-specific as far as desired goals and measured outcomes were concerned. I had my work cut out for me.

The end of Meeting Ritual

As the meeting was breaking up, my new friends informed me of the perennial custom; we all made our way—with the exception of the principal—to the local bar, and tradition had it, that the new junior member bought the first round.

The majority were married, no one spoke English of course and the most talked about topic of conversation was far removed from the meeting we had just been at; it had all to do with teacher union federation business, labour-management issues and the status of local contract negotiations—areas of conversation foreign to me, and in which I could not possibly participate.

Now and then they would try to draw me out; the person next to me or sitting across from me would attempt to open some talk in my direction. They were most intrigued as to why I would want to teach a bunch of unruly teenagers—and the most asked question of me—why in Senneterre, of all places?

We were in the pub well over an hour and I was still nursing my first beer when I got up to leave.

The Perrin Family

There wasn't much joy and spontaneity in the Perrin family, but it was a busy household. Mr. Perrin managed the local Caisse Populaire and he knew everyone in town. Mrs. Perrin remained at home and she knew everything and anything that was, or would be about to happen in town.

She collected my rent and she insisted that it be paid promptly, and in advance. The family was disciplined; went to church every Sunday; gave thanks to the Lord before each meal, and no one ever sat down to eat unless papa was at the table. If he was in the house, we all waited for him, and if he was not, Mrs. Perrin noted his absence; said grace, and then at the nod of her head we would start to serve ourselves. And there was little talk encouraged around the table.

First Day; "Good Morning Mr. Vincent"

I purposely stayed as far away from the door as I could, and let the grade nine class stagger in and get seated. I tried to remain casual and at ease, and therefore I engaged the next door teacher in quiet conversation. But some students were one step ahead of me—the girls—some greeted me by my last name as they passed by on their way to my class. Valerie had seen to it and had spread the word of my arrival.

When I walked in and made my grand entrance, the noisy class settled to a hush and the odd whisper. I went to the board, and with my back to them, I took a chalk in my left hand and I wrote my full name in as large a print as I could. I turned around facing them, and I said, "Good morning everyone," in a slightly unnatural tone of voice, and that was immediately responded to by a booming chorus of, "Good morning, Mr. Vincent." And that made my heart fill with joy. I remarked that they had pronounced, "Mr. Vincent" in the French manner and I gave them the English pronunciation.

To my surprise, they shouted out the greeting all over again, and louder—this time with the English version of my last name—and I fell in love with my grade nines.

The Complications of the Untrained Teacher

The upper grades were a different matter—they were not as adorable. I dealt with a variety of distracting issues; probably nothing that any other teacher had not faced any day in any class, regardless of instructional subject. I found myself lacking the repertoire of adequate responses.

I had envisaged, coming in, having to deal with a set of ideal students—all strong individual learners—and all at the same level of already acquired knowledge. That was far from the case. And there was the issue of motivation; some students had a desire to learn English, others could not care less, and what shocked me—they came right out and told me so. The other problem area, even in those students well motivated, was the fact that they all had a disparate and varied knowledge level with the language. Some of my grade eleven and grade twelve students had never had as much as one hour of formal English language instruction. I was upset and at a loss as to how to standardize my classroom teaching approach to the upper grades—at what level of complexity or comprehension to set a test, let alone an exam. And I did not want to teach to the test or to the exam—I saw that as short-changing them.

Unfortunately, I found myself teaching the upper grades to the lowest common denominator of ability, and this in effect brought the rhythm and cadence in the instructional day to a standstill. And I noticed the signs of frustration on the faces of the more capable students.

A more experienced teacher would probably have known how to resolve my dilemma, without losing the amount of sleep I did over it. Quebec was just beginning to introduce a seamless English curriculum, from early elementary grades to the end of high school. I was picking up and dealing with the remnants of the past's piecemeal approach. My colleagues commiserated with my problem and offered as much guidance as they could provide under the circumstances.

The Problem of the Age Differential in General, and that of Miss Perrin in Particular

The third problem that I faced with the upper grades was more serious for me than the other two, although it had absolutely nothing to do with pedagogy. Some of my students were almost of the same age as I was. That can be problematic; especially when interacting with female students. Some of my grade eleven and grade twelve girls were not interested in my English instruction skills or lack thereof—and they would let me know about it; some asked me to stay after class for supplementary tutoring; some asked me to their parents' homes on weekends for additional tutoring—when their moms and dads would be away to the cottage; and others simply came right out and asked me out for a date. All of which extra-school activities I firmly turned down.

Miss Perrin was one of the more importunate ones. On different occasions toward the end of November, I started to hear from some students that Valerie had an advantage; she was telling her friends that she was getting home tutoring and the hints were dropped that her relationship with me had advanced beyond the teacher-student scenario. I talked to her parents alone one night, after supper. They were very upset—not at the daughter—but at the teacher—how did I dare cast such aspersions on their daughter, and by extension; on them. No amount of explanation could mollify them. They called the principal and threatened to call his director.

When I sat in front of him the next day and pleaded my innocence, he seemed to believe what I said. I knew that his job was to protect the school—I was secondary. He shared with me the information that the rumours had reached his ears before Valerie's parents' call to him. He had not called me in before because he had attached, no credence to them. But a parents' phone call was different, it had to be addressed and we had had to have a meeting.

I learned from my colleagues later that day that I should have had a union steward with me when I met the principal—as a matter of fact, the principal should have seen to it that I had a union representative present during our talk.

I wondered later on if the principal was not trying to gently remove me from the school. The doubt lingered in my mind.

Another Defeat. Another Return home

Nothing further transpired over this incident, but it made my stay at the Perrin's untenable. When I left three weeks later to enjoy the Christmas vacations with my family, it must have surprised Mrs. Perrin to see me wrestling with my trunk down the stairs, but she said not a word. The cab waiting outside took me directly to the bus terminal. And I never returned.

When the school superintendent called me in Sudbury in mid-January I lied to him; I said my mother was seriously ill and that I could not leave home. He mentioned the fact that we had a contract, and I replied; "What are you going to do? Put me in jail?"

Needless to say, they did not forward my last pay cheque, and the accrued vacation time; and neither did I use their board of education as potential contacts on any of my future employment application references.

CHAPTER 19

I Ask for my Old Job Back

In my innocence, I had the temerity to call the Inco personnel office, thinking that I might have a chance to get my old job back at the machine shop. After being told to wait a few minutes, someone came on and asked me in an incredulous voice, if I was serious; and when I said that I was he cut me short, and said curtly that, no; the job was not available; that they had invested a lot of resources on me and that I had let them down. And with this, he hung up on me.

I had burned my bridges with the Canadian Armed Forces, burned my bridges with Falconbridge Nickel Mines; burned my bridges with Inco; and just recently burned my bridges with the Senneterre school commission. There were a lot of smoking embers behind me and I was still only nineteen years old—and there were still many more jobs to burn in the next nine months.

Father-in-Law is a Sceptic

My father-in-law-to-be would give a low chuckle, smile and shake his head in disbelief when I would relate—sitting at his kitchen table, enjoying a bottle of beer—all the different job experiences I had gone through, before starting my thirty-five-year career with the City of Sudbury. He must have wondered at the time what kind of man his daughter was getting involved with.

Electrical Work at the A&P Food Mart

In February, I turned twenty years of age and there followed a variety of jobs with different electrical contracting firms around town. There was a great amount of construction work about the city and tradesmen of all kinds were in great demand then. I would pick up the telephone, make a few calls and I would be working on the following Monday. I worked all spring and summer as an electrician's helper, installing the electrical fixtures in the new A&P Food Mart on Pine Street (now the home of Evans Home Building Centre).

In September, Monique, who now had her Teacher's Certificate, was moving somewhat reluctantly, up north to teach elementary school in the small town of Holetyre, Ontario.

I picked up The Sudbury Star one day and checked the employment section. The City of Sudbury was looking for a "Junior Assessor"—in those days the city did its own municipal property assessment.

A White Collar Job—My Application at the City of Sudbury

I went to City hall and spoke to Tony Arena, the assistant personnel manager—I did not waste the time of submitting a formal letter of enquiry for employment in response to the advertisement. I have always taken immediate action on anything facing me in life—and always taken the shortest route between two points. I filled an application on the spot and wrote the standard employment aptitude test.

Three days later I got a phone call from Mr. Herb Hatton; not the assistant—but the personnel manager himself. He says, "Ray, all our junior assessor positions are filled;" and I'm ready to accept the gentle let down of 'we thank you and wish you the best', but he continues, when I am about ready to hang up, and he says, "but we have a recent opening in the Welfare department for a field worker, would you be interested in social work."

I had no idea what I was going to say; yes to, at the time. I had not the slightest idea what a municipal welfare office did. All I saw was a desk, and me behind it with my blue or grey three-piece suit; white shirt and tie, "Of course," I replied, "I'm very interested." "Good," he said, "go have a talk with the welfare director at 150 Durham Street South. Her name is Simone Patterson; see her tomorrow at ten a.m."

And that is how I found the career I was meant to. Helping the poor and the marginalized. And I found the helping profession fulfilling and gratifying work. So much so that I spent thirty-five years at it.

I was to be helping people whose lives I knew very well. I knew what they were facing and where they came from.

The Office. Simone Patterson. And I Am Interviewed

The welfare office was downtown on Durham Street South, a block away from city hall. I later realized why it required a stand-alone office; away from the sedate bureaucrats at city hall. They would not have appreciated the ragamuffin down-and-outs of the city walking their hallways.

When I walked into the office at nine forty-five a.m., I could barely get in, it was so crowded. There were people—recipients—shoulder to shoulder, crowded into the reception area. I edged my way to the counter and I told the receptionist the purpose of my presence. She told me that Mrs. Patterson would see me shortly and she whispered an apology, "It's the first of the month," she said— it was October first—"and its welfare cheque pick up day; all single, unattached men have to collect their cheques here, and in person." They were being put on display for all to see—a public shaming it seemed to me.

Simone Patterson managed an office of eight staff; if hired I would be number nine. The job opening was an addition to complement.

Simone did not have one superfluous ounce of fat on her body. She was of medium height; thin, with angular facial features; with blond-dyed hair. And she carried a small body bursting with energy.

Simone had worked her way up through the ranks; she'd been with the city since leaving high school with her Commercial course diploma. She came from a working-class family. She had divorced early in her marriage; right after the birth of her only child. She had never remarried and she still lived alone. She was forty-two years old when I first met her. Her surname was deceiving: Patterson was her married name, which she had kept following her divorce. She was French Canadian and fully bilingual, without a trace of a French accent.

She told me later, that back when she had to raise her child, an English surname proved an asset in the workplace. So she kept it. Patterson would increase her chance at promotions, whereas the French maiden name of Brisebois, from the Flour Mill, did not stand a chance.

But make no mistake in that regard; Simone moved up through the ranks and got promotions, totally based on competence and intelligence.

Simone and I got along from the very first instant we met. Difficult to say why we had such a good rapport; it could be a combination of many things; her son had the same name as I did—Ray—and he was my age. But I think it was more than that—Simone detected a young man without affectation, who had come up from working class like her; someone who could relate to the persons and families the welfare office dealt with.

After the introduction she told me the same thing that the clerk had said—this was the first of the month—a busy time on cheque pick-up day.

She asked about my past work experience—she looked at my education background, and could not understand how I had been hired to teach—I offered no response. She commented on my personnel aptitude test scores and she said they were good; and the fact that I was fully bilingual worked in my favour—the great majority of welfare clients I was to discover later, were French Canadians.

She was aware that my knowledge of the municipal social services system was non-existent, but she said not to worry—I would be in training for six months—and, in her words—"I would be taught the ropes"—Simone's vocabulary was always clear and to the point, and her sentences short and crisp. She was a good communicator.

Then she asked, in a matter of fact manner, if I had the use of a car. No, I had not. Did I have a driver's license? No, I did not. Her facial expression changed, and I could see she was taken aback and puzzled. She leaned forward, gave me a painful look and said, "Ray, this job requires you to make house calls all over town; people apply for assistance and we go to their places to take the application and do an inspection. Personnel was aware of this requirement. But," she continued, after a short pause, and the energy returned to her voice, "we can keep your position office-bound for your first three months of training, and that should give you plenty of time to get your license."

I was in a slight panic—I had never driven a car in my entire life; not having a driver's license was the least of my problems—I had to learn to drive first.

"And," she said with a reassuring smile, "don't be in a hurry to buy a car, you can use my city-provided car to make your initial house calls; until you have your own vehicle."

There was no one in the whole wide world like Simone Patterson. I told her often that she was my surrogate mother. Very few employees can say that of their bosses—and mean it. And many years later, as she sat in the hall as an invited guest, aged but still full of energy; I repeated that heartfelt sentiment from the podium, at my retirement party.

White Collar Work and Blazing a Trail for Male Fieldworkers

Then, as we reached the final stage in the interview, she said, "In the entire history of the City of Sudbury welfare department, the city has never hired a male fieldworker; and I think it's time we did," she confided. She had a male deputy-director, but he carried a limited caseload of single male clients. And as she concluded the interview, she let out a golden bit of information that got seared in my memory. Maybe as an inducement and the fact that I had a grade thirteen diploma, she informed me that the city had just introduced a new in-service education policy—the city would reimburse an employee, his university course tuition fee if the course was work-related and upon successful completion of such a course.

I walked out of the interview, and foremost in my memory of the morning meeting was the issue of a driver's license, and what she had said about a city- sponsored university reimbursement program.

My interview was on Wednesday, October 1st, 1966. I received a call from personnel the next day telling me I was hired; and to report for work on Monday, October 6.

I was to be the office's first male fieldworker ever hired—and furthermore; the youngest fieldworker of either sex ever hired. And the first house-calling-inspecting fieldworker ever hired—who had no car—and, could not have driven one if he had had one.

Celebrating with my Friends—La Fiamma

The weekend of my hiring I took Guy Lavalle and the two younger St. Georges boys—my buddies from Hearne Street—for a little celebration at La Fiamma, downtown on Durham Street. I bought two bottles of Mateus 'pink-rose' wine and we had a great time. I was new to alcohol and I think I enjoyed the Mateus as much for the shape of the bottle as I did for its contents. It was a low alcohol 'rose' but I loved the feel of the bulbous shape of the glass.

La Fiamma was the cool and the trendy place to go to in those days. And the downtown was alive and vibrant, and if you wanted a night-life—the downtown was where it was at! It was a young person's place. And if ever Sudbury could boast of an "intelligentsia," it was where it tended to congregate—university students and the hangers-on of the want-to be-beat, generation.

You walked in from Durham Street level and made your way to the basement. The lighting was low, and checkered tablecloth covered tables awaited you; each centred with empty Mateus bottles stuck with lit and half consumed candles, with dribbling wax draped down the necks of the bottles. Fridays and Saturdays had live music of the folk and jazz variety. La Fiamma did not cater to the "Hippie" set, or the "Flower Child" generation—they, had opted out. La Fiamma catered to the eighteen to thirty crowd, who were career oriented, educated and yet, wanted to blend in with the cool and the hip. And the menu was hip and cool—two-person pizzas'; pasta; cheese and crackers; French bread and all kinds of wines; tea and coffee; that was it—no beer, no spirits, no gooey chicken wings; no heavy stuff. It was a wine lover's place.

Fred was down in the mouth that night; he lamented the day that he had accepted an office job with Trans Canada Credit—the finance company—Fred did not possess the hardness of heart, to work in that environment; calling people and telling them that unless they paid up or caught up on their monthly payments, he would summon the bailiff and repossess their furniture, or whatever else they had taken out on credit.

Finance companies preyed on the poor; if there were no poor people in this world, there'd be no finance companies. Fred, along with his two other brothers, was soft-spoken and of a gentle nature. Like all of us around the table, Fred came from a low-income background and we therefore empathized—particularly me—who had experienced my mother having had a winter coat repossessed. Fred would throw out the legal jargon that had become his daily vocabulary, and he said those words with disdain in his voice—power-of sale, repossession, foreclosure, consolidation, and garnishee—and he would say mournfully, "I don't know how long I can keep hurting powerless people."

Fred did leave Trans Canada Credit shortly after, and he moved away from the city of Sudbury altogether. I was to hear later that Fred became a successful Toronto stockbroker. I smiled when I heard that: Fred had switched camp—from preying on the poor, he had moved on to preying on the well to do.

I Find a Driving Instructor

That same night, when well into our fourth bottle of Mateus, I brought out my dilemma about having a city car offered me to work with, but not having a driver's license allowing me to get behind the wheel; Guy had piped up, "No problem," he said, "my dad can give you lessons after work and on weekends."

And he did. Guy's father readily accepted to give me lessons.

On To the Dancefloor behind Reg Wilkinson's

We left La Fiamma and made our way to the rear laneway, behind Reg Wilkinson's Men's Wear. You climbed a flight of stairs and landed on an upper floor recently converted to a lively dance hall. There were great dances being held there every Friday and Saturday nights. The hot Sudbury band, "The Beasties" were playing that night. I danced with this pretty, empty-headed blonde—all she could talk about was the "Beatles", or, the "Beasties". She turned her face up to me on the dance floor, and she drooled, "I just love 'The Beasties', don't you?" I almost puked. I led her back to her table and started to look for Fred and Guy. I found Guy soon enough, but Fred had gotten involved with a group of girls. Fred was a very handsome young man, and the last I saw of him that night, was when Guy and I came down the stairs of the club. He was waving to us from the open window of a car full of girls, and one of them was taking what looked like a pair of panties—and, ceremoniously proceeded to hang them up the exterior radio antenna.

If the Mateus had not helped to alter Fred's sombre mood; then what was to happen to Fred for the remainder of the evening, probably would.

Mr. Lavalle teaches me to Drive

Mr. Lavalle was a very nice, quiet man. He had been a long time taxi driver, and at the time of my lessons, he was a taxi dispatcher for the same company he had driven for. He proved a good teacher; by early November I had applied for my license and passed my driver's test. However, since I did not have my own vehicle, I kept on using Simone's city-provided car to make my house calls. That arrangement lasted until my marriage in July, 1968 at which time my wife and I purchased a car—a fire-engine-red, Volkswagen Beetle—in which you froze in the winter—but cheap on gas.

In Training—Learning the "Ropes" and the Rules

It was standard practice at the City, that new employees be put on a six month probationary period of employment, before being granted full-time permanent employment status. And so it was with me. For the first three months, I stayed office-bound, "learning the ropes" in accordance with Simone's training regimen.

It was an unwritten rule that indigent people requesting financial assistance, had to present themselves in person at the office (at the corner of Durham and Elgin) —no telephone calls, please. Another public shaming exercise, which went some way in keeping the caseload numbers under check.

In those days, keeping the welfare caseload numbers down was seen as a reflection of a good and competent welfare administrator. The rules became imperative, and unfortunately, the welfare applicant got lost in the shuffle. And all administrations in the province held to the same attitudes. The archaic "residency" rule made you look at the applicant, not as a poor person in need, but as a municipal cost burden that we ought to make every effort to pass on to some other municipality. The residency requirement was one of the first "rules" I was taught. It was mandated to be enforced. An applicant's immediate last three years of residence prior to his application for financial assistance was meticulously captured and documented, and if he had "broken" residence in the year preceding his application, then, whatever costs Sudbury incurred for a full year following the date of application, was "charged-back" to the last municipality he came from—an anti-welfare-client-dumping safeguard going back to the dark ages of the Elizabethan Poor Laws.

It was a bureaucratic tug-of-war game that all municipalities in Ontario engaged in till the early 70's; ostensibly to discourage financially strapped municipalities from dumping chronic welfare cases onto their more affluent neighbours' tax rolls.

And, God forbid you died twenty feet outside of your own municipal boundary—and you were indigent while doing so—then the municipality in which you had collapsed and died of a heart attack, had to pick up the burial costs. And that became another cause of dispute between different municipal welfare administrations—who would accept ownership of the body?

So I went to work for an agency meant to help poor people pay their rents and buy food to feed their children, and I quickly discovered that the formalities of the bureaucracy came first, and people in need came second. And the welfare official's decision was final—there were no appeal mechanisms in place at that time. The welfare director—tyrant or benevolent—was the unchallenged master of his kingdom.

To be fair, by the mid-70's, with the advent of the Canada Assistance Plan, provincial welfare reforms were eventually introduced; albeit, slowly and gradually. Mandatory assistance levels were put in place along with province-wide consistent eligibility criteria; archaic rules were removed from the regulations and, most importantly, a client's complaint Appeal's Review Tribunal was established. However, prior to the reforms, and all the archaic "poor-laws" era rules notwithstanding, I enjoyed the people-helping profession. Although the rules were puzzling and at times dictatorial; they were provincial Ministry of Public Welfare sanctioned, and until reforms came, workers in the field had to live with them.

After you waded through the red tape you still had people in financial need to deal with; people who had real feelings and emotions; looking to me to solve some of their problems. I made sure that I worked for them, and I made sure that they were as insulated from the shenanigans of bureaucrats as I could possibly make that possible. And when dealing face to face with families, in their sparsely furnished and cold apartments, or a single person in a small dingy room, I could do it. When I walked in, I left the bureaucrat outside of the door and had him wait for me to come back out.

I made it a practice very early in my fieldwork visits, never to open up my briefcase, and start documenting anything on paper; until I had had at least fifteen to twenty minutes of small talk with the timid person in the small room, or, the embarrassed family heads of households.

I owed my clients at least that much respect. And later on as a supervisor, I stressed the adoption of that practice to new caseworkers-in-training.

My First Three Months

My first three months were spent learning the internal office processes and procedures; meeting applicants at the counter and completing a 'referral' on their behalf. That referral was then passed on to a fieldworker, who then proceeded to make a 'home visit' within a few days, to complete a full application. The referral captured cursory information such as name, address, phone number, marital status and a brief past work history.

Louella, Hermine and Myra—the personal secretary; the counter clerk (who had received me on my interview day); and the bookkeeper—all, had a lot of fun at my expense in those first few weeks—which I didn't really mind; after all, I was new at this.

The office staff pretty well knew all recipients and return applicants—many on first name basis—so, when a lady applied, whose shady reputation as a lady-of-pleasure was well known to all staff; or when a perennial male never-do-well and jail-bird, presented themselves at the counter, and I dutifully proceeded to ask them about their immediate past employment histories, and got down to seriously record their responses; I could not help but hear the muffled giggles and titter going on behind me. And then I would do what came naturally to me—I would blush, beet red.

But I liked my colleagues, and they liked my freshness and innocence. This municipal welfare work was not an easy job; you were either meant for it or you were not, and having a good sense of humour was a great asset.

If during the screening and referral process, I came across someone in emergency need of funds for shelter or food, I had the authority to complete a form and requisition immediate assistance with a food voucher or the cutting of a cheque.

Along with my in-office orientation, I was assigned the daily courier job between the office on Durham, to city hall on Cedar Street—no e-mails, faxes or photocopiers in 1966. I would take the correspondence from Durham to city hall and vice-versa. This was a daily task which continued until I had completed my probationary period. It was a nice break, and I got to know the workings of city hall departments and the people working there.

I Share an Office with my Friend Elsie

The day came when I got my own desk in an office—shared with Elsie—one of my colleagues. This was in my fourth month of training. Elsie Jermyn was another staff who took me under her wing and guided me along. We not only shared an office, we shared daily jokes and frustrations. Elsie was fifty years of age and she lived alone with a high school aged-daughter.

Early Adventures in Welfare Work and my Colleague Smitty

I now made house calls to prescribed clients and carried a caseload. Simone's light green tin-box of a car—a Chevelle—was not the most comfortable, but it got me to clients' houses and back. I was slowly taking over Smitty, our deputy-director's caseload of single men, while he would concentrate on Specialty cases of nursing homes; hostels; the Salvation Army and Pioneer Manor, home for the aged.

Smitty Lapalme was not known for his charisma, diplomacy or tact. Smitty came into municipal social services very late in his life; in his early fifties, and he got the job through political contacts. Smitty had been a salesman and he'd been a city ward Alderman when the job of the deputy welfare director had come up—he had inside information and he lobbied—he applied for and he got the job.

Smitty was judgmental and severe. According to Smitty; you were on welfare because of three controllable reasons—you were either lazy; had no moral fibre in your body; or, you were an alcoholic. My father had none of those characteristics, yet he was penniless.

Smitty was particularly rude to down and out single men. He had no sympathy for their plight; and it was not unusual to hear some of his clients sitting in his office, plead for their cheques, and Smitty instead; would hand them a requisition to the Salvation Army for a bed, and a voucher to Slim's Lunch restaurant on Borgia Street for meals.

At those moments I would watch Elsie from the corner of my eye; she would cringe and shake her head. More than once she told me that his treatment of single men verged on the sadistic. From his point of view; Smitty was saving the department money, and stopping his client from cashing and drinking away his cheque. Totally erroneous and mean-spirited points of view.

I got along well enough with Smitty, but we had many a philosophical debate on the inherent goodness or evils of human nature.

Violence Breaks Out in the Office

One morning, after logging in my day's itinerary in the office home-visit book; closing my briefcase and proceeding toward the door; I heard loud, argumentative voices coming from Smitty's corner office. This was not surprising in itself; there were lots of clients' loud voices coming regularly out of Smitty's office. We had become inured to it. But this time it was different. There also was the sound of furniture being upset.

I caught the secretary's look of concern on her face and I decided to hang around the waiting room area for a while. The loud shouting voice was not Smitty's, it was his irate client now screaming that he did not want to sleep at the Salvation Army hostel; that he wanted his own cheque to pay for his room rental.

By the time I had made the decision to put down my briefcase on the floor and move toward Smitty's office, the assault had begun. The client had grabbed a heavy twelve-inch glass ashtray from Smitty's desk, and he had already struck the first blow to the back of the head. Blood was streaming down Smitty's neck, and when I walked in the office, Smitty had been pushed to a corner; he was pinned down behind his upturned desk and the assailant had his arm raised, ready to strike the second blow. I walked up behind him and shoved my arms underneath his armpits and brought my hands up and locked them behind and around his neck, and he was thus immobilized.

This man immediately quieted down; let go of the ashtray; sat on a chair and started to weep softly. Staff had called the police by then, and I took a stunned Smitty to St. Joseph hospital for sutures and medical assessment.

Smitty was back at work the next day properly, bandaged, but pale-faced—he was a heavy smoker and he had a heart condition.

The client was back at the North Bay Psychiatric hospital where he'd been a patient previously. Smitty refused to press charges. Elsie was gleeful, she said Smitty had it coming to him.

And I walked around wondering what in the world was going on here; where the only place my army training came in handy was in the white-shirted world of bureaucrats.

A Young man on his Way to Vietnam

A strange young man walked into the office one day, shortly after the Smitty incident. He was single, had made it by bus as far as his money could take him and was now flat broke.

He was headed to Buffalo, New York, to enrol in the US Marine Corps., and then hoping to be shipped to Vietnam. I was not going to refer him to Smitty, he'd be sent to the hostel. This was late in the afternoon and for whatever silly reason, I took him home to my parents where he had supper with us, and he slept over at our house. He met me at the office the next morning and I got an emergency cheque issued with sufficient funds for bus fare and food to Buffalo.

Out of thirty-five years of social work this was to be the only occasion where I got personally enmeshed with a client. When I talked to him across the counter I saw something in him that reminded me of myself. He was from Montreal. Exactly my age and full of my romantic ideals. I am sure he got to Buffalo, as I am sure he became a Marine and got deployed to Vietnam—that's the first place non-US nationals got sent to in those days. I am not so sure he made it out of Vietnam.

Every time I would watch the late news on the progress of the war, particularly during the months of the "Tet offensive", I would think of that strange young man. And I would be on the lookout, watching for his face on the gruesome TV images.

CHAPTER 20

Involvement with the Church Youth Movement

Sometime toward the end of November, I started to get involved with my church youth group. We met twice a month and it was held under the auspices of the St. Jean de Brebeuf church in the Flour Mill. This was a church-sponsored French Canadian Catholic youth group. It was for young people and led by young people of the parish; the group was shepherded along by a local priest acting as an ex-officio member.

From the pulpit and through bulletins; the church had called the youth of the parish to a congress at which a committee of nine representatives was created, and I was one of the nine voted in. The committee's purpose was to bring the youth of the parish together; to discuss topical social and cultural issues of the day, and promote understanding and problem solving by participating in large semi-annual plenary sessions. Committee meetings were held in the church conference room, and large membership meetings were held in the church basement social hall. One of the main jobs of the committee was to organize social functions—dances; seminars; and out-of-city trips to special events, and the likes.

The Blind Date. I Am Introduced to a Friend of a Friend

And that is where I met Odette Pharand—she was a sitting member of one of our committees. Odette worked at St. Joseph hospital and she knew my mother who also worked there, in the linen department.

Odette had a friend who needed a boyfriend, and then Odette went about selling the virtues of this girlfriend of hers to my mother, while at the same time telling me about how great Jeannine Lelievre was, and that I should give her a phone call.

My mother, now become a broker and go-between, started to mention Jeannine to me on one side while Odette advocated on the other; so, one evening I picked up the telephone and asked Jeannine if she would like to go to a movie. Her voice faked surprise at receiving my call, but she said yes, she would like to go to the movies. And that is how I met Jeannine Lelievre.

Wrestling with the Beginnings of a Relationship

Jeannine was an RNA at St. Joseph. She was tall and pretty, average weight, light blue eyes; blond and fair complexioned. And like me, she had just started to work. Her parents lived in Hanmer, but Jeannine shared an upstairs apartment with an elderly unmarried aunt, on Baker Street; a convenient ten minute walk to the hospital.

Since I did not have use of the city car after work hours, I walked to my first date with Jeannine, and we walked to and from the movies, not very far away from the downtown. She was a nice girl, very quiet and soft-spoken. We went out every other weekend or so. She was nice to be with and she was pretty, but this was not a passionate relationship; for whatever reason, this was not a relationship that I could move forward with. In my relationships I was always caught between honesty and commitment—in my heart, the two components had to be there for the equation to balance. I would never in my life commit to anything for the wrong reasons.

I was an innocent, and probably the most scrupulous twenty-year-old young man in Sudbury, and I could not help it. I would not permit myself to commit my feelings and emotions with another unless I was honest, body and soul. I would never allow dishonesty the light of day in any of my relations with women. First and foremost; I could not lie to myself; therefore, how could I lie to anyone else? Some weeks later, I had the city car for an entire week when Simone was out of the country on vacation.

Jeannine asked me to visit her parents with her—and as usual, I did not make the connection.

A Trip to Montreal

In early December, the church youth committee organized a three-day C.N., train outing to Montreal, to see a Canadiens versus Red Wings hockey game. I invited Jeannine; and Odette was taking her fiancé, John, along with her. This was a package vacation trip and the entire party was lodged downtown Montreal, at the C.N's Queen Elizabeth Hotel. We were a group of about twenty, with Father Mercier, tagging along as a chaperone. We picked up the train late on a very foggy evening at the Capreol station and we had a great time on board, all the way to the big city.

Interestingly; immediately upon arrival, Father had whisked away his white clerical collar, and up to the hour of departure back to Sudbury, Father Mercier was nowhere to be found; he had managed to vanish for forty-eight hours.

We got into Montreal late in the early hours of Saturday morning. John and I shared a room, and the girls another. We had a great afternoon that day; we saw the hockey game and then we had a light snack on the way back to the hotel, and all four of us ended up in the boys' room for a drink. We hadn't even finished our drinks when I stepped out of the bathroom to find myself alone with Jeannine. I did not have to ask where our friends had gone; I was not that innocent that I did not see the scene unfolding in front of me.

After talking a lot, both of us made our way to the window to enjoy the late evening skyline; things quietened in the room and it became uncomfortably embarrassing. I turned the TV on and the eleven-thirty news came on and we watched that; and then, by the time the "late movie" was about to start, I suggested to Jeannine that she ought to check in with Odette and see what was going on. When

John came in, shoes in hand, he was not amused, and without saying a word he went straight to bed.

The journey back to Sudbury was uneventful, with the exception that Jeannine and I joked a lot and we were on good speaking terms—we could look at each other in the eyes and laugh—whereas John and Odette were in the throes of a deep fight all the way home. They were married the following summer.

Jeannine and I continued seeing each other, but with less and less frequency, and sometime in early March, I stopped calling on her altogether; without forewarning and without notice.

But I felt at ease in my mind that I had not made any false promises and we left each other with more than our integrity intact.

A Quick Visit to Holetyre

Earlier that winter, I made the bus trip all the way to Holetyre to visit with Monique. This was a corner of the country as far, and as lonely, and as cold as Senneterre had been; except that this little remote corner was in Ontario. Monique boarded with a local family, and she was pleased to see me and she gave me a grand tour of her well-decorated elementary grade classroom.

I boarded the bus and headed home. I remember three things from my spur of the moment trip—the smile on Monique's face; the colourful classroom, and the bitterly cold and sunny day it had been.

A Clean-Cut Young Man Becomes a Full-Time Permanent Employee

By mid-April, my probation period was over and I got what—I was told later—had been my performance evaluation—a chit chat over coffee with Simone—very unlike those I was to perform later with my own staff; involving charts and point ratings and career planning suggestions; and advice for work improvements.

When I brought the inter-office mail to city hall that afternoon, there was a large brown envelope; those with a butterfly metallic clasp closing the envelope; that I was to bring to personnel. The young secretary was alone and while I had my back to her, ready to leave, she says, "Hey Ray, want to know what Simone has to say about you?" I turned around, and I didn't even have time to say a word when she blurts out, reading from my appraisal review sheet, "Clean-cut young man. Recommended for permanency."

She said this in such a matter of fact way; that I thought that this was information that the whole world was entitled to be privy to. Someone doing this today would be fired.

Retirement Planning at Twenty

I left city hall in a celebratory mood, stopped by Dino's hot popcorn four- wheeled stand, at the corner of Cedar and Durham; bought a fresh bag and made my way back to the office thinking all along how a 'clean-cut young man' ought to behave. I received my formal letter from personnel a few days later, containing the news, which I was already acquainted with. A month later I got a letter from our pension fund Plan informing me that given my age at start of employment, I could expect to retire on full pension, in October of 2011—which in 1967, to me, seemed like an eternity—but then the fine print at the bottom said that subject to the factor of 90, (age, plus thirty-five years of service), I could retire on full pension at age fifty-five, or, October 2001—more encouraging; but 2001 still looked so very far away.

Office Protocol and Statistics

We were not formally sworn to secrecy at the welfare office, but there was an unwritten rule that dictated that once you stepped out of the office, you left anything to do with the job, and particularly anything to do with client information and identity, behind; not to be disclosed to anyone—not even the mayor or a member of parliament—unless under court direction. And this I can attest to; we all judiciously adhered to.

People came to the office to file an application that I personally knew; we had thousands of hard cover files and many names were familiar to me; acquaintances or friends' parents, and I would not touch them. If a case was assigned to any of the fieldworkers and the applicant was personally known to us, we declared a conflict of interest and passed the case to someone else to manage.

What was not subject to secrecy, however, was the statistical data; the cultural demographics of our two thousand files active caseload. It did not really surprise me that although we made up thirty-five percent of the city's population; we Francophones, made up seventy percent of the caseload. After all, Sudbury's Francophones were, for a variety of reasons; last hired, and the first to be let go, in any work cycle. At least, from my welfare perspective, that's how it looked to me.

The other interesting bit of statistical information was that we had a disproportionately high number of single, unattached men on the caseload, compared to families; but I found out later that this was a phenomenon to be found in most caseloads right across the province, in effect; if you wanted financial security—get married—and, if female; don't have babies in your teens. Not a great sociological discovery, but facts corroborated out by field experience.

Louise and Arvind

Louise was eighteen years old that spring when she met Arvind at one of the YMCA weekend dances. Arvind Kumar Bansal was twenty-six and of East Indian background. He worked at Falconbridge Nickel Mines, in the assay and laboratory department. His parents lived in India, where his father was a real estate lawyer. Arvind had called at our house on a couple of occasions in the month of June; but my parents, myself and my sisters, did not pay any particular attention to this new friend of Louise's.

I noticed that he was personable and very charming toward my parents; particularly toward my mother. He was handsome, athletic, and gregarious with self-aggrandizing and boastful tendencies. He had very little discernible accent in his speech. However, he was certainly different from us culturally, and we all thought theirs was a chance meeting; one to be of short duration, the age difference being so wide and Louise being scheduled to leave town to attend Algonquin College in Ottawa in September, to take an Office Administration course.

He came into our family somewhat stealthily, like the thief in the night, which one does not realize has been lurking about, until the daylight hours have broken out the next day, and then one becomes aware of things missing here, and there.

Louise Wants to Party and Mother Proposes a Chaperone

I came home one day at the end of June, to find Louise upset and in tears; there was a house party being organized for the July 1st long weekend; a party to which she'd been invited to by Arvind, and a party to which our mother had said an emphatic, no to; she would not give Louise permission to attend.

The party was to take place on Whittaker Street, and most of those invited would be much older than her—people from the university crowd or already fully employed—and, mother found out that Arvind lived at that address. This was going to involve a much older set and there would be drinking going on; that, along with the location, did not agree with my parents. The party was scheduled to take place in a big, two-level house, the whole of which was rented out by five single males—the hosts of the party. In the eyes of my mother, this set up was nothing short of troubles waiting to happen.

So for the entire week leading into the long weekend, Louise was miserable and she kept on pleading for mother's permission to let her attend. My mother did not so much object to Arvind as much as she objected to Louise attending as an eighteen-year-old, amongst such an older and unsupervised crowd.

On Friday evening, the very last day before the big Saturday night party, and after much importuning, mother softened her position—she compromised—she said to Louise, "Now, if Ray wants to accompany you, and stay with you until he leaves, and you come back home with him; you can go." Louise jumped on my neck and it was a done deal.

I Chaperone a Sister and I Meet the love of my Life

I had no girlfriend at that time and I had the city car at my full disposal as Simone was away for two weeks, to someone's cottage. I had nothing better planned to occupy my time that long weekend and she was my little sister; so, of course, I said yes, I would accompany her.

My mother again had shown the mastery of her negotiation skills, and along with it; put me squarely on the path leading to my future wife.

The house on Whittaker Street north was a big two-story apartment building, located at the dead end of the street, adjoining Elm Street West. It still sits there today. Five single guys had rented the entire building, and they'd gotten together to host and organize this party—little wonder that my mother had not been keen on Louise's attendance.

We walked in at about seven o'clock p.m., and Louise provided me with a quick introduction to Arvind and a few other people there that she knew. I met Bridg Garg there for the first time—I was to become friends with Bridg many years later.

At this early time of the evening, I could see no more than a dozen or so people, and they were busy coming and going from the different parts of the main apartment. Both apartments had a common inner access, so that one did not have to step outside to move freely from one to the other.

Singles and couples kept on flowing in and out of the apartment throughout the evening. When we had come in, the music wasn't on yet, but some couples were sorting out some albums; looking through different stacks of records, and organizing them on top of the stereo cabinet. From the entry vestibule and past the clothes closet you had a full view of a large living room; to the right of which, a short connecting hallway led you to a small kitchen area.

Three girls were seated on a couch that had been pushed out of the way to make room for dancing and now stood against the opposite wall facing the entrance vestibule.

They were the keepers of the gate. No one could miss them as you walked in, and conversely, they could not fail to notice anyone walking in. And, as they had come to the party as single and unescorted—as I was to learn later in the evening—they had taken up a strategic location from which to tag and reference, any unescorted male party-goer coming in; all the while seated by themselves and pretending to be engrossed in conversation. However animated their conversation appeared to be, you knew that they were really not interested in the content of this conversation; when their mouths moved, their eyes were riveted toward the vestibule.

Louise had left my side and I casually scanned the room facing me, trying to appear as bored and as disinterested as I possibly could. I pretended not having noticed the three girls seated on the couch, but I made a mental note to ask the prettiest of the three to dance with me at the earliest opportunity—if she was available. And the opportunity was not long in coming—and she was available.

After depositing my bottle of wine on a nearby table loaded with liquor, the music had started in earnest.

She wore a lovely, sleeveless blue dress; blue from the waist down and blue with white stripes from the waist up. I could not keep my eyes off of her. Her hair was cut short with bangs just above her soft brown eyes. She was of average height, with a dark complexion beautifully accentuated by the shades of her dress. And the dress was perfectly cut, enhancing the features of a pretty figure. She reminded me of the heroines in the Russian novels I was reading.

She had gotten up from the couch and she was making her way toward the kitchen area, when I moved forward, stood in her way, and asked her to dance. She accepted with a charming smile. And, we danced.

Her name was Emily, she was a second-year St. Elizabeth School of Nursing student. She was at the party with two nursing student friends, and she directed her gaze toward the couch where they were still seated; but now engaged, talking to people who had just come in from outside. One of the tenants of the house had invited one of Emily's friends to the party and had asked her to bring along any other nursing student interested in the weekend get together.

We danced the next dance. And, any other dance either of us danced; we danced it together.

And I knew that night that something special had happened to me. I knew then, that I had found the person that I wanted to share the rest of my life with.

I was at this party ostensibly as a chaperone for my sister; I had walked in ready to play the part of the bored and disinterested tag-a-long and within an hour I was disarmed, alive and interested in wanting to know more and more about Emily. She was soft and yielding in my arms. There was no tension in the tiniest fibre of her body. I could see no one else in the room but Emily. There was no sound in the room, but that of Emily's voice. And no smell, but that of her fragrance. After the second dance—when most girls would withdraw to their awaiting friends or the powder room—she asked me if I wanted anything to eat—she had been on her way to the kitchen to make sandwiches when I had stepped into her path.

I thought I was the luckiest guy at the party, no other girl was offering to prepare food for any other guy there. What else could I want? I find a woman that I am falling in love with, and she volunteers to feed my stomach into the bargain.

I drove her home shortly before midnight. She had asked her girlfriends to sign her out in the registry when they were to be back at the school residence. When we reached her parents' house, I took her phone number and asked her if she was free the next weekend. She said she was, and I said I would call.

When I got home, my mother asked; with alarm and consternation, what had happened to my sister? Where was she? Without giving much of an intelligent explanation, I jumped right back in the car and went to retrieve my charge.

St. Elizabeth School of Nursing

The St. Elizabeth School of Nursing stood within fifty-yards of St. Joseph hospital. The eight-floor red brick structure contained classrooms, and private student room residences; a communal dining room area, and in the upper two floors was located the living quarters, and the offices of the Sisters of the Grey Cross—the Nursing School faculty and the hospital's owners and administrators. An underground tunnel or passageway connected the school building directly to the hospital, so that, students could go from the classrooms and straight to the hospital's first floor for their practical nursing experience, without ever having to take one step outside, and face the elements.

A First Date

Thursday of the following week, I called Emily at the Students' Residence. The call was answered by a lay staff at the main office and receiving area, and I was transferred to her floor; we made a date to see a movie that Saturday night—I would pick her up at her parents' home on Sandra Boulevard.

Students could go out at night, but they had a ten o'clock p.m. curfew; however, on three occasions per month, they were allowed to stay out until twelve, midnight. Furthermore, students who had families in the immediate Sudbury area could spend their weekends at home with their parents if they so wished. This was the case with Emily. And she was winding down her stay in residence all altogether; for the first two years of their three-year program, it was mandatory that the student nurse remains in residence; however, for the third and last year, the student could move back home on a permanent basis. By mid-July, Emily would be moving back home, and in the fall, begin the third and last year of her Registered Nurse (RN) program.

This was my last week with Simone's pale green Chevelle, and there would be very few future occasions when I would have the luxury of picking up my date with a City of Sudbury provided vehicle.

Sometimes I would have the city's, sometimes my sister Monique's, and sometimes we even used Emily's dad's car, but most times we walked; or, I walked the thirty-five minutes' walk to her house, and I took a taxi back home late at night.

Later on in our courtship, my habitual eleven-thirty p.m. calls to Queen's Taxi became so frequent and predictable, that the staff there started to have a little fun at my expense. Mr. Lavalle, my neighbour (and driving instructor), was the dispatcher at Queen's; he would answer the call for a cab, and without my having spoken a word, he would say, "Yes, we're on our way to Sandra; and, you're going to 20 Cabot Street." And that was before "Call-ID" became an available feature on telephones!

That first time I picked her up at home, she was ready and waiting for me, looking out of her living room bow-window. As I was driving into the driveway of the red brick bungalow, she was already stepping outside. I got the impression she did not want me to meet her parents, she was so quick to fly out of the house. Emily always wore the prettiest dresses. And she wore them to advantage. The colour combinations and the cut enhanced and magnified her very feminine features.

After the movie, she wanted to go to a bar for drinks and listen to a band. I resisted the suggestion for two reasons—firstly; I was really not familiar with "bars", and secondly; I was not comfortable with spending money for noise and intoxicating liquors, when what I was really craving for, was a quiet time with Emily; peace, and the enjoyment of intimate conversation with the person I was in love with. My mind was in a strange state: I did not really care what she thought of me—what mattered was that I was in love with her. Her feelings for me; if not an immediate reflection of mine, I felt confident, would take care of itself, given time—and, time was on my side. I suggested we go to Murray's on Durham Street.

She agreed without hesitation, and we walked over to Murray's for a coffee. We very seldom ever went to "bars" in our short courtship, although we went out to bars, had drinks, and listened to the different bands after we were married. I personally found bars a waste of time—not to mention money. The "bar scene" to me never presented a constructive opportunity for anything worthwhile. I found a bar as lonely a place as a bus station—you're surrounded by people, and yet, your heart aches with loneliness.

You could not carry on a meaningful conversation amidst the blaring noise and the fending off of the aggressive booze pushing waiters.

We talked for hours on that first night at Murray's. I let her talk for long uninterrupted stretches, about herself and her life. I was just happy to listen to her voice. She talked about her recent trip to Eastern Europe with her parents, the relatives she had met there, the sights she had seen; the adventures she had had and her impressions of the socialist regime of Slovakia. And she talked about her parents and her three brothers. At times, I found her a bit frivolous, and overreaching to make an impression, but I loved her the more for it. Indeed, I was happy just to listen; after a week of welfare work, where every hour of every day was filled with the sad stories of peoples' miseries, and hopelessness; children in need of love; clothing and food; and, having to deal with the unattended, rampant mental illness throughout much of the caseload; Emily's voice was like a sound coming from another world; a real and well anchored world, from which she came out and stepped into mine, depositing and unwrapping parcels of sunshine, joy, and laughter, onto my lap.

I took her home that night, walked her to the door, and I kissed her Goodnight. And when I turned, about to leave; she drew me back to her, encircled my neck with her arms, and kissed me, passionately. There was no mistake; I knew she liked me.

CHAPTER 21

I Meet Mr. and Mrs. Hatala

The weekend following, I called on Emily again—this time, without a car. Not the greatest way to impress a girlfriend's parents—arrive at the door on foot, and sweaty from the July heat.

Emily invited me in and there in the living room, I met Mr. and Mrs. Hatala for the first time. I shook hands with her father, slowly and deliberately, and looked into his clear grey eyes; and then I went over to her mother, and I did what we did at home; I put both my arms around her shoulders and I gave her a light kiss on both cheeks—the French greeting I was accustomed to. I detected a slight smile on her face as she slowly pulled away with all the subtlety that surprise could muster.

Emily was to tell me on our walk downtown that evening; that I must have pleasantly shocked her mom—none of her brothers had ever kissed and hugged their mother the way I had just done. This seemed strange to me since I had been brought up with plenty of kisses and hugs, and it was as natural—more natural, indeed—a gesture, than saying "hello", and producing a cold and unconvincing handshake.

Mr. John Hatala and his wife Mary (nee Ferenc), were born, raised, and had been married in Slovakia. They came from small rural communities in eastern Slovakia. They had four children, three boys, and a girl, Emily, the youngest. The eldest son, John, was born in Slovakia and he was already seven years old when Mrs. Hatala left the old country to join her husband, then living in Creighton. They were hard working, frugal, family-centred, loving parents. Mr. Hatala worked for Inco as a miner, until his retirement in 1969.

Emily's mother was the financial wizard in the family. She had no formal education, but she had an innate understanding of how finances worked. She could calculate interest on investments and she knew a good deal when she saw one. She knew the value of money and how to strike a bargain; and how to negotiate. Without her, Mr. Hatala would not have done as well as he did. She was a great money manager, and she was a great cook. She could make a great meal out of leftovers—nothing ever went to waste. And no one came close to her in pastry baking.

Our Walking Dates

We walked up Regent Street to Elm Street and then proceeded east to the downtown. She wore a beautiful orange coloured, short-skirted dress with a white square shaped collar. She was fresh and radiant with life. We held hands and I noticed the palm of her hand was damp and moist in mine, and I enjoyed the feeling of her skin on mine and the responding pressures of our hands.

Later, on our walk back to her house, she told me that she and two girlfriends were going to the Montreal World Exposition in three weeks' time. She would be gone for a week. I did not offer any response; it seemed natural enough for three friends from the same school to take holiday time together; a lot of people were travelling to Expo 67 that summer. I was only to discover later how painful that whole week without Emily would be for me.

And then somewhere along Riverside Drive, on our way back to her house, she slowed down the pace, looked up at me, and asked what I thought was a strange question; she asked, "Have you ever been awakened?" I did not really know what she meant—in what context—but I did not want to disturb the moment with questions. So I was hard put to provide an adequate answer, but I said after a while, that; yes, "I have been fully awake since the age of three," and proceeded to explain that I could clearly recall things and events going back to when I was living in Mud Lake; and that I considered myself fully awake to the world around me to the extent that, my God-given sensory faculties would allow me.

There was a long silence. I don't know if we were talking about the same things, but I was satisfied that in a way she had gotten to know a little bit more about me. That subject never came up again. I was probably a strange and different young man to Emily. I was certainly not complicated.

Monique Buys a Car and a New Teaching Assignment

A month full of happenings. In early August, Monique had received confirmation of a new teaching job in the small town of Rockland, outside of Ottawa; and Louise had received her acceptance notification to attend Algonquin College in Ottawa.

Monique had bought herself a brand new Chevrolet Malibu and the two girls were going to live together in a boarding home; while one would teach, the other would attend College. Monique would meet her future husband-to-be at that boarding house.

In mid-August, our mother had her first of many heart-related health problems. She had angina attacks and was hospitalized for two weeks to stabilize her condition.

At about the same time, Emily and her two girlfriends headed to Montreal to attend the Expo 67 World Fair.

I was still very involved with the church youth group, but the summer months were down times for the committee; organizationally, things got busy in the fall and winter months.

Emily's Absence and her Character

That one week of Emily's absence was to be, in my mind, the litmus test of my true feelings for her.

The absence proved more difficult to bear than I could have imagined. I could not focus on the day to day developments with any concentration or cohesion; my mind was all over the place; my thoughts always floated and made their way toward her without my having to make any deliberate intents in that direction.

Her absence helped to bring out the fine details of her character to the surface of the painting I was laying on the canvas. Emily was intelligent, loyal, sensitive, and honest to a fault. If she had to choose between; telling you the truth and hurting you, and not telling the truth and leave you in self-satisfied ignorance; she would tell you the truth.

I have never known Emily to wilfully deceive anyone. I have never known Emily to lie—and I have known her now for fifty years. She is compassionate, gregarious and inquisitive. However, her inquisitiveness may be her Achilles heel! Her inquisitiveness may, at first encounter, appear brash and obtrusive—if not intrusive—but that kind of conclusion would miss the mark by a mile. She asks questions of people—and sometimes, of perfect strangers—because she cares, and is interested in them; and she chooses to be genuinely concerned about them. She never talks about herself, she talks about them.

I used Monique's car and drove around town; I went to Chelmsford, twenty minutes northeast of Sudbury and visited Colette, who lived with her husband at her in-law's house. I did all kinds of things in my free time away from work in order to distract my mind. I found myself driving by her house on Sandra, knowing full well she was not home yet—in the hope that maybe she'd gotten home earlier than anticipated.

I had forgotten the exact date of her return, so one day I stopped by her brother, Andy's apartment, on Eyre Street, and enquired as to her return date. He did not know and he looked at me somewhat puzzled as if he had forgotten our introduction; I told him my name but he kept on repeating that she no longer lived at this address and that now she lived on Sandra Boulevard. Not getting anywhere with him, I bid him goodbye and went next door to her good friend, Betty Svarckopt. I knocked at Betty's door, and there I got some satisfaction. Betty told me that Emily was back in town that weekend.

If this had been a contest, I would have won first prize in the "forlorn" lover's category.

She had not been home more than two hours when I called her. I borrowed my sister's car, picked her up and drove her to Cabot Street to introduce her to my family. My self-consciousness about Cabot Street and low-rental units had disappeared—I was occupied in a professional career, and furthermore—Emily's judgment, I knew, went beyond the superficial.

Introduction to my Family

My family was surprised, to say the least. They had known, of course, that I had met someone and had been seeing this girl for the past seven weeks—but no one was aware to what height my ardour and seriousness had climbed to.

My mother liked her immediately; my father liked her friendly and open countenance and the fact that she had "good hips"—whatever that meant; but, my sisters were taken aback, and I sensed their aloofness and truculence come out, clear and unmistakable.

My sisters and I were very close, and I felt that their initial reaction was one of poorly masked resentment toward this intruder—they would have to share their one remaining brother in the family with an interloper. But these feelings of my sisters were of short duration. As they got to know Emily; they got to accept her and like her as much as my parents did.

A Proposal on McKenzie Street

Late one afternoon, as the sun was setting and reflecting on an early November powdering of snow; Emily and I were walking on McKenzie Street when, directly in front of the public library; I stopped; turned her around toward me, and I said, totally without preamble, "What I am about to say, is not idle talk from a crazy Frenchman. Don't waste my time; I would like to be with you forever, but if you're not interested—then, I would like to be free to move on." She looked at me with a broad smile on her face, and replied, laughing,

"Are you proposing marriage?" I kissed her and said, "I thought I just did."

We had met on July 1, 1967; were engaged in December of that year; and, married on July 13, 1968. Why wait when your heart and your mind are in complete conjunction.

I purchased the engagement ring from Birks on Durham Street, and the entire staff at the welfare office got to know about the event before my family—or even my betroth—ever got to know about it.

Sometime in November, during my lunch hour, I had stopped in front of the Birks' Jewellery shop window and looked at some displays of rings. I stepped inside and talked to a clerk. I had not noticed Louella Leblanc, our office secretary, following close behind me—and as I was to learn later—staying within hearing and within sight of what I was doing, as much as she could without being seen by me. I selected a beautiful engagement ring—a big blue sapphire centre stone, with two diamonds to each side, encased in a white gold ring. I put some money down on the purchase and used Birks' "lay-away" plan—I would have the ring paid before Christmas. A week later the bookkeeper, Myra, could not contain the office knowledge any further and she asked me about the ring, and who was it intended for? How long had we known each other? What was her occupation? And, so on.

When I got the ring out of the store, I was so proud of it, that I showed it to the entire office that same day. I presented it to Emily on Christmas day.

Getting to know My In-Laws

I got to know my future in-laws more intimately in the following seven months, and the more time I spent around them (and that was often), the more I got to appreciate them, and the more I got to love them. Mr. and Mrs. Hatala were unaffected, very warm and loving people. I got very close to them, particularly, Emily's father, John. I liked Emily's mother very much and although she gave the impression of aloofness and distance, I knew she loved the hugs and embraces—and I gave them to her at every opportunity. Emily's father was very kind and practical in all of his approaches and views on life.

His favourite words of advice were, "As long as you have a good roof over your head, and enough to eat at the table, count your blessings and be happy." He had an engaging smile that he mixed in with short, timely chuckles, and when he did he was at his most disarming and loveable.

My father-in-law got very close to our two children, particularly, our son Christopher. He was a great babysitter and companion to both of them. A strong father-son bond soon developed between him and me, so much so that, when he died in 1991, I must admit that I grieved more deeply and missed him more intensely than I did my own father at his death. Don't get me wrong, I loved my father, but my father-in-law was more of a father to me than my natural father had been.

Both of my in-laws were extremely generous to Emily and me; with their love, and with their unsolicited financial assistance when it was least expected, and when it mattered most to us at the time of receipt. They were great at anticipating the most beneficent time to come forward and offer their assistance.

My in-laws taught me that, indeed, a penny saved, is a penny earned. They also taught me the time honoured practice of east European haggling and negotiating over prices. They made a true believer in me that there is not only value, but reciprocal respect and integrity in haggling with merchants over prices—the merchant gets a sale, and the purchaser retains respect—failure to negotiate by a merchant, was seen by my in-laws as a failure to appreciate them.

I had always loved my mother's cooking—what young boy doesn't—but I had not really met great cooking until I had tasted of my mother-in-law's cooking. She could pull anything out of the fridge and make a great dish out of it, and her pastries were unmatched, particularly, her Slovak desserts.

My son and I would learn all about mushroom picking—the types and the various eatable varieties—from "Dzedo". And, if we were too early in the mushroom season, we went horse manure picking off of Fielding Road, on Fielding estate property. We would fill burlap bags full of manure to spread over "Dzedo's" and "Baba's" backyard garden on Sandra Boulevard.

The Cottage on Vermillion Lake

My in-laws had a cottage on Vermillion Lake and one day in early spring before Emily and I were yet married; my father-in-law and I set to lay the wooden dock back in the water. I must have impressed Emily's dad because he talked to his wife about my skill in laying the huge wooden side logs and keeping them running true and square—my old machinist skills coming into good use—keeping continuous right angles to each other to guarantee a straight line—I had done this by running 2x4's at ninety degrees to each other all along the length of the dock.

I found it always to be of advantage, without being mercenary, to try to impress future in-laws whenever honestly possible—you never know when you will need them on your side.

That cottage on Vermillion Lake was the site of many happy moments for me that spring, and the summer leading to our wedding. It was also the site of Saturday morning garden labours and assorted cottage maintenance work. However, I loved our time spent at the cottage. And we did so almost every weekend that year. I liked the time secluded alone with Emily and I also enjoyed the time spent with her mother and father.

But, weekends with her parents could not really be called relaxing occasions. Fridays after work, or, early Saturday mornings, the ritual would begin; we packed the large family sedan with food boxes and coolers; with beer and pop; pushed the lawnmower into the trunk; found nooks and crannies for linen, clothes and other assorted things, and headed for a weekend of cottage maintenance; grass cutting; lilac hedge trimming; and fertilizing and weeding the huge garden—in other words, a weekend of constant work.

Sometimes it was a joy, contemplating the return journey home.

When Emily and I could make it to the cottage alone, work was the farthest thing from our minds. I recall us being alone one weekend, and she packed a picnic basket while I went out and rented a canoe from the nearby marina.

We set out on the lake, on a lovely Sunday mid-afternoon, rowing pleasantly across the lake to reach the opposite shore for a romantic lunch together, when; with still a half hour of rowing left before reaching our destination, the wind picked up; the sky covered quickly and a downpour of rain started to pelt the open water. It was too late to turn back, so we continued our paddling as if nothing was happening. This was a warm day in June, the air and the rain felt mild and pleasant on our faces. We were drenched in no time, with heavy water droplets dripping down our noses.

But it was a memorable day, one of the happiest I had experienced in a long while. We were oblivious to the weather. We were laughing and happy to be sharing the moment together. By the time we reached the opposite shore; the wind had abated; the rain had stopped; the sun was coming out warmer than before and the water in our clothes was slowly evaporating in undulating wisps of steam.

I wanted time to stand still then and there; I could not imagine the existence of a happier moment.

I Am Tested: The Affair of the Diaries

But, Emily and I had moments of a different shade of colour prior to our wedding day. Since age fifteen, I had made it a practice to keep meticulous entries in a daily diary.

One day, as we were taking a walk in the neighbourhood of Byng Street playground, I made mention of the fact that I kept a diary. We had moved into the playground area and sat on the swings; moving in unison, to and fro, talking about nothing of great import; when she says very casually, "I would like to see last year's and this current year's diary." I was taken totally unprepared, and by complete surprise, because that was not a tentative, chance and frivolous request—this was a demand. She had repeated the request a second time before it really sank into my mind.

I said, "Emily, diaries are very personal things, are you serious about what you're asking?" She said, yes, she was serious; she would like me to let her have my last eighteen months' most recent entries. "But, you may be upset by what you read," I continued, looking at the ground moving swiftly beneath my feet, "and," I said, "there is no inherent benefit to our relationship, in your reading the entries; but there are definite risks." She did not respond. We did not speak much the remainder of the evening, and I made my way home much earlier than usual.

I called her from home later that night and told her that she would have the diaries. I had nothing to be ashamed of; nothing to hide.

I surrendered the diaries the next morning, as promised; and she held them in her hands for a moment, and turned them back to me on the spot, unread—it had been a test—one of many I was to be passed through prior to the solemn marriage vows. Test of honesty; test of loyalty; test of character and integrity. And I apparently passed them all.

Male Chauvinism and the IQ Test—A Lesson in Humility

One day, we were at the cottage and a test of another kind was put to me. Amongst the many magazines, old newspapers and assorted light reading material that people had brought with them over time, and had accumulated in boxes; was a book-size compilation of IQ test inventories—all of them, mathematical skill tests; verbal skills; logical reasoning and spacial relationship tests—they were all there.

According to the editor; these tests were purported to have a high degree of scientific, and statistical reliability—the test results were supposed to be a reliable measure of the entity being measured. So, Emily completed a segment; score it with the instrument appended at the back, and turned the test over to me casually, and asked me to do it.

And I did, fully confident that this was a cake walk. We scored it; compared the results, and to my consternation, she easily beat me. I immediately asked that we do another one, a different category. We did, and the same result prevailed—she beat me again. Now my pride and very manhood were under assault. So I asked that we do another one, and then another one, and another one hoping that I would finally get to balance the scales.

I had to finally relent, and abashed and much humbled, admit defeat. No amount of posturing and blaming cultural test biases gained me any credit.

I had always known that Emily was very intelligent, and that frustrating afternoon at the cottage confirmed it.

Another Irritant: The Youth Group

The other irritant, albeit temporary, in our pre-marriage relationship, had to do with my involvement with the Francophone Catholic youth group. Up to the month of April, I was still actively involved. We were to be married in July, and my activities with the church was a part of my life that Emily did not actually share in since she was not Francophone.

Sometime in March, I chaired a large seminar, an open plenary session of all associated French-speaking Catholic youth groups in the Sudbury area. This was a large gathering, with the local French CBC radio media present amongst other invited observers. I opened the ceremony with a four-minute rhyming speech or poem, containing in it everything that an opening four-minute address would have contained.

In the evening, when we had broken up into small working groups, there was a French CBC radio personality present at my table, and without much of a preliminary introduction to the proposal he was to make, he asked me if I would be interested in doing some radio program spots for the local station.

I almost laughed, but refrained from doing so—and I said, thank you; but no, I was not interested.

A Big Error of Judgement

Two sisters were on my committee; both, French elementary school teachers; one had a boyfriend, the other was unattached. In preparation for this large gathering in March, I was invited to the sisters' house on Vercheres Street to work on the program agenda. Most of our committee work was done in St. Jean de Brebeuf's meeting room, but it was a nice change to go out to a private home and do some work there.

I met their parents, and we moved to a sitting room to work on the agenda; the list of invited guests; main themes for discussion, and so on. As I was getting ready to leave, somewhat late into the evening, the single, unattached girl, asked me if I was free at some date in June—she needed an escort to one of her friends' wedding.

They were two nice girls and came from a very upstanding French Canadian family; I don't know what short-circuited in my mind: my desire to please overcame whatever ounce of common sense I may have had at that moment—because, I said yes, I would go. She was glowingly pleased and I felt instantly miserable.

On my way home, I realized I had just made an inexcusable blunder of immeasurable proportion. I walked in the house and I disclosed everything that had just transpired, but a short half hour earlier.

My mother was sure I was pulling a joke on her; but my sisters, who knew my social awkwardness and naivety full well, wasted no time in jumping all over me and lambasting me with unprintable, well-deserved abuse.

Within another half hour, I called the girl's house and laid out the true state of affairs—I was engaged to be married in July. The girl at the other end was speechless. No one knew at the youth group that I was engaged to be married—no one was aware that I had so much as a girlfriend.

CHAPTER 22

Father Lemire Sets Out to Investigate

The word got around fairly quickly. Within a few days, I got a call from Father Lemire. Father Lemire was a new arrival at St. Anne's church, downtown. He was very young, and he'd been made the chaplain of the Sudbury Francophone Catholic youth groups. Father Lemire was from Montreal, and he looked straight out of the seminary. We had already met and we were closely involved together in coordinating work since his arrival in Sudbury, in January; he also did pastoral care work in the parishes—it happened a few times that I would bump into Father Lemire when I made my welfare house calls—he tended to the poor's souls while I tended to their more mundane needs.

He was of average height, of a slender and delicate build; soft facial features and soft of manners and voice; and he wore his dark, wavy hair, shoulder-length; he was what women would consider, handsome. If not a priest, he could have been a poet.

His phone call; however, was not poetical, it was to the point and unequivocal. He wanted to meet my fiancé. He knew she was not French Canadian from the reports he'd received. He did not say so in so many words, but he wanted to test her catholicity; her character; the circumstances behind our engagement; and the reasons as to why I had not made my engagement a matter of public knowledge—in other words, he wanted to know—was she pregnant?

All this came through clearly to me in the phone call, although the tone of the conversation was of the most benign and casual nature imaginable. Father invited Emily and me out to dinner at Cassio's, on Lorne Street—and he, or the parish—was picking up the tab.

It was a great dinner and a great meeting. Emily—as I knew she would—swept him off his feet. By the time we left Cassio's I thought he was in love with her. Or at least, he'd been mesmerized. I had purposely not mentioned to Emily my earnestly felt suspicions as to the real motives behind this dinner invitation. But, as those cottage IQ tests had indicated—she was indeed much smarter than me—she had divined Father Lemire's whole scheme before she had even set foot in the restaurant.

To be fair to all concerned, by mid-April I had handed in my resignation from the youth group.

Planning a Wedding

From January, onward, the search had been on to find an appropriate reception hall for our wedding guests. We were to be married at my in-law's parish church; at St. Clements, in the west end; and after much debate and running around, the Silver Beach Tavern, on Long Lake Road, was selected as the place to receive our friends and relatives to join us in the celebration of our marriage.

The wedding party was comprised of my brother Ivan, as my best man, and two ushers (one of which was Arvind, Louise's boyfriend); Emily had a maid-of-honour and two bridesmaids. And as required of us; Emily and I enrolled in the Catholic "marriage course". I went into the course program skeptical and blasé as to the need for such an exercise—but, I came out of it convinced of its value for any young couple contemplating marriage. Everything was discussed in a frank and open manner; and in a group setting—with local experts in the field of finance; law; emotions and, yes—sex.

The question as to where the newly married couple would set up their residence after the wedding was quickly settled. My in-laws owned a four-plex apartment building on Eyre Street south, (where Andy lived), and we would rent a fully furnished, one bedroom apartment from them. The money saved from not having to immediately purchase furniture, we would put toward the cash purchase of our very first car—a fire-engine red Volkswagen Beetle.

Ray A. Vincent

The Bridal Party and my Mistake

In early June, Emily's mother organized a "Bridal Party" and she charged me with a—I was to find out later—very important job.

I was to purchase a long strand of white silk ribbon, four inches wide and at least six feet long. On this ribbon was to be typed all the names of the ladies providing a gift to the bride-to-be, at the Bridal Shower. My mother-in-law liked a little pomp and ceremony, and she had seen this display of ribbons atop and circling the presents at other bridal showers she had attended—and there was no way she was going to be outdone by any of her Slovak lady friends—particularly, by Mrs. Tomchik. Problem was, no one had told me of the social importance of the printed length of this blasted ribbon.

Sure enough, I got a six foot, four inch, white silk ribbon; but when I had finished typing in all of the ladies names; neatly crowded together—first mistake—one below the other—it left four feet of unused, dangling silk, which I thought would not look good at all; so I did the practical thing—I cut off half the ribbon away. Second, and very big mistake. When unsure, one should always solicit advice. The memory of this event and my handiwork with the ribbon would follow me for years. Needless to say; my mother-in-law was furious when I unveiled the ribbon at the house, and she let go a volley of Slovak words in my direction, that my wife-to-be politely refused to translate for me.

The Stag Party

Two weeks later, the bridal shower was followed by my stag-party, held at the Slovak Hall on Alder Street. My brothers-in-law, John, Andy, and Paul, organized the evening, although Andy did the majority of the local Sudbury work since John and Paul lived out of town.

This stag thing was all new to me—I had never attended a stag party and knew nothing of its purpose. I had no idea what it was meant for, or why my presence would be necessary.

I stayed at Andy's for a while until it was thought fit that I was ready to be introduced at the hall. Emily's older brother John came to pick me up at around seven p.m., John knew a fish out of water when he saw one. He put his arm around my shoulders as he led me to his car, and he said, like a big brother would, "This is just a bunch of guys getting together for a drinking party and some poker games; just behave as if you already knew everyone there," and, he continued with a wink, "they won't know any different." Well, there was a lot of both going on—cards and drinking. I knew no one there except my father-in-law, his three sons and their uncle Balint. No one from my side was present.

I was surprised when at the end of the evening, Andy came over to me and handed me an envelope. There was some money in it for Emily and me.

Aunt Balint's Impassioned Objections

My mother-in-law had a sister, Emily's aunt Balint, who live in Creighton. Emily's mother never divulged this anecdote until a year or so after our marriage. This story became a proof to me about how much her mother believed in our marriage, and how aware she was about the depth of my love for her daughter.

Aunt Balint had also been born and raised in Slovakia. But unlike her older sister, she had witnessed the atrocities and privations of world war two. She had immigrated to Canada immediately following the conclusion of the war. She wore the "babushka" on her head much more frequently than my mother-in-law would. Her English was almost non-existent and when she spoke her own tongue, she spoke in a high pitch, and screeching-like tone of voice; all the while flashing the two gold teeth in her upper jaw.

Two months before the wedding and one week before the bridal shower party, she called at my mother-in-law's; and, no sooner settled in the living room, she did what they did in the old country when a suitor was not to someone's liking in the family. She pleaded with her sister to break-up Emily's engagement before, she said, a big mistake would be made, and they would all have to suffer some irreparable embarrassment. Feeling she was not getting anywhere with her sister, she called in her brother-in-law and repeated her entreaties and warnings.

"Think about it," she had said to my in-laws, "he's French Canadian; his parents have no money, and," she would continue, clasping both hands to the sides of her head, screeching in her inimitable fashion; "he doesn't even own a car!"

My mother-in-law listened but remained implacable. She said nothing then, and she never said a word to her daughter. My mother-in-law had always been in favour of this love marriage.

Aunt Balint did come around eventually—she had no choice—I became a favourite of her husband's.

A Slovak Custom: "The Blessing of the Bride"

Earlier, on the morning of the wedding, Emily's uncle and aunt Balint, were at her house; and when Emily was fully dressed in her wedding gown, uncle Balint officiated over the ancient Slovak custom of the "Blessing of the Bride"—I was not present of course; but Emily told me it was a solemn and a tearful event felt by everyone present. It is a moving ceremony performed by an elder of the family. The elder invokes the blessings of our Lord to favour the young woman who is moving on to a new stage in her life. Only the immediate family and Emily's bridesmaids were present in the living room, when her uncle laid his hands over her head and recited the special prayers; beseeching the Lord to look favourably on her marriage. And Emily cried throughout.

Of this special custom; Emily was to tell me later, and how privileged and protected she had felt.

The Reception

Some two-hundred guests attended the reception. Emily's relatives from the USA were present and congratulatory messages from Slovakia were read out. Two of my brothers, Pete and Louis, had opted not to attend.

Emily's brother Andy acted as master of ceremonies. We were happy that Andy had volunteered to be our master of ceremonies—big Andy was never at a loss for words—in any environment.

The live band was great and the food was even better. I was disappointed that some of my brothers were not present, but this was not their day, it was Emily's and mine. We had a great day, a great reception, and even greater happiness.

In my enthusiasm, I made one small strategic miscalculation. It is a tradition in most eastern European weddings; prior to the meal being served, for all the guests to form a line, men, and women; and move forward toward the awaiting bride and groom; everyone swaying to the sound of a "zardash" and personally extend congratulations to the bride and groom. Good manners, expect the groom to offer each presenting guests with a "shot" of whiskey; to which the groom also partakes—while pronouncing the "Die Boze" greeting. Every guest clicks glasses with the groom, and they down their drinks on the spot.

No one had told me not to match everyone drink for drink—after the first few drinks, I was expected to go through the motions only; using my empty glass. After a dozen or so full-fledged "Die Boze's", Andy tapped me on the shoulder and whispered in my ear to go through the motion only, or I would never make it to the President Hotel bridal suite. And I stopped just in time.

"Make her Happy"

My sister-in-law, Vera; Emily's brother John's wife, was in the guest procession and she came up to me; kissed me, and when we hugged, she put her mouth close to my ear and she said, in a voice full of tenderness and earnestness, "Make her happy." I have never forgotten those three words. I made her a promise that I would—and I have always tried to live up to that promise.

Vera was a good judge of character. Sometime earlier, after my first introduction to her and her husband John; after she'd gotten to know me a little more, and watching me and Emily's interactions with each other; she had blurted out to a room full of people, "These two are like two peas in a pod." It proved a very fitting expression, describing Emily and me.

A Great Party

The live music was great and my wife and I danced all night—the atmosphere was more that of a great party, than a wedding.

Following tradition, everyone formed a large circle; Emily donned a "babushka", and for a cash donation, anyone, man or woman, could enjoy a short dance with the bride.

Around midnight, when the party was still going strong, Emily and I left the reception to go to her parents' house and change into our "going away" clothes. When I got the signal from one of her US aunts, I picked up my young wife in my arms, carried her across the dance hall floor to a waiting limousine outside. Emily's six-year-old niece, Tammy, leaned over to her mom and said, "Poor Uncle Ray, he's going to hurt his back."

Once we got to her parents' house, we found her mother was already there waiting for us. I realized shortly why she was there—she and her sister were adding up the money-gifts—some of that money went toward paying cash for our first car. But they were doing something else which intrigued me, they were recording everyone's name in a book, and what each had given—a handy reference, since one day she may be attending one of these peoples' children's weddings.

The "Bridal Suite", the Wedding Night, a Recovery Period

We returned to the reception hall after having gone through our change of clothes and bid goodbye to our guests. We got to the President Hotel on Elm Street, well after one a.m. What I had rented out the week before, as the "Bridal Suite" was nothing but a regular room. We were too tired to argue with the front desk clerk for a change of room.

We were both exhausted from the full day—particularly Emily—and all the dancing. Emily's legs and feet were hurting her. I had showered, undressed and lay in bed, waiting for her to come out of the bathroom; and, when she did, she stopped by the bedside; bent down, and to my amazement, she completely disappeared from view. After a few moments, I saw a pair of feet poking up over the mattress, with toes wiggling and muffled moaning sounds coming as if from under the bed.

I stood up in bed and looked over her side; she was lying flat on her back; legs propped up against the mattress. She looked at me with a shy, apologetic smile and said, "I'm sorry, Ray, but my feet are just killing me." I laughed; got out of bed, and took up the exact same position alongside her.

Emily and I have always gotten along so well because we always complemented each other. There was no rush—we were going to be together forever. Some people have marriages, while others have arrangements; ours was to be a marriage.

After the next morning's breakfast at her parents', with them and her relatives; we took leave of them all and we were off to Quebec City; with a short initial stopover, to introduce Emily to Belleterre and the comforts of the "Chateau".

AFTERNOON

The West End: Eyre Street

CHAPTER 23

The Newlyweds Deal with Distractions

For Emily, this would prove to be something of a working honeymoon; her final exams for her RN designation were to be taken in early August; therefore, along with clothes for a two-week vacation, she had to take with her an assortment of relevant nursing textbooks. I had two weeks of paid vacation and I was due to be back at work on August 2nd.

Our itinerary called for a one day stop in Belleterre, where we had a room reserved for us at the "Chateau Belleterre"; then four days at a secluded cottage at Lac D'Argent (a gift from my sister Rose and my brother-in-law, Rosario); and then off, for a full week in Quebec City.

The journey to Belleterre was uneventful enough; however, once we arrived there, late in the afternoon, the place was hectic with traffic and people moving about all over First Avenue. Some type of festival was being celebrated, and there was an inter-county baseball tournament going through its playoffs and championship game. With all this activity, the small town had almost doubled in size for that weekend. And not only was the hotel within a hundred yards from the baseball field, it was booked to capacity—but we had a reservation. This was not the time to show Emily whatever sights were worthy of attraction in my hometown—first and foremost, we needed rest and relaxation.

Emily and I were tired and we meant to go to bed not long after supper time. We did return to our room shortly after supper, but we could not find a moment's restful sleep due to two singular events: we were bothered by loud voices coming from outside; and the blaring lights from the night game on the baseball field and the noises from the game itself. I had to get up from bed to close down our window.

And there was something else that caused me some unrest; I had purposely parked our brand new, shiny, red Volkswagen, at the front of the hotel so it would be in full view from our window, and allow me to keep an eye on it.

I was concerned when I saw a group of three or four young men; circling around our car; peering inside through the windows, and my concern turned to dismay when I saw one of them try the handle of the driver seat door. I got their attention by tapping on my window, and opening it, I shouted—in French—for them to get the hell away from my car. Finally looking up and seeing me, they dispersed.

I looked toward the bed and there was Emily, sitting up in her alluring honeymoon dainty nightdress, looking annoyed and impatient.

I was distracted by the events going on outside the hotel, and to the utter frustration of my fresh young wife, I could not bring myself to concentrate on the events that should have been taking place inside our room.

Every fifteen minutes or so, I would spring out of bed, part the curtains and scan the parking lot, and at every random voice heard outside—I would repeat the exit from the bed—and there were a lot of people coming and going outside, as this was the conclusion of the championship game.

Needless to say; my young wife, whose head had been full of romantic anticipation when we had entered the room, was not pleased with me; or with these hooligans from Belleterre.

I found myself under the stress of a quandary; attend to my wife's importunate and not so subtle hints, or protect my newly purchased private property from theft, or break-in? —And I opted for the latter—I got dressed, went out to our car and drove it a five minutes' walk from the "Chateau"; to Second Avenue—and parked it in Uncle Alfred's driveway.

After getting back to my room, full of anticipation for peace and conjugal intimacy, Emily said we had another problem, and she motioned toward the wall against which the head of our bed rested. A full-blown post-victory party was underway next door. The walls were literally paper thin; this was an old structure, and room-to-room soundproofing insulation was not the required code it is today. However, by one-thirty, the party wound down, and peace and quiet returned—but only temporarily—I recognized the voice of Henri Lacroix coming from the other room; one of my childhood friends. I did not recognize the girl's; whose voice moaned in ecstasy, on and again, till the early hours of the morning; accompanied by the drum-like poundings of their head frame slamming against the wall, not a foot away from our ears.

At daybreak I went and got our car—never saying goodbye to uncle—we breakfasted bleary-eyed; and we checked out and headed to Bearn and thence to Lac D'Argent; for the awaiting seclusion; and the legitimate and uninhibited, sexual orgies awaiting us there—or, so we thought.

Lac D'Argent Intimacy Shared with Intruders

The sun came up on a cloudless July morning—it promised and delivered, a clear sunny day. The roads leading to the lake were unpaved and led deep into the hilly and heavily forested country. We approached the cottage from a sandy winding road, and at about twelve o'clock noon, we came to a stop underneath two massive pine trees standing guard at the back of it. The key was found where I had been told I would find it—in the outside privy, under a pile of magazines.

There were not a developed lot, or other cottages, for many miles on that side of the lake; except for a rough looking fisherman's camp about fifty yards away, owned by Rosario's brother, Charles; and which Charles intended to finish in a fine, all-weather residence someday. The cottage was an ideal quiet getaway hideout for a newly-married couple; it had hydroelectric connection; running hot and cold water, and although without a flush-toilet system in place; it had a lovely sandy-silvery beach (hence, the name "Argent"); with a dock running out to about chest high water level; and a canoe, with paddles and life jackets, tied up alongside the dock. And the refrigerator and cupboards had adequate food for at least a week.

We unloaded the car; put on our swimsuits; packed a lunch, and headed out on the water for a canoe trek. We had a light wind, with barely a ripple on the water. It was a glorious day. We made our way up the lake, following the gentle contours, enjoying the view, the rest and the relaxation. We were the sole occupants of this vast domain of dense forest and quiet vistas. We paddle for about an hour and then struck out for a sandy beach at the foot of a gently rising hill, at the middle of which was a horizontal, flat rock formation—a perfect place on which to have our lunch. We beached the canoe; brought the lunch basket to our perfect little nook nestled in the bosom of the hill, and we went back to the beach for an invigorating swim—a good, old-fashioned skinny-dip. Then we went back to our food; spread out the blanket we had taken along to sunbathe, and had lunch—in the nude, no less—and then after lunch, and some frolicking under the hot sun; we stretched out on our backs to take in the sun's rays and enjoy the afternoon.

And that is when, lying on my back for no more than ten seconds; just when I was about to close my eyes and catch some sleep, that I noticed the glint as if the sun was reflecting on some distant mirror.

The Fire Warden

We had had our lunch halfway up the hillside, without noticing anything out of the ordinary; however, when I lay on my back, the hilltop stared at me, and on the very top of the mountain stood a Fire Warden's watchtower; and you could just make out the silhouette of the Warden scanning the territory with his field glasses. The poor man was only doing his job that day, and we had provided him with an unexpected bonus; a free pornographic exhibition. I never saw Emily move so fast.

"A Fire Warden's job is a lonely job," I said; "we brought some excitement to his daily monotony." I laughed, but she was not amused. Once back in the canoe, she said, "This is unbelievable, we're hundreds of miles in the bush and we still can't find privacy." And she plunged her paddle with a purpose, sending sprays of water crashing on me, sitting in the stern. "Can you believe this," she continued, resting her paddle and letting it glide through the water, "we're barely married forty-eight hours and we can't find quiet time together."

Surprise! Surprise!

We slept well that night. However, well before the sun had risen over the hills the next morning, our sleep was briefly interrupted by the sound of voices and the reflection of headlights against our bedroom walls. Obviously, someone had arrived late and was settling into the fishing camp next door. Things got quiet again shortly after, and we fell back asleep.

We were awakened early in the morning by a robust knock at the door. There, on the verandah, with beaming smiles on their faces, was my best-man—my brother, Ivan—with his wife; my sister Rose and her husband; and another couple, friends of my brother-in-law—they were all here to do some fishing. After a few shouts of "Surprise!", "Surprise!" we were invited to have breakfast with this unexpected, and unwelcome horde of people. We joined them for breakfast, but Emily excused herself as soon as she could upon finishing her meal. She was out of sorts by all these recent developments—and she certainly had a right to be. She said curtly, that she had to study for her exams, and closeted herself with her books for the balance of the day.

The honeymoon was not following the Hollywood script as pictured in the movies.

Ray A. Vincent

We Pack It In and Move On to Quebec City

We consulted briefly about what to do next; and very early the next morning, without wasting time with breakfast, or taking leave of my relatives; we quietly packed the car; left the cottage key on the table, and we were on our way to Quebec City. We had ten days left before I was scheduled to return to work, and Emily had but three weeks before her final exams.

If the first few days of our honeymoon got off to a less than desirable start, the journey to Quebec City, and our time spent there, more than made up for it. The Laurentians and the stops along the way were beautiful. We had a wonderful time—time together alone and in love. We took all the mandatory tourist excursions of the city—"en-Caleche"—we had lovely dinners in the Old City. We walked into shops and bought personal things and things meant for our new home.

Because of her dark complexion, Emily always looked pretty in pink outfits and variations on that shade of colour; one day, in a Ladies' clothing store, she tried on a burgundy coloured fall and winter coat with a natural white mink fur collar, and the white fur running down to her waist; she simply looked beautiful in it. We had looked at kitchenware in a previous shop, before entering the Ladies' store. She had a heartbreaking decision to make—my young wife opted to put our money on the household expenditure.

There were lots to see and do, and we fell in love with the city, but Emily made sure that we went to bed early, and that we got up late. She would not be the first bride to get pregnant on her honeymoon—but she behaved as if she wanted to make sure that she would be one of them—so much so that I started to question my capacity to match her natural inclinations.

I considered myself blessed; I had a wife who was both, emotionally and physically passionate and liberated to the fullest extent of the word. Emily was one of the most mentally healthy people I had ever come across. She was even- tempered and had an amazingly well integrated and well-adjusted personality. She proved what I had instinctively felt all along—going back to that first fateful evening of our chance meeting—that there were no "hang-ups" in the girl. I was to discover that very little flustered her; she took everything in stride and she saw the world for what it was—Emily wore no coloured glasses. Anyone who got to know Emily loved her. At first, I thought that being a nurse had shaped her personality, but I realized quickly how wrong I had been; her personality actually shaped how good a nurse she was to become.

And the more I got to know her mother, the more I understood where Emily's character and personality came from. If being in love is suffering from a bout of "temporary insanity", as some psychiatrists would have us believe; then, I have been "insane" for the past fifty years. And I bless the Lord that no one ever attempted to press a "cure" upon me.

Return Journey Home

We were on our return journey; somewhere between North Bay and Sturgeon Falls, on the TransCanada Hwy 17 heading west; less than an hour from Sudbury, when I noticed that it had been unusually quiet for a long while. I quickly glanced in the direction of my wife, and I was met with a pensive, somewhat sad looking countenance. I thought I saw tears rolling down her cheeks. I slowed the car down; turned to face her, and asked, "What is the matter?" she looked at me, laughing through her sobs, "Well," she exclaimed; "I'm not going to my mom and dad's house. It just hit me. This is all so new. I've never been married before." I burst out laughing, "I would hope you haven't." I said, taking her hand.

"And by the way," I continued, reassuringly, "neither have I, and we'll do just fine." And we did.

The Start of Married life—The West End

The apartment building at 285 Eyre Street South was in an older part of town; an area of town where many immigrants of Italian descent had congregated slowly, as if by osmosis; but now they made up the majority population of the surrounding neighbourhoods. The houses were kept tidy, inside and out, and the yards well-groomed and well flowered.

Our apartment was a three room, plus bathroom, fully furnished flat; located at the front, and facing the street of the four apartment building complex. You accessed the apartment through a fully covered front entrance porch. The porch was glassed-in on three sides and we kept colourful potted plants there. We also used the porch to give our babies some fresh air on sunny winter months, by laying them there for short periods of time; well covered in their prams; while they were asleep. The front door opened onto a wool-carpeted living room, to the left of which was our bedroom. The small kitchen area (where we took our daily meals) and the bathroom were located off the living room.

This was my first, independent living space, and I was very secure and at home in it. We lived in the front; two single people lived in the two small fully furnished apartments upstairs; accessible to the left of the building through an exterior side door which led to the stairway. There was a large two bedroom apartment at the back, occupied by Emily's brother Andy, his wife Inge and their daughter, Tammy. Our rent was eighty dollars a month, all utilities included—another sign of my in-law's generosity. The building was an old structure, but well-constructed, and the original exterior of imitation brick-stucco cladding, had recently been redone in solid brown bricks. We had a large backyard, on which fresh sod was thriving, and in which a healthy and tall apple tree gave out abundant crops—from which Mrs. Svarkopft, our neighbour, made great pies and shared them with us. Separating the backyard from the laneway, was a two car garage and some outside parking space for two additional vehicles.

We are Happy and the Failure of the "Rhythm" Method

We were happy on Eyre Street, and we laughed a lot—so much so; that Andy once commented on it, and asked what all that muffled laughter and giggles coming out of the front apartment was all about? We had our first child, Christine, born in September 1969, while we lived in that front apartment.

That pregnancy had been unplanned—thanks to the Catholic Church's "rhythm method" of natural birth control; as taught in the mandatory marriage course—but nonetheless, very much welcomed. Our second child; Christopher, was born while we were occupying the back apartment, three years later.

Emily Becomes a Registered Nurse

Shortly after settling in, Emily passed her Registered Nurses exams successfully, and she was offered employment at St. Joseph Hospital immediately. She became an Operating Room nurse in September, 1968.

Return to Work and Union Involvement

When I returned to work, the news was out that the Canadian Union of Public Employees (CUPE), had been ratified by the non-management employees, as the sole bargaining agent for the outside and inside staff working for the Corporation of the City of Sudbury. I was informed by my colleagues at the welfare office of this development, and furthermore; I was asked by them to be their shop steward. I accepted the trust and honour bestowed upon me by my friends. And at my first union meeting, held at the Steelworkers Hall on Frood Road, I was voted on the executive as one of two trustees required on the executive board. I was to have a seat on the city CUPE union executive, until my promotion to management, in the fall of 1973.

The Job Evaluation Procedure and Help from Unexpected Quarters

One of my first tasks at the welfare office, as a union representative, was to try to raise the level of union consciousness—what was the purpose of unionism—and more particularly in our case; raise the awareness of the big wage-gap disparity between municipal social workers in Sudbury, compared to cities like Hamilton; Windsor; Toronto and Ottawa. We did exactly the same kind of work but got only seventy-five percent of the salaried compensation they received. I quickly realized that one of the main reasons for this wage disparity had to do to a great extent with the make-up, or the composition of the workforce when analyzed along gender lines. Ours was eighty percent female; whereas, our comparator cities showed a sixty percent male versus a forty percent female split. Male workers in the sixties tended to be the main household wage earners—and they were, therefore, more militant in union activism and more demanding in contractual wage demands. And the record showed that male-dominated union shops enjoyed better wages and benefits than their female counterparts.

I held many after-hours meetings with my female colleagues and we drafted a job review request to be forwarded to the personnel office. We used a job evaluation mechanism jointly set up and agreed to between the employer and the union.

As the shop steward, I met with our immediate supervisor, Simone Patterson, after work one afternoon; and presented our self-evaluation and points rating score. I don't know if Simone was simply tired, or just understanding and good-hearted—but she accepted all our arguments and signed-off on all the documents requiring her signature; which, in effect; meant that she endorsed our position.

I heard later from Simone, that Herb Hatton, the director of personnel, had a fit when he received our submission—duly endorsed, and signed by our boss.

Within six months; which involved meetings with management; a job study; and a point rating system, we obtained full salary parity with our southern Ontario brothers and sisters working in the field of municipal social services.

Where women are secondary wage earners at home, the motivation to climb up the wage ladder is quasi-non-existent. The self-confidence and the assertiveness required of women at that time;

to take management to task on critical issues, was not at the same level of intensity as that shown by the men. They did not possess the men's aggressive stance and general confrontational approach to labour-management issues.

Although my union involvement was of short duration, I enjoyed it—I learned a lot about people, the workplace dynamics, and its politics.

In my second year, I attended the CUPE National Congress in Ottawa, and during one of the session breaks, the Sudbury Local President came to me and said that the French national CBC network was looking for some comments in French—and the Sudbury contingent put me up as a reluctant volunteer—I gave the short interview, in which I thought I had embarrassed myself with the French language. But to my surprise, on my return to Sudbury, my French-speaking colleagues and my sister Carmen (who always watched the French CBC nightly newscast); all said I had expressed myself and answered the reporter's questions, decently well.

Passing "The Duchy" on the Left Hand Side at Murray's

We had a routine following every monthly union meeting; we either went to the pub on location at the Steelworkers Hall, where we drank copious amounts of ten cents glasses of draught beer; or we went to Murray's for coffee and talked over the past meeting's proceedings.

One evening we decided to meet at Murray's. I had a coffee, but I realized that something else was being offered; by the union President—no less—without preamble or ceremony; Terry had lit up a joint, taken in a deep toke, and it was passed from one union brother or sister to another—and it made the full circle, unbroken—in effect; we "Passed the "duchy" on the left-hand side" all evening. And no one found fault with anything that had transpired at the recent union meeting. This was not the highlight of my union involvement, but it certainly was one of the more memorable ones.

Ray A. Vincent

Father's Reaction to an Engagement

Shortly after my wedding, Arvind and my sister announced their engagement. My father had remained quiet and in the background throughout their courtship; but now, the tiger had been awakened. My dad came out of his shell. As was his wont, my dad never said anything unless the gravity of the moment compelled him to take a stand—and then he would.

As long as the relationship had not taken a turn to the serious, my father was quite happy to let things be; however, when Louise came in one day flashing a ring, things took a detour, and warning signs filled my father's mind. He took Louise aside, and said, "Do you know what you're doing? Married women in Arvind's country follow their husband ten paces behind them. I cannot allow this to happen."

This was one of my father's most shining moments. I was impressed when I heard this conversation. My dad may have been quiet, but he was a man who was always aware of what was happening around him. Louise broke the engagement within a month. There may have been more issues factoring into the broken engagement besides my father's intercession, but he was certainly a significant contributory part of it.

The turn of events did not sit well with Arvind. There were issues of ethnic customs and pride that came into play, which no one in my family ever considered. East Indian culture saw the breaking of an engagement by the woman as a shameful event, cast upon the man and the man's family. Arvind went through some emotional turmoil for a while, but he did recover and went on with life. He eventually married some years after—an East Indian woman— through the customary mediation of a family arranged marriage, back in India. She was to join him in Sudbury, but unfortunately, this marriage lasted only one year, it ended in divorce. He shortly thereafter returned to India, and married again through the same family arranged nuptials—and this marriage proved more successful. Arvind had three lovely children from this marriage, one of which is a practicing lawyer and another is studying medicine. He and I have remained on friendly, speaking terms to this day.

Monique Gets Married

Monique picked up the marriage scene where Louise left it, on the stage. Monique got married in 1969, to a young man she had met while she was teaching in Rockland. He was a medical student when they married. He completed his internship shortly after and they moved to Barry's Bay, where he opened up a general family practice.

Doctor Joe proved to be a good family physician, but a poor husband. And my sister Monique did the best possible thing—after raising and doing an admirable job with their four boys—she divorced doctor Joe. Unlike our sister Rose, who hung on to a poor marriage; always hoping to change and reform an abuser; Monique ended her marriage for all the right reasons.

Hair: The American Tribal Love-Rock Musical

At the end of June, 1970 we attended a theatre musical performance, which left an indelible impression on my soul; not only through its beautiful lyrics but much more from the cultural-moral message it left on my mind.

We travelled to Toronto and stayed one night at John's in-laws, on Euclid Street. That evening, we went to the Royal Alexandra Theatre and saw the live performance of the musical "Hair".

I was mesmerized by the music, the performance and the message.

The musical "Hair" was all about the Hippie counterculture and the sexual revolution of the 1960's. The stage cast or "tribe", were a talented and energetic group of barefoot; big-haired; bell-bottomed; bearded and pot-smoking challengers of the American conservative social establishment.

I loved every minute of it: from the opening scene, when a performer crawled over to Emily and asked if she had "any money to give him"—to the closing scene, when new ground was broken in musical theatre when the cast invited the audience to join them on the stage, for a "Be-In".

Emily would not step onto the stage and join in the hand clapping, and the singing of "Let the Sun Shine"—but I did. And it was wonderful.

The musical won many awards for its performance; and the songs—Aquarius, Good Morning Sunshine, Hair, and my two favourites; Let the Sun shine and Easy to be Hard, became anthems of the anti-Vietnam War peace movement.

The musical played to a record non-stop 53-week engagement in Toronto.

Mother's Poor Health and the Return of Money Woes

By early 1969, my mother's health was failing. It had deteriorated to the point where she could no longer hold on to her job at the hospital. Her heart was diseased and she was on nitroglycerine tablets. Her colour had changed to the facial skin pallor of the cardiac patient; her breathing was shallow and laborious, and her normal and natural strength was waning. My father was sixty-seven years old, without a pension except for his small Old Age Security, and a small Canada Pension Plan monthly cheque. My mother was without income from any source, and she was only fifty-nine and Louise still lived at home. They saw themselves again living in poverty.

I Call my Friend at COMSOC

One day, in the spring of 1969, I picked up my office telephone and called my friend, Peter McKay. Peter worked for the Provincial Ministry of Community and Social Services (COMSOC)—the provincial welfare system which granted long- term assistance, to disabled persons and sole-support mothers.

Now, Peter McKay was not a male person; she was a female with a heart of gold and she had the compassion of the Buddha. To anyone asking the question, she would answer that her parents had always wanted a boy, so when she came along, they called her "Peter"—low on the credibility scale, but she held to this explanation as long as I knew her. If "she" lived in the liberated more of today, she may be more forthcoming.

I explained my mother's health to Peter, and her inability to hold employment. Peter made the house call, completed an application and left my mother a medical form for her cardiac specialist to complete. Within two months my parents were receiving a small provincial welfare pension cheque, plus drug and eye care coverage. This subsidy would disappear when my mother turned sixty-five, at which time she would be able to receive the Old Age Security benefits.

My work in municipal social services was moving in a positive direction. I enjoyed the work—I was a natural fit. I enjoyed my clients; whereas some of my colleagues were intimidated by them. I understood them, and they trusted me. They saw me as motivated to help them; as an approachable person, and not as a representative of the government bureaucracy. My colleagues respected me and my boss liked my fresh new approach—what else could an employee wish for?

I considered myself very fortunate, indeed. Simone was very protective and methodical in the unfolding of my training and development; prior to my marriage, my caseload was composed predominantly of single men and intact family households—that is, fathers and mothers with children.

However, marriage, in the eyes of Simone, somehow added a level of competency to my overall performance; it now, for some mysterious reasons, endowed me with the ability to take on a complete caseload. I had now, by marrying, successfully completed a certain "Rite of Passage"; affording new capabilities to the male social services caseworker; I was now allowed to visit, counsel and plan an assistance program for single girls; unwed mothers and female sole-support parents.

Simone told me later that; as her first male caseworker, and given my age and my unmarried state—it was not the single female clients, she was concerned with—rather; it was my innocence that she did not wish to put at risk.

I truly loved Simone for things like this. She was, indeed, a second mother to me.

CHAPTER 24

Urban Renewal and Socio-Economic Times in Sudbury

Sudbury was experiencing an economic "boom" phase at that time; the mid-sixties to mid-seventies. And there was a strong push for Urban Renewal projects in Canada then, and the Borgia Street rundown slum areas qualified under the tri-level government funding programs.

And, so started the rape and razing of Borgia, Vercheres, and Keziah Streets—Borgia Street and the Market; the New Queen Hotel and Paris House Hotel, were torn down and obliterated along with their entire neighbourhoods. These predominantly poor and welfare cases concentrated areas, were done away with by the rumbling bulldozer; to be replaced by the City Centre Mall; new commercial and government buildings, and roadway improvements.

But progress devastated many people and households, as some three hundred houses were expropriated and put down. For four years, the downtown was a boiling pot of construction activity, where the noise of heavy equipment went on, from morning till late at night. And work was plentiful for anyone with a good, strong back.

"Bebe" and Orval Want to Work

I had two clients with peculiar interests and a strong desire to work in that construction bonanza. Both were single, unattached individual males in their mid-thirties. Both laboured under some aspects of social-psychological handicaps.

"Bebe", was a well-known fixture in the Flour Mill; everyone knew him and took special care of him. He was tall and skinny; seldom talked—unless he was swearing at some teenager—and he suffered from a type of nerve-muscle problem, which was triggered by; and became quite evident, when he walked—and "Bebe" walked, and walked—all day long; from Notre Dame Avenue to the downtown core, and back—constantly. And, "Bebe" did not appreciate company; he walked alone.

"Bebe" may always have walked alone, but that does not mean that he was unaccompanied. He carried three articles, or props, constantly along with him on his incessant perambulations; an extinguished, half-smoked cigar; hanging precariously from his upper lip; an ankle length, beige raincoat covering his thin body; and, in his left hand; a rolled up copy of The Sudbury Star newspaper; with which he kept punching the vacant air in front of him as he walked—as if he was swatting at some invisible fly. And, "Bebe" was not a casual walker; his walks were what the fitness enthusiasts of today would call "power walks".

"Bebe" had been telling me for some time that he had a dream, an overwhelming ambition; and that dream was to work on the downtown Urban Renewal construction projects, for any one of the many construction companies operating there at the time.

He showed up in my office one day, and he said, "Cut off my welfare, Mr. Vincent. I don't need it anymore, I've got a full-time job with the Urban." Now, "Bebe" had been on welfare since age eighteen, I knew darn well that this was nothing but idle daydreaming on his part—so, I wished him the best of luck, but took no action to cut him off assistance.

Sometime after lunch, on the Friday afternoon of the same week, I received a phone call from one of the foremen with Dravo Construction at the Urban Renewal site, "Mr. Vincent," he says, in an agitated voice, "you gotta come down here and remove this son-of-a-bitch, before he kills himself or injures one of our employees" and, he continued, "if you don't want to do it, we'll simply call the cops."

For the past week, "Bebe" had showed up for work well before any other employees had arrived at the work site, at around six-thirty; armed with a long-stemmed oil can (the type you see in old railway pictures), and he would go to the heavy equipment—from bulldozers to huge eight-story cranes—oiling any moving parts he could reach. At first, they humoured him by letting him be, until the work crew and machine operators were ready to put the machinery in motion, and then they would whisk him away. It's when he became obdurate and wanted to hold his ground; when he started to pester them to remain in the middle of the action, that they forcibly began to remove him—but like a cork pushed under water—he kept on popping up.

And after a series of removals, he had produced my professional calling card out of his pocket; saying that I had gotten him this job, and he was going to see to it that I would not be disappointed in him.

I got in my car and picked up "Bebe"; I drove him home and told him that I had just fired him from this job. He looked disappointed for a while, then his mood picked up and he said, "Well since you're responsible for firing me—just make sure I get my welfare back."

And then, I worked very hard to get Orval hired on the Renewal site. Orval had been sober for a whole year—so he told me—and he was ready and fit to return to the workforce. I convinced my contact at Canada Manpower to have a look at Orval, and could he please do me a favour; place him in construction, since this was all Orval had done all his life.

Jim Stelmach owed me some favours—I had assisted many of his referrals by expediting the process. Jim called me later, and said, "Listen, Ray, I'm not as sure as you are that this guy is off the booze, but against my better judgment, I just placed him. He's starting to work tomorrow."

The next day, at one-thirty p.m., Jim calls me, "Ray," he says, in an exasperated tone of voice "don't ask me for any more favours. Your guy reported to work alright; as scheduled, and he was early, but by twelve o'clock noon; he was fired. And," he said, irritated, "I'm left holding the bag; I now have to work hard to repair my credibility with this employer."

Apparently, when Orval sat down for lunch—his, was a liquid lunch. When he'd opened his lunch pail, his "lunch" consisted of a half "Mickey" of whiskey and one full bottle of cheap wine.

Paddy the Irishman is Afraid of the Wild Indians

Along with the economic boom that Sudbury was in, came the wide open hiring practices of both; Inco and Falconbridge Nickel Mines. The mines were hiring and going far afield to secure the manpower they needed.

My friend, Paddy Walsh, from County Tipperary, had left Dublin sometime in the early summer of 1967. Paddy spent the first three months in Toronto doing odd jobs, before deciding to try his luck at mining work in Sudbury. So Paddy went to an Employment Agency on Yonge Street and got hired on the spot for Inco. He was to report to the Sudbury hiring office on Frood Road, on Monday, September 16th.

Bent over many a pint; young Paddy was cautioned by his Toronto friends to be ever vigilant, and very wary of Sudbury—it was a rough mining town; with a lot of violence, and trouble-making drunk Indians roaming every downtown street, looking for an opportunity to "roll" someone.

Paddy was nineteen years of age; slightly below average height, and weighed no more than 150 pounds, soaking wet. He combed his dark black wavy hair sideways over his head, with a curl, always managing to wisp over his forehead, over the left eye.

On his first day in Sudbury, Paddy finds the Frontenac Hotel on Durham Street, and he has a few pints with the locals seated there. And in his thick Irish brogue, he enquires of those around him; where could he get a room or a boarding house in Sudbury. The friendly folks direct him to a rooming house on Elm Street, under the management of the Frontenac Hotel ownership. He deposits a week's rent at the office, and he's given his key, and Paddy resumes his seat with his new found friends, and he orders another pint.

He slowly, and casually, introduces the subject that's been weighing heavily on his mind since the bus rolled into town: how safe are the streets of Sudbury? His friends around the table want a little bit of fun at his expense; so they exaggerate the rambunctious nature of the city. And when Paddy brings up the word "Indian"; they all raise their voices in unison and cry out, "For God's sake, stay away from the Indians; they'll get you drunk; and then they'll steal your money, and the very clothes on your back; you'll be lucky to walk away with your life."

Now, my friend Paddy is no coward, but visions of being "rolled" by a gang of violent Indians scared him silly; all those Western movies he'd seen back in Ireland didn't help either; what with the howling and the scalping, and those arrows-pierced bodies of white men—all this kept on flashing before his eyes.

After a good supper, Paddy walked up Elm Street, carrying a suitcase of personal belongings in one hand, and his beloved "Squeeze Box" in the other. Paddy could be out travelling the four corners of the world, but he would always have his accordion—his "squeeze box"—by his side.

He registered and he made his way to his room on the third floor; where he intended to get a good night's sleep, before going to the personnel office the next morning. And in a short while, Paddy is fast asleep.

Sometime well after midnight, he is roused from a deep sleep by screaming, shouts, and terrible noises coming from the hallway outside his room. He sits up in bed, expecting the worse; and when the loud crashing blows of fists banging on the door begins—he is convinced, and terrified—the wild drunk Indians have heard he's in town; and they're coming after him.

By the time he's put on his pants and grabbed his wallet; an ax has struck the wooden door and broken right through. Without a doubt, he's under attack, and he's practically a dead man now; and what a way to die! Head split open by the wild men of Sudbury. His next moves are dictated by instinct; before the second blow strikes the door—he grabs his precious "squeeze box" and he dives headlong under the bed.

When the Firemen finally entered his room, there was already a heavy black smoke rolling on the hallway ceiling.

Paddy was rushed outside; and he watched along with the other roomers, as tongues of flame consumed every floor, and every room in the building. The fire had started on the floor below his. There was no loss of life, but Paddy lost everything he owned—with the exception of a pair of pants; his shoes; a jacket and his beloved and inseparable "squeeze box".

He stored his accordion in a locker at the downtown bus station and spent that night at the Larch Street Salvation Army hostel.

The next day he was met by a cool September morning, and he had to present himself at the Frood Road hiring office, with a pair of shoes without socks; and a light T-shirt and a jacket on top—and he got assigned to work immediately.

Paddy went on to work for Inco until full retirement; first as a miner, and he concluded his career as a "hoistman". He also married a Registered Nurse and they raised three beautiful daughters.

For many years, "Paddy and His Patriots" was a very successful, and a favourite Irish band around Sudbury; much sought after by St. Patrick's Day party organizers.

Paddy did well for himself and his family. Paddy still lives in Sudbury; he became a friend and running companion.

Favours to my Boss: And Happily Given

My relationship with my boss, Simone Patterson, never waned; on the contrary, the bond of friendship and trust grew stronger. We had a mother-son, kind of understanding. And one day, this presumption on my part was demonstrated.

Simone had moved up the ladder in positions of responsibility within our provincial organization—the Ontario Municipal Social

Services Association (OMSSA) —an umbrella organization in which all municipal social services administrative officers had a membership.

This was a Friday and Simone had taken the day off to entertain a high-ranking provincial official—the Deputy Minister of the province's Ministry of Community and Social Services—an important man. He was scheduled to have dinner; prepared by her in her apartment at Ramsey View Court. I got a call from Simone around two-thirty p.m.; she sounded cool and relaxed as usual, "Ray," she says, "I have a favour to ask of you. Leave the office at three o'clock, go to the liquor store and pick me up a bottle of Crown Royal. I would really appreciate it," she continued, in the same tone of voice, she would have used to ask to make a special house call on a welfare family.

It never occurred to me that this was a strange employer-employee request. I did not take offence. I was proud that my boss could count on me to perform a favour that was over and above the call of duty. It appeared quite natural and straightforward to me.

She was my boss—a good and generous one at that—and I owed her for the many favours she had bestowed upon me. She had believed in me; she had given me a job that I loved; she had facilitated my getting reimbursed for my university costs, and she had let me use her car to perform my job when she had no obligation to do so. I was happy to do whatever I could to help her; all she had to do was ask.

Many employees today would rush to file a grievance through their union, against an employer making such requests of his or her employee. But ours—Simone's and mine—was a special relationship. She could have called upon a host of other people to run to the liquor store for her—her private secretary, her son, her daughter-in-law, a female employee, or Smitty, her deputy-director—but, she had called on me, and I felt it was akin to a friend asking for a personal favour.

At the end of May 1969, at its annual general meeting, Simone was elected by her peers to head OMSSA as its President. In May of 1970, Sudbury hosted the annual provincial conference, and Simone, as its President, had to give the important opening address—which usually set the theme and the tempo of the four-day conference—in front of the three hundred plus delegates attending the annual get together. A month before the conference, Simone asked me one day if I could meet in her office, immediately after office closing hours. When I sat down in front of her, the first thing she said to me was that I was under no obligation to consider her request—and she repeated that often in our ensuing conversation—she asked me to help her write her President's address—her speech. She talked about the issues to face municipal social services in the coming years, and she gave me a rough, written outline of what she wanted to talk about.

I spent some time over it that very weekend and handed her the completed speech Monday morning. She read it and she liked it. Not one sentence was changed. And that Friday night, in late May, she delivered it beautifully. I was in the audience. She came to me later that evening, before the dinner banquet, and gave me a hug. She said that delegates from the big cities—which meant Toronto and Ottawa, were coming to her wanting written copies of her address.

This was in the month of May; in July of that year, I started my Laurentian University study program, leading to my Bachelor of Arts degree; with a major in psychology and a minor in sociology. My first intercession course was a summer offering, and classes were not available in the evenings, only during daytime hours. Simone said, "No problem, Ray; take the time you need, we'll cover your caseload for the month of July." Fall and winter intercession courses were held in the evenings, well after working hours. And when I handed in the receipts for the course fees, along with proof of successful completion, seeking reimbursement from the City; Simone was in my corner—advocating for me at personnel and treasury—seeing to it that I got reimbursed, in accordance with the professional in-service education policy adopted by the City, a few years previous. Some employees at the City had very difficult times in getting reimbursed; in fact, some did not. G.P Grandbois, who worked in the Treasury Department, had a constant fight on his hands when it came time to seek reimbursement. His boss was not on his side. He finally gave up asking. But then, not everyone had

Simone as their boss. Simone never forgot a favour received and she always reciprocated when the occasion was appropriate.

Louise Gets Married

My sister Louise had met a young man, and the relationship progressed to an engagement, and then to a marriage, in 1970. The romance had started at the Sudbury Public Library—that was where they had met for the first time. Russell was not a Sudbury native, he was from Sault-St-Marie. His parents came from Italy and Russell had been born in Italy; he was a young child when his parents had immigrated to Canada. I had called Father Lemire and inquired if he would officiate at the wedding ceremony, but he could not do it since he was leaving town for a month; however, he suggested a retired priest from the parish. This priest was in his eighties and could barely stand up, but he managed to complete the ritual. They were married at Saint Anne Church, downtown, and a small family reception was held at Cassio's.

An Empty Nest and a Marked change in our Parents

Louise was the last child to leave the nest and I noticed a marked change in my parents—particularly in my mother. In the short space of five years, the last four remaining children had taken leave of mom and dad. It was an emotionally difficult time for my parents. For a while, they seemed shell-shocked, and my mother's health started to show signs of deterioration. She lost her enthusiasm and that spontaneous energy she usually carried about her. Not only was she unwell—she looked it. She lost her physical strength and that vivacity that was always present in the tone of her voice—the voice had faded to a whisper. Her eyes looked tired, and the skin on her face lost its elasticity. Her facial colour took on a grey, ashen hue.

She had the classic colour and the physical characteristics of the cardiac patient.

The Consequences of an Empty Nest

Louise's leaving the household carried another consequence affecting my parents, which, actually proved beneficial for them. My parents now occupied a four bedroom unit meant to accommodate a family of five or six individuals. However, since Sudbury Housing Authority rules did not allow for my parents to be dislocated until adequate, and appropriate alternative housing was found for them; they remained in that large apartment until they were transferred to a new, Seniors residential complex—thanks to Urban Renewal—downtown, on Louis Street. This was an eight-storied apartment building, just recently built. It was modern, secure and close to grocery shopping and professional offices. It had ample parking spaces for children visiting to park their cars in, to allow them to go and see their parents; and a large basement recreation and communal room, where we held many birthday parties. My parents were happy with their new living quarters, and; therefore, so were their children.

Our Second Child and We Make a Purchase

By mid-July, 1971, tests confirmed that Emily was expecting our second child; due to arrive January 1972.

We started to discuss a change of address to accommodate the new forthcoming addition to the family when Emily's parents came over one day in August; invited themselves to remain with us for supper—small apartment, notwithstanding. I suspected something was up by the constant smile on their faces since their arrival—but I had no idea what it could be. They lived a five- minute drive away from us. So, over dessert and one last shot of whiskey, they let the cat out and laid out the proposition—would we be interested in buying the apartment building?

The offer package, and its terms and conditions, as presented, was a virtual gift—it could not be deemed a purely financial transaction. This was a four-plex apartment building in very good condition; offered to us for twenty-seven thousand dollars; with four thousand dollars down as the down payment—two thousand dollars of which, was a traditional first-house-buying gift—that all their children got; so actually, our contribution to the down payment was only two thousand dollars. Furthermore; they would hold the mortgage on the basis of an "open" mortgage; and, to cap it off, the mortgage interest rate would be in the low single-digit range (when most mortgages at that time were in the mid-to-high teens). Enjoying an "open" mortgage meant that we could pay any amount over and above, the two hundred dollars a month they demanded, and the excess paid would be applied directly to the balance of the principal. This was a deal only generous parents could give you.

A Gold Mine, By another Name

We were all in lawyer Yankovich's office, on Durham Street, a few weeks later, to close this—in my mind—unbelievable development. My in-laws had sold us—more appropriately—given us; a literal gold mine. We would live in the rear apartment rent-free, and the rents from the other three units would easily make the monthly mortgage payments, and any excess rental income generated I applied to the open mortgage.

We were twenty-five years old when we bought the building, and we had just turned thirty when the building was ours—free and clear of mortgage indebtedness.

The purchase of the apartment building carried some added responsibilities, and mature, sober thinking in everything we did, but without a doubt, the purchase proved the most important event in our lives, and it led us directly on the path of financial security and independence.

My wife and I were both frugal and future-oriented. Conspicuous consumption behaviour was never part of our personality. We always lived by the rule that if—you could not afford it—you did not need it. And since we lived for tomorrow; we, therefore, planned for tomorrow.

My In-Laws and their Generosity

There were many other occasions when my in-laws stepped forward, and without being asked; opened their hearts and their cheque books to Emily and me. And I was always grateful—I never took their generosity for granted. Sometimes I was embarrassed to take their offers of money, but I took it; knowing full well that they knew it would be used to benefit Emily and our young family, and not myself personally. Throughout my life, at critical times on the journey, I have been blessed by our Lord in having had the good fortune to find good people around me; always ready to offer me their love, encouragement, and assistance.

The Sudbury Slovaks

Slovaks are a peaceful, fun-loving people; aggression and animosity are not in their character makeup. They love to eat, drink and merriment—particularly, with company around them.

Although the Slovak Hall on Alder Street was still a viable and busy place for the Sudbury Slovak community, the Slovak Friendship League of Sudbury did not boast of a large membership, and it was on the decline. Like most other ethnic Societies in Sudbury in the 70's, it was experiencing a decreasing membership for a variety of reasons. The incoming migration of Slovaks, Finns, Croats, Ukrainians, and Poles had practically come to a standstill; and the younger generation did not have the same ardent interest in keeping the vestiges of cultural symbolism, as alive and active as their parents once had. The older generations were going through the end of their life cycle, and then, intermarriages with spouses of non-Slovak descent also was a factor in the slow, but inexorable decline of the

Slovak Hall; and the Halls of all the other cultural groups in town, for that matter.

However; when Slovak families gathered together, in their homes, or at picnics, or at the annual midsummer weekend Slovak pilgrimage, at the Martyr's Shrine in Midland—organized by the Slovak Jesuit Fathers of Toronto—Slovaks knew how to have a good time. Those were occasions full of family love, joy and fellowship.

Slovak men—and, probably most eastern-European men, love to sing—get a few of them together on a social occasion; put a bottle of rye whisky on the table, and some cold sliced meats and bread; and within the span of a few raised, "Die Bozes,"—the rich bass and baritone voices would burst into spontaneous and happy singing. And to their voices, would soon be joined the high-pitched sopranos of the womenfolk.

I loved sitting amongst such happy people, come together to celebrate life—the Hatalas, the Balints, the Brugoses, the Tomchiks, the Urbans, the Mantiches, and many others. Even though I did not understand one word of the song, my heart knew it was about the homeland; hard work; sacrifices; pretty girls left behind, and love. And I shared in every toast lifted from the bottle. In no time, I was to become a Slovak—if not in body, then certainly in spirit.

The Position of the Sudbury Landlord in the 70's

If you were a student of human behaviour; welfare casework was an ideal position from which to observe society, but being a landlord in Sudbury in the early 70's, also provided you with a wide and rich field of study material. The vacancy rate was practically nil. Landlords charged exorbitant rents for a common hovel. Sudbury was in a "hiring" mode—the local economy was booming. I felt sorry for the many people who presented themselves at my door; responding to an advertisement for an apartment for rent; the newspaper in hand, enquiring about an apartment that had been rented, hours before.

People would present themselves at the offices of the Sudbury Star, hours before the first edition was due to come off the presses, to make sure to be first off the mark, with the "Apartment for Rent" section secure in their hands; and they would call, or show themselves in person at the landlord's door. From three p.m. onward, my phone would ring constantly. It was easier to give a rejection over the telephone; it's the face to face enquiry that was more difficult to deal with. On some days, round about supper time, a queue would form outside our door, with a half dozen apartment hunters waiting in the line; only to be told that the apartment was no longer in the market. I knew from my welfare work that most of those people were from out of town; they had jobs either with Inco or Falconbridge; and that some would end up sleeping in their cars that night until an apartment or room would turn up.

Tenants of all Shapes and Colours

You took your chances on the people you rented to. None came with recommendations. Some were clean, fastidious and responsible. Others, who presented a reasonable and clean exterior; ended up being some of the filthiest tenants imaginable. Our best tenant was a black girl (that I had been reluctant to rent to, from the beginning), who worked as an RNA at Extendicare York Nursing Home. She was the cleanest and quietest tenant, we ever had.

We once rented to an elderly and retired gentleman and his wife. They were from Newfoundland. He almost burned my building down through his smoking and alcoholism. I had to call the police on him once—in a fit of alcohol hallucination, he was screaming and running after his wife outside the house; shotgun in his hand, threatening to kill her. That; did not impress the neighbours. I quickly called Bill, his son, who lived in Garson, and told him that he had thirty days to get his parents out of the back apartment. And he did.

And then there were the pimps who parked their "employees" in my upstairs furnished apartments. I put a stop to the male traffic going up and down the stairs, as soon as I found out my upstairs was being used as a brothel. And then there was the tenant who asked me to fix a leaking faucet; and when I entered the apartment in his absence, to do the repairs, I was met with a veritable jungle of thriving marijuana plants, in various stages of growth all over the place—I shut down that kind of business also pretty quickly—and without providing any access to legal "due process", or giving them any time to appeal to the provincial Landlord and Tenant Dispute Resolution Panel. They were summarily evicted.

A Baby Emergency

We had our first baby-related medical crisis in the front apartment, six months after Christine's birth. Sometime after supper, we had visited at my sister Colette's, now living on Danforth Avenue. We returned home later in the evening and put the baby to bed. She started to cry by one a.m., and Emily detected a slight fever; by two-thirty a.m., the fever had increased and the baby was in distress; crying and thrashing about. When we put on the full light and looked at the baby, we had a sudden shock; the baby started to go into spasmodic convulsions—brisk, repeated shakings of the arms and legs. Emily shouted over her shoulder, "Call the ambulance," which I did, while she stripped the baby naked and put her down in a bathtub full of cold water.

By coincidence, our family physician, Dr. Kosar, was on call at the General Hospital that night. The baby was quite stable at this time and in good condition. Dr. Kosar took me aside and asked, "Don't you have a car?" to which I responded, yes, I did, and then he said, somewhat cross, "it would have taken you half the time to get here, had you taken your own vehicle; there was no need to call an ambulance." And he continued with his lecture, stern and unsympathetic; "Ambulances are for emergencies, and furthermore" he said, wagging his finger, "you had a nurse by your side all the time." Dr. Kosar was of Slovak descent and had been my in-laws family doctor for a long time, and had known Emily since a child—he was a very good doctor. He explained that convulsions in babies are a normal body reaction, triggered in the brain as a defence mechanism against a rise in body temperature—the homeostatic response to sudden rises in body heat. "But," he said in a more conciliatory tone, "immersing her in cold water was a brilliant move." He prescribed antibiotic drops and sent us all back home.

To Dr. Kosar, it may not have been a medical emergency, but to new parents, watching an infant convulse in front of them, it was. And I would strongly recommend a rush to the closest hospital, to anyone meeting with the same circumstances—but take, if possible, your own transportation.

Emergency of Another kind and the Undiagnosed Infected Appendix

We had an emergency of another kind; this time when we occupied the back apartment. The children were playing in the backyard and Emily was taking the sun, in a short sleeveless mini-dress, reclining lazily in a lawn chair.

I decided it was time to mow the lawn. We had had a family backyard barbecue the day before, with Emily's parents and her brother Andy and his family. Somewhere in the deep grass, someone had dropped an empty can of coke. I never saw that pop can lying buried in the grass, and neither did I see it flying out from under the lawnmower—it flew out with such tremendous speed.

I heard some kind of metallic crunch, and then, the scream coming from Emily. The can; shredded in a jagged metal shrapnel, had flown forty feet and ripped Emily's exposed underside of her right forearm wide open, from just above the wrist to a few inches underneath the biceps. I rushed in the house, grabbed a towel and covered the open bloody gash. And while Emily applied pressure and stemmed the bleeding, I had Mrs. Svarkopft over to sit with the children while I rushed to the hospital.

Twenty plus stitches later, she was back home with a mended arm. We were fortunate on many fronts; firstly, no arteries, ligaments or tendons had been severed; and secondly, the projectile could have hit her in the face and eyes; and thirdly, the children playing around her were not hit.

Another medical adventure having to do with Emily occurred while we lived in the back. This was the issue of the undiagnosed infected appendix. She had been complaining of lower abdominal pain for some time—and Emily does not complain of pain needlessly; she has a very high pain threshold. The doctors at the emergency ward were getting tired of seeing her, and they disputed her self-diagnosis of inflamed appendix attacks. One doctor on call sent her home one day with a prescription for sedatives—treating the acute episodes as psychosomatic—bouts of female hysteria.

One late afternoon, she could not tolerate the pain any longer and we called her parents to come over and sit with the children. That same evening she underwent emergency surgery to remove, what was by now, an appendix about to burst and cause life-threatening septic problems.

CHAPTER 25

Laurentian University

My studies at Laurentian University were going well. I was achieving good marks in all my subjects, and Simone still delivered as promised on reimbursement of course fees. And I enjoyed the experience of learning as I had never before done. I loved the research and the freedom to think at whatever depth or dimension my mind wanted to pursue.

In particular, Dr. Patchett introduced me to general Psychology; Dr. Persinger to the science of experimental Psychology; Dr. Abdul Zia to the love of learning history and attending fun, post-exam parties at his personal residence; and, to Professor Hildegaard Mahant, I owe the courage of my convictions; when I stood up to her when she threatened to fail me on an essay, because, she maintained; it must have been plagiarized since the English language used in my paper was—in her own words—"so archaic". She would not accept it. So I produced another paper in twenty-four hours; on a totally different subject—but in the same writing style, and "archaic" English—and she accepted that one and gave me a reasonable grade.

I was awarded my Bachelor of Arts degree in Psychology at the Fall Convocations of 1974. Emily and our children, my parents and in-laws were in the audience. A graduation party was organized for me that evening, at Emily's parents' house. I enjoyed the university—to this day; I have retained and I regularly use, my library reading privileges on campus.

THE CHRONICLES OF A JOURNEY

A Network of Community Contacts and an Offer to Teach

It was a long standing practice in municipal welfare offices, to offer practicum field-placement to Social Work students who came from either, the community colleges, or the university; in order that they gain practical experience and comply with their degree or diploma requirement.

Sudbury was no different, and I was selected to be these students' supervising officer while they were on placement with us. Although I still carried my full caseload, I enjoyed my interaction with the students—most of which's experience with poverty issues was through television documentaries. Acting in that capacity, I got to establish some very good contacts with these institutions' social work faculty members; and the Deans of the departments.

In June, the Dean of Cambrian College's French language, social services program approached me, and asked if I would take up the teaching of one introductory social services course, focusing on government-based social services programs—to be delivered entirely in French—and I accepted.

It was one evening per week, with a light workload, and it brought in extra income—which I discovered later, went back out as additional tax payable. But, it was a good experience for me and I did it for one semester. I did not return for the second semester; although it was offered to me again. Even though the workload was light, I found the preparation time required; my full-time job; my university course study demands; and, my young family, all mitigating against providing a good learning experience to my college students.

Another issue factoring into my decision not to pick up the second semester, had to do with the language of instruction—my facility with spoken French had become rusty, to say the least—for years now, I only spoke French in the presence of my parents—and the saying, in reference to languages, is quite true; "If you don't use it, you lose it!" You lose something along the way when you attempt to speak it in French, but think it in English first—something falls by the wayside.

Henderson Scores the Winning Goal

That was a memorable day: September 28, 1972. I will never forget—neither will most Canadians of the time—the day that Paul Henderson scored the winning goal—the Canada-Russia hockey "Summit Series".

I was at a client's house on Leslie Street that day. When the third period got started, I put away my papers and my briefcase, and I joined the whole family and we glued ourselves to the TV set. When Henderson scored, to break the tied-up game and win the series—with thirty-four seconds left in the game—we were all jumping and hugging in the living room. How proud we all were then to be Canadians. From the father, whose family had had to turn to the state to pay the rent and provide food for the table; and, to myself, an agent of the state—at that very moment we were all together; dancing with joy in our hearts; without the hint of any apparent social differences between any of us.

Some Casework Regrets and Pangs of Conscience

In retrospect; I can recall two salient, if not painful, regrets early in my social services casework. One involved the prosecution for welfare fraud, of a poor, down and out couple with children.

If you were the recipient of social assistance, you were legally obligated to declare any income coming to you on a regular basis—this money would be deducted from your monthly welfare entitlement. The wife, in this case, was in receipt of a monthly Workers Compensation (WCB) pension, and she was not declaring it. This fact was discovered two years after they had been in continuous receipt of assistance. The monthly WCB amount was relatively small; however, I was told that due to the length of time of the offence, I had to file a complaint with the local Crown Attorney's office—which I did. The case was duly prosecuted and the client found guilty. And, to my dismay, since the application was in the husband's name—he was equally penalized.

Now he had a criminal record and it would make his getting any employment that much more difficult—and they would; therefore, stay on welfare for a longer period of time.

That case affected me. It bothered my conscience. Even though what the office did was legally correct; it seemed to me that the personal and family consequences of the conviction were quite above and beyond any social harm done to society as a whole. We had contributed to making a poor family's living conditions much worse than it had been. This was a regret based on having taken action.

My second regret occurred, when I did not take action as I should have done, given the circumstances—the regret of omission.

This was early in my career. I made a house call; my first of the day, at about ten in the morning, at McCormick Village—a Sudbury Housing Authority, low-rental project.

I knocked on the door numerous times but received no response. I knew someone was in the unit since I could hear movement and noises coming from inside. So, I persisted and knocked with greater force; then after a while, the door was slowly, and hesitantly opened to me—by a six-year-old girl in pajamas. I walked in and dropped my briefcase by the door, while I called my clients' names; no one answered, but someone was slowly shuffling their way to me from the living room area—a stark naked, and filthy from head to foot, four-year-old boy. I pushed my way further into the house and found the place littered with dirt and foul smelling, with many days of food scraps all over; in plates; on the floor; and on the kitchen table; wherever there was any space in between empty beer bottles, there was debris, dirt and decomposing food, and the fetid smell of alcohol was everywhere. A one-year-old baby was asleep in a playpen which reeked of urine and excrements. The playpen stood at the foot of a stairway. There were cases of empty beer bottles on the kitchen counter—cases of twenty fours—and whiskey and gin bottles on the living room coffee table.

I found them in the living room—the children's father and mother—both passed out from alcohol intoxication. The mother was sprawled on the couch, half dressed, and she was mumbling and coming to; the father was lying on the floor with only his pants on, semi-conscious; his red face not far removed from spatters of fresh vomit.

I had known that he was an alcoholic, but I did not know that his wife was a companion to the disease. She made room on the kitchen table to allow me space to open my briefcase and record my observations. I mentioned to her that I was duty bound to call the Children's Aid Society. She broke down in tears and pleaded with me; she mentioned that her husband would kill her if he lost the children—he had been a crown ward himself as a child and he had gone through the CAS placement system; moved from foster home to foster home; abused and abandoned.

I did not report them. I walked away disgusted and upset. I should have filed a report. A serious error of omission caused by walking away from professional objectivity.

And, when I got home later that afternoon, the first thing I did was to go to my children and press them hard to my chest.

Pete and Claire Back in Sudbury

One day in 1973, my brother Pete from New Mexico, showed up in Sudbury. He was in town for a month, to set up Claire in the Ladies Wear business. He would help her get the store started, and then he would return to the States. The store was located in the neighbouring town of Chelmsford, and it did open up and did fairly well.

I visited them one day at my lunchtime, as I was making welfare house calls in the area. They rented a house in the Whitson Garden subdivision. They were not a happy couple. Terry was not with them; he was working somewhere in the U.S. They never smiled throughout my one hour stay with them. They looked like an estranged couple just going through the motions of a marriage. This was the beginnings of a divorce.

Pete left town at the end of August to return to his job demands in the U.S. And he and Claire never lived together thereafter. He had come to Sudbury to set her up, and to deposit her where he had originally found her; in Chelmsford, where her parents and her family still lived.

Brother Charley Acting up Again

And from another front came difficulties of another type; from our brother, Charley—and it affected my mother and father in a terrible way; for they simply loved Charley's children—Michel and Claudia.

One evening, while I was sound asleep, I received a phone call from Charley; his conversation was difficult to understand over the noise coming out of the bar at the Ambassador Hotel. He was on the pay phone; how he had gotten there I didn't know; he didn't own a car and he could not have driven himself there if he had had access to one since he did not drive. He was asking me for money—for fifty dollars. That was a lot of money then, and I did not have that amount on me, but I did have twenty dollars. I should have refused him and hung up on him. But I did not—he was my brother.

I drove to the hotel on the Kingsway, and there he was; seated in between two women I did not recognize. He was red in the face and he sheepishly took the twenty dollars without saying a word.

Charley had separated at about that time. He had come home late one afternoon after work, to find the upstairs apartment on Dell Street completely empty of any furniture. His wife and his children gone, and without an address as to their whereabouts. "She was considerate," he would say, relating the event with sarcasm in his voice, "she left me the cat." Which she had. I did not blame Margo for leaving him—no one in our family blamed her—we all thought she had done the right thing; for herself and the children.

Our brother had been battling pathological personality disorders for many years. I found him a small basement apartment on Frood Road; and to his credit, he kept on working, on and off.

However, what my siblings and I took great exception to, was the fallout, or residual effects of the separation. Overnight, he disowned his flesh and blood—he never once, ever after, communicated with his children—or allowed them to communicate with him. And Margo struck back—she forbade Michel and Claudia to communicate with their paternal grandparents—or their paternal uncles and aunts, for that matter. It devastated my father and mother—particularly my dad who adored his grandchildren. It broke his heart. What a sad, selfish and cowardly move on the part of both, Charley and his wife.

For a year and a half, he struggled with bouts of mental illness. One morning I had to come in late for work because I had taken Charley to the General Hospital psychiatric ward. He was prescribed some anti-psychotic medication. When I talked to him that night on the phone, he said that he had flushed all the pills down the toilet. I was beside myself.

My mother called me at home on a Saturday afternoon, and she asked me to come over. Charley was at their place on Louis Street, and he was talking about things she could not understand. She said that some people; strangers; were out to hurt him, and she wanted to know what could be done. Could we call the police and have those bad people arrested? I said I would be right over, and I made my way to Louis Street immediately.

Once there, I realized quickly that there were no bad guys coming after him—he was in a deep schizophrenic, delusional state—he saw people watching him all over—hidden behind clothes racks at Eaton's at the City Mall—waiting for him; seated in unmarked cars—the RCMP and the CIA wanted him for questioning on some drug deal. He talked feverishly and in an extremely convincing manner. Anyone not knowing him may have given his predicaments, some amount of credibility. At times he would be calm and measured, and then suddenly become wild-eyed, and agitated. He would not stay still for a full minute. For the past few weeks, he had started walking-binges all over town.

I took him to the General again, and I called his family physician, Dr. De La Riva; who had his office in the Flour Mill. And this time Charley took his medications and did not flush them away.

Although Charley remained somewhat affected throughout the remainder of his life, with paranoid-persecutory symptoms—the crisis bouts were interspersed with periods of stability—he managed to maintain a productive work history—in between episodes of bizarre behaviour.

He later moved to Elliot Lake and worked for Denison Mines and Stanleigh Mines, until those operations' final closures in the mid-80's. He worked until age sixty-one and died of mining-related chest obstruction (COPD), and of the compounding consequences of chain-smoking—at age seventy-five. Never having once spoken to his children since the day of the empty apartment—never having heard the sweet sound of the babbling of his grandchildren. What a fool!

An Unlikely Event— A Tornado Hits Sudbury

On the morning of August 20, 1970, I followed my usual routine; I had picked up my mother and brought her to our place to babysit Christine. I was on my way to work when the radio announced an incoming storm of some severity. It was coming in from the west.

And what a storm it turned out to be. Within a half hour, a tornado packing winds in excess of one hundred miles per hour—a category 3 (out of five) on the tornado force measurement scale—had bulldozed its way through Lively, Copper Cliff and parts of the south end of the city.

The storm left six persons dead, over eight hundred injured, and caused an estimated $15 million dollars in property damages, destroying many houses in the vicinity of Lively; and, at that time in 1970, Inco was in the process of building its smelter's Superstack; the structure was still being worked on when the tornado struck it—nobody died of the six masons working on the stack that morning, but many came near to heart attacks as the towering smokestack swayed back and forth.

The west end of town was not affected by any significant property damage. Our house was fine and so were our neighbours'. The ferocity of the storm was intense for a short while, and it packed a punch while it lasted ten to fifteen minutes.

Driving around the path of the storm, one could clearly see the severe damages to property. However, that fall when I went out grouse hunting, in the areas around the Fairbanks Provincial Park; behind Walden; the damages to my favourite hunting spots took a personal dimension. Large swaths of forest, of both, deciduous and coniferous stands, had been levelled flat; as if some big foot had stepped on a collection of twigs—one hundred yards wide and miles long. Where my walking trails had been—they were now impossible to locate, totally covered up—obliterated.

New Ways in Municipal Governance

Throughout the province, in the early 1970's, there was talk of rationalizing the manner in which municipalities governed themselves. There were debates everywhere in the media and at the dinner table; about the pros and cons of Municipal Regional Governments. The Sudbury area municipalities were not excluded from the fray. The Regional model of municipal governance came to Sudbury in October 1973. And with the introduction of this two-tier level of municipal organization, came the amalgamation of the City of Sudbury welfare department with that of the District of Sudbury Social Services Administration Board, or DSSAB—the latter; heretofore, charged with the responsibility to deliver services to the small outside towns, and organized areas. This meant joining two operations into one. It was organizationally difficult and stressful, but it was done smoothly and successfully.

When the dust settled, I would retain my job as a welfare caseworker, but now I worked for a much larger municipal organization—both, in terms of numbers of employees, and geographical territory of service.

A Competition for a Supervisory Position

But these developments also meant enhanced opportunities for career advancement. The office doubled in size overnight, and there was a need for a Supervisor of Field Services.

Smitty Lapalme, as the deputy director of the city welfare office, was seen as the logical selection; but Smitty carried a lot of baggage. Through the years, Smitty had accumulated a history of negative reports—reports that had made their way to the desks and the ears of officials at the provincial Ministry of Community and Social Services, at Queens' Park—mainly to do with his mistreatment of clients. I also applied, and I had the support of the Ministry consultant who had been sent to Sudbury to oversee the smooth transition of the amalgamation process.

The District welfare Administration Board met at the end of October; and the next morning the news was out, that I had been promoted to Field Supervisor.

Smitty was not happy with the decision. He told me that week that he'd been subjected to some kind anti-French, Anglophone conspiracy. That he had not been selected because he was Francophone.

I did not feel it was appropriate for me to remind him that, I too, was Francophone. Notwithstanding his deep disappointment, we remained good friends. He did not blame me—he told me so—he blamed the waspish anti-French "conspiracy".

The Selection of a Director and a Compromise

With the joining of two offices; Simone Patterson, our director with the old city operation, found herself in a more delicate situation. She was non-union, and had no protection; the District Board already had its director in Paul Schaak, and there could not be two heads to one body.

A compromise was found—she would become "Associate-Director" until such time as one of them retired. Both retained full and identical salaries. I noticed that, although they were equals, and

Simone had a greater seniority standing in terms of directorship years of service compared to Paul; one of them was somewhat more equal than the other; Paul always made the final decisions on operational matters—this had a lot to do with the male-female disproportional distribution of power prevalent in those days.

Paul Schaak

Paul was very honest and straightforward. He was an indefatigable worker, his capacity for work was phenomenal—the German in him. When I first met him, he sported a brush-cut hairstyle, and he was a big smoker. He changed his haircut to the standard, flat and parted on the left style, and he stopped smoking for health reasons later on. He was of average height, and muscular in build. Paul must have loved the colour brown; because, even though he had a whole wardrobe of suits—they were all in different shades of brown. Paul had some political association with the Conservative Party, both, provincially and federally. He had married a French-Canadian girl, and they raised a great family.

A New Organization and a New Address

We were now away from Durham Street, as we physically joined the District Welfare operation, located on Larch Street. It became immediately obvious that the office space on Larch was inadequate to accommodate the expanded organization. It had had barely enough square footage for Paul's staff; let alone now, with the added demands put on by the additional incoming City staff.

Within six months we were moved to new quarters—atop the Sudbury Steam Laundry operations on Walnut Street—not an ideal location, but it gave us the space we needed. The new location was away from the downtown core and it offered a large amount of floor space. But, there were some logistical and technical problems to deal with. There were access difficulties for clients, since bus transit to our new site was very poor; and clients had to climb a steep and long stairway to reach our floor; furthermore, we had no elevators and physically handicapped clients faced tremendous challenges; and the heat and ventilation systems were antiquated—we froze in the winter; and we suffocated in the summer. We put up with these inconveniences in the knowledge that we were in temporary quarters—a brand new City Hall was well into its final phases of construction, on Brady Street; and we would become a tenant of that new building. Our move to the new, ultra-modern building, was planned to take place in 1976—a little more than a year away.

A Director on the OMSSA Board

In the spring of 1976, I attended the annual OMSSA conference being held in Toronto, along with Paul Schaak and Simone. There was a large gathering of delegates that year—mostly because it was being held in the "big city". There happened to be vacancies on the board of directors, and at the business session of the conference, I was nominated from the floor by my new boss, Paul Schaak; to be elected as one of two Northern Ontario sitting representatives. As there were many nominations; we had to have an election, and I was elected by my peers. I was to remain on the board of directors for seven consecutive years.

A Difficult Period of Adjustment

My first twelve months in management proved difficult and challenging for me. At times, I discussed with Emily if I had made the right decision. I was yearning for the security and the comfort of my old job. I was blazing a brand new trail; neither welfare offices—Paul's or Simone's—had had a Field Supervisor position in place prior to my coming on the stage. I had no footprints to follow. I was on my own. In effect, I created the position as I went along. People who came after me, following further organizational expansions—

Jean, Ray, Mary and others—accommodated easier to the position, because by that time there was a pattern for them to follow.

By being on the management team, I had lost the security and accustomed workplace behaviour of the unionized position. I had become severed from my union colleagues. Even on coffee breaks, I now felt alone. And prior to my promotion, I only had to take care of myself; now, everyone's problem on the large caseload team, became my problem to solve; every field service issue, became my issue. My job was no longer a Monday to Friday, nine to five, assignment anymore. I had to put in whatever time that my area of responsibility demanded.

In return, I got an increase in salary; a private office; secretarial services; a monthly car allowance; and an extra week of vacation per year.

And, the biggest bonus of all—my mother and father were extremely proud of me—the boy from Mud Lake was going somewhere.

It took me a year of learning; by trial and error; before I started to feel comfortable and competent in my new position. And after that first year, it was fairly smooth sailing and I enjoyed management, and I never looked back. Finally, I was now in a position to put in place ideas and strategies that I had wanted to see implemented from the first day I had become a caseworker—I have always found it much easier to lead from the front, than from behind.

New Areas of Responsibility

My new position required that I step in some time and resolve client-worker conflicts and interaction problems; either to do with regulatory interpretation or good old fashion personality clashes. Some of those situations, at times, involved clients who had been, or were now, friends of mine—either at Sheridan Tech or from the Flour Mill—and it was difficult for me not to show a bias. But whenever there was ambiguity, or where I had clear discretion, I gave my client friends the benefit of the doubt and ruled in their favour.

But when the case was clear that they were in contradiction of the General Welfare Act and its Regulations, I ruled bureaucratically and upheld the rules—in fairness to the legislation and all the other clients that we serviced.

My position also required that I plan, and directly manage newly hired caseworkers' orientation and training.

Poor Jane Boniakowski! Jane was tall and thin and she carried a grade school teacher-like look about her. She always had a serious and nervous demeanour, and she talked in short, crisp sentences. And, the more tense she became the sentence length would shrink accordingly, and the redness in her face flared up.

I took her out for her first introduction to field visits, one cold mid-January morning—in my, barely holding together; red Beetle Volkswagen. Beetles were unlike most cars in the engine cooling department—they were air-cooled, and the fan blower in my little red "bug" was not functioning properly. But, what really frightened my passengers was the visible two-by-four piece of lumber, running front to back, under the right edge of their seat; positioned in that fashion so that the seat would not fall on the road.

And I was taking Jane that morning to the Onaping Falls-Levack area of the district—probably the coldest part of the territory. It took twenty minutes before we got any semblance of warmth coming into the cabin. Just around Azilda, I nonchalantly reached underneath my seat and handed Jane a scraper. "What's this for?" she asked, somewhat puzzled. "Would you mind scraping the windshield in front of me," I replied, "I can barely see through the window." And Jane started frantically scraping away with all her might—at this point, she felt her life depended on it. The inside volume capacity of the car was so small, our body heat and exhalations froze immediately on the frigid glass a foot away from our faces.

By the time we reached Dowling, some heat was coming out of the vents, and we had ten-inch portholes of vision on both, the driver and the passenger side. By the time we had completed our field assignments and made our way back to Sudbury, my new rookie was mighty quiet; stomping her frozen feet onto the floor, and sporting a red nose and rosy cheeks.

Later in the afternoon, as we underwent a short debriefing in my office, Jane took my arm; and said, with a very compassionate and serious tone to her voice; "Ray," she said, "you must take that menace off the road—you're either going to kill yourself, or kill some innocent person driving the same roadway."

Over the years, Jane never missed an opportunity to relate to her colleagues, the hair-raising experiences of her first field trip with her supervisor, and the evils of an air-cooled engine.

Now, Ray Read had much more pleasant experiences to talk about after his first outing with me—and it had nothing to do with a sexist nature on our part. We were in the pleasant heat of mid-summer, and I decided to stop over at my house around lunchtime, where Ray and I could have sandwiches and iced tea. I showed him the house and the building in general, and then we sat down to lunch. This must have impressed Ray, because, whenever he would talk about his training and first field experience, he never talked about the great things he learned—he always brought the talk, to the great iced tea that I had served. But, Ray must have learned some things of significance from me—a short time later he became our third Field Supervisor. Ray and I have remained good friends, well into retirement—and he still talks about the visit to my house—and the iced tea!

Paul Schaak Recommends Me to a Directorship

Paul Schaak—now my new boss—came to me one day and told me that the Algoma District Welfare Board was looking for a new welfare director, and he asked me if I was interested in the job—it was mine if I wanted it. Paul had a great reputation amongst welfare administrators, and he carried a lot of respect in the field—and a large amount of influence. If I wanted the job; he would recommend my name to the Algoma Board selection committee, and advocate for me.

I thanked him sincerely. I was honoured, but hesitant. I told him to give me a few days to think it over.

I discussed the offer put to me by Paul with my wife. Within three days I got back to him.

I turned down the job offer and the huge promotion—and for many; and considered reasons. I loved Sudbury, and to relocate my young family to the small town of Thessalon, outside of Sault-St-Marie, where the Algoma District welfare office was located; did not appeal to me. Emily and I had our parents in Sudbury; Emily had a full-time nursing position in Sudbury; which she would have to quit, and there were no hospitals in Thessalon to regain employment in a profession she loved; the small town of less three thousand people had none of the amenities that Sudbury had to offer; in terms of educational and cultural resources, which to us was important for our children.

Paul understood my position and the matter was not discussed further. My friend, David Court; a caseworker with the Algoma District Board, ended up getting the job. I could have been welfare director at age twenty-eight, but I never regretted our decision.

CHAPTER 26

We Plan a Visit to Slovakia

In 1962, Emily and her parents had taken a two week trip to Slovakia (Czechoslovakia at that time). They had confined their trip to the Slovak part of the two-part country—the region where all of her parents' family was located. One day, Emily's mother and her father suggested a return visit. One that would see Mrs. Hatala, Emily and myself and our two children, now six and four years of age, travel to the old country. Mr. Hatala stayed behind in Sudbury; he applied the cost of his flight toward the purchase of two airline seats for our children.

Emily arranged the itinerary; we would spend two weeks in Slovakia, visiting relatives and historical sites—she and I would make side visits—one to Prague, on the Czech side, and another, to the Tatra Mountains in northeastern Slovakia. Her cousins, Joe and Milan would accompany us on those short trips, and they would act as our guides and interpreters—Emily could speak and understand the Slovak language, but it was restricted to the village dialect; whereas, her cousins had the facility of the urban, higher school grammar. Emily could get by anywhere with her village language dialect and straightforwardness—she made a lot of the city Slovaks smile and chuckle in the process.

We would wrap up our Slovak trip with a four day stay in the jewel of Austria; the city of Vienna, and then head back home to Canada.

THE CHRONICLES OF A JOURNEY

Babushkas and my Mother-in-Law: The Black Market Entrepreneur

For my in-laws, and for most Canadians of eastern European descent for that matter, a trip back to the old country—now under the yoke of a repressive socialist, communist regime—meant that you brought with you, suitcases full of presents from the free economy system of government you were privileged to be living under.

But my mother-in-law went one step further. She decided she would show me the business side of her character—and, she decided she would show the local Slovak village ladies, how the economy really worked in the free world. She brazenly ventured into the world of the "black market". She would be a visitor, and, an entrepreneur—and risk going to jail for it.

Months before the trip, she'd been writing to her sister and various other close relatives in Slovakia, asking them all one basic question—what was in short supply for village ladies over there? —What were the personal items in great demand? The replies came fast and furious, and all agreed—there was a great demand for "Babushkas'" (that is, female headscarves, or kerchiefs), nylons, and plastic tablecloths.

But the greatest need being voiced—particularly, in the villages we would be visiting—was for babushkas. The word "Babushka" in the Slavic family of languages (Slovak, Russian, Ukrainian, Croatian, etc.) denotes 'grandmother'. Hence; the elderly and the married village women vied with each other; as to who could own the prettiest and most colourful headscarves or babushkas'. It was not unusual in the pre-socialist days to have individual villages identified by the distinctive and unique colours and patterns imprinted on the "babushka".

The socialist government had put out an edict forbidding the production of "babushkas" since it represented the past; backwardness and a bourgeois lifestyle; whereas, the socialist state propaganda was all about being modern; a step ahead and forward-looking. The regime went to great length to force people to break away from tradition and the old ways of living. No one went to church in the cities, and gradually, churches were even starting to close in the villages.

Wearing a pretty babushka did not only satisfy a certain amount of female vanity; it also signified that this village woman was married and unavailable to men, or she could be a widow.

This whole symbolic structure was seen as archaic, and a throwback to the capitalist-created class struggle. We noticed in our travels through the country that, anything that smacked of the 'old days' was discouraged and frowned upon.

But the village women would go to any length—the local authorities be damned—to get themselves babushkas—and the more colourful they were; the better. My mother-in-law was aware of all this, and so she wrote back that she was coming to them with "babushkas" to satisfy all tastes.

Mother and Daughter Go Shopping on Queen Street

So one Saturday, a month prior to our departure date; Emily and her mom went downtown Toronto; on Queen Street and the ethnic neighbourhoods around the Euclid Street area, and they bought hundreds of dollars' worth of kerchiefs (babushkas by another name). They filled two suitcases full.

I could not understand what was going on—but Emily told me, "Trust me, my mother knows what she's doing." My mother-in-law was to step into the shady world of the "black market".

She would sell an item that was in great demand in the villages—she would become the "babushka" queen from Sudbury. And she did sell her babushkas; all of them; two suitcases full, in exchange for Slovak currency; the Koruna—and she made a little fortune by Slovak standard of living—which she turned over to Emily and me, with a big smile on her face.

Emily had been right; her mother did know what she was doing.

THE CHRONICLES OF A JOURNEY

A Chance Meeting in Vienna and on to Slovakia

We left the Toronto International airport in July of a late afternoon; bound for Vienna—where I met a distracted, and seemingly upset Sudbury lawyer, Elmer Sopha, in the Viennese airport terminal. He was changing planes on his way to Budapest. Elmer was a great orator and courtroom lawyer—if not performer—he was such a good lawyer; I saw him more than once, intimidate judges with his booming voice. And he became a good politician.

From the Vienna airport, we transferred to a bus; crossed the bridge over the Danube, and made our way to Bratislava; the Slovak state capital, located very close to the Austrian border—less than an hour's bus ride.

And at the Austrian-Slovak border, I got my first taste of Soviet style hospitality awaiting us on the Slovak side—border guards toting AK-47 sub-machine guns, slung over their shoulders by leather straps. Everyone's luggage was disembarked for inspection, and for the first time in my life I had a panic attack—those damned "babushkas"—I was sure our party was all headed to the closest jail.

When they got to our luggage and unzipped those carrying our personal travelling clothes and things, they spent some time rummaging through them; by the time they got to the luggage of babushkas they were pressed for time; opened them, and a gave a cursory look at the contents—the young man asked in a bored and disinterested voice—what those were all about. Emily responded, flashing him a disengaging smile; "Presents from Canada, for family and friends," she said, with innocence and milk and honey flowing from her voice. The young officer smiled back; closed all the suitcases and moved on.

The Reluctant Socialists and Encounters with the Underground Economy

We were fortunate that we were dealing with Slovaks at the border. Slovaks were reluctant socialists. They had become enmeshed in the Bloc because of the vagaries of war. Slovaks are a docile, and peaceful people; over the centuries they had had to adapt to living under the subjugation of one foreign master or another. They had developed culturally effective survival mechanisms. The young soldiers milling around the bus were carrying their weaponry nonchalantly; with an air of embarrassment and without the least sign of aggression. Seemed to me they were dying to strike a conversation with the passengers, but held back for fear of their superiors—many of them, I'm sure, had family living in America or Canada. They gave me the impression that they'd rather be home to their beer and loved one than here playing the part of the soldier.

Our journey still had a very long way to go. Our ultimate destination was the farm country villages of eastern Slovakia. We were now in Bratislava, on the far western reaches of the country. Emily's cousin, Joe Kochis, met us at the bus terminal in Bratislava and he was to escort us to the airport, and from thence we would fly to Kosice; a large city within an hour of our destination—the village of Secovska Polanka—where my in-laws' family lived.

While waiting for the plane in Bratislava, we made our way to a restaurant—we were famished—where we had the worst, thin, watery, beef noodle soup imaginable—two to three thin, leathery strands of beef in a bowl full of brown water. Emily's cousin smiled sheepishly at the fare and said; "Welcome to the Peoples' restaurant food. But," he continued, "Slovak beer is the best in the world." And it was.

In the restaurant, I had my second introduction to the socialist system of daily life—and it had nothing to do with the terrible food being handed out.

The official rate of exchange of a Canadian dollar to the Slovak "Koruna" at that time, was one dollar to seven korunas. Any bank or commercial enterprise in Slovakia would give you nothing more than seven korunas for your dollar; however, people on the streets would gladly give you thirty-six korunas for your one Canadian dollar, and even more for an American greenback. Here was the oddity of their system—people in Slovakia had lots of money; lots and lots of korunas—but, practically no consumer goods to buy with them. To buy foreign made, highly desirable consumer goods—and there were state-owned stores (Tuzeks), selling them—folks needed foreign currency—dollars—to transact any purchases in these stores.

So, after finishing my "peoples' soup", I went to the washroom. I was still standing in front of the urinal when the headwaiter came in and he stood there quietly, some ten feet away from me; clad soldier like in his black and white staff uniform; with a big bill-fold, hanging at his belt. There was no one else in the room, but the two of us. By our way of dress and the English spoken; he had easily picked my party as one from America. When I turned to face him; he opened his big restaurant wallet and pointed to all his korunas, and he said in broken English; after looking nervously behind him toward the closed door, "Please, gentleman, thirty-six korunas-one dollar." You did not need to be a linguist to understand what he meant. I was more than happy to trade, given the poor government exchange rate of seven to one. However, my wife carried all of our travel money; I had about one hundred Canadian dollars on me, so I showed him the contents of my wallet and I said, "One hundred," and in the best Slovak I could muster, I ventured; "moja Zena, peniaze," (my wife, has money) as I pointed toward the door. He understood me, and after looking over his shoulder to the door again, he nervously counted out three-thousand and six-hundred korunas; took my money and quickly turned about and left.

Soviet Bloc residents would go to great lengths to accumulate American or Canadian currency—their only means of buying luxury goods.

When I went back to the table; flashing the wad of money all the way back for all to see; boasting of my good fortune, Emily's cousin's face turned very dark and severe, and he said something in Slovak under his breath to Emily and her mother. What he had just said, was, "Tell Ray not to do that, and put the money away out of sight right now. If the authorities are alerted, he could get five years for that, and the waiter ten to fifteen." I quickly stopped celebrating.

Arrived in Secovska Polanka

Once landed in Kosice; two other cousins were waiting for us and took us in two vehicles, and drove the five of us, plus luggage, to our final destination—Emily's aunt Elizbetha, in the village of Secovska

Polanka. It was very late in the night when we arrived. There was much kissing and hugging, and many women with babushkas and smiles with mouthfuls of glinting gold teeth. And when we lay down to bed it was well past midnight.

The house was privately owned by her aunt and it stood on a long, narrow piece of land on which was a big cultivated garden at the back. The entire house; foundation and walls, were constructed of large cement blocks, with walls a foot and a half wide. The exterior walls were all stuccoed and whitewashed. The inside walls of the house had been whitewashed but recently, probably in anticipation of their Canadian visitors, and so our room was filled with uncomfortable dampness. What was our bed at night, converted to a sitting room couch, or a bench in the daytime—and this was a normal living arrangement in all the villages we visited.

Restless sleep and a Socialist Morning Serenade

I did not have a restful sleep, and I was awakened very early by the noise of two unusual sounds. One came from the street outside, and the other one seemed to come from directly under the house, or the basement; if they had one. It did not take long to realize that the noise from outside did indeed come from the street.

Spaced apart by approximately one hundred yards; anchored firmly to the hydro poles, were huge, loudspeakers bellowing lively martial music, and now and then, a party comrade would cut-in, exhorting the workers of Slovakia to greater production in the workplace; greater efforts to achieve the quotas set for the year; and it would end with a little song about peace at home and throughout the homeland, before returning to martial music—good, old-fashion socialist propaganda. More than a bother to my sleep, I found it disgusting to my spirit.

The scratching and grunting noises from underneath our bedroom proved a lot more tolerable and benign. And it did not come from a basement—the house had none—it came from the big pig Emily's aunt kept in the backyard. Its den was in a small shed attached to the rear wall which extended underground, well below the foundation.

The Simplicity of the Slovak Countryside

I had no problem in accepting the village way of life and its living conditions. It was a new, and for me; enriching experience. Farming communities anywhere in the world are rustic and simple in their lifestyles, and Slovak villages were no different. I had come to visit and meet a people that I loved, and I had come to be with them on their own terms. If we had wanted the modern, big city life, we would have booked a fancy hotel in any of Slovakia's big cities—and there were a lot of them. I met loving and extremely warm people. Their hospitality was amazing. Everyone opened their hearts and their houses to us, everywhere we went. They all reminded me of my in-laws.

Socialist Restrictions

Inasmuch as I loved Slovaks as individuals, I very much disliked their authoritarian form of government. We, as tourists, could not move about the country unless our destination and reason for travel were duly reported to the local authorities beforehand. Our time schedules, from place to place, had to be made known in written form. Our passports surrendered at hotel desks. And we were told not to openly, and within the hearing of others, criticize the government.

A Sale had taken Place

Even though I had gotten up early that first morning, my mother-in-law had been up and about much before me. And hordes of women were filing in and out of the house. Those coming in were going directly to the front sitting room to meet Emily's mother. I was surprised to see so many women, of all ages, coming so early in the morning to get reacquainted with Mrs. Hatala. Why not come and visit around lunchtime?

I found out later that they were not old lost friends; they were women come from far and wide—from this local village and from outside villages—to bargain for a "babushka"—and as many as they could get their hands on.

By breakfast time, my mother-in-law's two suitcases of kerchiefs, nylons, and plastic tablecloths were sold out—as a matter of fact, most of the "presents" had been already sold in advance of our arrival.

And she handed Emily a stack of Slovak korunas which would finance our trip to Prague, and the Tatra Mountain resorts. Emily overheard one of her aunts' say; that the stack of korunas represented more money than the average annual income earned by a Slovak worker.

A Visit to Prague and the Tatras on Babushka Money

Our plans called for Emily and I fly to Prague with her cousin Joe and his wife, and spend four days there; and after our return to Secovska Polanka; spend four days visiting local relatives, and then leave for the High Tatra Mountains with her other cousin, Milan, and his wife. Milan had his own car. And while we were absent, touring the country—Emily's mother acted as a nanny for our two children—a great arrangement.

Joe Kochis; Emily's cousin, was older than his brother, Milan. He had four children, two girls, and two boys. Neither he nor his wife spoke one word of English. Both were metallurgical engineers. They were great fun to be with. They always saw the comical, or the irony in the socialist way of doing things, and were quite at ease talking privately about it. Like his brother, Joe and his wife were card- carrying party members—more for their children's sake than theirs. Party members' children got ahead of the queue—the better schools; the better jobs—the privileges.

We flew with them to Prague and we had a great time in this beautiful Eastern European city—the "Paris" of the Communist Bloc. We went to the theatre and saw the live performance of a play full of anti-Russian political satire.

I was amazed at the efficiency of their public transit system. All conveyances were fast, clean, and on time—and cheap. One price took you anywhere in the city—and for the full day. Emily and I were paying all costs—ours and our hosts'.

Prague is one of the most beautiful cities in the world. And even more so at that time—it had kept its old world charm. At that time it was one of the few cities on the planet that had not submitted to the American fast food influence. On our last night, we went to an exclusive hotel restaurant—where the communist high-class was known to congregate.

A Meal for Joe to Talk About back at the Factory

We sat down at seven p.m., and when we rose to make it back to our hotel, it was past midnight. Compared to North American prices, everything was cheap in socialist countries.

We started off the evening with authentic Russian vodka and caviar, and then we went on to the most expensive entrees they had—which, when compared to our costs, was very modest—and we had wine and fancy pastries. The vodka was so pure and refined that we had it by the glass full—unadulterated by any other liquid—and it drank as smooth as a glass of water. However, when I stood up halfway through the meal, although my mind was crystal clear and my speech unaltered, the muscles of my legs would not obey the commands of my brain—I could not immediately stand up—it took some time and much coaxing.

When the check came; I casually looked at it and passed it on to Emily. She reached for her purse and counted out seven-thousand two-hundred korunas— korunas of "babushka" money—and laid that on top of the bill, plus adequate gratuity. Emily's cousin and his wife were beside themselves—their combined monthly incomes did not equal what we had spent in the restaurant. They were speechless for a moment; and then, they would burst out laughing. Cousin Joe again showed his great sense of humour. He asked the head waiter if he could have a copy of the bill—he had to show this to his coworkers back at the metallurgical plant—unless he had a copy, they would not believe him, he said. And the waiter gave him a copy.

My mother-in-law's foresight and "black market" acumen, had provided us with korunas sufficient to pay both couples' return airfare to Prague and back; and funds for hotel accommodations; tourist attractions and fancy meals. And we had korunas left over, sufficient to underwrite the other side trip to the High Tatra with Joe's brother, Milan.

Whereas Joe, the engineer; drove a Russian made, four-cylinder Skoda; Milan owned a French Renault—and he was very proud of it—although Renaults are no vehicle to brag about. But, it was the fact that he was different—and that was a big deal in socialist societies—from most of his countrymen—that mattered to him. He stood apart and he was a visible individual in a society that disparaged individualism. Socialist regimes tried hard to bury the individual. Milan was a high school teacher and his wife Marianka worked as a librarian.

But Milan had a talent that made him a lot of money—he was a musician. He was a guitar player, lead singer, and bandleader of the local "Rock Band". Playing Rock music in a socialist country made you an instant personality and in great demand. He made more money playing for teenage weekend dances, and weddings, then his teaching job brought him. Hence his ability to finance the purchase of the Renault, and a government flat full of American and Western European furniture and odds and ends.

He disliked the communists with a passion, but like most of his professional countrymen—he had little choice but to tow the party line. But Milan's lifestyle, the personal successes, and coming into the limelight too often did not take long before they started to attract enemies.

Twelve years after our visit, Milan left his wife and walked away from his marriage. He defected to Canada—to Sudbury, to be exact.

We travelled to the Tatras with Milan and his wife—again, financed mostly by black-market babushkas. And again we had to deal with the stone-faced bureaucrats to get travel documents and authorization. Milan made a special visit to some officials in Kocise to get the paperwork expedited—I would not be surprised if he bribed a few people—not an unusual occurrence in communist countries at that time. One could always move ahead of the queue if you had money in your fist. And again, we had to surrender our passports to the local authorities, to be returned to us only when we came back. Socialists love control.

In the Tatras, where the country had prime tourist attractions and an impressive mountain range—the Alps of the Carpathian mountain range—all shops and vendors shutter their businesses after seven p.m. One evening after supper, the four of us went out for a walk. There were many tourists walking about. It was still warm under the setting sun and very pleasant. Emily suggested we proceed to the ice cream vendor, we had seen at the street corner, on our way to the restaurant. A cool ice cream cone would make a great after dinner dessert. But when we got to the street in question—the vendor had locked-up his kiosk—and he had gone home. When I mentioned this commercial oddity to Milan, he laughed and said through Emily; in Slovak, "Welcome to the communist way of life! No personal incentives to work hard; no rewards for showing initiative—as a matter of fact, it is discouraged," he said throwing up his hands. "The ice cream vendors and the sausage vendors—all vendors—go home to their families at six-thirty. And they couldn't care less if they sold one hundred ice cream cones or sausages, or a thousand of each—it's all one to them—they get the same pay; not one penny more." And he shook his head and laughed.

Ray A. Vincent

First Impressions

Everyone worked slowly and methodically. No one in government or commercial establishments understood the concept of "service", or, "customer oriented behaviour". And everyone wore the same grey, drab-looking clothes; and lived in the same grey cement block and government-owned high-rise flats; where the small closet-size privies smelled; the elevators malfunctioned most times, and electricity would blink on and off at random throughout the day. Welcome to the Peoples Socialist Republics. The people themselves were beautiful, but I would not have wanted to live there—I would have looked for a way out.

The villages were much more pleasant. Although still centrally controlled—churches were being compelled to close, and the eyes and ears of government informants were everywhere—yet, they were much happier than their urban compatriots. They had their garden plots; they had plenty of food and beer—although I looked for it, I saw no evidence of food shortages anywhere in the country where we went—they had their "vinarens" (wine shops) and their karchmas (pubs), and they had decent pensions in their old age. The older men and the babushka-clad women were the happiest of the lot. Compared to the hardship and privations forced upon them by war and political strife—their present life, even with restrictions—was the best they had enjoyed in many years.

The Cousins, Joe and Milan

Joe's relationship with his wife was as different from his brother Milan and his wife, as were the differences of the motor cars they owned and the lifestyle they led. And there was little of family resemblances between the two. Joe was much older and happy and laid-back. You could sense the love and respect the couple had for each other. Milan was younger, unhappy with the political and economic state of his country and it came through in his comments and relations with his wife and children. He was restless and high strung. He was a man looking for something beyond the present horizon. Milan had been a promising athlete in his high school and university years—once a time national record holder in the eight-hundred-meter run. But his track accomplishments were not up to the standards of elite runners coming from other Communist Bloc countries. He was slender, of average height, balding from the top of his head and he was a person who was always anxious to please and anticipate the needs of those around him. The marriage; with two children, a boy, Marek; and a daughter, Blanca; was to founder and lead to his leaving the country for Canada, in 1992.

When Emily and I left the Tatras, to rejoin Emily's mother, and our two children in Secovska Polanka, it was time to repack our luggage; say our goodbyes; and head for the last leg of our trip—a four day stay in Vienna—out of babushka money; but full of rich memories. Emily and I were to return to Slovakia in 2006, by ourselves; when the country had amicably separated from their Czech brethren and was adjusting to the vagaries of the world of the "free economy".

Vienna—Pictures of the Western World

We landed in Vienna after one p.m. in the afternoon. And you knew immediately that you were in a Western country. There were colours and billboards everywhere. People were smiling and laughing. You saw no soldiers carrying sub-machine guns at waist level. For some ineffable reason, you actually felt free. And, government officials and clerks, and servants of the free enterprise system, actually offered their services—it was their job to help you, and they saw to it that you were made aware of it. What a contrast to the system we had just left; where every official was a sourpuss expecting you to do him a favour; and hand him a bribe; and where they were intent on letting you know that you were not welcomed.

But, give me old Prague any day—even in that socialist era—even the Communists could not extinguish the spirit of old Prague. Prague has, and still retains that untouched, old world charm. Make no mistake; Vienna is breathtaking, somewhat like Venice is, but in a very different way. Whereas Prague was the calm, sedate, jewel-bedecked royal matron of Europe; Vienna was the glitzy, veneered, effervescent and showy courtesan—the pretender. And in Vienna—everything was very, very expensive.

We stayed three nights in a great hotel—the St. StephensPlatz Hotel—right in the centre of the city. We were very fortunate to have Emily's mother with us. It gave us a great amount of freedom to crisscross the city and stay out late at night if we chose to. Staff at the hotel thought we were very well to do—after all, we carried our private nanny about with us.

Our first full day we spent all together, taking in the mandatory tourist tours of this marvelous city, and its historical venues. Late in the afternoon, as we were making our way back to St. StephensPlatz in a horse-drawn Caleche, Emily asked the driver, "Where do you and the Viennese people go for supper?" He appreciated the question, and he was more than happy to show us; he turned a corner and went up a side street, and he pointed to a nondescript basement restaurant, which he said served the best goulash soup in the whole world. He proudly hopped out of the Caleche and proceeded to open the carriage door for Emily and her mom—and my mother-in-law picked that time to thank him—she unceremoniously stepped right onto his instep by accident, and the poor man winced and hobbled on one foot for some time. I felt compelled to give him a handsome tip. And he was certainly right about the delicious homemade food of the establishment.

We went there that night for supper—and then every night until our departure. You walked down a damp stone stairway, at the bottom of which you were met and escorted to a table. The restaurant, the food, even the staff—all was rustic; comfortable; unpretentious and friendly. The food was great and the atmosphere enchanting. Our children, Christine and Christopher, and even my mother-in-law thought they were in some Austrian Disney World. Halfway through the meal, a group of local gypsy violinists and their female singing ensemble came out, making beautiful music as they moved from table to table, the melancholy strains lagging behind them, well after they had left the scene.

On our last night, we left the children with Emily's mom and we went out on the town. Coming out of a bar around closing time, we jumped on a streetcar just to see the city night lights and the people, as it meandered through the city. We were on an adventure. After a while, we noticed that more people were exiting than were coming onto the tram; and the streets were getting darker and the houses farther spaced apart; and, in fact, we were moving to the outer edges of this large city. The streetcar conductor slowed to a stop, came into our compartment somewhat agitated, waving his arms frantically and shouting in an imperious voice, "Finito! Finito!", and he was making the universal sign language for sleep—pressing together the palms of his hands and resting his head, overtop of them.

He was telling us that this car was going no further—in fact, he was going home to sleep. He had reached the end of his line for his shift, and he was telling us—foolish Italian couple that we were—to get off his street car so he could lock up.

When we stepped out it had started to rain a soft, gentle rain. I found it romantic, it reminded me of Vermillion Lake in the canoe, but Emily found it anything but. She was scared. It was dark, rainy, and very few houses with lights on around us. By chance, a taxi had come to deposit a fare across from where we were. We hailed it and got to the hotel room where we found the kids—and the nanny—fast asleep.

We returned to Sudbury tired from a long trip, but also refreshed and invigorated—our lives enriched by the experiences we had gone through. The best sociology class and a complete study of the humanities; is that one achieved in the broad classroom spread out for you, within the travels to other countries.

Looking for New Living Quarters

We slowly began to look for the privacy of a single-family dwelling. Our children made some good friends on Eyre Street. Christine was attending grade one at St. Albert elementary school, just up the street, and she spent that whole summer playing house with Barbie

Zuppan; who lived at the corner of Eyre and Douglas Streets. And both, Christine and Christopher made friends with the Ballance children who lived two houses from us.

A Family with Problems— Children with Problems

The Ballance family rented a small, cramped apartment, in which they squeezed four children and two adults. Mr. Ballance worked at Inco and spent all of his spare time building a wooden structure at the back of his pickup truck. He called it his "camper", and he meant to go travelling the country on his holidays; him and his wife in the front cab, and the kids sprawled at the back in the "camper". It was incomprehensible to me how all six would manage to sleep through the cold nights in the made-shift camper. He was a migrant worker come to work for Inco in the hiring spree of 1967.

    The three boys and their little sister spent most of their summer outdoor playtime in our backyard that year. Most times they looked wild, unwanted and unkempt. One late afternoon, Carl, the eldest, kept on hanging around the backyard, not wanting to go home when the younger ones had already made their way to the house for supper. I went outside and told Carl that he should be home. But he was reluctant to move from the playthings and the sandbox, and then he turned his big sad eyes to me and said, "Mr. Vincent, my dad doesn't like me." I wasn't sure if I had heard correctly, and I asked him, "What do you mean?" and, with that doleful and sad look on his face, he replied, "When my dad doesn't like us, he throws knives at our mom, and he was throwing knives at our mom again when we left the house and came here." I took him in for something to eat from our own table.

    And that night before bed, I hugged my children again.

    I could never understand how we allow people to marry, who do not love children. These are people who put themselves first and their family, second. They should be castrated. And this selfishness goes right across the income spectrum. I knew a young lady whose father was a doctor, and her mother a practicing professional and polite society standard bearer—the vice-chair of that year's United Way campaign. One evening, as I was leaving the downtown Holiday Inn, after some function, I saw this same teenager panhandling outside the hotel. She probably recognized me, and it gave me the incentive to approach her. I went up to her and I asked, "Do you want a ride home?" "No, thank you," she replied, "I have a house, but I don't have a home to go to." And this was not rehearsed—this was straight from her heart. I had difficulty finding sleep that night. Her face and her response haunted me for some time.

Until people start to realize that in life, it's not what you say that counts, or how much money you make, or do not make; it's what you do that matters, and only until then; will we begin to resolve personal and family problems.

The West End: Haig Street

CHAPTER 27

The New House—the So-Called "Jewish Synagogue"

Our house on Eyre Street was paid-off; our family was growing, and we were cramped for living space. The kids shared one bedroom and they occupied bunk-beds—Christine was now seven, and Christopher was four years of age—we were in need of more room. And the time was right—we were mortgage free, and we were saving money. We spent the winter and spring of 1976, looking for a house. A private house, without tenants living within a few feet of us. Without hearing people's voices talking through the walls, or stomping the floors with their feet overhead.

We found a house we liked; on Haig Street—or, as I would tell our friends—the Caruso Club Street—then everyone would know its location. The house was two blocks away from Emily's parents, still in the West end of town, basically the same neighbourhood as that which we enjoyed on Eyre Street. It was an ideal location for us; close to Emily's parents, and the free, and the best childcare service that came with this close proximity to them. St. Cecilia Catholic elementary school was at the west end of the street, and well within safe walking distance for the kids; Our Lady of Perpetual Help parish church next to the school; the Byng Street municipal playground, (where Emily had asked for my diaries eight years earlier), was next to the school; and we loved the Italian flavour of the area—in short: everything conspired to make it a great place to raise the children.

The house at 515 Haig Street was less than a year old in construction. It had been put on the market as a "private" sale—there were no real estate signs stuck on the lawn outside. Renzo was a proud man and he had not wanted his Italian friends in the neighbourhood to know that he was selling.

Renzo Zuliani was a reputable house builder. He had demolished an old structure right down to its foundation and rebuilt a brand new house. That newly-built house was originally meant to be his own private residence. However, his life was being upset at the time with marital difficulties—his wife was leaving him and she was going back to England; and therefore, Renzo had decided to sell, and remove himself back to Italy.

We bought it; conditionally: that he build a fireplace in the family room and a library in the den—which he did. We bought the house for fifty-eight thousand dollars, with the Royal Bank holding the first mortgage. The monthly mortgage payment was three-hundred and seventy-eight dollars (principal, interest, and taxes); our monthly rental revenue being generated from Eyre Street, was one thousand dollars a month. In effect, Eyre Street paid for our mortgage, utilities, and maintenance. We banked the excess in our savings account; with which we topped-up our annual RRSP contributions.

Everyone was happy with the new house—except my in-laws. They were not overjoyed with the ultra-modern look of the design and style. The house had been architecturally designed for a purpose—Renzo's wife was an artist—she had had a lot to say about how the house was to look. But my in-laws couldn't care less about architectural design and style—they called our new house, the "Jewish Synagogue". However; what was important was that Emily and I liked our "synagogue".

The design and style of the house; inside and outside, was quite unique and modern for its time. But there was one obvious misfit; and that was the fact that it was located in an old area of the city—this was a house, whose modern design should have placed it amongst Lakeshore properties, or at the very least, in a newly built subdivision.

But we loved the house and the unpretentiousness of the Italian neighbourhood—where we, and our children, made very good friends. The Caruso club was at the east end of the street, and the Byng Street playground at the foot of the hill; at its west end. Our new place was halfway up the Haig Street hill. It gave us seventeen hundred square feet of living area; three bedrooms; a fully finished basement where my den was located; and an upper loft with a sitting area, with bedroom and bathroom. French style pocket-doors separated the entrance vestibule from the dining room, and similar pocket-doors separated the small kitchen from the dining room. The exterior walls were finished with stucco-clad panels and cedar shingles. It had a carport on the left front of the house—no garage. Although the lot was not large, it was reasonably landscaped, with a large Colorado blue spruce standing guard at the front, and a small backyard with a rear patio-deck accessed by sliding doors.

We loved the house, and as promised, we got the children a little dog from the city animal shelter—Blackie—a half poodle and half terrier, little puppy.

For the first year or so, we had both children use the second bedroom on the main floor as their room. Emily and I occupied the other, and we left the loft bedroom and upper area as a guest living space. The two main floor bedrooms had sliding, double-hung "Bolak" windows—those that operate with moving cables and sliding guide mechanisms. And the bottom of the windows sat low; very close to ground level.

It did not take Christine and Christopher long to realize that if they opened the windows, and unlocked the screens, they could casually crawl right out of the bedroom, and gallivant outside at their leisure. There were a few evenings following our move when Christine would come to us and put out the alert that; her pajama-clad brother was strolling down the sidewalk, heading to Edna Street—with the little puppy; Blackie, happily galloping behind him.

Andy: the Self Made Man

Emily's brother, Andy, and his family had moved to Mississauga the year of our move to Haig Street.

Andy had opened his own retail paint and wallpaper store business on Barrydowne Road. He had previously managed the store of a large paint and wallpaper Canadian distributor, "ToneCraft Ltd"; that store operated under the trademark name of "ToneCraft-The World of Colour". Well, Andy decided to leave the management of ToneCraft's store and strike it on his own. He would open up his own competitive business in the paint and wallpaper retail trade—a few hundred feet away from his former employer, now become competitor—under the ingeniously creative name of, "The House of Colour"—and in no time, he was served with legal papers; threatening lawsuits for trademark infringements, and breach of employment termination contractual agreements. Andy was unceremoniously forced out of business. He could not take on the big multi-national corporation. The family moved to Mississauga, where Andy remained self-employed, developing and marketing a variety of tools and applications for the paint and wallpaper trade.

He was an unusual person. He was a character right out of Dickens. There was a lot of Wilkins Micawber—from David Copperfield—in Andy. Always in debt, yet recklessly cheery and self-important, feckless and a man who loved the sound of his own voice. And like Micawber; Andy was relentlessly optimistic, and he fairly well adopted the Micawberian principle that "Something was bound to turn up".

He was big, he was tall; and he was loud—and he made it a point to be the centre of attraction. He weighed-in at two-hundred and eighty plus pounds; he stood six feet four inches at a minimum, and he had a crushing handshake—which he loved to exercise in the company of men—while flashing a big grin on his face—whenever an occasion called for a shake of the hand. He was dark brown haired, with brown eyes and a sallow complexion. And he wore his father's gentle smile as a constant fixture on his face.

Deep down; he was a gentle giant dressed up in a big show of hustle-and-bustle. And he was Emily's favourite brother. He loved her and he was very protective of her interests; I never saw them angry at each other; she could get him frustrated and exasperated at times—but never angry.

He was a self-made man. He was bright, and he had great business drive—and just like Mr. Micawber—Andy was always looking for that next great financial bonanza—just around the perennial corner.

He would tell me often that he would be a millionaire before a reached his fortieth birthday. He loved ideas; practical, money-making ideas. He would spend nights thinking of some product to invent, or improve; if already in existence. He was charismatic and very gregarious; the sort of person that would dominate a room, or a floor hosting any event—his size and loud voice could not fail to draw attention. I never took offence when he would talk about bureaucrats in a disparaging way—he saw us as totally unproductive, and a net cost burden on the economy. He was partially correct in his assessment, but I would always remind him that bureaucrats were a necessary evil, contributing to the smooth functioning of government—particularly, in the transition years. I would ask him, "Would you want the fate of your business in the hands of politicians and the vagaries of influence? Or, in the hands of law-and-rule abiding bureaucrats?" Then he would laugh, and exclaim, "You answer just like a bureaucrat!"

Andy had two passions in his life; his children, and speculating on the stock market. The former brought him great joy; the latter brought him nothing but grief and eventual marital difficulties.

He was typical of self-made men—he was in terrible need of recognition. He wanted so badly to make a mark for himself in the world—to be looked up to by his better-educated friends.

I very much enjoyed Andy's company. Not only was he fun to be with, but he could tell great life stories—and he had a bag full of them! He was honest, seldom rude and he never swore; and the fact that he wore his feelings and emotions on the cuff of his sleeves, did not bother me—it made him that much more real, and endearing. And like a true Slovak, he enjoyed his beer and his whiskey. Once I had him introduced to the great fishing in northwestern Quebec, he became an annual August fixture around the fishing camps at Lac Simard. He and his family became participants in our big, annual fishing get together on our favourite lake; a few miles from Belleterre. And there; sitting by the campfire, he would let go with his stories—true stories, of funny things that had happened to him over the course of his hectic life, set in different and colourful settings and on a variety of stages—but he was always the main protagonist—front and centre.

Milan Visits Canada

A few months after Andy's move to Mississauga, cousin Milan from Slovakia was sponsored to a two-week visit to Canada. The trip was fully paid for by my in-laws; they paid for Milan's airfare and they gave him some spending money. Most of his stay in the country was spent with Andy, in southern Ontario. The visit did not wear well on Andy—his wife had not expected that they would be the primary hosts. And she did not like Milan from the day she met him. From the very outset, Inge did not take to Milan. She thought he was a user and a manipulator; he had come into the country with a shopping list of things he wanted Andy—and by default—his relatives—to buy and pay for. Eastern Europeans still had the impression that North American streets were paved with gold, and that everyone here was extremely well-to-do. For starter, he wanted Andy to buy him a brand new Gibson electric guitar (Milan was a musician). That did not sit well with Inge, nor, with Andy, for that matter. There was a whole list of other things—some he got, and some he did not.

Thankfully, Milan only spent a few days in Sudbury; chauffeured around by a tired-looking Andy. Most of his time was spent with Andy and John, between Mississauga and St. Catherines where John lived.

Andy was not saddened to see his guest leave, and for that matter, neither was Milan. I don't think he was overjoyed with his first taste of a free and open democratic society—in Slovakia, he was a big-shot; whereas here, he would have been a very small fish in a very big pond. After his shopping list was crossed out, and his luggage full of North American made goods, he departed; back on his way to Slovakia.

A month or so later, I was to meet Andy over someone's birthday occasion, and I took the opportunity to enquire about Milan. Over a cold beer, I asked him, "Have you heard back from Milan yet?" He burst out laughing, and after looking round to make sure that his wife or kids were not within hearing range, he said, "Well, I just got a letter from him," and almost unable to contain his big, wide grin, he continued, "and boy, is he ever pissed off at me. Seems like that money I spent on his going away present—that which came personally from me—got him into an awful lot of trouble with the Slovak border security people." Of course, I had to ask him the obvious; what "personal" presents was he talking about, that had caused so much trouble? We had all bought Milan something to bring back to the old country with him; for himself, or relatives back there.

"Well," Andy continued, winking and smirking his way into the plot, "he asked me for things he could easily sell to his buddies back home, and make a lot of korunas in the process—a babushka-like gambit," and he had to stop the narrative, he couldn't restrain his laughter. Finally, he picked up where he had left off, "So, I drove to Buffalo the week he was due to leave, and came back across the border with an arm-full of porno VHS cassette tapes—the newest thing on the market—all varieties, all "genres"—as the sophisticates would say—and I told Milan that 'These will sell like hot cakes'".

The letter went on to explain how Andy's "personal gifts" almost landed him in a communist jail.

His baggage was stopped at the Slovak Customs and thoroughly searched, as incoming luggage usually would be—everybody and his grandmother who has been out on a visit to a capitalist country, bring something in from outside. The pornographic tapes, although well hidden amongst clothes, were discovered. But as the fortunes of the time would have it, the two young male customs officers were more interested in discretely impounding the porno tapes, than in putting a poor school teacher—a comrade—in jail. And they stood to make a small personal fortune in the bargain. The hot contraband goods were removed; along with other confiscated items, and added to their personal collection—the well-known and widely practiced socialist "bonus" system of remuneration—otherwise known, as graft and corruption. And they let an anxious and sweaty Milan, walk away peacefully.

More about the Hatala Brothers

As mentioned previously, Emily came from a family of four children, and she was the only girl born to Mr. and Mrs. Hatala. Her brother John was the eldest; then followed Paul, and then Andy.

John lived in St. Catherines, where he and his wife owned and operated a retail furniture store—and where we got all our furniture, wholesale when Emily and I got married. All four children were quite different from each other, in temperament, and general outlook on life. John was more like his father in many ways; he was quiet, conservative, gentle and soft-spoken. He had the perfect temperament with which to raise four girls.

Andy was the boisterous risk taker; and Paul, the pompous and arrogant little man with an overriding Napoleon personality defect.

Paul was another character of Dickensian proportions. He was the walking; breathing; a caricature of a man. He was highly intelligent but had not completed high school through sheer laziness. He was corpulent and of short stature (which his mother attributed to the fact that, when a child, he had fallen and bitten his tongue).

Paul had suffered an accident at work—he had frozen both feet while out on a winter survey assignment with the Ontario Ministry of Highways—all of his frozen toes, from both feet, had had to be amputated. He recovered well, but he walked about, ambling with a duck-like gait. He eventually went back to work with the Ministry and remained with them until retirement age. He handled his handicap very well. With the help of specially made shoe prosthesis, he did everything an able and fully-footed person would do; with the exception of running—and oddly enough; he had been, and remained, a very good dancer.

But Paul's downfall was his overarching brash and arrogant personality. It was a compensatory set of behaviour brought about to a large extent, by his physical handicaps. Paul was intellectually bright, but unfortunately, very lazy. If it needed effort behind it, Paul would shy away.

Alone with me; Paul was mild and even-tempered—a friend, and a gentleman. However, with his friends and a group of his peers present, he became a different person; it seemed to me that because of his small stature, he had to find ways to bolster his ego—and he would swagger; become boastful; arrogant and argumentative. Paul very much wanted to blend in with his Anglophone community of friends; and to such an extent, that he actually distanced himself from the acknowledgment of his Slovak and eastern European heritage—he saw his cultural roots as an embarrassment—if not to be denied; at least, not to be advertised openly. He made no effort, like Emily, Andy and John did; to learn the spoken dialect. And when he was offered an opportunity to travel to the Old country with the family, in 1962, he passed on it, and stayed back, alone at home.

I would humour him and let him have the floor when he wanted to deliberate and expand on anything—even when I knew that he was wrong—and then he was in his element. But Emily was not so magnanimous; whenever she realized that he was wrong or putting-on-the-dog, or belittling someone—she would not let him get away with it. So the two clashed quite often. Emily would not stand for his know-it-all pompousness—and at times the animosities became very public and heated—to the point where Emily got to dislike him with a passion; which for me, made my social interactions with Paul, at times difficult and embarrassing.

And Andy's feelings toward his older brother Paul, pretty well mirrored Emily's. Andy and Emily simply would not tolerate his arrogance and hogwash. It was unfortunate that Andy and Emily fell so often into Paul's trap. I saw Paul for what he was—a weak and insecure person—trying to project an image of himself that was as shallow, as the fishing reefs on Lac Simard. Yet, they fell for it all the time.

Paul and his family also became a month of August regulars at Lac Simard.

And Paul had habits which he found difficult to drop: he could not pass a sale, a bargain, a swap, or a garage sale—and he loved his ten to fifteen cans of diet coke per day, and his cherry-flavoured cigarillos.

He was swarthy; rotund and short; and he sported a full, bushy moustache. And when he pushed a cigarillo in between his moustache and lower lip and pitched his straw hat over his head; picked up his fishing rod and gingerly boarded my boat—I couldn't help but laugh out loud—he was the perfect picture of a short and fat Mexican. And he loved fishing, and like his brothers Andy and John, who also loved fishing, he was not good at it. But we all had a great time together in the boat nevertheless.

Paul had two girls, and they became two fine young ladies. He was to divorce the mother of his two girls when the girls were teenagers. His first wife had left him to begin a lesbian relationship; a relationship which proved sound and of a long duration. Paul managed to retain custody of the girls. In a series of sad developments, Paul's two girls proved to have been the unfortunate recipients of the collateral damage emanating from the marital breakup.

Paul remarried a few years after his divorce. He married Patricia; a widow who already had four dependent children—all teenagers—with her. It made for extremely difficult times—in terms of assimilation and accommodation. Paul, from the very beginning, would attempt to assert his authority over Pat's children. His intolerant and dictatorial manners were not well received by the step-children. And from the outset; friction arose. And it made for extremely difficult relationships between the new parents. The environment became so unbearable, that slowly, some children began to leave the newly-formed household.

Paul and Pat had accumulated some property—an apartment building on Whittaker Street; a lakeside cottage, and their private home in Walden. Paul died at the relatively young age of sixty-one, and by that time his relationship with both, Andy and Emily, had been mended.

Emily asked him in private; and specifically, if his financial affairs were in order—and, were her two nieces—his daughters; Lisa and Laura—appropriately looked after in his will? He told her on his deathbed, not to worry—his girls were looked after he had said. He said Pat would see to it that they receive an equitable share. Well, it came to pass that the girls were not appropriately looked after.

For a man who boasted about his knowledge of the ways of the world, he showed himself pretty silly, and a trusting fool. He had not requested an impartial and professional evaluation of his net wealth, nor made any specific provisions for his girls. He had left their compensation at the sole discretion of Pat, their stepmother; to be doled out by her—as she saw fit—and in amounts to be determined by her! And so it happened that the girls got jilted. They got very little from their father's estate. Paul was a foolish man in life; and a foolish man in death.

New Office: New Hospital: Community Involvement

In 1977, my office had new quarters, on the third floor—the West Tower—at 200 Brady Street; the newly constructed City Hall building. My office was perched atop Brady Street, right opposite Golden Grain Bakery. Unsolicited by me, my office was a corner office—anyone familiar with the bureaucratic pecking order; having a corner office is a big thing—a bureaucrat's status symbol. It was at the south end of the floor, and somewhat far removed from the noisy hurly-burly of the reception area. Not only was it a quiet area of the floor, but I was strategically located, surrounded by my field staff. By this time we had an addition to the supervisory staff numbers. Due to an increasing staff complement, we had hired a new field supervisor, Jean McTaggart. Jean's office was located at the northwest end of the floor.

Also that same year, Emily transferred to the new hospital on Ramsey Lake Road—Laurentian Hospital. She was an Ambulatory Care nurse for a few years and then she moved on to the Recovery Room—where she worked until retirement, in 2004.

I started to get more involved with community agencies. I accepted the invitation to sit on various boards of directors as a representative of municipal social services. In this way, I became a member, and treasurer of the Sudbury Community Service Centre, which had Penny Early-Tough as its executive director. The Centre's main focus was on credit counselling and advocating for debt repayment negotiation and consolidation. I appreciated the agency's mandate very much since it benefitted people in poverty; and by extension, my clients particularly. I headed a committee to draft the agency's first constitution, which was adopted by the membership at its next Annual General Meeting.

And I got involved with the Byng Street community Playground Association. My involvement was based on two main reasons; firstly, I was a parent with two young children who, I believed strongly, should enjoy the outdoors and play outside with their friends as much as possible; and secondly, I believed I had a duty to make those opportunities happen if I could. I had enjoyed the outdoors without the burden of stifling parental oversight, or guidance, for that matter—but living in a large city was not the same as living in the backwoods of Belleterre. Kids in big cities need shepherding. And I have always felt that I should be part of the solution, and not become part of the problem.

CHAPTER 28

The Byng Street Playground Association

So I went and attended my first Playground Association meeting, sometime in the fall of 1977—held at the playground clubhouse. And without really realizing what had just happened—I was elected president.

The meeting was mostly attended by women, with but a sprinkling of men. I knew some of those present; the neighbourhood ladies—Mrs. Comba, Mrs. Mariotti, and Mrs. Volpini. Mrs. McGuire, the outgoing president, made it quite clear that the playground's fate was in trouble. It had problems with numbers and the city was targeting it for closure. That kind of future was becoming the fate of many of the city's playgrounds. Organized sports teams were on the decline, and parent volunteers were not answering the call for help. I noticed a few young people in attendance—one of which was Walter Michelutti. Walter was still in high school, but he later became a driving force in getting the teenagers of the neighbourhood to join the playground hockey teams, and to help with the daily work needed to keep the playground a viable resource for the children of this area of the west end.

No one present wanted to see the playground close, yet when it came time to nominate and elect a new executive board; few volunteers came forward. I put my hand up and volunteered, and then followed Mrs. Comba; and then Mrs. Volpini; and a few other interested parents—those with young children. Everyone present, including the teenagers, pledged to help, with the raising of the rink boards; flooding the rink; scraping off the snow, and generally give a hand in the day to day maintenance of the rink, and the clubhouse.

Our Executive Board

Once elected to the board, I found myself acclaimed as the new incoming president. Cathy Comba would become our treasurer; Mrs. Mariotti; our secretary, and Al Sizer (who would one day become a city Alderman), was appointed as our sports director. And Mrs. Volpini would be our clubhouse manager; which meant managing the canteen and the smooth functioning of the clubhouse—including discipline and enforcing rules (this was a paid employee position, funded by the city's Park and Recreation Department). The incumbent paid into the Employment Insurance scheme and therefore, collected unemployment insurance over the spring and summer months.

The Playground "Do-It-All-Man": Not a Paid Position

When I went home that night my in-laws were at the house. I informed everyone—with a smile on my face—that I was now a President—of a playground. My in-laws thought that this was a paying job and asked how much my weekly salary would be. My wife thought this meant attending a meeting or two per month over the winter season—little did she realize the title of "president" was honorific only. What I really was, in fact; was head-maintenance man; head snow shovel-man; and midnight flooding and ice-making man. I also became the discipline and rules arbitrator. And I was to become the first person kids and adults came to; to adjudicate disputes and grievances. And I became the late night contact person, and recipient of neighbours' complaints; when they felt that there was too much noise coming from the shrill and happy screams of the children, having a late night game of shinny. So much for the glamour and prestige of being a playground "president".

Dad "Owns" Byng Playground

But, our children were elated. They were putting a totally different spin, and interpretation, to their father's position as "president". They went to school the next day—a school at a stone's throw's distance from the playground—proudly boasting to all their classmates—that overnight—their father had now become the "owner" of Byng playground.

Instantly, they became the much sought after "stars" of the whole student body. They enjoyed their new found status for a few days; but by Friday; Danny Zuliani had asked Mrs. "Willie" Gregorini if, "Mr. Vincent really owned the whole playground?"—the teachers quickly put the ownership of the playground back into the community's hands.

The Winter Carnival and Nick Dellelce to the Rescue

The Playground Association's first meeting was an important one. We needed a new snow blower; and for that purpose, our treasurer, Cathy Comba, who worked at the Bank of Nova Scotia on Durham Street, secured the playground a loan sufficient to purchase the machine—which we promptly did. The loan would be repaid with the profits from the canteen, and various fundraising events held throughout the years—the most important of which was the annual winter carnival. We raised a lot of money for the playground through our annual "Winter Carnival"—a weekend fundraising event, held in late January, or early February—filled with food; hockey tournaments; and fun activities for kids of all ages. The neighbourhood ladies baked and donated all kinds of hot food; which they then sold from the clubhouse, all weekend long.

Al Sizer, and Emily and I, met one afternoon in our living room, planning our first carnival. We came up with all kinds of fun things for children enjoy—then Emily suggested to Al, that we should rent out ponies from some farm in the Valley, for kids to ride on—for a fee—Al chocked over his coffee, "Emily," he said, "think about it. Where am I going to get those ponies? How am I going to get them to Byng? How am I going to shelter them? And feed them? And," he continued, throwing up his arms in the air, "who is going to clean up all that horse manure?" We all had a good laugh at Al's expense, and Al was much relieved when we went on to other business.

Part of this other business was to go and solicit Nick Dellelce—a big businessman, and a mover and a shaker in town—for assistance in providing us with a trailer, which we would locate next to the clubhouse. We anticipated big crowds and we needed more space.

Nick Dellelce was very good to us—well beyond our expectations. Al and I went to see him at his office on the Kingsway, two weeks before the carnival weekend. We fully expected a rejection—let alone the chance to talk to him. However, as soon as he realized that we were from the west end; he gave us of his time, and of his resources. Within a few days, he had his men tow a big construction trailer to Byng, and they put it right alongside the clubhouse; close to the Hydro pole. They went up and connected to the Hydro line—without authorization from any authority—so that now, we had heat and comfort in the big trailer. And when the carnival was over; Nick quickly removed the trailer. I have always been grateful to Mr. Nick Dellelce. Mr. Dellelce was a benefactor and a good friend of the west end.

Gambling and Bootlegging—For a Good Cause

That trailer brought the playground a lot of money over the weekend—overnight; it became a moneymaking, gambling and bootlegging joint. Al brought a big "Crown and Anchor" wheel from somewhere, and I brought in bottles of rye whiskey; which we hid in the cupboards. Parents would come in from the cold January winds, holding on to a steaming Styrofoam cup of coffee, as their kids played outside; and for a few dollars, they'd get their "Cafe

Royale" served to them; while they tried their luck at "the wheel'. We were totally unlicensed, and what we were doing was illegal—but Al and I were young and fearless—and we were somewhat emboldened by the fact, that we were not doing this for our gain—we were doing this for the kids and the playground.

With the money raised, we got the sport teams free sweaters and free playground jackets; and we went on to buy an audio system with loudspeakers, to project music to the outside rink, to which singles and couples could skate to; and we had scheduled to repay the loan over a period of four years—we had the snow blower paid-off in two years.

The second order of business at our first meeting was to set-up an action agenda for our Sports Director. Al Sizer was given a free hand to organize as many sports teams as he saw fit, and to contact interested volunteers willing to take over those teams; as coaches and managers.

The third order of business was to advertise and convince the west-end families that Byng Street playground was alive and well, and most importantly; parents were being solicited to register their children for activities being offered over the coming winter. Muriel Mariotti contacted both, St. Clements church, and Our Lady of Perpetual Help; and had our efforts advertised at the pulpit, and through church bulletins. And I had handwritten information notices photocopied at my office, and I delivered the bundles personally, to our neighbourhood public and separate elementary schools.

Byng Street Wants Mrs. Volpini

The last order of business, was to appoint Mrs. Volpini, clubhouse and canteen manager—the canteen and clubhouse manager ordered supplies to put up for sale in the canteen; kept the clubhouse tidy and clean, and enforced rules and discipline.

The appointment of Mrs. Volpini proved a more difficult undertaking than I had thought it would be. This was an hourly-paid, casual, City of Sudbury Parks and Recreation position. The Playground Association could recommend an individual, but we could not hire the person outright—that decision was made by "Parks". To further compound the problem of getting Mrs. Volpini appointed to a job she had been doing now for a few years, was the fact that some coterminous playgrounds had closed recently; whose clubhouse managers had more service seniority than our Mrs. Volpini. But I was adamant, I wanted Mrs. Volpini. And I knew that those casual seasonal jobs were not "union jobs", and furthermore, I knew a few people at Parks and Recreation—and so did Al Sizer.

I called Fran at "Parks", but she was not in to take my call. So I talked to her assistant, and I told her of our board's recommendation of Mrs. Volpini. Before the day was over, Fran called me at my office; two floors up, "Ray," she says, "you cannot have Mrs. Volpini. There are two other persons with much more seniority, who've been bumped out of work because of closures—and they are first on the placement list." I listened patiently, then I said, "Fran, there are no union protocols that need to be followed here; you will not be facing challenges and grievances. The selection should be based on playground-community recommendation—the board wants Mrs. Volpini; the children and parents love her, and I want Mrs. Volpini. And," I continued, "the Volpini's house and backyard, backs right onto the playground. Your other folks would have to travel some distance, whereas she can yell at the kids from her kitchen window."

Mrs. Volpini was confirmed as hired the next week. Every time I would step out of the cold and walk into the clubhouse, she would stop whatever she was doing; and with her ruddy face shining a big smile at me, she would exclaim, "Hi, there chief! You want-a-cuppa coffee?"

The Good Young Men of the West End

I had never met, and I have not since met; such a nice, mature and helpful group of young men, as those young men who lived at home with their mothers and fathers, in my new neighbourhood in the west end.

Walter Michelutti, Mark Trevisiol, Fred Narduzzi, John Rumball, Forest Fraser, Earl Fraser, Frank Stradiotto, Sandro Zuliani,

Curtiss Webber, Gary Trebb, Bob Brooks, Tony Sanchioni, Dave Nicholson and Carlo Cardamone—they, amongst many others, were great young men to be around; who rallied around me and Al Sizer, at the time of our Byng playground days (1977-1982). They helped around the rink and the clubhouse—and most importantly—they made up the core of two consecutive City Midget "A" Championship teams. They were fine young men. They were good hockey players and good representative ambassadors for the west end of town. Their parents ought to have been proud of them—I certainly was.

Walter Michelutti and Carlo Cardamone

Two young gentlemen, in particular, ought to be singled out. Walter Michelutti, was the midget team coach, and he was behind the team bench for both championship years. Walter was mature, well beyond his years; a student at St. Charles College at the time; he was seventeen or eighteen when he took over the midget team. Walter was a fiery competitor, a good coach, and motivator, and he had the respect of the entire team. He was a great young man, with a solid character, and he amazed me with what he could do—and he amazed me with the level of maturity he displayed at all times.

The other young man whose actions were exemplary was Carlo Cardamone. My esteem and love for Carlo grew from the first day he made his appearance at the rink. Truth be told—everyone I knew, who knew Carlo; loved him.

The first time I met Carlo was in my first year as president. It was a Saturday in early December when we were getting the first frosts and setting up the first floods. This giant of a teenager, with a big bushy afro-like crop of hair on his head, walks into the clubhouse, and he makes his way directly to me, and he says; in a voice much too soft for his size; "Hello, are you Mr. Vincent?" I acknowledged the greeting and the enquiry; I said I was Ray Vincent. "Mr. Vincent," he said, "what can I do to help? Give me any job, I'll be more than happy to help out." I was dumbfounded—that attitude from a kid of about sixteen years of age—and although he had the body of a twenty-year-old—it was an amazing thing to hear. And my heart was filled with joy, just looking at him. "Well," I said—I still did not know his name—"open the back door, and take the T-bar out, and unwind the water hose and pull it right up to the rink gate." And he went into it with alacrity; pulling at the heavy gauge rubber hose.

I looked at him awhile through the side window, and I turned to Mrs. Volpini, and asked, "Who was that?" She propped her elbows on the canteen counter and resting her chin in her open palms, she said, "That's Carlo—Carlo Cardamone."

Carlo was that unusual kind of person, who did not wait for you to ask for help—he anticipated you—he knew the work that had to be done, and he was the first one to come forward and volunteer—and all this coming from such a young person, never failed to amaze me.

To you; Walter Michelutti, and to you Carlo Cardamone, my bow, and the tip my hat.

It made my heart feel comfort in the knowledge that we had such fine young people in our midst. I wish I would have gotten to know the parents of all those young people. I'm sure these young adults were a reflection of those hard-working; brave and family oriented parents; whose families were prevalent across the west end at that time. I saw myself in a lot of those young people—after all, my parents were not immigrants, but that was in name only, but as a statement of fact—they certainly were.

The Children Settle In

Our children made good friends in the Haig Street west end area. There were many young families all around us at that time. It is not the same neighbourhood today. The ethnic blend has changed a lot and the younger people have moved to the suburbs, and their parents have gone on to retirement homes. Christine spent many hours playing with Tammy Dubruiel, Laurie Trebb, Anna Melchikilesch,

Trina Tallon, Lisa Verelli, Nadia Sechetto, and of course, many hours with her cousin, Anne Greco, who lived across the street from us.

Christopher developed quick friendships with the Zuliani boys, who lived down the street (particularly David), and David Diapolo; Justin Kusinskis; and the boisterous St. Amand kids from across the street. And we were fortunate to have very good neighbours to the left and to the right of us—Mr., and Mrs. St. Pierre and Mr., and Mrs. Weir. And Jeannie and Gord Ward up the street.

Cousin Joe Kochis Visits Canada

My in-laws thought that since they had invited and funded one brother's trip to Canada, a few years back; they ought to do the same for the older brother, Joe. So, in the summer of 1977, Emily' cousin Joe Kochis arrived from Slovakia for a three week visit. Emily and I were to be his hosts for a week; Emily's parents for another week; and Andy and John in southern Ontario, would pick up his last week.

We met him at the Toronto airport. We could pick out his flushed, smiling face amongst the hordes of travellers walking through customs. He recognized us and waved.

We travelled back to Sudbury immediately after loading the car with his luggage. He couldn't stop from smiling and exclaiming at the congested traffic; at all those silver specks flashing under the setting sun as we came out of the airport exits; travelling the 401 and 400 highways.

He was amazed at the never-ending series of lakes, on either side of highway 69, heading north to Sudbury. He was an engineer and he was intrigued by the mechanical concept of the "automatic" transmission driven engine, and the missing pedal on the floorboard—the clutch.

After two days in Sudbury to spend some time with Mr. and Mrs. Hatala; we packed the car and took him on the road—first, to Ottawa, then Montreal, and then up from Kingston to St. Catherines, to see John, and thence to Mississauga to meet Andy.

THE CHRONICLES OF A JOURNEY

A Slovak Not Impressed with the Pace of the Game of Baseball

In Montreal, we went to the Big O, to watch the Montreal Expos play a baseball game against the New York Mets. After quietly studying the game for three or four innings; Joe leaned over to Emily, and said something in Slovak and the expression on his face was serious and somewhat depressed—but Emily chuckled at what she'd just heard him say. So, of course, I was curious to hear what he had said that was so funny; she said Joe had just told her that, "This American game called 'baseball', would never catch on in Europe—it's just too damned slow—and boring!"

Of the two brothers; Joe was much more relaxed, and he was grateful for the hospitality shown him. He was easy going and very good company, and unlike Milan, he did not produce a shopping list of preferred and expected gifts from his hosts.

Emily and I were to see him again; that time in Slovakia, a few years after my retirement; when we rented a car—an 'automatic'—and travelled the country with his lovely niece, Marja; acting as our tour guide. Joe was to die of cancer, a few years after our visit.

Louise moves Across the Street

My sister Louise and her husband Russell moved across the street from us in 1978—the era of double-digit mortgage interest rates. My mother liked Louise's move since she could now visit her two children and her grandchildren; all in one visitation call.

My mother's health was getting worse—she was constantly out of breath—but she put up a good face on it—our mother had never been a complainer. My mother's main irritant was that Russell was not the passionate and ardent gardener that she was. My mother did not believe that a domicile was a family home; unless it had a garden or flowers, behind or around it. She would say to me, "What kind of an Italian is he? He doesn't want to clear any ground for a garden, and he won't so much as raise tomato plants in the backyard." She liked Russell, but I think she liked a well-tended garden even more. And of course, she loved Anne and Lisa. I enjoyed having my sister right across the street from us. We socialized over the weekends and had many a wild card games of poker, or "Rummoli".

And while Christine played with her cousin Anne, I would lift Lisa on my shoulders and we would tour the playground and the neighbourhood streets. After a few years, Russell got a job in the mines in Elliot Lake, and the family moved there in 1984.

CHAPTER 29

Time Has Come to Sell the House on Eyre Street

The apartment building on Eyre Street was becoming somewhat of a burden. Sure, it was bringing a good monthly revenue, but I had to contend with the hassle of running after tenants for rent arrears; the constant demands of repainting and repairs; complaints from one tenant about another tenant—one tenant even broke into his neighbour's apartment and stole valuables—which the aggrieved tenant thought I should be held responsible for—he contended that the door locks were not sufficiently secure.

So, we decided to sell; pay off our mortgage on Haig Street with the proceeds of the sale, and put in the bank what was left over. There was, to be honest, another—if not the overwhelming reason, for my wanting to sell.

The Consequences of Childhood Trauma

It was my morbid fear of debt. It was a phobia that got its roots well implanted by Mr. Riendeau of Belleterre, when I was but a young boy—"Tell your parents that they're charging more on the weekly food account, than the weekly payments they're making on it." Even today, in advanced years, the scene replays frequently; disguised yet still potent; in dreams that hover on the nightmarish.

Carrying a mortgage on the house on Haig Street, became a source of constant anxiety. I had an abhorrence of debt. I saw carrying debt very much akin to losing my freedom—I felt shackled and in somebody else's power. My wife and I were probably the last persons in Sudbury to apply for a credit card—Andy thought there was something wrong with me—and, indeed, there was. The hotel clerks would look askance, when, after having registered, I'd open up my wallet to pay in advance, when everyone paid after the fact; at checkout time.

I knew full well that I was affected by childhood events, but I was powerless to repress the consequences. People around me, I'm sure, thought me extremely stingy, since I would not spend money when we had no scarcity of money available to us to spend. I have always kept my cars until they would begin to deteriorate beyond repair—however, when we bought a new vehicle, it was paid for in cash—no finance company for me!

There were many other consequences that found their origins on the artifacts of life experiences; my father was constantly employed, and then unemployed—work—lay-off—unemployment insurance. An ongoing, repetitive cycle. His last twenty years of work were a series of employment at minimum wage, interspersed with long periods of unemployment—so that, when I secured permanent employment with the City of Sudbury, I vowed not to put my family through the same distress—I worked steadily for thirty-five years; until retirement—while taking only six days off due to illness—otherwise, I was at work.

And I sent our children to English language only elementary, and high schools, because of my early negative classroom experiences—the grade nine English class; when only three months removed from the province of Quebec; without a word of English at my command—I was asked to stand up in the room, and recite a section of Shakespeare's Macbeth.

However, my life may turn out, I will never regret the fact that my adulthood was very much shaped, and conditioned by my childhood. I would never trade in the magic of my childhood experiences.

We find a Buyer—But, He's a Bum!

So the building on Eyre Street found a buyer. With the down payment, we paid off the mortgage on Haig Street.

But the buyer could not come up with the entire sale price of fifty-seven thousand dollars; so we decided to hold the balance in our favour, by holding a second mortgage; which he was to pay at two hundred dollars a month. Richard Pharand was our lawyer, and we put the transaction in his hands.

After a week or so, I get a call at my office from Richard, "Ray," he says, in his gruff voice, "I did some research on this guy—your buyer. Ray, I got to tell you, he has a bad history—this guy's bad news—he's a bum," he put out bluntly over the phone. "What do you want me to do? We don't have to go ahead with this," he advised, "we can back out and move on to someone else." I thought for two seconds, and I said to our lawyer, "No, Richard, let's go ahead with the sale now; I'll take my chances." I was so set and determined to get rid of the building.

And Richard Pharand was found to be absolutely right. The guy turned out to be a bum. And a bum of the worst kind at that. Years after; his wife and children ended up on welfare. And he defaulted many times on his child support payments, then; as he had had a habit of defaulting on my second mortgage payments on numerous occasions.

For the first year, he made his mortgage payments on time; but thereafter, they became erratic. He became unreliable. I would wait one day past the due date, and when the payment did not appear in our account, I would call him. And this became a constant and repetitive battle. One day, when running after a payment, and getting a chance to talk to him, I suggested he remortgage the building and pay off my second mortgage; and put himself in a position to only carry a first. Interest rates had gone down, and he had a good payment history on the first mortgage; so he should be able to convince his Credit Union to remortgage the place. He agreed to follow up on the suggestion.

So one day, shortly after this conversation; Richard calls me again. "Ray," he said, "the bum is ready to settle the second mortgage, but he's got a problem; the Credit Union is coming up five-thousand short on the refinancing—so basically, they're asking; are you willing to take a five grand loss?" By this time, I was so fed-up with the "bum", that I said to Richard, "Yes, let's go ahead. I'll take five thousand off." "Are you sure you don't want to think this over?" he asked. "No, let's go ahead. I want this guy out of my life," I replied.

But, the "bum" hung around, he was not to be out of my life quite yet.

A year later, he calls my house; wanting me to pay half of the cost to replace the basement weeping tiles—he said I was partly liable. I wasn't going to call Richard on this—I told him to fuck-off and I hung up on him. I never heard from him again.

A Good Lawyer

I have nothing but good thing to say about Richard Pharand—he was a Flour Mill boy and he came from working-class parents. Richard was very good to the average French Canadian working man in the community—so was then-lawyer Randy Lalande; who is now a judge—and he is well respected by the trade union movement. And he was an excellent lawyer. Richard did not have the free-flowing eloquence of an Elmer Sopha, but Richard's style was clear and direct. He got to the issue, and he cut through the peripheral noise and nonsense; like a skilled surgeon would with his scalpel.

My first contact with Richard Pharand came this way: I was serving on jury duty one day—well before he started acting for us on our sale of Eyre Street—and the case involved his defence of two men—miners—accused of buying a snowmobile with the knowledge that it was a stolen item. I was immediately impressed with his jury panel selection behaviour. He picked and challenged with skill and circumspection—with a keen flair as to each person's societal leanings.

This was one of Pharand's earlier cases in his career. The two guys had met the seller; everyone sitting over a beer at the Nickel Range hotel, and they had bought the snowmobile there and then.

And of course, on the stand, they denied knowing that it had been stolen. I'm sure the jury—like I did—had the guys convicted in quick order.

But then Richard did his concluding summary address to the jury: he said something like this; looking at us individually, and straight in the eyes, he said; "Think about it,"—he did not say, "ladies and gentlemen of the jury"—no, he came right to the point, "think about it," he reiterated, "two guys are having a cold one after a hard day's work at Stobie. They meet someone who wants to sell his snow machine, and the price is not cheap, but they'd split the cost fifty-fifty. There is nothing suspicious here. They are not buying something for a fraction of its market price. They are boyhood friends, and like friends, they'll share the cost and they'll share the enjoyment of the machine over the winter months. Now, I'm asking you to put yourself in their position," he concluded, "isn't that at all possible? Isn't that what friends would do? Doesn't the picture agree with you—two friends over a bottle of beer; meeting with someone and talking about the coming winter and ice-fishing and snowmobiles? Isn't that just possible? Think about it!" he exclaimed; closing with the same statement he had opened with.

And he sat down. He had successfully sown the seed. There was a doubt.

We acquitted the two buddies, because yes; the scenes painted by Richard Pharand were quite possible. But driving home; in my heart of hearts, I knew that the two rascals had always known that they'd been in possession of hot goods. But a good lawyer had got them off.

A Family Vacation to Gaspe

We had bought a new car the previous year; a Chevy Malibu, and we decided to take the family on a vacation to eastern Quebec—to the Gaspésie; see Perce and then stop in Quebec City on the return journey, and take in all the historic sites. First, we stopped in Montreal for two days, and from the hotel lobby, we booked a bus tour of the city and the surrounding historical features.

Ray A. Vincent

A Pervert in the Elevator

On our very first day in Montreal, an incident occurred which upset me, and shook me out of my complacent innocence. This was in the late afternoon; we'd been in for a few hours after checking in, and the family was comfortably settled in our room, on the eighth floor. I had gone to the fifth floor to fill up a bucket of ice cubes; and when the elevator stopped to pick me up on its upward transit, I boarded it and moved to the wall opposite the doors—I sensed immediately that something was not quite right.

There were three passengers present; two teenage girls; and a man in his late thirties or early forties, slender and of delicate stature. The girls were obviously agitated, and they were pressed together alongside the elevator command panel; with panic-struck expressions on their faces. The man stood three feet to my left, with visible beads of perspiration on his forehead.

He was Caucasian; black-haired; and very well dressed in a three-piece suit; he had a crisp, well-trimmed moustache and a goatee covering his chin; he was breathing heavily; his hands were trembling and now and then he would wipe a braid of hair away from his damp forehead. He gave the impression of being an educated professional—a doctor; a professor; an artist—someone along those lines—maybe invited to Montreal to give a lecture—or a performance.

No one spoke. The girls never moved their eyes away from him, they kept them riveted on him at all times. And they did not address me—I wished that they had. The elevator was set to stop on the seventh floor. When the doors spilled open; the girls bolted out, like horses rushing out of a burning barn—wild-eyed with fear. The man followed them out—and, I followed him. The girls now were running, down the left-hand side hallway; he walked in their direction, and I stayed with him, following closely behind, ice cube bucket in hand. The girls had managed to put some distance between themselves and their stalker, and when they reached a certain door; they stopped, and they began to frantically bang on the door, all the while crying out to those inside, "Open the door! Open the door!" The door no sooner opened than the girls slammed it shut behind them. I stopped a few doors from theirs, and I could clearly make out the horror-stricken voices of the girls inside. The man continued walking past the girls' room, and he proceeded to the very end of the hall where he vanished through a set of doors leading to the emergency stairwell.

I took the elevator up to the eight, where I found the kids watching TV. I felt like I had just come out of a dream. I told Emily; "I have just witnessed something strange and scary."

About forty minutes later, while Emily was sorting out the clothes that she wanted the children to wear in the dining room-lounge, and getting them ready for dinner, I went to the bar for a drink; meaning to be back to them shortly—and there, seated not far from me; sipping on a martini; was my man—my well-dressed man—the elevator pervert!

With the exception of the hotel incident, we had what I thought, a very good—although tiring—vacation. We got to see a lot of new scenery of our beautiful country, and we experienced new cultural attitudes and made contact with a lot of history. But once home I was taken aback by the children's assessment—which was quite different from mine—"Please, mom and dad," they said; almost in unison, "next time you want to go on a history trip, you two go ahead—but leave us behind with our grandparents—we have all the history we can handle at school during the school year—we don't need more during summer vacation."

Children in Minor Sports

Our son, at age eight, was probably the fastest skating, hockey-player in his age group. At the very outset, as an Atom age player, he tried out for, and made; the Triple "A" Atom team—the elite "travelling" hockey team of Atom aged players, representing the Sudbury Minor Hockey Association. What he lacked in stick-handling finesse, he more than made up with speed and scoring ability.

I never told my son, "You must play hockey, or, you must play soccer." He would come home from school, and say; "So and so, is playing hockey; or, so and so is playing soccer, and I would like to try out." Then we would take him out to the tryouts. However, I always said, "Do your best." And when I saw he had some talent; I encouraged him.

Good coaches—coaches with their players' best interest at heart are a very rare commodity indeed. Most coaches have but one goal; and that is, to win at all cost. Those kinds of coaches are in minor sports for themselves—for their egos. And they are users of children; the kids are the means to their ends. Christopher was fortunate to have started in minor hockey, and soccer with children-loving and skills-developing coaches—Oscar Boudreau and Herve Tremblay in hockey, and Frank Malvaso, in soccer.

I kept a log book, in which I recorded Christopher's personal achievements and statistics so that he could monitor his progress. I loved the games of hockey and soccer, but I never told my son, "You ought to work on your skills development, so as to become a professional sportsman." I encouraged him to do his best at anything he ever took a liking to, and I knew that he was good at sports—and without a doubt, his being good and recognized with achievements and awards—was flattering to my ego. And sometimes; when I think about it all, I wish it had not been so flattering to my ego. Maybe I did push him after all—and pushed him too hard.

By Midget age, he had lost interest in competitive sports—hockey, and soccer. He switched to the less competitive high school league. And I was perfectly happy with his decision, and he would not play any sports throughout his university years. Not everyone is destined to become a professional athlete. Life has many and much broader playing fields on which to exercise whatever talent God has been gracious enough to bestow on one. Christopher went on to become a school administrator—a high school vice-principal.

Our daughter Christine was a good athlete in her own right. She played in the City Girls Softball league, while in high school and she enjoyed it; even though one year she broke her ankle while sliding in her attempt to steal third base. She went on to play soccer at the University of Windsor.

Andy's Misadventures on Lac Simard

Our August family fishing trip to Lac Simard had become an annual event—and as I write this, we are in our fortieth consecutive year. The lake is close to the village of Moffet and within fifteen miles of Belleterre. Initially, we rented a rustic cabin and a boat and motor from the lodge outfitter. Later, Emily and I purchased our own fishing boat, powered by a good seventy horsepower outboard motor, and an attached trolling motor at the transom. The trip to the fishing camp became the occasion for an annual family get together, from Emily's side of the family—John, Andy, and Paul would converge at the lodge and, along with them later on, their married children and the grandchildren.

And the visit at the fishing camp became a much-anticipated event. We started to talk about it and plan for it, back in early spring. It was a great place to relax and to socialize—and do some good fishing. We shared a lot of good times and stories—led by Andy, of course—around the evening campfire. The ladies would talk about what ladies usually talk about when gathered in a group; and the men would expand on the day's fishing success, and on the latest fishing techniques and theories; some of which were made up on the spot—not to mention, the big ones that got away. And there were always some memorable misadventures to recount and embellish upon if no one had been witness to the event.

The Trolling Motor that went Quiet

Andy had just purchased a new nine horsepower trolling motor. His son, John Paul and my son Christopher, decided to secure the motor to the stern of a canoe and go out on the lake, in front of all the cottages and take it for a spin. A group of cousins; all teenage girls, were paddling their canoes on the quiet lake. The boys, in a burst of bravado, circled the quiet canoes; and proceeded to tighten the circle and create waves and mayhem. The more the girls giggled and screamed; the higher J.P., revved the motor, and the more he tightened the circle.

According to my son, on board with J.P.; suddenly there was complete silence in their canoe—the noise of the screeching engine could not be heard. J.P., still held the bent over position of the helmsman, with his torso thrust forward, arm extended back toward the motor and hand clenched firmly around the tiller control handle—but, when my son looked past, and behind J.P., he noticed that something was missing—the motor mount bolts had become loose on the transom—and the motor was now making its way to the bottom of the lake.

Further Misadventures

One year, Paul brought a big boat to camp—newly purchased—that got swamped with water during bad weather, and sank to the bottom of the lake—fortunately; in only six feet of water—it was still moored to the dock. And on another occasion; Andy blew the piston heads off the inboard-outboard motor he had just recently purchased (a used boat and motor), and he had had to get towed back to camp. Over the campfire that night, he went on at length, blaming the Jew from Oakville who had sold the boat to him—but we all blamed Andy for not putting enough oil in the gasoline mixture.

Now without the use of his big boat, he was forced to rent a seventeen-foot aluminum boat that came with a twenty-five horsepower motor.

A few days later, late in the afternoon; past eight-thirty p.m., at a time when most boaters are getting off the lake and heading to camp; Andy pulled anchor and was making his way back from fishing on the big lake—almost an hour away from the lodge. Within twenty minutes, the motor on his rental unit failed. Andy had John Paul with him, but because they were the last ones to come off the lake and head for camp; they found themselves unable to hail any other boat for help. They drifted helplessly in the wind and waves until darkness came upon them; and when a storm had begun to stir.

When they got close to the southern shoreline, where the shoals and fallen trees made that stretch of shore dangerous to approach; Andy yelled through the wind for J.P., to cast the boat anchor overboard; in order to slow down, and arrest the progress of the boat, and avert a crash against the fallen trees and other obstacles littering the shore.

J.P., swung the anchor and line over his head, around and around, and with a mighty heave, cast the anchor as far away from the boat as he could—and J.P., was a mighty strong boy. The anchor flew through the thick darkness, and the line attached to it followed obediently—but there was a problem—in the darkness of the night, neither had noticed that the opposite end of the heavy gauge nylon line was not secured to the boat.

So the line followed the anchor, whipping the air around it. And Andy and his son heard the dead splash of the anchor as it came crashing through the surface of the lake; and when they reached down to grab the line to pull it taut against the anchor; they discovered to their horror—that there was no line to be found anywhere.

They were in total darkness, and it was now getting close to midnight. They were being slashed and scratched by the wall of fallen tree branches against which the boat slammed.

Back at the lodge; by that time everyone was afraid for their safety; we knew something had happened; that they had most likely met with a mechanical breakdown of some sort. Andy's daughter, Tammy, was very worried about the safety of her father and brother.

Claude Gemme, the lodge owner, called for a quick meeting of all his guests, to inform them all of the state of affairs, and, to call out for volunteers—who would go out into the blackness of the night and attempt to find, and bring back; the lost party?

Two hands sprung up as soon as the request for volunteers was made—two Americans from Cleveland, Ohio—one was a Baptist pastor on vacation with his family, the other; a computer analyst. And without hesitation, they sprung to action. The night had gotten stormy. It was windy, with rain falling now and then, and with absolutely no light; the night was black as ink.

The two had a great amount of experience with the lake—they had been regulars at Lac Simard for many years. And they had a good and steady boat, equipped with an inboard compass system—and they knew the compass readings needed to get them through the river channels on their way to the big lake. They would navigate the nine miles of water, totally by compass and the help of a heavy-duty flood light.

When they finally made their way through "the narrows"—a pass through the connecting lake system, no more than a hundred-and-fifty yards wide, they directed their floodlight to the right, and they saw a faint response—the flicker of a light in the distance—Andy had a small flashlight with him, and it caught the rescuers' attention. They slowly made their way toward the stranded boat; transferred the wet and cold fishermen to their own boat; attached the disabled boat to a towline, and got them safely back to the lodge in the wee hours of the morning.

My admiration for the selflessness, courage, and resourcefulness of Americans, soared that night

And that rough southern shoreline, where the bay received Andy and J.P., became known by every one thereafter, as "Andy's Bay". It is a point of reference, which not only assigns a known location on the lake, but it also conjures up many memories; some of anguish, and some of laughter.

CHAPTER 30

Rose Leaves Her Husband

In July of 1980, Rose made the fateful decision—she bundled her four children, and she left her husband. She made the right decision, but as it happens too often, she took too long in making it. She had given us advance notice of her departure date from Bearn; so we were able to find her an apartment on Whissell Street—in the Flour Mill—the haven for Quebec ex-patriates. A friend of hers whose husband had a truck moved her belongings. Of the four children, two were still in elementary school, and two in high school. The eldest, her daughter Lise, was in high school, and Yvon, the oldest boy, would commence high school in the fall—the French public high school; McDonald Cartier. The two younger boys, Claude and Marcel, would attend a French separate elementary school; a short distance from their house on Whissell.

    I referred an application on her behalf, for general welfare assistance—I duly declared a conflict of interest. I stayed away from involvement in the case adjudication process, and the caseworkers involved did not report to me. The caseworkers and the supervisor involved were not aware that she was related to me. Rose and the children were deemed to qualify immediately for financial assistance. Later; I referred her name to the Mothers' Allowance branch, and she also qualified for that program and she was granted a monthly allowance—Helvi Lundgren was her Community Social Services caseworker. And a good and compassionate social worker, she was.

    Rose's four children faced a set of four difficulties to deal with; the sudden estrangement from a father, which they, naturally, loved;

and, having to adapt quickly to a new community, with no one to depend upon at the outset, than themselves. The children looked sad and lost—they walked about, zombie-like.

I knew very well what they were going through; the road would be difficult indeed. The four looked out of place, and they had problems of adjustment in school; their French was not in synch with the Sudbury spoken French, and even their manners differed from the friends they made. I told them to be patient, things would sort themselves out. They had youth on their side—just like I had had—and they managed, and they survived their first year.

A Reconciliation

However, before the end of the second year; Rosario was in town, pleading for a reconciliation. And Rose; under the pressures of poverty, and the demands of raising four teenagers alone—gave in—she was back in Bearn before the start of the second school winter semester. She had gone through two separations but had never found the strength to go her own way.

More Community Involvement

As Christopher became more involved in minor hockey, I became interested in the inner workings of the minor hockey scene in Sudbury—who led the organization? How were priorities set? What were the priorities? Were programs set up with kids and parents in mind, or was the focus primarily organizational? —So, as I usually do in such circumstances—I got involved.

I attended its annual spring AGM, and I ran for election to the board of directors of the Sudbury Minor Hockey Association (SMHA). I was nominated by Denis Gauthier and Oscar Boudreault—and I got elected on the first ballot. I remained on the SMHA board from 1981 to 1987.

We had a large board, with a full-time, paid executive-director, in Blaine Smith; all other duties were performed by board member volunteers. I was happy to see that the work and efforts of the SMHA were player-focused. What was beyond the control of the board, was parental attitudes and their in-rink behaviour. Sports parents—hockey parents, in particular—do horrible things and their children suffer for it.

I have seen parents with stopwatches in their hand, checking if the NHL bound little darlings were getting the same ice-time as another teammate. I have seen a parent go to the team bench during a game; rip-off the team jersey off of his twelve-year-old son, and fling it in the face of the unsuspecting coach. In my line of work, these parents would have been charged with child abuse. I always considered myself fortunate that my parents never attended any of my sports activities. They had the grace, and the courtesy, to let me be and grow without interference.

Some coaches also bring problems to minor sport—but they are nowhere the egregious problem that parents are. Coaches can be screened and selected, and they must attend certification programs—and they can be removed—whereas parents must be accepted for what they are—and very seldom can they be removed.

For the same reasons that I ran for the board of directors of the SMHA—I wanted to know who did what, and why? —I ran as a trustee on the Sudbury School Board. Our children's elementary school, St. Cecilia, had been identified by Superintendents, as a school slated for closure, and its students to be bussed to other community schools. We went to all the meetings and asked questions, and the answers from board officials were paternalistic and inadequate—so I decided to get involved—I ran in the fall elections—and I got elected to public office.

I always believed that one should be part of the solution—or, at the very least, that one should try to be so. The school still closed as scheduled—but I did eventually get some straight answers from the staff. I served on the board from 1981 to 1986, and then again, from 1998 to 2006. I serve as vice-chair, and as board chairman for three consecutive years, 2001 to 2004. If you believe strongly in something, don't stand by on the sidelines—get involved. The view is much clearer if you are standing in front.

Following the same attitude and philosophy; I accepted the invitation to join, and I became a member of the advisory board of the Canadian Mental Health Association; and I sat on the board for the years, 1987 to 1989. This proved a valuable experience and a resource for me—it made me a better social worker—and it brought direct benefits to my clients.

A Sibling Dies

The year 1982 was a sad year for myself and my siblings, and more so for my parents. After fighting a battle with lung cancer—which had quickly spread to his brain—my wedding's best man—my brother Ivan, died, at age forty-nine. His disease was directly work-related—the first of my other three brothers to die from work-related environmental causes. The mining environment; the toxic gases; the smoke and the dust—all took their toll.

My mother and father were in deep sorrow—the first death of one of their ten children. My mother's health would not permit her to travel all the way to the state of Idaho, where Ivan had worked his last years, and where his wife and children still lived. Colette flew to Idaho and attended the funeral on behalf of the family. I was to learn many years later, that some of his ashes made their way to Mud Lake—where Pete and Colette, and Ivan's wife, Berthe, had them scattered, in accordance with his wish.

A Break-In and I Catch a Thief

In the mid-eighties; Christopher was now in his PeeWee Triple "A" hockey age group—and along with Triple "A" hockey came a lot of out of town tournaments—a lot of winter weekends on the road travelling—and, consequently, a lot of money expenditures.

One particular weekend was coincident with the school March Break, and the team had competed in a tournament held in North Bay. We had returned to Sudbury, late on Sunday afternoon. We were often out of town because of hockey, and being a cautious person, I usually left the outside light turned on; furthermore, I also left some lights turned on inside; and the radio would be left on, with the volume turned higher than normal—all to deter the potential break-and-enter.

On our return home, we found the house warm, welcoming, and safe, as expected. The next morning my son and daughter went to school; I went downtown to my job at city hall, and Emily, at around nine-thirty, went to the kennel in Hanmer to pick up the dog. And when she pulled back in the driveway, at about ten-forty-five, things looked normal enough.

However, when she put the key to the door, everything was anything but normal. The door jamb was split, from ceiling to floor level—without turning the key, or applying any forward pressure, the door swung open of itself. She took a step into the vestibule and she froze—and Blackie stood still by her side and growled. From where she stood, she could see part of the dining room area and part of the dining room floor. A large, open tablecloth laid spread out on the floor, between the dining room hutch and the table; and various things had been placed on it—her Lladro figurine collection, and her Czech fine cut crystal ware amongst other things.

We had a telephone on the wall, next to the vestibule entranceway, and she reached for it to call my office—and, that's when she heard a distinct "click" on the line—as if someone was picking up a telephone receiver in another area of the house—she dropped the phone; picked up the dog; and ran to Mr. and Mrs. St. Pierre—our next door neighbour.

"Ray," she said, with fright in her voice, "come home right away, someone is in the house." Living where we did in the west end, I was home within fifteen minutes. The police were already at the house; detective-sergeant Balloway and detective Bignucollo. And it seemed that, while Emily was at the neighbour making her phone call, the thief had made his escape. In the hurry of the moment;

however, he had left behind him, still on the floor; the sheet loaded with loot.

My den in the basement, where I did some paperwork, and all the bedrooms, were in shambles. Every single dresser drawer had been pulled off its runners, and its contents spilled out, helter-skelter, on the floor and on the beds. Emily was in tears—all her jewellery was gone—some very valuable in terms of money—and some of great personal and sentimental value—her engagement ring; her school of nursing graduation pin; and some family keepsakes, amongst others.

The police took a report, and carefully dusted for fingerprints, but we were told by detective-sergeant Balloway, in a very forthright and honest manner; that they would do their best; but very few of these culprits were ever apprehended; and that the jewellery they stole was quickly exchanged on the street, for money or drugs: the best we could do was to check the pawnshops, and hope for a reasonable settlement with our insurance. Both of which met with disappointment.

Obviously, Emily was very upset by what had happened, and she was also annoyed at me, that I seemed to be taking this in stride. In "stride"; that is, until the evening of the break-in—when I prepared to step out for a walk and realized that my winter jacket, and the matching blue scarf, were missing from the closet. Now, the break-in had become personal—and I was pissed!

The very next Saturday morning, our son had a noon-hour hockey practice at Cambrian arena. We dropped him off, and since we had quite a lot of time to kill, Emily had suggested we go for a coffee and a sandwich at the "Borgia Market" food court; in the City Center Mall. Those were the days of the "busy" downtown; before the merchant exits to the suburbs and the supermalls—and before the takeover of the downtown mall by the Call-Centre industry. The Borgia Market food court was a hopping place, with people constantly coming and going.

She had said, laughingly, "Who knows, we may catch our crooks there." It was a busy time of the day; we picked a table and sat opposite each other.

Halfway through our coffee, I looked at her squarely in the face, and I said, "Don't look around just now, but my jacket just sat down, three tables behind you." And sure enough, a young man sporting a large Afro hairdo had sat down at a table occupied by two young ladies.

"Sure, sure…" Emily said with a smile, "Eaton's has probably sold fifty, maybe hundreds of those jackets in Sudbury alone." And she dismissed me again with her smile; obstinately refusing to look behind her. I bent over to her with emphasis, and whispered, "I'm telling you, Emily; it's my jacket, and he looks like the type that would break into anybody's house."

Now, I have to admit that up until then, I had been pretty calm; but my heart skipped a beat, after what came next. "Holy shit," I whispered in disbelief, "here comes my scarf."

And sure enough, another young man had just stepped off the escalator and was making his way toward the trio behind Emily—proudly wearing my scarf around his neck. This was weird; I felt like I was watching a movie; with these live scenes unfolding before my eyes. I just sat there, watching their animated conversation. I had no idea what to do next—until the fellow with the jacket rose to leave—then, I said to Emily, "I'm going to follow him—you call the police to get here, and pick up the guy with my scarf." And then I got up and followed my man.

Again, I was watching the movie. He went down the escalator—I was right there behind him. He walked through the mall—I followed him at a distance. He stopped to look through a shop window display—I would do the same two shops away. He stepped outside and crossed Elm Street, at the post office—so did I. To my dismay: he boards a Sudbury Transit bus on Lisgar Street; well—so do I, picking a seat way in the back.

We meandered through the west end, Lorne, and then, Gatchell.

He gets off on Irving Street—I get off at the next bus stop, and quickly retrace my course back, till I catch sight of him turning onto Morrison Street. He enters an old grey stone tenement house—I knew the house from my welfare fieldwork days—it had a long, narrow hallway, connecting directly from the front door to the back door. I thought he suspected of being followed, and he was taking the front door, in order to escape through the back. So I entered the building right behind him, in time to see him close the door of room number ten. I stopped in the hallway for a moment and heard voices coming from that room. Quiet, measured voices of two, or three persons. He had no idea he'd been followed.

Not far away from the tenement house, at the corner of Lorne and Clemow Street, was a phone booth—still there to this day. I called the police station, and without giving me time to say much, my friend, detective-sergeant Balloway says, "Your wife called, we have the young guy with the scarf, and he's admitted to everything, and he's also identified the friend who was in on it."

"Well," I said, "I'm calling from Clemow at Lorne, and I know where you can pick up his friend."

The unmarked cruiser picked me up, and we proceeded to the rooming house. In the car, Balloway asks, "Can you make a positive ID on your jacket? We have no search warrant." And he looked less than optimistic. "Easily," I said, "check the contents of either pocket. I'm a regular pipe smoker, and I know there are pipe tobacco strands at the bottom of each."

I remained in the car, and Balloway's partner came out with a grin on his face; he said, "We called the station from inside—they're sending another cruiser—we have our man, but there's another fellow holed up in there who's wanted on a Canada-wide warrant."

It took some time for the case to come to trial. There followed a few more interviews with us at the house. The last interview was memorable. One evening, after supper, about a month or so after the arrests; I was outside, pushing snow off the entrance of our driveway. And without my being aware of it, a car was creeping slowly forward, up Haig Street; it was behind my back, moving forward ever so slowly, hugging the curb: then, this loud-speaker-amplified command booms out of the front hood of the car; startling me and causing heads to pop out of houses in the immediate neighbourhood—"Freeze, double-o-seven!" it screamed, "drop that shovel!"

There, through the windshield, I could clearly make out Balloway and his partner; laughing their heads off.

The case went to court in mid-spring. A conviction was registered, calling for six months of jail time.

As a sad footnote to this story; one of the young men convicted for the break-in—he, with my scarf—was none other than Carl Ballance of Eyre Street days—the young child who had been terrorized by a physically abusive father.

Needless to say, my jacket and scarf were recovered, but practically none of the jewellery. I say "practically" none of the jewellery—for the following reason. Sometime in early June, a client was causing a disturbance in the reception area. His welfare cheque was being held up, and he demanded to speak to a supervisor. So, I had him shown to my office. He was not a happy camper, he came in huffing and puffing with grievances; but from the very first moment he walked in, I purposely barely paid him any attention—my eyes were riveted to his left ear.

I offered him a chair; all the while keeping my eyes glued to his ear. He sat now, quiet and composed, and I still kept looking at his left ear. I even craned my neck slightly forward to get a better look. The young man was by now distracted by my behaviour, and he looked over his left shoulder, expecting a staff person to be standing there behind him; someone he had not heard coming in. Finding no one there, he turned back toward me with a puzzled look on his face.

And then I told him, "That's a beautiful gold, double-looped earring you've got there—my wife would sure like to know where the other one is." And I reached for the phone.

He answered, "Balloway here," and I responded, "Double-o-seven, on duty, sir!"

Speaking to Students and the Chairman of the Board Not Impressed

As part of a good public relations strategy, my office would encourage its supervisors to go out in the community, and speak about our services and the various outreach programs we had available. As the senior supervisor, I was the designated agency spokesperson. I would go out and speak to schools of social work students, at Laurentian University and Cambrian College. I established some good contacts with the academic staff, and I used the opportunity to advertise the work we did and lay the foundations of a recruitment program for the hiring of new, energetic young staff. At every chance I had, I solicited young graduates to join our ranks and apply for employment with our department—in the eighties and the nineties, caseloads were reaching all-time highs, and additional staff was in demand.

On some occasions, we were invited to a high school to speak to a social studies class. The chairman of our welfare board, Sterling Campbell; happened to be a high school teacher at Sudbury Secondary School, and he asked me one day, after a board meeting, if I would address one of his classes and speak about the social problems and issues round about Sudbury—from my perspective—as I saw them.

The operative guideline for me, was his own words; "problems, as I saw them." Therefore, my speech; in front of an impressionable group of young people, was more philosophical than bureaucratic—I did not follow strict government policy talking points—I shot from the hip. I meant the speech and the following discussions to be freewheeling and based on actual field observations. I was armed with some statistics and a whole lot of emotional assumptions. Sterling, as the class teacher; was present, and he was seated at the far back of the room.

And I could see that he was not pleased with neither; the tone of the speech; nor, with the flow and content of the question and answer period that followed.

I talked about poverty and its effects on children and young adults; I talked about the economic struggles of the working class; the privileges of money; that rich people got richer, and poor people got more children; the barriers which some ethnic groups in Sudbury, and, particularly, our native Indigenous peoples had to face every day of their lives; the bias in our educational system favouring children from white middle class homes—and then the bombshell—I quoted passages from Paul Vallieres', "White Niggers of America", in reference to his thesis on Canada's treatment of French Canadians.

I caught glimpses of Sterling at the back; red-faced; squirming with anger and discomfiture. Sterling was an elected ward alderman sitting on council, and chair of my board—and what I was saying was not complimentary—it was radical. But I had not been asked to go to the school to sing the praises of the system—I was going to say it the way I saw it—and I did.

As the bell was on the verge of ringing to announce the movement of classes; Sterling rose and gave the customary, if curt, 'thank you' to the guest speaker, on behalf of the class; with the scraping of chairs and desks, few heard what he said—students were crowding around me asking a host of questions—some of which were personal in nature; there were single students in receipt of "student welfare" in the audience; and some lived at home with fathers and mothers in receipt of monthly welfare assistance; and to those individuals I handed my calling card, so that they could call me and put their enquiries in full privacy.

The next time I met Sterling Campbell at a welfare committee meeting, he never raised the matter of my talk to his class. And he never invited me to speak at the school ever again, either—next time; he invited Simone Patterson—she was much more conventional.

Mother and Father Not Doing Well

My mother and father were not doing well. My mother's health was failing evermore; she could barely do her housework—today, she may have undergone surgery for heart valve replacement procedures—but at that time she was a poor candidate for surgical intervention; her age and medical conditions made heart surgery, a very risky proposition.

And my father was not feeling well; the x-rays had found lesions on his lungs, and when I called Dr. Lafond to find out more information, he said bluntly; "Well, your father has lung cancer, and you know of course that lung cancer is fatal: nothing can be done." This was at supper time; he hung up on me; and I returned to my meal without much of an appetite—my mother, out of concern for her husband, had asked me to place the call—and now I would have to communicate the doctor's diagnosis, and prognosis to an already frail, elderly woman.

I never forgave Dr. Lafond for his insensitivity—and later on; as we all suspected: his false prognosis. My father was left alone; no treatment programs were put in place for his supposed lung cancer. His eventual death, later on, was totally unrelated to a cancer of any kind—my father was to die of a blood clot in the lung—a pulmonary embolus.

Mother Goes Shopping for a Casket

My mother called me at work one morning; she asked me to go over to the apartment, and have lunch with them; on my lunch hour. When I walked in, I found her in a cheerful and upbeat mood. The same could not be said for my father; my dad's mood was quite different—he sat at the table, somewhat depressed and sulking over his soup. And my mom said, without any opening preamble, "I want you to drive me to the Cooperative Funeral Home, we're buying a pre-paid funeral and we have an appointment—I have to go sign papers and select the coffins." This was my practical mother at her best. Unemotional and straightforward to the issues.

Throughout this, my father did not say a word; he did not even give me a look—he kept his head down, quietly sipping his soup of canned Habitant pea soup.

"He doesn't want to go," my mother said, looking at my dad, "it's too depressing for him—he's been down like this for the past two days."

So we drove to the Cooperative Funeral Home, at the corner of Notre Dame Avenue and Lasalle Boulevard. Once there, I introduced my mother to Roger Delongchamp, one of the funeral directors. Roger was well known to me; we had socialized together—his wife, Arlette, worked at my office—the best clerk-receptionist we ever had.

Tall, soft-spoken Roger, walked my mother through the benefits of the pre-paid funeral program—and they are very significant.

My mother was attentive and very at ease; she asked a few questions about the priest; coffee and sandwiches; the reception, and other pertinent and sundry details.

"Now, Mrs. Vincent," Roger said, after the papers were signed, "we'll proceed to the upper-floor showroom, where you will select the two casket models of your choice. Of course," he added demurely, "you could let your executor do that when the time comes—if that is your wish."

"No, no," mom said, "good heavens; they may pick something we wouldn't like—or, pick the cheapest—to save costs." And as she said this, she looked at me with a grin—and I did not fully appreciate the humour.

So, there she went, walking up and down; through rows upon rows of different types of coffins. I could not suppress a chuckle—but there was my mother at her irrepressible—she did the 'Goldilocks and the Three Bears' thing—my mother had never lost her flair for the theatrical.

She would approach each coffin and put her hands inside the velvety interior, and feel for the padding; softness and imagined comfort; and she would say out loud; expressly for Roger and I to hear, "No, this one is too hard," or, "no, this one is too soft," and then, finally; she looked at Roger and me and exclaimed, "yes, this is the one, feels just right!"

CHAPTER 31

Institutional Confinement and Upset Parents

Over the next few years, my parents' conditions got progressively worse. At that point in time, our sister Colette worked at the Extendicare Falconbridge nursing home. Colette worked in accounting, but she had a certain amount of influence with the Admissions department. She had managed to get our parents admitted—although they would not be sharing the same room—they would be in the same building.

Colette had not consulted with any of her siblings on these decisions and developments affecting our parents. I was not happy; I thought the move to a nursing home was premature, and the accommodations in separate rooms, simply terrible.

Because you are older does not mean that you have lost your feelings of love, and your need for closeness. This was a loving couple who'd been together for over sixty years—and now; we ripped them apart with an unplanned separation. How callous could we be?

My father was very upset—he kept on looking for his wife. Overnight; his soul mate had been wrenched away from him. He was very depressed and walked about the hallways, dazed and lost. He knew how to get to my mother's room, and he would spend entire days there; in her room, seated in the rocking chair we had brought from home; moving away only to attend to meals and the bathroom. Late into the evenings, after hallway lights-out, staff had to guide him back to his own room, on the second floor.

My father was confused and very low-spirited. He did not understand what had happened to them—one day they are living happily in their little apartment on Louis Street, and the next day; they wake up to a different world.

My mother was more open to change—after all she was the one who was physically incapacitated—although one day, shortly after they'd been admitted and I had dropped in to visit them; she said to me in response to my comment that she did not look happy, "Well, why should I be? Look around you," she had said in her inimitable way, "this place is full of old people—I don't belong here." Her comment was funny, but sad indeed—it said a lot.

Nursing Homes

And she was right—they; both of them, did not belong there. Nursing homes are appropriate institutions if you require nursing care, but not if what you need is a retirement home. Otherwise, one should not be there. Nursing homes are immediately depressing to the spirit. They are smelly ghettoes, where the smell of bodies pervades the hallways; and they are full of old and sickly people; people that children, or the state, wants to put away and out of sight. Nursing homes are hospices by another name; they are places you go to while awaiting death. If not, upon admission, then surely shortly thereafter, the spirit dies.

How We Treat the Elderly

An injustice had been done to my parents—an injustice very much akin to elder abuse. We proved again that we did not have my parents' best interest at heart. Colette and all of us for that matter were looking after our own convenience. Our parents' demands on our time were becoming more pressing and exigent—they were old and we had no need of them anymore—for babysitting our children, or to entertain us, or feed us at meals of their own preparation—so we put them out of the way, so we could have more time for ourselves.

Most grown-up children are selfish and mean to their parents. However, beware! What is done to aging parents has a way, of later being visited on the children. Hurt a good friend, you are insensitive; hurt good parents, you are damned!

My Father Fights for his Life

I received a phone call, early one morning at work. Colette informed me that our father had fallen and broken his hip; and he was now at Memorial Hospital, awaiting surgery. Three days post-surgery, the hospital discharged this elderly man back to the nursing home—too quickly I thought, given the seriousness of the surgery—they gave him the bum's rush—no physiotherapy or rehab programs in place—they needed the bed: he was discharged.

The hospital discharge occurred on a Monday. Two days later; Thursday of the same week, early in the afternoon, Colette called me from the nursing home—our father was in critical condition, desperately fighting the fatal attack of a pulmonary embolism—a blood clot had travelled from the hip surgical area and had made its way through the bloodstream, and lodged itself in an artery of the lung. For a man of my father's age—the consequences were usually morbid. Only the week previous, our father was alive and well: and now he was fighting for his life.

When I got to the nursing home, he'd been isolated in a room where they put residents who were awaiting death. Colette was in the room, along with Dr. McMullen; the home doctor. The only sound in the room was my father's laboured breathing. It was a large room, devoid of any ornamentations; no pictures on the walls or knickknacks on wooden stands; no potted plants on the floor; with the exception of a round table with five chairs, set apart against a far wall; and there was the gurney with my father, occupying the centre of the floor area—he had a light bed sheet draped over him, from his feet to just below his chin. Dr. McMullen was seated, alone, at the table by the wall, with face averted; my sister Colette was standing by our father, holding and stroking his hand.

I went to the opposite side of the gurney, facing Colette. Her face was red, showing the stress of grief. Our father was slowly dying by asphyxiation—and right before our eyes. And we were powerless to help. It was not a pretty sight. His eyes were staring, wide open; fixated to a point somewhere on the far ceiling, at the end of the room. His face was pale and damp. His breathing was laboured, and he breathed in with great distress—in hard sucking efforts—and when his chest decompressed, he let out a faint moan with every expiration. This was my first time of coming face to face with death. And I never felt so small and helpless in all my life.

I made my way to Dr. McMullen, and asked him why he wasn't doing anything—why was my father not being rushed to the hospital for some emergency intervention? Dr. McMullen raised his head: and I will never forget the sad look on his face; "There is nothing that can be done," he replied gently, "your father is now in a coma; he is unconscious, and he will die before the night sets in."

And sure enough; he breathed his last breath, October third, 1985; at about the same time most folks in Sudbury had put away their dinner dishes, and turned on their TV sets to watch "The Cosby Show"; "Dallas"; or "Cheers".

I went to work the next day, feeling a numbness in my heart and in my mind, and I went through the motions—I even attended a Board of Education committee meeting. It was my way of handling grief—to walk through the pain. I wanted to have nothing to do with my feelings; I felt sad, guilty, and angry; and I turned back to my running shoes, and long-distance running.

If my father's death, and the circumstances surrounding it, had happened in the United States—the hospital and a host of people would have been sued. My father was discharged too early from the hospital, and; furthermore, he had not been placed on a course of anti-coagulant medication upon discharge—and if he was; in my opinion, the nursing home did not see to it that his medication was administered to him. All actions open to litigation. However, at the time it was the farthest thing from the family's mind. After all, we're Canadians; we are expected to be meek and mild, and accept things as they are presented to us—to complain and demand explanations is thought rude and impolite.

Ray A. Vincent

Mother Trying to Manage on Her Own

Within a month of my father's death, my mother moved to the Finlandia Koti retirement home, on Fourth Avenue. She was only at Finlandia for half a year; she said she wasn't happy there because there were few people who spoke French at the home—but, there were other reasons; which she was shy to talk about—the monthly cost was too high for her to afford. Finlandia Koti is a beautiful and very well run rest home—the best, in quality and the best administered in Sudbury.

Mother Grants Power of Attorney and Growing Unhappiness

Colette got my mother to agree to give her full power of attorney over all of her affairs. My mom never consulted with her other children about this important matter. And that is when mother removed herself from Finlandia, and made the move to Colette's house—again, without talking to any of her other children about any of this. Things were fine for a few months; however, one day I took her to my house for a weekend stay, and she confided in me that things were going sideways. She was depressed and cried often. She missed our father very much; she maintained that we had abandoned her; that Colette was cold and indifferent; and that Colette's daughter, Lise, actually showed open displeasure at the fact that our mother had moved in with them. She related incidents when her granddaughter went out of her way to be mean to her—to the point where mom said she wanted out of Colette's house.

My niece, Lise, was in her early twenties, and she was of a vile temperament at the best of times. I believed every word that mother told me—my mother was not a complainer, and she would not have brought out those kinds of charges unless she had valid grounds upon which to base them. My relationship with my niece, Lise, could never be the same thereafter; to the point where I could not tolerate her presence in the same room with me.

THE CHRONICLES OF A JOURNEY

Sad News from Rose—A Tragedy

Other sad news befell the family shortly after these developments. As related previously, Rosario had convinced Rose to reconcile; and he had brought his family back to the Bearn homestead.

They owned a lakeside cottage (where Emily and I had honeymooned); and he and Rose also owned a large woodlot—where he harvested pulpwood, which he sold to the Temiscaming paper mill when prices warranted it. On the wood lot in question, he had constructed a little house and he had cleared an acre of land, which he and Rose developed into a large, and a bountiful vegetable garden.

One day in late spring, he told Rose that he was going to work on the garden plot. He did not show up at home that evening—this was not, of itself, unusual—he had the little house to sleep in. However, he did not show up again on the second and the third evening. Then, some concerns were raised. Rose sent Yvon, the eldest of the boys, to go out there and seek out his father. Yvon went to the lakeside cottage first, thinking his dad may have gone fishing after working hard in the big garden.

Rosario's truck was not at the cottage; Yvon did not bother to go in; he turned his car around and headed for the woodlot a few miles away.

The truck was parked by the front door. The front door was unlocked, and very little was disturbed in the house; the bed was neatly made up as if no one had slept in it. Yvon went through the back door, and from the elevated verandah, he had a good view of the tilled garden in front of him. There was a bundle of dark clothing, some fifty yards away, laying there on the damp garden earth.

He approached the clothing and saw his father lying face down, with a thirty-ought-six hunting rifle alongside him.

Later on at the wake, I will never forget my sister Rose's strange comments; "Imagine," she said greatly perturbed, to a gathering of ladies from the church of St. Placide, and the immediate family gathered around her, "the audacity, and lack of decorum on his part; to do what he did while we're in the middle of the 'Holy week of

Mary'—how can we concentrate on our daily prayers and novenas?. Couldn't he have waited a couple of weeks?"

She was standing no more than ten feet from the closed casket—"He did this just to spite me—the animal!" she continued, with great indignation in her voice. She took the suicide as an affront—an embarrassment to herself and her family. She completely missed the act of despair—the deep human tragedy.

The Sudbury Masters Running Club

I had gone back to running, but that was only as a casual, weekend activity. When work became increasingly stressful and sadness started to wend its way into my heart—I did not go to the doctor's—I joined the Sudbury Masters Running Club (SMRC).

For quite some time I had watched, with some interest and curiosity, Billy Rossetto, an employee with the Sudbury public board of education, who worked on the fourth floor of the west tower; and Louis Moustgaard from the Region's engineering department. Punctual like good clockwork, every noon hour Billy and Louis would make their way; jogging bag slung over their shoulder, to the club's running room, located inside the confines of the Sudbury Arena.

I joined and started to run with the Sudbury Masters, on January 27, 1987—and I continued my membership—and deep friendships—with the running club, for a long unbroken period—well beyond my retirement from work.

For a very small annual fee, you got a key to the runners' room and you became—ipso facto—a club member. And the group ran every work day, Monday to Friday, singly or in various clusters of runners. We met at noon hour—our lunch hour—and we ran outside on most occasions.

The membership was composed of different professional people who worked within, and around the downtown core. We came back from our run; we showered; got dressed again and went back to work—refreshed, having washed-off the stress of the morning and ready to take on whatever would come at us the rest of the day.

We ran; we talked; we joked; we solved each other's personal problem—marital, or financial, or both; we even tackled the important world issues of the day—and we managed to solve those also—it's amazing the problems you can resolve when your body's bloodstream is racing to your brain, loaded with endorphins!

Besides providing a venue for exercise and fitness, leading to a healthy lifestyle and stress reduction; the SMRC also had a philanthropic mission in the community. The club organized fund-raising running events throughout the year—the largest, in terms of participation numbers and fundraising achievement, was, at that time; the annual Ramsey Tour Half Marathon and Five km., road races. Monies raised by the SMRC through those events were given out as bursaries and scholarships to an athlete in need of financial support; attending either Laurentian University or Cambrian College. The SMRC has donated hundreds of thousands of dollars over the years to the cause of student-athletes.

A Special Group of Men

A nicer group of men I have never found anywhere else. The atmosphere around these men was more than friendly, or collegial—the bond was special and unique; it was mystical and brotherly; it came from the sharing of personal experiences and the common love of running. The relationship between runners is difficult to explain—it's like that welding of feelings between soldiers who have gone through, and survived; the fire of battle. Runners can read each other's minds better than any other two people—with much more ease and accuracy than a spouse could—the relationship is special.

The Sudbury Masters Running club was founded by Mike Narozanski and Louis Moustgaard, back in the early 70's; many of us at the club—including myself, ran seven days a week, and went out to run in competitive races and marathons; all over the country and the USA. Sudbury's rugged and hilly terrain provided the ideal training ground for long distance road running—and Sudbury became well known across the province for the competitive quality of its master road runners—for every distance, from 5 Km., and 10 Km., races; right up to the full marathon.

The Annual June Pilgrimage to Louis' Cottage

The SMRC was more than a running club for master-aged runners; it was a genuine fraternity—a brotherhood. We ran together and we socialized together. Our get-togethers have become so important, that we have ritualized them. Even now, when most of us are retired and well advanced in our years and have stopped running; we still get together as a group, up to three times a year—where we laugh; reminisce, and take the liberal opportunity to exaggerate our past athletic exploits.

Louis Moustgaard still opens his cottage for us on Lake Penage, on the third Thursday of June, each year. Few things make me feel happier than to meet the boys at the camp, and see Louis, with that impish smile of his, draped all over his face.

The Sudbury Masters has been a big part of my life—not only have they made me a better person, but they have also made me understand more deeply what real friendship is, and what it is founded upon.

So here's to you: Mike Narozanski, Louis Moustgaard, Bill Thompson, Gerry Rouleau, Darryl Mathe, David Innes, Mike Wisniewski, Steve O'Neil, Peter Best, Bob Delfrate, Murray Giusti, Bill Rossetto, Kurt Gelbhar, Bobby Potvin, Dan Welch, Paul Washchuk, Alfio Grottoli, Vic Dunn, Mike and Francis Sheridan, and Paddy Walsh.

I thank you all very much to have given me the honour, and the pleasure, to have known you.

CHAPTER 32

Our Mother Dies

My mother died of heart failure, in the middle of the night, January 13th, 1988. She died alone; not surrounded by loving family, as she had deserved to be. There were no last whispered loving words; no pressing of the hand; or a gentle kiss goodbye on the forehead. A life of love, sacrifice, and pain closed; her praises unsung; her virtues and hard work, taken for granted; a woman who never asked for anything in return, went quietly away, alone, in the middle of the night.

It took me a long time to realize that persons like my mother, are very few in the world. She loved—and expressed that love at every moment of her life—and expected nothing in return. That's as close to sainthood as one can get.

However, the lack of bedside family company could not be helped—she'd been at Memorial Hospital for two weeks—she died around three o'clock in the morning. The hospital had called Colette and Colette had called me right away. Mom was already dead before any family could reach the hospital.

I returned to bed that night feeling numb and cold at heart; thinking—we are so shallow, selfish, callous and insensitive. What a sad commentary to cast upon a family of ten children: a mother and a father, who gave their lives and souls to us; and only two children at their bedside, in their last moments of life.

Ray A. Vincent

An Embarrassing moment

An embarrassing moment occurred when the family proceeded out of the church; but a moment, which few people noticed, who were not close to the front of the cortege, marching behind our mother's coffin. In the church vestibule the funeral director picked up the crucifix lying atop the coffin and moved forward to hand it to me, but I motioned and pointed to Rose; the senior of the sisters present. Colette unceremoniously thrust herself forward at that time and made a grab for it, and then Rose came up and took a firm hold of it so that we had the beginnings of a tug of war beside the body of our dead mother; a few quick muffled words were exchanged between the two sisters, and Colette relented and reluctantly let go of the crucifix.

A Meeting with Colette and another Embarrassing Moment

Two weeks after mother's death, Colette called me at work; asking to see me at lunchtime. Once seated at the table, she produced a sealed envelope and pushed it toward me. "What's that?" I asked.

Colette had mother's power of attorney and she was the executrix of mother's will—a copy of which I, nor any my siblings, ever saw. "That," she said, taking the envelope and putting it in my hands, "is half of what was left in mom's bank account—$283 dollars. After settling her bills, she had $566 dollars left in her account—$283 is your share—after all; you and I did most of the work around mom."

I was speechless and disgusted. I deposited the envelope back in front of her, and I got up and I left the restaurant.

None of my siblings expected any money from our parents—they had none to bequeath. If there was some insignificant amount left, it should have been forwarded to a charity—not surreptitiously split amongst two children, and slid over a table top in a sealed envelope. That was an insult to the memory of our parents.

THE CHRONICLES OF A JOURNEY

Some Serious Running

After mother died, I started to run with a vengeance—forty to sixty miles per week, seven days a week. I knew it was compensatory behaviour, but I needed the outlet to keep my emotions under control. There were also things happening at work which drove me to the comforts of the streets and into the arms of the running club. And my friends and family began to worry about me.

People were worried; I could tell by the way they looked at me—particularly if they had not seen me for a while—from January to May, I went from 198 pounds to 160. I assured all those with the overly solicitous look, that I was not sickly with some terrible illness—it was the running snowballing effect, I explained—the more I ran, the more weight I lost—and the more weight I lost, the easier and more enjoyable the running became; therefore, I ran more, and so on and so forth; until they seemed to understand the situation.

I now weighed 155 to 160 pounds—my high school weight—my heart rate at rest was 38 to 45 beats per minute—I was super fit—my stress level was down to nil, and my productivity at work spiked ahead.

I ran two marathons, the year of my mother's death—the Massey Voyageur marathon in July; my first at the distance of 26.1 miles, and I broke 3 hours; with a time of 2 hours, 56 minutes. I ran my second marathon in October—the Detroit International Marathon—in a time of 2 hours, 50 minutes. While in Detroit to run the marathon, Emily and I took the opportunity to visit with Christine, who had just started her first year at the University of Windsor. Her main impression of the race was that "She'd never seen so many skinny people, all gathered together in one place at the same time." And earlier that year, I had done a personal best 10 km., road race—the Cambrian College spring run—in a time of 35 minutes, 38 seconds.

I lost myself in running—but I found peace of mind and a new dimension to my life.

I organized my training runs carefully so that they had the least possible amount of interference with family life. I ran during my lunch hour; before supper time, and on weekends early in the morning; so that at the end of most of my weekend long runs, I came back home and I would find the family still fast asleep.

An Addictive Activity—Sports Anorexia

Emily did not mind my running addiction—and, it had become an addiction—a sports anorexia of sorts—as long as I enjoyed the activity and it did not take family time away from us.

I faced two medical inconveniences directly connected to my intense running; at the beginning, I had bouts of hematuria—bright red blood in my urine—which worried my nurse-wife greatly—but that phenomenon was running related, and not a urological pathology, and it cleared away with time. The other incident was the tear of my right Achilles tendon during a long run, still a mile away from home, in the late 90's. It was at that time—when I had to take time off running—that I discovered how physically addicted and mentally dependent I had become to running. I actually experienced real withdrawal symptoms—physical discomfort; anxiety and sleep problems—I sadly missed my daily fix of endorphins. However, once I got to discipline myself, to the point where I controlled the running, and not have the running control me—I proceeded to have a long and enjoyable relationship with road running.

A March Break in Florida

That late winter, at the high school March Break, we took Christopher and a friend of his and Christine's, Mike Fay, to Clearwater Florida, for a week in the sun. Mike joined us on a separate flight later in the afternoon of our arrival, but we returned to Sudbury on the same flight. We enjoyed the vacation, the heat, and the relaxation; and the boys enjoyed the cheap American beer (by the full shopping cart) and the American girls at the beach. We had a rented car and we toured a bit.

Mike Fay was a nice young man and a friend of the family, but he always gave me the impression of a lost puppy looking for some good owners to adopt him. He always carried a sad look about him. Mike came from an Irish immigrant family; there were five children in the family. Mike's father was a well-respected doctor in Sudbury, he was a specialist in liver and kidney diseases—a nephrologist; the only one we had in northern Ontario—and he travelled to clinics throughout northeastern Ontario doing consulting and dialysis work.

Mike was fun to be around because he was so spontaneous and genuine, but he had one weakness; he loved to brag about his downhill skiing prowess— and indeed, he was a very good skier.

I was at the beach with the boys on our second day of our arrival in Clearwater; I stayed well away from them since they were paying court to a group of pretty teenage girls, but I was close enough that I could overhear some of the conversation. And the conversation was about where the boys came from; what they did back home for fun, and subjects of that nature. When Mike mentioned that he and Chris spent most of their winter weekends downhill skiing—which wasn't true as far as our son was concerned—the winterless girls hooed and aahed with admiration. And then the girls asked the names of the ski mountains the two heroes were tackling around Sudbury; and then Mike, always the fast thinker, came out with the name of the best mountain of all; he said it rivalled Whistler in British Columbia— Sudbury's Mount St. Adanac! Needless to say, the girls were impressed.

And, for those not familiar with the Sudbury ski scene: the Sudbury Adanac ski hill, in the heart of Sudbury, has a maximum vertical elevation not surpassing 239 feet!

The Regional Municipality wants Control of the Welfare Board

In 1987, the Regional Municipality of Sudbury (The Region) made a direct assault, for a complete takeover and control of the District of Sudbury Social Services Administration Board.

Senior bureaucrats at city hall—with the full consent of the board's chairman, Sterling Campbell—began to isolate Paul Schaak from the directorship of the department. There began a concerted effort by the Region—headed by Mark Mieto, as senior staff—to remove Paul from his job. Months of dirty tricks and internal political shenanigans began. Paul was a Conservative political party supporter, and he had been appointed to his job many years ago, by a conservative provincial government. Mieto and Campbell were Liberal supporters. Furthermore, it was no secret that Mieto had aspirations for Paul Schaak's job.

Political Intrigues

Paul was under extreme pressure—the caseloads were increasing—and the board had to revert to some significant bank borrowing to meet monthly expenditure demands; while waiting for the next month's provincial subsidy payments to come in; but since the subsidy payments were based on a budgeted amount related to a lower caseload; we were always underfunded and dependent on the bank. The monthly reports to the board showed a growing bank debt, due mostly to high prevailing interest rate charges on the bank bridge-loans.

The Vultures Move In

The Region saw an opening; an excuse for a takeover bid. The DSSAB budget was in a deficit—therefore its director was incompetent. The logic of the predator.

The Region complained to the Administration Board about the ballooning interest debt load to the bank, and the consequent budget overrun. The time was ripe for the Region to ask for direct control of welfare administration within the Regional Municipality of Sudbury. Pressing the point of poor fiscal management; senior staff with the Region, with the support of Sterling Campbell—the

DSSAB board chair—convinced the board to have Paul removed from his dual directorship with Simone Patterson.

Simone was never a party to any of these backroom maneuvers; she was as shocked as any staff was. Late one Friday afternoon; Mark Mieto, as the Region's Health and Social Services top civil servant, and Sterling Campbell, came to our offices on the third floor of the west tower. They conferred with Paul and Simone under closed doors—the meeting was short; the announcement was quick and direct: effective immediately, Paul was removed from his director's position and all duties attached to it (but he was to retain his full salary and benefits); and Simone was designated as the sole agency director.

An Interim and Unsolicited Promotion

On their way out of the office, Sterling Campbell stopped by my office and closed the door behind him. He apprised me of the latest developments and informed that as of next Monday, I would carry the title of acting deputy-director, until such a time as things got sorted out.

They were on the floor not more than a half hour. They had set off a bombshell and quickly departed. Union staff was whispering, but they went on with their regular duties and stayed the course. But the supervisory staff was shaken and upset. We loved and respected Paul.

Paul Down but Not Out

Paul Schaak was an incredibly honest and hard-working man—and he was very proud—and he would not kowtow to the Region's marching orders, without looking into his legal options.

However, people with less integrity, and with a whole lot of career ambitions at the Region—someone who wanted his job—went to work to oust him from his position. But these people with the cloaks and daggers faced one slight unforeseen inconvenience; Paul's position was a provincial political appointment, and therefore, he could not be removed without the province's consent—you could not fire what you did not hire. So they switched their tactics—they tried to get him to resign out of his own volition; and to this end, they harassed, humiliated and embarrassed him—they opened up new bags of dirty tricks.

Dirty Tricks and the "Dungeon"—the Vanguard of Constructive Dismissal

If Paul would not resign and leave on his own—and he would not—then, they would make life difficult for him; every day of the week—they decided that they would isolate him.

When he reported to work one day, his office was locked and Mieto told him that he had been seconded to work for him and that from now on he was to report directly to him. He was given a dingy little cubbyhole of an office, downstairs, on the first floor; in between the flower shop and the travel agency. He had a desk; a telephone; his own chair, and one chair beside the door, for "guests". He told me jokingly that he had misbehaved, and therefore, he'd been relegated to the "basement"—and now, he'd have to work his way back up.

I said, "No, Paul, you haven't been sent to the basement—seems to me you've been sent to the "dungeon". He laughed—he still had his sense of humour.

And there, seated at his desk, he was told by Mark Mieto, to write "papers" on various topics to do with the municipal and the provincial social services system—something a teacher would assign a first-year Cambrian College, social services student to do—a "paper", on the history of General Welfare Assistance in Ontario; a "paper", on Special Assistance; and a "paper", on Supplementary Aid; and a "paper", on the Canada Assistance Plan and its impact on provincial-municipal cost sharing; and a further "paper" on the role of municipal social services in emergency disaster response.

Embarrassing tasks to ask a man of his accomplishments and the status he held in the field, and right across the province. It was a clear case of workplace abuse and an abrogation of due process. It was vicious, and it shouted for a counterattack through litigation.

Unfortunately, Paul's personality and character were very far removed from the confrontational. He said nothing as long as Mieto's directions were supported by the DSSSAB and its chairman: he obeyed and performed the menial tasks; if they'd asked him to sweep his office floor—he would have done it. But Paul was no fool; he was highly intelligent, and quietly; alone in his cubbyhole, he was planning his next move—his counterattack.

The Counterattack

First, and without any advertisement of the fact to anyone—he secured the services of a good labour lawyer. And secondly—and most importantly—he arranged for an appointment with the assistant Deputy-Minister of the Ministry of Community and Social Services, at Queens' Park. The annual OMSSA-AGM was being held in Toronto that spring of 1988. As a member of the Association, Paul had a right to attend and he was allowed to do so. Attending the full proceedings of the AGM was the farthest thing from Paul's mind—he was going to Toronto, not for the OMSSA conference—he was going to Toronto for his meeting at the Deputy-Minister's office, where he would meet with John Sweeney's assistant.

While he and I were driving alone in my car, on our way to the conference; he told me about the special meeting, and he asked me if I would do him a favour and attend the meeting with him. He said my memory was better than his, and I might find the experience interesting. I liked Paul and I had the greatest respect for him—I told him that I would be more than happy to accompany him to Queens' Park.

But, Paul was so wily and mentally sharp: I realized later that it was not my memory that he'd wanted at the meeting—he wanted a witness (probably suggested by his lawyer), to what was to be said at the meeting—someone he could later call upon to give evidence, if that ever became necessary.

John Sweeney, the Deputy-Minister, and his assistant deputy knew all the details of the shenanigans being played out in Sudbury—they had the information file on their desk, and they'd been briefed prior to the meeting. And Paul was aware that they did.

The province always appointed (the provincial appointee) a voting member, to each District Welfare Board it created; across the northeast and the northwest of the province. These appointees were a direct funnel of information to the Minister's office. The Sudbury board appointee was Lionel Demers, from Garson, a good conservative party member; and Mr. Demers had kept the Deputy-Minister's office fully apprised of all the nasty intrigues going on in Sudbury.

Assurances

The meeting at the Minister's office had not been a long meeting, but one that made Paul break into a smile—a smile I had not seen on his face for a long time. We left the meeting with unequivocal assurances that Paul had the full support of the Ministry and that he would retain that support as long as a District Welfare Board was in existence in Sudbury, and as long as there were no legal causes to have him removed: after all, the government of the day was a conservative government, and Paul was one of their own—Campbell and Mieto were in the other camp.

Armed with these assurances, Paul's lawyer fired a letter to the board chairman, Sterling Campbell. The contents of the letter were dealt with "In Camera"—in private, away from the public and media scrutiny since the matter was a personnel issue. The outcome was favourable to Paul.

Reinstatement—A Vindication

After eight months holed-up in Mieto's "basement dungeon", Paul made a happy entry (not long after the board's "In Camera" session), back on the third floor and into his old office—fully reinstated. His return came about a week after the special personnel meeting of the board. And Simone reverted back to her original positions.

Eventual Amalgamation

The Regional Municipality had lost the first round in the political battle for control—but it would eventually win the war.

They let Paul keep the directorship; and the DSSSAB its existence, until Paul's full retirement at age sixty-five—and then; with Paul out of the way, the vultures came swooping down; Mieto and his gang moved in. With the provincially appointed director now retired, and with the political and public will behind them, the DSSSAB was amalgamated into the Health and Social Services department of the Regional Municipality of Sudbury—the general manager of which became none other than, Mark Mieto. The bureaucrat had expanded his kingdom.

Simone Patterson, my dear old boss, remained in active employment for a few years after Paul's retirement, as director of social services, reporting directly to Mark; and I continued as her deputy. Simone retired in 1989, and her replacement was put out to an open competition.

An Open Competition for the Directorship

The staff expected to see my appointment as the director as a natural progression and a matter of course—but, Sterling Campbell and Mark Mieto thought otherwise. My sympathies and loyal affiliations with the "old guard", did not sit well with them.

The now vacant position of Director of Social Services was advertised province-wide and through the Association (OMSSA) newsletter bulletin. I applied for the position. I went through pre-selection, and there were now two finalists left standing for the job—myself and Harold Duff.

Harold had a solid work background; he had worked as a caseworker with the city of North Bay; and his most recent employment had been as CEO for the municipalities of Newmarket-King City, north of Toronto. Harold came in with good administrative skills—and Harold was hired as our new director.

Harold Duff—A Good Man and a Very Competent Director

I was disappointed and it hurt at the beginning, but it hurt less and less, as I got to know Harold Duff. Like myself, Harold came from a large working class family, —good Irish Catholics—and he was a northern Ontario boy from Kirkland Lake. Harold's brother, Dickie Duff, had played professional NHL hockey, and some of his playing career had been spent with my beloved Montreal Canadiens.

Harold was gifted with superior organizational skills: Paul and Simone may have had strength in people skills—but they could not touch Harold in the areas of organization and planning. Furthermore, he was honest and fair; and he took pride in getting things done. We were alike in many ways, and we got along exceedingly well from the very first day of our meeting.

Harold came in with a big advantage—he owed no one any favours. He could mold the organization in accordance with his vision—and he proceeded to do just that; to the utter dismay and upset of the union, whose president of the local was a staff member in our office.

The union executive had gotten comfortable; they were used to a more casual and easy relationship with both, Paul and Simone, whose leadership styles were quite different—they were directors of the status quo—they were not directors of goal setting, ideas or innovation. Harold was; and when Harold had an idea or a goal in sight, he did in fact consult; but after that process was exhausted, he forged ahead—you went along, or you were left behind in his dust. And I liked that kind of management approach; it got things done;

innovations and procedures that were focused on enhanced service delivery to our clients; in increased productivity; and in greater accountability, finally got to see the light of day.

At work, Harold was all business; but after working hours he was congenial and very approachable—and like the good Irishman that he was—he loved to talk, and he talked fast and with heated animation.

Had he not been my boss, Harold and I would have gone on to become fast friends. The last thing I wanted was to compromise our relationship and set up conflicts of interest affecting either of us. However, we did have a good relationship at work, and a continuing friendship after both of us retired. We went grouse hunting in the fall and we visited each other—but I always felt that we could have been closer—and I would have wanted it to be so—had it not been for the fact that we had a boss-subordinate relationship at the professional level.

Reactions from Colleagues

I was aware that some supervisory staff at work—those who had seen me as an adversary (some that I thought were my friends), were actually inwardly grinning with glee when I did not get the job; and they were hoping that I would receive our new boss, with bitterness and open acrimony. I disappointed one or two of them—Harold and I became friends quickly.

Workplace Observations

It helped that we were very much alike. We liked goal setting and getting things done. We had a degree of mutual respect which was never put in jeopardy. There never was anything avuncular about Harold: if you did your job, and did it well—you never got any complaints; however, if you came to work expecting to mark time, and then collect a pay cheque—you could expect to hear from Harold.

I have always been of the opinion that your employer owes you nothing, except commensurate compensation for your production. The employer-employee dynamics is really the other way around; you have to show up first and deliver the goods before you should expect to be given compensation, or reward.

Strange to say; but in the same way that I have never met a woman that I did not like; I cannot honestly say that I have ever had a boss that I disliked. If you are going to work for someone, isn't the job that much easier to do if you get along?

Accepted in the Society of Freemasons

In the winter of 1988, after soliciting membership in, and being sponsored by two gentlemen that I held in high esteem—Marvin Streich and Lloyd McTaggart—my name was brought forward as a candidate for admission into the fraternity of The Order of Ancient, Free and Accepted Masons of Canada, in the province of Ontario. I was duly voted on, in proper form, and accepted into the secrets and mysteries of the order, in February 1988, as an Entered Apprentice. By the fall I had been raised to the 3rd degree of a Master Mason.

I was one of the very few French Canadian, and Roman Catholic, in the order. And by the ensuing year, I travelled to Hamilton for a special convocation of the Moore Sovereign Consistory, held at the Scottish Rite Cathedral where I was conferred my 32nd degree in the craft.

Belief in the Three Essential Pillars

I had always believed strongly in the three essential pillars of Masonry, which are; virtue; morality; and brotherly love. Now I had an opportunity to not only practice these character traits with like-minded men but also to celebrate them allegorically. Nickel Lodge no. 427 gave me the stage upon which to exemplify what I believed in.

I realized fairly quickly that the fact that Masonry had very few French Canadians in its ranks, had nothing to do with any sort of formal edict restricting the admission of French Canadians into the brotherhood: the reasons stemmed from misunderstandings—most French Canadians I spoke to were under the impression that there were rules within Free Masonry, barring their application for membership; and some told me that, if their parish priest ever found out that they were Free Masons—they would be summarily excommunicated from the bosom of the church. All these assumptions are patently misleading and incorrect and do not reflect the truth.

The number one entry criterion into Masonry is that one (the candidate) must believe in the existence of a Supreme Being—in the existence of God—the omnipotence of the Great Architect of the universe. Freemasons are God loving folks—so much so that, if you later embrace atheism, the order can remove you from membership. Freemasonry accepts good, free-willed individuals of any nationality and ranks in life. We have labourers, miners, tradesmen, farmers, teachers, doctors, lawyers and bishops and kings in our company—all are equal once they enter the precincts of the lodge.

Freemasonry is not an esoteric, subversive, secret organization: nothing could be further from the truth—Freemasonry is an open, international and multi-faith organization with some secrets in its rituals.

CHAPTER 33

My Father-in-Law

The first signs that Emily' dad was not well started to appear very gradually, very slowly; they were more noticeable by those of us who did not live with him; Emily's mom took a little longer to appreciate the subtle changes.

The past twenty years that I had known Mr. Hatala, were very close, warm, loving times in my life with him. The strong bond between our children; particularly Christopher, and their grandfather, was rich in loving care and understanding.

I learned a lot that was important from my father-in-law; nothing in the way of practical, car or house fixing skills; but more importantly, the appreciation of simple things; nature, the harvesting of wild field mushrooms; a walk through the bush; laughing, and enjoying the company of friends and family; good homemade meals and a good drink with company; keeping quiet, when joining the conversation would not be helpful, or when it would not increase the enjoyment of those around you; a toss of the head and roll of the eyes upward to signify displeasure; and when happy and joyful, smile—smile his soft, childlike disarming smile—the smile that radiated love all around him; and I learned from him that you never have to swear to make your point; in fact, he would say, that by swearing, you lost the argument; that swearing is not manly, but a sign of weakness.

And I learned from him the true value of working steadfastly, without complaint, with patience; that the hardships at work and the disappointments; and the sacrifices made, were tolerated for reasons beyond yourself—they were for your loved ones; and he taught me the importance of saving my money—for my loved ones.

THE CHRONICLES OF A JOURNEY

He was a deep book full of knowledge on these important subjects. He never wasted his time talking about politics or world affairs, or the latest blockbuster movie—he and my mother-in-law never sat in a movie house in their entire lifetimes. He never spent his hard earned money on the "Big Boy Toys" his French Canadian colleagues at work did—on snowmobiles, boats and motors and the latest gadgets. He never wasted his time in talking about how bad Inco treated him; he was content and happy that he had a job to go to—and a paycheque to raise his family with. He never complained about the state of world affairs—about the Russians; the cold war; the Cuban missile crisis; or concerned himself with about the space race, and the proliferation of nuclear weapons.

No; even though my father-in-law was keenly aware of world events, he considered them ephemeral and beyond his control: he concerned himself with what was close to home; to what was close to his heart; to what mattered to him—his family and his grandchildren. He concerned himself with the important—the unimportant—he left to the experts to worry about. In his wisdom, he really knew what life was all about—he knew what really mattered.

I quote his favourite phrase to my friends sometimes, and they smile in polite but shallow understanding; "Ray," he would say, in his east European accented English, and with his grey eyes aiming somewhere above my forehead, "Ray, the only thing you need in life, is a good roof over your head, and enough money to put food and drink on the table, and clothes on your kids—anything else the good Lord gives you is a bonus." My father-in-law was not a philosopher—he still went on his knees by the bedside every night and recited his prayers—he was not educated or sophisticated, but he understood what life was all about.

And when he said "drink on the table", he did not mean water or milk—he meant the eastern European staple—a good bottle of rye whiskey!

I loved my father-in-law for the simple and beautiful person that he was. Ours was the bond between father and son—god knows I loved my own natural father—but my love for my father-in-law was greater.

Ray A. Vincent

The Early Signals: The Incidents

So when he started to act strange and show some early signs of senile dementia, I was upset and concerned. A series of things happened which led the family to a decision to have "Dzedo" admitted to a nursing home.

Mother and father-in-law still lived in their home on Sandra Boulevard. One day, he took the bus to go to the downtown Canadian Tire store. He was to be back within an hour; he was gone all afternoon, and he said to his wife when he finally got back home, that he could not locate the return bus (a trip downtown he had taken many times before), and he walked in the house carrying a foul smell about him—he had soiled his pants.

And that same summer, I took him out to one of his favourite activities—we went blueberry picking on the hills beyond Fielding Road, in Walden. We were picking a patch together when I moved on a bit farther away, and we continued picking methodically. We had been separated for about twenty minutes when I stood up and saw no signs of him; I went on to higher ground and I still could not see or hear any of his movements; I shouted out his name and got no response. I then went searching for him; he was not far from where I had left him; he had fallen to the ground and got himself wedged in between two large boulders, his coffee tin of berries a few feet away and blueberries spilled all over his chest—he had tried to salvage his berries.

He did not say one word when he saw me coming toward him—he looked dazed and confused. I got him up, and after seeing that he had no broken bones, I gave him some water, and we went straight to the car, and home. I was shaken up.

One day, after the blueberry incident, Emily's mom called the house—Dzedo had disappeared—we called the police. He was located, walking the hills behind Princess Ann public elementary school, at the end of Douglas Street west.

At one time, over the winter, he was very restless and difficult with his wife; and Emily's mom called the house again—we lived a bare four minutes' drive away from their house; and in order to calm him down, I took him for a car ride all over New Sudbury, and the Minnow Lake area. He never uttered one word throughout the drive. On our way back to his house we stopped for a traffic sign, at the intersection of Douglas Street west and Whittaker; dzedo looked all around him and exclaimed—out of nowhere—the first vocal sound he'd made since I'd picked him up two hours earlier, "Boy, has Copper Cliff ever changed!"

I said nothing and drove on to his house. I told Emily that night that her dad would need some monitoring, if not constant surveillance.

And he started to hide money, and personal things like his wallet—and forget where the hiding places were—and he would walk all around the house, like a child looking for a lost toy, or the hidden Easter chocolate treats. We found the hiding places—in different closets—in the pockets of different pieces of clothing.

At that time, Paul owned an apartment building on Whittaker Street; in consultation with Emily and their mother, it was agreed that baba and dzedo would sell their house to Paul—with the four children getting an even division of the sale price—and the old folks would move to one of Paul's first floor apartments. Mr. Hatala could no longer look after the big house on Sandra, and that would be a more fitting living arrangement; it had a large kitchen, a living room and two bedrooms. But it did not take long for my mother-in-law to call again. Her husband would walk into her bedroom in the middle of the night, and just stand there, hovering over her bed—or, wanting in under the bed covers. She could not get any restful sleep. So the next day I went in and installed a lock on her bedroom door.

Dzedo Pees on the Floor and Walks away from the Party

The following summer, Andy, and Inge were celebrating the occasion of their twenty-fifth wedding anniversary. Their kids were putting on a party at the family home in Oakville, in honour of their parents. I drove to Oakville with my family and my in-laws.

Andy had a big house, and we all—my in-laws and ourselves—stayed at Andy's. Emily and I and our children, in one bedroom, and my in-laws in another. That first night, I awoke to some loud voices—upset voices. Andy's wife, Inge, ever the fastidious and fussy person, was beside herself—dzedo had gotten up in the middle of the night, and confused with not knowing where he was—he had proceeded to relieve himself; standing up against one corner of the bedroom—he'd peed all over the wall and onto the plush floor carpeting.

The dinner party was going to be outside, under a big rented tent which covered the entire front driveway. With the garage doors open, and the garage serving as larder and pantry; it was an ideal set up from which to serve the catered meal.

It was a beautiful and warm late afternoon. It was a large gathering of family and friends—the Kurdels from Sudbury had made the trip. We were all having a good time, and the drinks and the toasts to the guests of honour were aplenty.

We had sat down to eat and we were not yet halfway through our meal when my father-in-law decided he had had enough of this: he was leaving—to go back to Sudbury—270 miles away. He had gotten up from the table, and had made his way to the sidewalk—and had begun to walk away, up the street—and surprisingly fast. No sooner had I seen him rise up from the table, I knew he was up to something and I was right behind him.

He had made up his mind that he would not stay; he would walk, and he had made up his mind that he would not turn back. My father-in-law was a very strong man, he'd been a miner all his life; he had a powerful back and powerful legs. I could not forcibly hold him back; and for whatever reason, no one from the dinner table came to help me—these developments had happened so fast, that very few people were aware of anything unusual happening at all.

He would wrench his arm away every time I touched it. I was alone with a strong man intent on keeping on moving right ahead. I increased my pace and moved a few feet in front of him. He never said a word—his gaze was fixed somewhere ahead of him, and he had an angry expression on his face. When he slowed down, I put my hand on his shoulder and I said, in as normal a voice I could summon up, "Dad," I said, "let's go back and have a beer, and talk to Emily, Christine, and Christopher." He stopped and I kept the pressure of my hand on his shoulder—I don't know if it was the thought of seeing my family, or the promise of beer, that did the trick—but he walked the two hundred feet back to the table with me; quiet and obedient like a chastened child.

One day in the fall, I picked up Mrs. Kurdel at her house on Eyre Street and drove her to my in-laws to play some cards—my mother-in-law loved to play cards. I stayed in the apartment with them, watching TV to while away the time, knowing that I would be needed to drive Mrs. Kurdel back home. My father-in-law was seated at the head of the table, concentrating on his hand, when I noticed Mrs. Hatala's countenance change; and it did not take long before I got an unmistakable whiff of her concern—dzedo had soiled his pants. I told the two ladies to keep on playing, while I guided my father-in-law to the bathroom.

I had him stand in the empty bathtub and I stripped him naked of all his clothes, which I bundled up and put in the sink. I then turned the shower on, and hosed him down from head to foot. And again, he said not a word; he was as compliant and as docile as a sick child is wont to be when sickly—the last two years were as if he had lost the power of speech. After towelling him down, I put his pajamas on him, and lead him to his bedroom where I put him to bed.

When I went back to the living room, the two ladies were still seated with the same set of cards in their hands. They had not made any moves in their game ever since the incident.

Admission to the Nursing Home

Before Christmas, 1988, Mr. Hatala was admitted to the Extendicare York nursing home.

We visited regularly and you could see that he was upset and angry. One day, a few weeks after admission, I went alone to see him. He looked at me straight in the face and said, "Ray, who the hell put me in here?" for a man who'd been struggling with confusion—he was very lucid now. My heart hurt with sorrow when I replied, "The doctor; the doctor said, this was the best place for you." He then looked resigned and defeated.

It was a lie and then it was not a lie. It was a cover-up. I felt sick to my stomach—I had betrayed a friend. And I felt ashamed throughout the drive back home.

The Runaway

But, that was not the end of his protests. He ran away a few times— and I quietly cheered in the wings. Nursing home staff would immediately call the house, or our places of work; telling us that he'd disappeared—and then shortly after, they'd call back that they had found him, in his pajamas; walking down Regent Street, heading north—the right direction, toward home and his wife.

He would watch for his opportunities, and then make his getaway dash to the emergency exit staircases. As a matter of reluctant and last recourse, and for his own safety, they had to restrain him to his chair at meal times. But these actions lasted only a short time; after some months, he stopped running away and the restraints were done away with altogether.

The Sixtieth Wedding Anniversary

In the spring of 1989, we celebrated my in-laws' sixtieth wedding anniversary at the lovely Snow Flake restaurant, facing Ramsey Lake at Science North. It was a big gathering; all the children and grandchildren and many friends had joined with them to celebrate the event. We had taken my father-in-law out of the nursing home for the special occasion. As usual, he was quiet and within his shell—but he smiled now and then, and he seemed happy to be surrounded by family and friends. Emily was seated beside her mom, and I was next to her. The children were with their cousins. It was a noisy and busy place. There were speeches and toasts by Emily and her brothers, and general merrymaking.

"Who Are All These People"

I noticed Emily's father lean over to his wife, and say something to her—the few words he'd spoken all night. Emily overheard the question and her mom's response, and a strange expression came upon her face. I did not hear a word because of the noise.

Emily puts her mouth to my ear and said, "My god Ray, dad just asked mother who all these people around the table were? And she told him, 'dzedo, you old fool; these are all your children and grandchildren.'"

My Special Friend Leaves Us

My special friend passed away on April 2, 1991. After the church service and the interment, family and friends gathered at Cassio's on Lorne, for a meal and fellowship.

I was in pain and deep sorrow. I could not understand how his sons, and Emily included, could smile; socialize; and joke with these people around them. I had just lost my best friend; I was not in a joyful mood. I left the restaurant before dessert was served. I opted to walk home by myself and I made my way through the back streets of Gatchell, depressed and tearful. And I got home before Emily and the company staying with us, had arrived.

I did not sleep well that night, and around two a.m., when my family and our guests were asleep, I slipped out of the house and got in the car. I took highway 17 west and drove to Massey and back. I went back to bed shortly after four a.m.

Ray A. Vincent

A Defector in our Midst

Mark Kochis, Emily's second cousin from Slovakia—the son of Milan—had been in written communication with us for some time now, wanting an invite to come over and visit Canada. Mark was twenty years of age, and his written and spoken English was very good indeed. Mark had saved and accumulated the funds to pay his own way to the country.

He needed a formal invitation from us to confirm that we would welcome him, and look after him during his vacation stay— he needed the written invitation to show the socialist authorities back home—otherwise, he would not be allowed to leave Slovakia. He was a young man in which the Soviet-bloc country had invested a lot of resources, in terms of child care, health services and education—the investment had to be safeguarded. They wanted to know where he would be staying during his three-week stay in Canada; he was a young man with potential; they wanted him back.

Older folks returned home, but young people tended to stray. His mom and dad were still in Slovakia—usually a good deterrent against defections.

On a sunny July mid-Saturday, in 1990, Mark arrived at the Sudbury airport. Christine had a summer vacation job in Windsor, and Christopher was also working out of town during his university summer vacation; planting trees north of Chapleau. We would have plenty of room for Mark at the house—and three weeks would go by very quickly—but our young man would soon inform us of a slight change in vacation plans.

The Announcement

On his first day's arrival, Emily and I took him out for dinner, at a restaurant on Lasalle Boulevard—after all, his visit was cause for celebration.

Mark was of average height, with brittle, light sandy hair; very slender and of delicate body frame; blue-grey eyes on a rather pale and sickly looking facial complexion. However, he was energetic and enthusiastic in speech and general deportment. He was young and ready to tackle the world.

It was still early in the evening, when we were getting the last of our coffee and dessert; Mark folded his napkin neatly on the table and he said, "I have something to tell you right away," and he said this in his clipped, school-learned English—with subtle hints of lessons right out of audio-taped-accented British English: I was bracing myself for a request for money.

"Please," he continued, "don't get angry at me. You will certainly think I deceived you, but that was never my intent." We still did not know what he was driving at; I still thought it was money.

He looked at us full in the face; in genuine innocence and honesty, and he said, "I never, from the very beginning, had any intention of ever returning home. I am defecting to Canada—I destroyed all my Slovak documents and my return ticket in flight, and I flushed them down the airplane toilet." Then he took in a deep breath and he seemed relieved of a big weight off of his shoulders.

Needless to say, Emily and I were speechless for a while; but we accepted the bombshell with composure and we put on our best face. "Well," I said, somewhat out of breath, and looking at my wife and then at her cousin, "we have three weeks to get things moving—it'll be tight—but first things first; you and I have to go the Canada Immigration office downtown, first thing Monday morning."

He looked at us with a smile—and I was hoping he'd burst out laughing, and cry out, "Got you! This is a big joke!"—but no, he meant business; "If I cannot stay in the country," he continued, matter-of-factly, "I'll be moving on to Australia. I have some American dollars." He had no idea how expensive a ticket to Australia would be, and I doubted very much that he had that much money on him—not to mention the difficulties he would face, having destroyed his documents—if he really had.

It was quiet in the car on the homeward ride. Emily was perplexed; Mark was taking in the Sudbury night lights and I was mulling over a plan for Monday.

Ray A. Vincent

We take a Plan to Canadian Immigration

I went to work as usual that Monday morning, but at ten o'clock I took two hours off work and went home and picked up Mark. I had my plan—we were going to apply for "political refugee status".

We proceeded to the Canada Immigration office on Lisgar Street, atop the post office. I walked in with my charge and we sat down in front of Bob Leclair, an immigration officer—I had asked for Bob specifically. For a civil servant, Bob was the nicest and most decent person we could have been assigned to. He was easy going, humane and understanding. I knew Bob from my work at social services; the welfare office had had at times, occasions to call his office for client status verification, on sponsored immigrant welfare applications.

We explained the circumstances and asked Bob about filing an application for "political refugee status". He turned to Mark and asked him one clear, straightforward question, "Mark," he asked, "have you ever been persecuted by the Slovak authorities? Ever been put in jail, or threatened, for your political or religious beliefs? And, if so, could you prove it?"

The answer from Mark was a clear and quick, "No"; to all of the above.

"Then, since you are absolutely not running away from Slovakia for political or other persecutory reasons," Bob said, "you stand no chance in front of a federal Refugee Panel." And that was the end of that plan.

Bob Leclair's Plan

And, as we were disconsolately getting ready to rise, and leave as defeated petitioners—Bob raised his hand, in a motion for us to sit down again—and at his most humane and helpful; he said, "But, there is another way—apply for 'Landed Immigrant Status'—if granted, it would allow you to stay in the country; permit you to work, and give you time to get the process of applying for full citizenship underway."

I asked about how one applied for a 'Landed Immigrant Status' certificate.

"There are," he said, "hurdles to jump over and hoops to go through. And there is some red tape. First, you need a sponsor; secondly, and most importantly, you cannot apply within Canada; you must apply from outside the country of intent—in Mark's case, he would have to apply from the United States—and only then is the application processed—and it's not fast; it takes time."

We were inflated, and then somewhat deflated again.

In order to buy time, I asked if Mark's visitor's permit could be extended beyond the initial three weeks. Bob had some discretion, and he extended his stay by one additional week—to four weeks.

We had until mid-August to get the nearly impossible task done.

Emily's Mother has some Contacts

Over dinner that evening, we talked about, and reviewed the full morning's proceedings with Immigration. Emily's mother was at the table with us. She had some contacts—she had some priest friend amongst the Slovak Jesuit community in Toronto. The Slovak Jesuits had a long-standing and fully funded program; a program approved by the federal government, and dedicated to the sponsorship of needy Slovak immigrants—she would call them the next morning—and she did, with great results.

The Slovak Jesuit Fathers agreed to sponsor Mark—and he was very fortunate—this program was being phased-out, and he filled the last seat available. All his lucky stars were aligned in perfect conjunction.

A Trip to Buffalo, N.Y.

The second hurdle to master was to go to the USA to file his application for Canadian Landed Immigrant status, at a Canadian

Consulate office. So we took Mark to Toronto to meet with the Slovak Jesuit Fathers first, to pick up his sponsorship confirmation documents; and then we dropped him off at Emily's brother John, in St. Catherines—next door to Buffalo, New York. John would take over the second leg—he would take Mark across the border at Buffalo, N.Y., and get him to the Canadian Consulate there to file his immigration application.

This was done, and we had already burned two weeks of the four allowed to complete the process. We had a big problem; we were running out of time.

The bureaucracy marches ever so slowly. Even though he had filed his immigration request, all in good form; outside of the country, in Buffalo; it did not mean that he would get an immediate answer—it could take many weeks, if not months before an answer on his application came through.

We were running out of time. It was now almost mid-August; we would need another month's extension, at the very least—or Mark faced deportation out of the country.

Another visit to Immigration and a Different Reception

We went back to the Canada Immigration office and asked to see Bob Leclair again. We were told that he was not available; he either declared a conflict of interest since he knew me personally, and he put the file in someone else's hands; or, he was really away—I never found out.

We were not lucky—the file was on the desk of Al Abercrombie—the local Immigration office Unit supervisor. Mr. Abercrombie was not helpful—he was downright rude and hostile to Mark's request. We had no sooner sat down than he made it clear that he wanted him out of the country—and the sooner the better, as far as Abercrombie was concerned. The open file on his desk showed that Mark had been to the US and that he had filed the proper papers at the Consulate, for Landed Immigrant status—but without an adjudication yet.

He looked at Mark and said, "You have four days before the expiration of your visit; we have no decision yet from Ottawa on your application; and furthermore, you have no sponsorship papers from anyone—I'm afraid you'll have to go back to Slovakia, and await Ottawa's decision from your home country. That's the best we can do at this time." He concluded with a smile.

Then Mark reached into the leather folder on his lap and pulled out the signed sponsorship documents from the Slovak Jesuits. The Slovak Jesuits' sponsorship program was a federal government approved, long time honoured program, that had served the federal politicians in Toronto very well. Wise and ambitious bureaucrats knew not to step on political toes—it was not a good career move for aspiring civil servants.

Abercrombie was not a happy man. He was shaking with anger. "I see," he said, perusing the paper with careful scrutiny; "listen," he said, looking at Mark across the desk, "you have four days to bring me a hard copy proof of a flight ticket to Bratislava; departure dated six weeks from today. If you do that before the expiration of your four days; I'll extend you another six weeks—without the ticket confirming departure, I'll have you removed from the country."

That is how small-minded, dictatorial-muscle-flexing bureaucrats behave. And that is how this self-important mandarin ran his small castle. He was no better than the Eastern-Bloc autocrats that Mark was trying to get away from.

A friend to the Rescue: A ticket Produced

On the first floor of city hall, on the immediate right-hand side as you came in from the water fountain concourse (there at that time); were a variety of commercial shops; there were a flower and curio shop on one side, and a full-service travel agency, on the other. The next day after our meeting with Abercrombie, I took Mark to the travel agency and we talked to Jasmine, an acquaintance and a friend of one of my staff.

Jasmine was a sales agent with the agency. We were there to enquire about the cost of a plane ticket—Toronto to Bratislava, Slovakia—and I explained to her the whole story of Mark and Abercrombie; the reasons for the ticket—I spared no details. She was sympathetic to my young friend's plight. "Well," she said, after doing a little research, "the cheapest ticket, for the date you want it for; by Lufthansa Airline; Toronto to Bratislava, one way, is $9,700 dollars." That was a lot more than we had anticipated, and she stood there looking at our downcast faces.

"But listen," she said cheerfully, "I can print out the ticket now, don't pay anything; do what you have to do with it, but"—she cautioned, "you must bring it back to me before we close shop today—then I can cancel it. If you do not, you'll have to pay for it."

In life, a man like Abercrombie—was part of the problem. Whereas, an innocent young lady the likes of Jasmine—was part of the solution.

Mark told me later, as we walked back to the travel agency with the victorious ticket in hand, and a 'thank-you' card with twenty dollars of Mark's money in it, destined for Jasmine, "What a wonderful country Canada is!"

The temporary 'on loan' flight ticket produced the agreed upon extension from Abercrombie, and now everyone could breathe a little easier.

With the Landed Immigrant status certification would come a 'work permit', and an Ontario Health Insurance card; but the certificate was not in yet—and Mark wanted to work—at anything, as long as he was kept busy—he was not lazy, and neither did he want to live off of charity.

Cortina Pizza Offers to Help

Emily and I knew the Massotti family very well: they were the owner-operators of a Sudbury district chain of pizza restaurants—Cortina Pizza. I went to talk to Tony at the Martindale Street restaurant and pizza shop, and I asked him, "Do you have a job for a hungry, hardworking young immigrant from Slovakia?" Tony had been there, he'd been a young and hungry immigrant at one time; I recall his story of his first landing in Halifax, he and his brother penniless; on the train to Montreal, eating white Canadian bread—thinking they were eating white cake.

Tony replied without hesitation, "No problem, bring him here to me tomorrow morning." And that's how Mark started his first job in Canada—making pizzas at Cortina Pizza—or, at least trying to—he told me he spoiled quite a few on his first attempts—and the staff around him having a good laugh at his expense.

The Social Insurance Number Caper

After a few days on the job, he came home after work (commuting to work and back, with Christopher's bicycle), and he said, "The payroll girl is asking me about something called 'an employment insurance card number'; she's asking me to bring it to her, so she can make out my cheque." It took me a few seconds to think this out, and then I replied casually, "Tell her she'll have it the day after tomorrow." And I changed the subject to the art of pizza-making.

How One Finds a SIN Number

At the municipal welfare office, if an indigent person died in the city, without next of kin, or anyone coming forward to claim the body for burial purposes—the Coroner's Act of Ontario obligated the municipality to bury the deceased individual, and pay the funeral home the cost of such 'indigent burial'. And there were many such burials—two or three per month. Through an agreement with the local funeral homes, we paid a set fee for their services.

A file was opened and closed in each case and put away for record keeping. Each file contained personal identifying data, a case history, and information as it pertained to welfare eligibility. And of course; each file contained the deceased person's Social Insurance Card (SIN) number.

    I dug up (not literally) a dead man's case that had been closed for at least seven years; jotted down the deceased's SIN number on a piece of paper; and that evening after supper, I went to Mark's bedroom, knocked on the door and when he opened it I handed him the paper, "Here's your SIN number," I said; "give it to the payroll girl. And when you get your new SIN card with your immigration papers from Ottawa—make sure you destroy this piece of paper." He gave me a knowing smile and we never talked about it ever again—that is, not until 2008, when Emily and I met Mark and his wife Esther in Seattle; and we reminisced and laughed about his Sudbury adventures—and he thanked us again profusely for all we had done for him. I told him that sometimes living up to my motto, 'Be part of the solution and not part of the problem', could land one in hot water.

A Waiter at the Snow Flake Restaurant

Mark did not stay long at the pizza shop. When he finally got granted his Landed Immigrant status, and his legitimate SIN card, he got a job which he was perfectly suited for—as a waiter at Science North's Snow Flake restaurant. A great restaurant where the tips were very significant. Mark had all the attributes of a superior waiter—he had a continental flair about him, and an engaging accent; slender and good looking—he made great money on tips.

An Amazing Young Man

By October, he had his own apartment; a small upstairs three-room apartment at our neighbour's, Mr. and Mrs. Weir next door to us.

    Now that he was allowed to remain in the country, he would apply for full Canadian citizenship later on; but he had no intentions of remaining in Sudbury for long, in our 'sleepy town', as he called Sudbury.

Over the winter of 1992, he applied for admission at the University of British Columbia, and he was accepted. In late spring he went to Andy's in Toronto—he was in the market for a used car—and Andy, the wheeler, and dealer, was the perfect person to direct him to the best deals.

Mark came back to Sudbury within a few days, with a very good car—a 1988, red, Nissan Pulsar with a T-Bar roof—a sports car—and Mark told me later, "For a kid from a socialist Commie country, it may as well have been a Ferrari!" He kept his job at the 'Snow Flake' till the middle of August. At the end of the month, he loaded up the little car from the floor to rooftop, hugged and kissed us goodbye; got in his car; honked the horn, and was on his way west to embark on the next chapter of his life.

He told us later, it was a five-day road trip. He travelled through Sault-St-Marie and he hugged the northern US border, heading westerly. The young man was no fool; the highways were better; gas and motels, and food were cheaper. It was a great travelling adventure for him; memorable in his mind was the 'Big Sky' country of the state of Montana.

Mark successfully completed his university degree, graduated, and got employed by the Royal Bank of Canada, as an RBC financial advisor—a job he still holds today. He married Esther Valencia, and they live happily with their young son Lucas, in Vancouver.

We visited with Mark and Esther in Seattle, when Emily and I were there to pick up a cruise ship. Mark had taken time to drive to Seattle and spend a day with us. And not a birthday goes by; his or ours, without a phone call from either of us. We are very proud of Mark—an amazing young man.

CHAPTER 34

Christine Starts to Work

Children's developments and the direction their lives will take are difficult to predict at the best of times; and I was in for a few surprises—sometimes unhappy, heartbreaking surprises. At other times, blended with happier notes.

Our children grew up as very normal, average teenagers; they were not spoiled; they were not abused; there was nothing precocious or unusual about them. Christine graduated with her Bachelor of Arts degree from Windsor University, and shortly thereafter, secured employment with Levelor Inc., as an account manager. The company's Head offices were in Toronto, and Christine chose to live in a high rise apartment complex in Mississauga, in order to be in closer contact with her clients; and this meant constant driving in southern Ontario.

As a graduation present, we had bought Christine a small car that very summer of her graduation; and a small car it was—a 3 cylinder, General Motors "Sprint"—good on gas, but as fast as a snail; it did not live up to its name in the "sprint" department. Her girlfriend Caroline joked, that on a steep hill, she could overtake Christine easily, riding on her bicycle. When Christine took her boss out with her, during training and orientation sessions, he was petrified; these were Toronto and GTA highways, and he told her after their first day out, "You're gonna get killed before the end of your first month on the road, with this toy car."

The next week, she was driving a big company van, which came with an expense account to her credit.

Our Son and his Adventures

By grade 13, Christopher had quit all involvement with any sports; he had a girlfriend; carried his long, and wavy curly hair well below his shoulders; and smoked cigarettes, and whatever else he could lay his hands on. His circle of friends was like-minded; leaning to the cool, unconventional lifestyle.

What example, he patterned himself upon, I could never figure out—it certainly was not aligned with me. Instead of being my friend, he became his mother's friend and confidante; he became someone who lived with us; who watched his manners like a good boy while at home; who was polite around his parents—but someone who placed the feelings of his peers, above those of his parents. Sometimes I thought we had taken in a boarder in the house.

In a very subtle fashion, but quite noticeably, his vocabulary started to change; his sentences became curt and spiked with the ubiquitous word "man". This word, "man", became interjected at the beginning, or the end of each sentence; or, at both, the beginning and the end—it drove me crazy—I thought I had a coloured man from the ghettos living with us.

He applied for admission at the University of Guelph and his application was accepted, and like most first-year student, he lived in residence. Both our children always had summer employment as students. The agreement with them was that, they would pay for their tuition costs with their summer job incomes—which also left them some spending money—and Emily and I would cover the costs of books; residence and meal plans; travel and other pocket expenses—our children never had to resort to government student loans (OSAP); they graduated from university, debt-free.

The Repetitious Mini-Withdrawals

Twice per month—coincident with my pay cheque dates—I deposited spending money in Christopher's bank account, which he accessed at his end in Guelph. I do not think that Christopher was aware that at my end, I held the bank passbook—so that I could easily track if I wanted to—all of his withdrawal activities and patterns. And they were interesting, to say the least—particularly on Friday and Saturday nights: a continuous series of withdrawals, all spaced fifteen to a half hour apart, for small cash amounts through an ATM; with amounts varying from ten to thirty dollars. When I enquired about this some years later, he laughed and said that the Friday and Saturday nights were, "pub nights"—made a lot of sense to me.

In his second year, he was adamant that he wanted out of students' residence; he and some friends would move out and rent an apartment in town, and share costs.

I did not like the idea, and I was against it from the very beginning, even though it would mean a net cost saving to Emily and me; and I told him so. However, he was twenty, going on twenty-one, and I gave him some credit that he possessed a reasonable amount of sound judgment.

Our Son runs a Bootlegging Joint

In the spring of his second year, we went to visit him at his new living quarters. I was not impressed, and his mother was very upset; he and his friends had turned the upper floor apartment into an "after hours bar"—in other words, a bootlegging joint—complete with a posted price list on the wall; specially printed "members' cards", which only select patrons were privileged to carry around with them. You gained entry by being a 'club member', or the friend of one. And our son was the main bartender.

How he would find time for school studies and research time for his papers, was beyond my understanding. What else was being sold there "after hours" made me cringe?

Emily gave him an ultimatum—out of there within thirty days—or the flow of all parental funds, for now, and ensuing years, was to be shut off.

And he moved before a month had passed from the date of our visit; to a new address and with another friend. The new address was a single detached house, fully furnished, and with a full basement.

I become More Involved in the Community

In 1993, I was invited to sit on the Advisory Board of the Salvation Army. The 'Army' in Sudbury ran a men's hostel; a second-hand store with clothing and furniture; and, an aftercare facility for those on alcohol rehabilitation. There were many good Sudbury citizens, and very good people indeed they were, who gave of their time and sat on the board; not the least of which around the table were the likes of Geoffrey Lougheed and Bob Fontaine. All board members had a genuine desire to be of help to the Army in particular, and to the community in general.

I got to know the men and women of the Salvation Army; a more selfless and sincerely philanthropic organization would be hard to find. They indeed carry out a service to God, through their daily mission of assistance to their fellow human beings. And they do it every day, without any bias or prejudice to any creed, colour, race or nationality.

I have participated in many door-to-door campaigns for many different organizations, and as evidenced by the reception I was to receive, the mere mention of the word "Salvation Army" opened up a greater number of wallets and purses to the cause of the Army, than any of the other organization put together. One day, as I was doing some "Red Shield Appeal" canvassing, an older gentleman told me the story his dad had told him: his father had been a veteran of world war two, and he had told his son that the "Sally Ann" was the only benevolent group going to servicemen at the front, giving away personal effects of toiletries without questions; and without ever asking the men which church they "belonged to?" which, he said, was unlike the behaviour of the other clerical groups coming around.

Ray A. Vincent

Christopher becomes an Educator

Our son completed his degree at Guelph, and he was accepted at Canisius College in Buffalo, N.Y., in the Teachers' College program. Emily and I were happy with this career choice, and we agreed to fund his entire tuition and residence cost—and being a private U.S. college—it was expensive. But it was a great teacher's college, run by the Catholic Jesuit Fathers—we were happy for Chris; our son had seen the light (or so we thought) —so we had no hesitations in helping him, and we gave him our full support.

He spent the summer in Sudbury with us while waiting for the commencement of school at Canisius. We had put many of his personal belongings and furnishings in storage in Guelph. He may have need of some of those in Buffalo, and it was thought wise to keep them closer to the U.S. border, for easier access. And he still had some articles of clothing with his friend at the house in Guelph. Those we would pick up when we visited the storage bin.

A Disturbing Phone Call

One evening after supper, three weeks into his stay with us in Sudbury, a phone call came to him from his friend back at the house in Guelph. Our son took the portable phone and walked out to the outside patio deck to handle the call in privacy. When he walked back in the house, he had a ghost-like pallor on his face and his hand was shaking when he deposited the phone back to its cradle. Then he sat down and told us.

The friend, with whom he'd been sharing the big house, was the caller. The friend had just been busted for operating a "grow-op" in the basement of the house, and Christopher was implicated; in a closet, inside one of his jacket pockets, the police had found a rolled up bundle of cash. His friend was charged and was due to appear in court—and the police had said that they wanted to speak to our son in regards to the bundle of money, and his role, if any, in the "grow-up" business. His friend intimated that he, Chris, may also be charged since he had been an inmate of that house and that the large quantity of money found in his jacket pocket was certainly suspicious, if not incriminating.

I got Chris to call his friend back, and get the investigating officer's name and phone number. I called the Guelph police station and made an appointment for early in the next week; Chris and I would go and speak to him in person.

I was hurt and disappointed; we had been used and deceived. I had no doubt that our son knew about the marijuana; and that he had used, and maybe even sold, some. But this was a time that called for defence, and not accusations and hand wringing. The often quoted saying in regards to getting your kids in sports in order to keep them out of trouble with the law; particularly the saying, "Put your kids on the ice, and keep them out of hot water," in direct reference to hockey—is a lot of bunk.

However, there were some positive aspects to Chris' position. He had graduated and he had officially moved out of Guelph before the police actions involving his friend occurred. He was accepted at Canisius and he already had a residential address in Buffalo. And he was now living in Sudbury—difficult to prove that he was involved in the grow-op in Guelph when he was not living there.

A Meeting at the Guelph Police Department

The day before leaving for Guelph, I told Chris to put a clean, crisp white shirt and tie in the suitcase, plus his full suit and dress shoes. I wore my usual tweed jacket, with shirt and tie. And we left the driveway early in the morning, bound for our scheduled one-thirty o'clock, afternoon appointment.

At the outskirts of the city of Guelph, I pulled into a gas station, and Chris took the luggage in the washroom where he proceeded to change into his interview clothes—dress shoes; dark suit; and matching shirt and tie. We had to impress upon the officers that; here was a good middle-class young man; enrolled in a private school run by Jesuits; who would be taught by them, on how to properly teach their children one day.

We were seen promptly at the time appointed. I was allowed to sit in with my son. The tenor of the meeting was tense and formal at the beginning, but it became more cordial and relaxed as Christopher's situation was explained and made clear; that he had left the house in question over a month ago; that the primary tenant had only been Chris's friend since the day that he had moved in with him; that they had not moved in together; that the marijuana plants were already in place when he'd moved in; and the closing clause—that he was due to attend teachers' college in the fall.

They asked about his clothes in the closet and the wad of rolled up money found in his jacket pocket; Chris said that he had left some clothes behind, because he may want to travel from Buffalo to Guelph to visit friends on the odd weekend; there being a very short driving distance between Guelph and Buffalo. As to the money found in his jacket, he denied ownership of it; Chris suggested it may have been put there for safekeeping by the owner of the grow-op. They asked who else lived in the house, and Chris stated that there were only two legal tenants in the place—he and his friend—but that different persons were constantly coming and going throughout the day, and on a regular basis.

It became evident from their line of questioning, that they were more after incriminating evidence against his friend than trying to find cause to charge Christopher with any wrongdoing. However, as an enraged parent, I held some hope that they'd throw the book at him also.

They then told Chris to go, alone, in a side room; and there to take his time, and write by hand; a full and complete deposition of all he knew of the marijuana growing operation; and of events as they unfolded at the house, from the first day he moved in it, to his last day of residence there.

They cautioned him to write nothing but the truth since the document would be filed in evidence when the charges against his friend were prosecuted in court. I was not allowed to go in the room with him, but once completed and signed in front of the officers, I would be allowed to read it.

When I asked the officers if he would be required to testify in person, they said it was unlikely. And he did not have to; his friend pleaded guilty—and that was the end of that.

We returned home to Sudbury immediately upon walking out of the station. It was to be a quiet five-hour drive. The silence was interrupted once; and that was when Chris said he was, "So sorry, that he had 'ratted' on his friend."

Then I lost it and exploded—after a week of stress and suppressed anger—he had just pushed the wrong buttons.

I looked at him and shouted, "What friend?" I told him his so-called "friend" had almost ruined his future entry to the U.S. to attend school; almost ruined his career goal to be a teacher; almost ruined his reputation and, almost caused great embarrassment to his family; and more words expressing my complete disappointment in him. When I had finished my rant, I was red in the face and beside myself with anger.

A Drive to Buffalo and More Upsets

When Emily and I drove him to school in Buffalo in early September, I was still seething with anger—but I kept my mouth shut. On our arrival, we stayed in a hotel downtown and we proceeded to the school residence first thing in the morning.

Things did not augur well. On our way through the downtown streets of Buffalo, I got involved in a car accident—my fault—my bumper clipped a car in front of us and to complicate matters—both front airbags in my car deployed. My brand new Chrysler Concorde was still mechanically sound, so we limped the rest of the way to the students' residence. I had to borrow scissors from the residence Home Supervisor, in order to cut away the bags from the steering wheel and the passenger dashboard. And, as I was getting about to unload the car of boxes, clothes, and kitchenware, my son added to my ill humour: Chris says, "You know, mom and dad, I can do this program next year—I've put you through enough trouble already—we can go back home; if that's ok with you."

And that's when I lost it again. "There's no fucking way you're coming back home with us. You've been accepted here; you're here right now—you're going to do what you have to do to successfully complete this program—and that's the end of this discussion." And I threw a few boxes around.

The room accommodated two students; it was large and clean; with two bedrooms, a living room and a kitchen. After unloading, we all got back in the car and we went grocery shopping—and we bought lots of groceries.

When Chris came home for the Christmas vacation period, he was doing well at school. This was a one year program and he would be done by the end of May 1995. He returned to school after the Christmas break; driving his own car—we had let him have our second car—the Dodge Spirit.

A Successful Career in Education Notwithstanding

A few years after his graduation, Christopher went back to Canisius for a second term; this time to study for, and earn his Masters of Education degree.

Upon graduating with his teacher's degree, our son came back home to Sudbury. In order to get his Ontario Teacher Certification, Chris needed to complete a student placement program supervised by an Ontario board of education. I contacted Gord Ewing, the director of education with the Sudbury District Public School Board—I knew Gord well, from my days as a school board trustee. Chris was placed at Churchill Public elementary school to do his teacher training, and after completion, he was certified to teach by the Ontario College of Teachers.

Christopher got employed by the Dufferin-Peel Catholic Board of Education as a high school teacher shortly thereafter, and he is presently a vice-principal with that board. Chris became the youngest staff member ever to be promoted to that position.

Elected Trustee of the Sudbury Catholic School Board

In 1996, I ran for election to the Sudbury District Catholic School Board and got elected. My ward, or trustee area in the municipality, took in all of the west end of the city; plus Gatchell; Copper Cliff and Walden—areas where I was very well known to the predominantly Italian neighbourhoods.

I had been asked by many to run as city alderman, but the municipal election rules would not allow it—a municipal employee could run for office as a school board trustee, but he was barred from running for his local town council, in order to eliminate the potential for conflicts of interests.

The Costly Business of Education: Duplication of Services

School boards in Ontario are strange political creatures—and very expensive ones at that; the very cause of which is duplication of services. And the province of Ontario is fully aware that it is spending an excessive amount of taxpayers' money to satisfy and pacify, very powerful special interest groups.

Throughout the province, most cities of significant size have four school board entities, whose main offices could be located on the very same street! This state of affairs translates into four separate, and autonomous, bureaucratic fiefdoms and empires.

Behold, an English language public school board building; an English language Catholic school board building; a French language Catholic school board building; and finally, to be politically clean and cater to the voters at large, a French- language public school board building; and in the near future, I predict the emergence of an Aboriginal Indigenous peoples' school board building—potentially, all alongside each other, on the same street!

What this means, in real and practical terms, is the actual quadrupling of administrative costs. Sudbury has four separate and distinct buildings to house the bureaucracy; we have four separate and distinct Directors of education, costing the rate payers in excess of six hundred thousand dollars in combined salaries per year; we have at least ten Superintendents of education spread over the four boards, costing the rate payers close to $1.4 million dollars per year; we have four separate and distinct Human Resources departments; we have four separate and distinct maintenance and janitorial departments; and we have four separate and distinct secretarial, information technology, and a variety of other support staff groups.

When I had the temerity to suggest, through many letters to the editor of The Sudbury Star, that boards of education should start looking for "economies of scale" and significant cost savings through inter-board service consolidations, resource sharing, and amalgamations—housing everyone in one building, and rationalizing and sharing services—I was applauded by public school supporters, and crucified in the press by the Knights of Columbus and other Catholic organizations. One person went on to write in the newspaper, that I ought to be excommunicated from the church. And the French community got into the fray—calling me a traitor to the cause, and telling me to read the British North America Act; the Act purportedly (I have not read it), guaranteeing French language and Catholic education rights in Ontario

And then I started to get disturbing phone calls in the wee hours of the morning, with silence at the other end when I picked up the receiver; and pizzas delivered to my door which we had never ordered.

All these complainants purposely missed or misunderstood my position. I was never against French language schools or the presence of catholicity in the classroom. My issue was with duplication, and it's taking sorely needed funding away from core education and the upkeep and upgrading of educational facilities. My issue was in the making of educational mandarins wealthy on the backs of school children. My point was that you need not have four separate, and very costly entities, to deliver French and Catholic education in our province—education rationalization has been done in other jurisdictions.

If the will was there, you could have one administration, respecting the rights and integrity of all student groups and their parents; and accomplish the goals of the four disparate groups as they exist today.

The main roadblock to the achievement of a rational; advanced; and solidly funded public education delivery vehicle; are the powerful vested interest groups; and the pandering and weak-willed politicians. These put their self-interest ahead of those of our children.

I finally saw the beginnings of common sense at the latter part of my tenure on the board—someone was listening after all. Heretofore, four separate yellow school buses would pick up different kids standing on the same street corner—that changed in the late nineties: one bus for all the kids on that same street corner; regardless of the language of instruction, and regardless of religion. The same bus would now bring the kids to their individual schools—the Sudbury School Transportation Consortium was born; the amalgamation of school bus transportation had arrived, saving millions of dollars province-wide. We could do the same thing for other education-related services, and recycle the millions saved, back into kids' enhanced education programming.

Sister Rose Dies

A sad event early in the spring of 1997; after a long and courageous fight with cancer, our sister Rose died at the age of sixty-seven. She was buried in the little village where she spent most of her life, alongside her husband Rosario. She left behind a daughter and three sons—all in early adulthood.

Ray A. Vincent

Christine Gets Married

Another memorable event in 1997: the marriage of our daughter Christine, on October 11th.

While working in Toronto for Levolor, Christine had met a young man the previous summer. They had met playing in a recreational softball league.

We respected her choice of the kind of man she chose to spend the rest of her life with. However, he was the farthest removed in character and attitude from the person I was—but then, she was not marrying me. He was self-centered; he was not educated; or skilled in any trade, and he did not understand the value of money. Troy never appreciated the concept of 'planning for the future'; living for today was fine with him. Troy could look after his personal appearance very well indeed, but where things mattered—around his house, in regards to maintenance and upkeep—he behaved as if he were a tenant.

Shortly after their wedding, Christine and Troy moved out of their apartment in Mississauga and moved into a newly built house, atop the hill in Hamilton. Emily and I provided assistance toward the down payment, and we purchased the essential household appliances for them; the fridge and stove, dishwasher, washing machine and dryer.

CHAPTER 35

A Right Wing approach to Welfare

In June 1995, Mike Harris' conservative government was elected to power, with Harris taking the helm as premier of the province. One of his major election campaign promises had been the "Common Sense Revolution" approach to fiscal management; and, the reform of welfare services; the overhaul of the General Welfare Assistance Act; and the transformation of welfare assistance from a perception of a citizen's right, to the concept of the "social privilege"—hence, the birth of the Ontario Works Act of 1997.

Ontario Works was introduced and was to be administered by municipalities through our social services departments. Ontario Works was a last-resort income support program for the poor set up to replace what we had delivered in the past—it still delivered a welfare cheque, but the cheque to an employable individual was now contingent: the client was now to become actively involved in his employability and job search, in order to qualify for financial assistance.

Prior to 1997, persons requiring financial assistance received support under the General Welfare Assistance Act. While the Ontario Works program purported to better respect peoples' dignity, build self-esteem and promote independence, its origins came out of a right-wing political philosophy, as a workfare program under the Mike Harris agenda. The approach and thrust of the program when first announced had great popular support—finally, the street said: "Welfare bums" will be made to earn their assistance cheques. Participants were encouraged to be actively involved in the community and get retrained for suitable employment.

Under Ontario Works, the client "Action Plan" became of foremost importance—and I was elated with this approach—finally, a concrete and practical method to assist people in finding employment; something many of us in the field had wanted for a long time. The cranking up and mailing of cheques month after month, year after year, did not lead people on to the path to employment; some of us thought it contributed to a loss of client motivation toward employment. Skills training and retraining initiatives, employment counselling and employment services delivered by the municipality and outside agencies should prove more effective.

In Sudbury, we blended both approaches within the delivery of Ontario Works: in-house employment counselling services, and referring clients to outside specialist resources.

The "plan" was to identify and address an individual's barriers to employment. It was a benefit for persons 18 years and older and single parents regardless of age. What many of us liked about the program was that in order to qualify for financial assistance under Ontario Works, the client had to be willing to participate in employment services; programs and related activities; unless, of course, unable to work due to medical reasons.

The program was results-oriented in its purpose, aims, and goals; however, to be successful, we needed available jobs out there in the community, in which our clients could move into, once their training phase had been completed; and, we also needed well motivated, program-enthused and willing staff to embrace the new concept to make it work.

Unfortunately, not all staff fell in love with Ontario Works. Some saw it as a purely political initiative by a right of centre government—which it was of course—but this reality, of itself, did not mean that the program was flawed in its intent, just because someone named Mike Harris supported it.

One key staff, in particular, our manager of employment services, took a stand in which she rejected the philosophy of the new program, and she refused to implement any services which would facilitate the introduction of Ontario Works and its related services to our client base.

A Back Door Promotion

Mark Mieto did not take lightly the fact that one of his subordinate staff—and a manager—was bucking the system. He acted swiftly—he removed her from her job—and demoted her to fieldwork; a major demotion.

The day before he was to meet with Beverly, and inform her of her removal as the head of the Employment Support Services Division, he met with me and offered me the position—a promotion. I told Mark to give me time to talk to my wife and I'd get back to him the next morning. I accepted the assignment and moved to the Employment Support Services office at the corner of Elm and Elgin Streets the very next day.

We Need Jobs

We were in the heydays of "Call Centres"; municipalities were tripping over each other in the race to go and court Call Centres, to open up in their cities. Call Centres usually hire people by the hundreds; therefore the plan was to bring in a call centre in the city, and through the Ontario Works program, have our clients fill the positions to be opened up. But before we could place our welfare clients into call centre jobs, we had to show a prospective employer that we had a job ready (and bilingual) workforce.

To that effect, I contacted Cambrian College, wanting to meet with them to discuss what, if any, training programs the College could set up for our clients. Cambrian College was very receptive, able and willing to meet our needs; and through their cooperation, we set up a training course for potential Call Centre operators. This was good business for Cambrian as it increased their enrollment and their revenues, and the cost of the program would be provincially funded.

Now we had a pool of trained and skilled "Call Centre" workers waiting for eager employers to scoop them up. And the last piece to the puzzle remaining to be put in place was the most important—we needed to convince a Call Centre company to move into town.

Ray A. Vincent

Shopping for a Call Center. Invited to an Evening Social

And to that end, Mark Mieto and I went to Toronto—shopping for a Call Centre company. We travelled to Toronto together. Once checked in we went to our separate rooms to freshen up and agreed to meet at the hotel restaurant for dinner.

After dinner, we went to the bar for a drink. Mark was a tall, well proportioned, handsome man; and Mark travelled with a reputation—he loved the ladies—particularly ladies he got to meet when travelling out of town without his wife. There were two very beautiful, well dressed and highly made-up women in their mid-twenties, at the opposite end of the bar. Mark knew right away what kinds of "ladies" they were, and he asked me if I minded if we ordered them drinks, ahead of our going over to talk to them. I smiled and excused myself saying, "Order the drinks if you wish, but I'll pass on the joining them Mark, I'm up tomorrow morning at 6:00 a.m. for my morning run"—which was the truth. And with that I finished my drink and took my leave, telling him I'll meet him for breakfast.

When he finally showed up for breakfast, I was in the last touches of finishing mine; and he looked awful; he looked rough, red-faced and bloodshot-eyed—like a guy who'd partied all night with ladies picked up at some bar the night before.

The Sales Pitch: Omega-Direct

We had set up an appointment to meet the executives of Omega-Direct; a large and growing "outbound" Call Centre business with various established Call Centre offices, in and around Toronto. Our job was to convince them that coming to Sudbury was good business for them; that Sudbury was a good place for a big Call Centre operation; that Sudbury had the required infrastructure; that Sudbury's Ontario Works clients were college trained in the rudiments of work in Call Centres; and furthermore, that many were fluent in both official languages. In effect, what we were saying was that Sudbury was ready to receive a Call Centre employer.

And then Mark waved the irresistible carrots—free accommodations in the vacant police building at the corners of Larch and Paris Street; financial subsidies toward office furnishings and computer connectivity; and the biggest and sweetest carrot of all—the payment of an amount, to be negotiated, subsidizing Omega-Direct for every hour worked by any of our Ontario Works client that found employment with them. A sweet deal for the company that would see the government picking up close to fifty percent of its labour costs. Any company executive that was not salivating at this point was probably brain dead.

These were the incentives that brought Omega-Direct to Sudbury and produced in excess of eight-hundred-full time jobs to the community—most of them going to our welfare clients.

The funding subsidies came from the Regional Municipality of Sudbury, from the province of Ontario, and from my Ontario Works Employment Support Services budget; and even though it was time-limited and on a per client basis, the program was effective in providing needed employment and a work environment for a lot of people in poverty. However, when the funding subsidies phased out over time, we witnessed a retrenchment in employment levels to a significant degree. Our detractors said, "See, we told you so, Omega-Direct was only interested in the free money while it lasted."

But I would answer, "Talk to the hundreds of our clients who had been unemployed for years, and who got the opportunity of a job, and gained immeasurably in work experience, and transferable skills in the process."

A Contract Needs to Be Drafted

It is interesting, and sometimes highly frustrating to witness how the bureaucracy works. When Mark and I returned from Toronto after our successful meeting with Omega-Direct, and before Omega-Direct would start hiring our job-ready clients, we had to have a duly signed Purchase of Service Agreement contract drafted and presented for signatures by both parties—the municipality and the company. The iron was hot and we could not delay the hammer strike.

Time was of the essence. We had a company ready to commit and we wanted to show them that indeed, we had our money where our mouths were.

I contacted the municipality's solicitor's office located on the third floor of the central tower at city hall, and told Heather Salter, our solicitor, what we needed to have done. She said she would talk to Mark (my department head) and get back to me.

We needed this contract document completed and ready for signatures within two weeks; Omega-Direct executives were coming to Sudbury to visit the Call Centre location; check out the computer infrastructure; and go over the agreement, hopeful to sign off on it prior to their departure back to Toronto.

A week went by and I hadn't heard anything from legal yet; I called Heather and enquired as to the progress of the contract; there was a pregnant pause, and her response, when it finally came, left me speechless. She said, "Not been around to it yet, but if you bring me a draft of what you want in it, we'll get working on it right away." I felt like slamming the phone down.

I asked my secretary to pull out a couple of purchase of service agreements we had in place, with community agencies that provided fee-for-service work for our clients. I shoved them in my briefcase and went home. Using them as templates, I drafted the complete purchase of service agreement between the Regional Municipality of Sudbury and Omega-Direct—from the opening preamble to the "Sunset Clause" at the end of the document. Next morning, my secretary typed the whole contract and by noon I had it on Heather's desk. I did not spend any time with her—my buddies were waiting for me at the Running Club.

Two days later, four copies were on my desk, straight from "legal"; it was on the legal department's stationary, with an attached note from Heather Salter; a one- liner saying she had reviewed it, and all was in order.

I read the document line for line, and compared it with my midnight draft—not one word had been altered.

Saving Taxpayers Money, not in the Bureaucrat's Interest

Nine months into my new job as Manager of Ontario Works' Employment Services, I received a call from Mark, asking for me to drop over to his office. His office was at the opposite end of the floor.

When I walked in he was pouring over a set of department budget spreadsheets lying on his desk. He lifted his head from his deep study and motioned that I take the seat closest to him. "Hey, Ray," he said with a fleeting smile on his face, "what the hell is this?" and he tapped on a section of the spreadsheet, as he turned the whole sheet over to me.

That was my $2.1 million dollar budget. I took great pride on how I had managed it; nine months into our fiscal year—and underspent—everything in the black; I was on my way to end the year with a nice surplus. Municipal taxpayers would be very happy with me.

But, I was to learn the fine art of bureaucratic fiscal management pretty quickly.

"Ray," he says, looking at me without his smile this time, "this looks bad; we can't have this, we cannot end the year with a surplus. When we go through finance committee, fighting for next year's budget allocation, they'll cut you back; they're going to make a case to shrink your budget down to your current year's actual expenditure. We cannot lose money; no, we must "grow" the annual budget—and that applies to every budget moving forward. So," he continued, with a little of his smile returning, "go out there and spend—I'm sure you need new office furniture; new staff computers; a new photocopy machine; purchases of staff training and education seminars: go and get them; the budget must be fully utilized by year end."

And spend, I did—I got brand new furniture for my office—better than Mark's. I purchased new office equipment and I had a staff quiet room constructed, soundproofed, where one could retreat to in times of stress and lay down on a couch, and relax.

More Community Involvement

I enjoyed and learned a lot about my community, and organizations whose main goals and objectives were to help people in need.

When approached and solicited by my friend Murray Giusti, I joined the board of directors of the Rockhaven Recovery Home for alcoholics and substance abuse clients. I got involved; I headed a committee to draft the agency's internal procedural handbook, and I became the chair of the board the next year.

At that time I also joined the Sudbury Training and Adjustment Board (LTAB); a more useless body one would have had difficulty in finding. It was an advisory panel set up by the provincial government of Bob Rae, during his short-lived and disastrous NDP provincial government days. Its main function was to advise the provincial government and the Regional Municipality, of current and forecasted labour market trends in the area; and identify labour force training needs to meet current and forecasted demands. It was to do this by gathering labour market information and data, compile statistics and draw inferences as to future training needs in the community, and project in what directions labour demands were headed. And it was to present those findings and recommendations to the two levels of government through a voluminous "Annual Report".

The objectives looked great on paper, but it was totally ineffectual in its main mandate; there were many problems, and the main one was timing. By the time the information was collected, the data analyzed and the inferences and the conclusions formulated into an annual report—a year or two had gone by—it was late, stale and redundant information. Secondly, and somewhat the cause of problem number one was that it was woefully understaffed—it had an executive director and one secretary—that was it!

The group around the table was large and representative of labour unions, management groups, and government agencies—but the overrepresentation of labour skewed the discussions—it became political at times. Granted, the board was composed of a lot of nice and congenial people, but people without any authority to effect change or influence politicians.

The advisory body moved in a vacuum. We had great philosophical discussions that led to nowhere; and we had great luncheons and dinners so that in my mind it became—"The Group that Loved to Eat"—because we did a lot more eating than productive work.

We lose a Good Woman: Mother-in-Law Dies

We lost Emily's mother on March 15, 1998. She lived to be 93 years of age. A beautiful person, and like my own mother—never a complainer. She was not known for showing a lot of exterior manifestations of emotion, but she was a warm hearted, generous and kind woman. What she kept in check as far as outward show of emotions, she let out in great outbursts of cooking prowess in the kitchen—she was a great cook—and if "baba" had cooked it, everyone crowded in around the table.

In her last year; Emily, Paul and I took time to see her every other day at Pioneer Manor rest home; and in her last month I went over after work and fed her supper.

She passed away in the early afternoon, with Emily and I, and Paul and his wife at the bedside.

Charged with Looking after my Neighbour's House

We were blessed with good neighbours; and Harry and Marry Trebb from across the street were also good friends. Their son Gary had played in net for our championship playground midget hockey team, and Laurie, their daughter was a very good friend of Christine. As had happened in our own household, Harry and Mary's children had grown up and gone off to school; and they'd found work out of town, so Harry and his wife had been alone at home just like we were. They had four children; one was a lawyer, Ronald, who lived in Sudbury; Gary was working out west; Spencer was deceased, and Laurie worked in Toronto.

That summer of 98', Harry had decided to visit his brothers in Saskatchewan—Harry's birthplace—and Mrs. Trebb would go and visit relatives in Elliot Lake. They were to be gone three to four weeks. Both Harry and Mary were in their mid-seventies, and it made a lot of sense that they would make plans to visit kin and siblings before it was too late. And since Mary was only going as far as Elliot Lake, she was expected back home much sooner than her husband.

Harry came to my house the week before they were due to leave, and asked me if I would pick up his mail, and keep an eye on the house in his absence. No problem, I said; that is what good neighbours do for each other.

Ten days after they'd been gone, I got a call from Emily at work. She called just before lunch and my departure toward the running club; "Ray," she asked, "are the Trebb's moving?" I said, "No, Harry would have mentioned something to me about it."

"Well," she continued, "there's a big moving van in their driveway; stuff's being moved out; just thought I'd let you know."

Within fifteen minutes I was pulling my car into our driveway. I walked across the street to the Trebb's—I was the guy entrusted with looking after their house, and there was the Allied Neely Van in their driveway being stuffed with their things. I was sure I was going to interrupt a robbery in progress.

Moving company people wearing the Allied Neely Van crest on their shirts were moving furniture out of the house. I stopped one of them on the porch landing and asked him what was going on. He looked puzzled by my question, and he suggested I go in the house and talk to Mr. Trebb—under whose direction they were working.

The Mr. Trebb in the house was Harry's lawyer son—Ron. I introduced myself and he looked abashed and embarrassed: he proceeded to tell me that he was acting on behalf of his mother; his mom was leaving her husband—a senior citizen marital breakdown at age 76—with the kids out of the house, to boot! He anticipated my next question, and said, "I'm calling dad tonight."

Just when I thought welfare work had thrown everything weird for me to see—this ranks up there with the case of the mother and daughter sharing the same putative father of their children and, living happily together in the same household.

I walked into my house where lunch was waiting and I said to Emily, "Sit down for a minute, have I got something to tell you."

Office Automation: A Consequence

Computer automation had been introduced in the department for some time now; it speeded up case processing, and client cheque production; it made possible for direct bank deposits of clients' cheques directly into their accounts; and provided us with a wealth of month-end statistical data.

There was even talk of eliminating the mandatory home visitation; a client and family verification procedure that had been with municipal welfare agencies back to the old days of "Relief" client assistance programs.

With automation came decentralized case management and; with decentralized case management came decentralized case authorization, and with decentralized case authorization, came more client payment decision-making into the hands of caseworkers, and in my view; a weakened system of supervisory monitoring and fraud control. And in those days, our main concerns were with attempts by clients to defraud the system; we never in our wildest dreams gave any thoughts to internal, employee fraud.

Ray A. Vincent

An Inside Job

A few years back we had hired a young, honours graduate from the University of Windsor's School of Social Work program. Ours would be her first job upon graduation. She was young, single, blond, blue-eyed and very pretty. She was gentle and soft-spoken; carried a shy, quiet smile about her; was well liked by her colleagues (and popular, with the male caseworkers); she was very intelligent and low key; she never said a controversial word at the monthly staff meetings, or said much at the regular team meetings; and she was a quick learner—the perfect employee—every supervisor wanted her on his team.

The caseloads were high and increasing; supervisors would screen well in excess of forty case files on a daily basis. Supervisors relied on casework accuracy from the staff, and because of the work overload, very few case audits were carried out, very few spot checks were actually done.

Well, it did not take long for our young, demure and so polite caseworker to figure out that she could take advantage of a wide-open system.

She took advantage of two things: supervisory work overload and, the automated system of client cheque direct bank deposit. She started to create fictitious client cases—for every twenty or so, legitimate cases, she would slip through one totally bogus case for approval; and, she would have the fictitious client cheques directly deposited to her own bank account—it was the perfect internal welfare fraud for its simplicity.

If supervisory staff had been awake at the switch, we should have realized that some of the case histories did not make sense; that something was not quite kosher. Her bogus cases were meant to generate large cheque amounts; hence, they were all of unusually large families in composition; some of them had the same underlying narrative—travelling through town and stranded with a car breakdown, with babies to feed; or, a large family whose father had absconded; no food in the house and a high rent bill to pay.

Later on, when we checked into the fraudulent cases and the information documented, not only were the families fictitious—so were the city addresses provided: the street existed but not the house numbers recorded. And what should have raised another flag—none of the fraudulent families had any phone numbers.

Our young lady started to wear high-end designer clothes; she vacationed in Hawaii and other exotic places; and she bought a house on Algonquin Road. The poor girl began to feel the need for some kind of a cover, she eventually would have to account for her new found wealth. Staff talked openly in the lunchroom about how fortunate she'd been to have inherited money from her granny; and how generous an aunt our young girl had—to have bought her a brand new car.

We did not discover the fraud—the banks did. God knows how long this would have continued if one day a bank employee had not called our office manager.

The person from the bank had said to Trudy, our manager, "There may be absolutely nothing wrong here; this probably involves one of your caseworkers acting as client "trustee", which is unusual, but it happens and it's fine—but we would like you to confirm if this is so."

And the jig was up. That is how the can of beans was spilled—all of her numerous fictitious clients' cheques were being deposited to accounts across town, held in her name.

The case was brought to the police, and when confronted she admitted to the whole scheme. She was charged with fraud for an amount in excess of $350 thousand dollars. At trial, she was convicted; slapped on the wrist with house arrest and probation and a restitution order; the house was turned over and expropriated by the city.

A welfare client gets jail for stealing less than a thousand dollars—she got house arrest for a year—welcome to white collar crime justice! So much for equal justice before the law!

Interestingly, in this case, there was practically no press coverage of the event and the ensuing court proceedings. Two things were at play here: the city did not want negative and adverse publicity, it wanted no embarrassment—and neither did CUPE, the young girl's union—it would look bad for the membership. Both organizations had contacts with the press (and the press is unionized); one would not be far off the mark to suggest collusion to ensure a tight wrap on the story.

CHAPTER 36

The Boston Marathon

April 19 1999 was a special day; it was the occasion of the 103rd running of the Boston marathon— I had qualified to enter the race, and I was there at the start line located in the small town of Hopkinton; and the 26.2 miles would run through other towns and villages, before ending in downtown Boston.

Emily and her brother John and his wife were waiting for me at the finish line. It was not my best marathon finish time—but then, neither was I ten years younger. I was doing well by the halfway point, with a time of one hour twenty-six minutes—and then dehydration set in, and the wheels came off—it was a warm humid day, and I had trained in the cold Sudbury winter weather. But the fact that I had qualified for, ran and completed the Boston was gratifying enough for me.

A special Year: a Grandchild and a Retirement

And, 1999 was to be a special year for me for other reasons; it was the exciting year of the expected birth of our first grandchild; and, after thirty-five years of municipal social services work, I had decided to take my retirement, effective October 6th—the same day and month I had started my career with the city of Sudbury and had gotten to meet Simone Patterson.

In early summer, with only a few months away from retirement, I found it difficult to concentrate at work. My mind would wander far afield, into the unknown territory ahead of me. And then in June, Christine called Emily and my thoughts turned to an entirely new set of preoccupations.

A Medical Complication

The birth of our first grandchild was not to be a normal one. The routine obstetric ultrasound screening had determined that Christine was to give birth to a baby boy, but there was also something else discovered—baby Noah was to be born with a Congenital Diaphragmatic Hernia (CDH) condition.

When Christine called Emily in the early afternoon, she was in tears and her voice was breaking. Statistics showed that babies born with neonatal diaphragmatic hernias had a 67 percent morbidity rate. Little Noah had a 33 percent window; the majority died shortly after birth.

A congenital diaphragmatic hernia is a birth defect of the diaphragm. The diaphragm is that wide, flat muscle band which separates the chest and abdominal cavities. Little baby Noah had a large hole in the diaphragm and this malformation allowed the abdominal organs—the stomach, intestines, liver, spleen, and kidney—to push themselves into the baby's chest cavity, hindering proper lung formation and breathing. While in uterus, baby did not need its lungs to breathe, because the placenta performed this function—however, if the lungs are too small or constricted at birth, little Noah would not be able to provide himself with enough oxygen to survive.

This was explained to Christine and Troy, pre-delivery, and they were given two options—either of which the hospital would carry out—abort the pregnancy, or go ahead to term, and deliver the baby and trust in the expertise of one of the best pediatric surgeon in the country—if not in the world—Dr. Peter Fitzpatrick.

Emily asked Christine if we should go ahead with the planned preparations and furnishings of "baby's room", and; furthermore, if we should go ahead with the planned "baby shower"—and she answered in the affirmative to both questions; she was going to do she said, what "baba" Hatala would have done in similar circumstances—baba would have faced events head-on, taken it one day at a time, with hope and with resignation.

Christine and Troy were very fortunate in the fact that they resided in Hamilton; home of the McMaster Children's Hospital, which had a pediatric neonatal surgical Specialty and, most importantly, where Dr. Fitzpatrick, head of pediatric surgery, practiced his skills. A great pediatric surgeon, and an even greater human being. Dr. Fitzpatrick presently is a professor of pediatric surgery at McMaster University.

Upon delivery, baby Noah was immediately placed on a ventilator, and within twenty-four hours Dr. Fitzpatrick and his team went to work to save this little life. The organs that had invaded the chest cavity were manually pushed back to their normal location, and the hernia closed, and the baby was then transferred to the intensive care pediatric nursery.

After three weeks post-surgery, Christine and Troy brought baby Noah—our "Miracle Baby"—home. The surgery was a complete success; Noah developed normally; did well at school and in sports activities. When only 33 percent of CDH babies survived, Noah went on to compete in provincial swim meets for his club; played competitive hockey from atom to midget level.

May God bless and protect people like Dr. Peter Fitzpatrick.

When we celebrated Noah's first birthday, I wrote a letter to the editor of the Hamilton newspaper—The Spectator—which was published, thanking Dr. Fitzpatrick and his wonderful team. This was a letter written on behalf of the "Miracle Baby".

I Retire

The day of my retirement came October 6, 1999. The day of my last appearance at work, Mark had come to my office and he'd said, shaking my hand warmly, "Ray, go around the building, say your goodbyes and get the heck away from here; go home; we'll all see you at the party."

The retirement party was held at the Caruso Club, and it was no surprise; I knew well in advance. I had mixed feelings. I was happily and voluntarily moving into early retirement; I had the full pension factors of age plus years of service, but I was sad; I would miss a job I thoroughly enjoyed doing, and I would miss the comrades-in-arms that I was leaving behind at the office. People may say different about their retirements, but I saw my retirement as a sad event.

My heart was agitated with emotions as I walked toward the podium to say my little speech—my farewells and my thank you's. I surveyed the room, and strategically seated together in the centre of the floor, not far from the podium were my truly dear friends—Simone Patterson, Paul Schaak, Herb Hatton (who'd said back in October 1966, "But, we have an opening at the welfare office, would you be interested?"), Smitty Lapalme was also there at the table, and Lou Leblanc and Mona St. Jean from Durham Street days.

All my sisters were there and my brother Pete, and so were our good neighbours Mr. and Mrs. St. Pierre, and Mr. and Mrs. Ward. All my colleagues from work were there in attendance and a good number of retired staff. The Sudbury Masters Running Club was well represented and my dear friend, Bill Thompson, took the podium later on their behalf and said many kind words which I much appreciated.

And it gave my heart a leap of joy to see our daughter Christine and her husband Troy, coming in through the hall doors, pushing a stroller in which our "Miracle Baby" was fast asleep.

To my disappointment, our son Christopher had opted not to attend.

DUSK

CHAPTER 37

A Mischievous Deception

And then came the much dreaded year 2000. The year when at one millisecond past midnight on January 1, 2000, the cyber world as we knew it was supposed to suddenly come to an abrupt standstill.

Throughout 1999, the Regional Municipality of Sudbury had spent hundreds of thousands of taxpayer dollars in order to make its computers, so-called "Y2K compliant". Overnight, the IT department achieved celebrity status. Once relegated to a nondescript corner of the building, it was now very high profile, up and centre and in much demand.

Much of the concern revolved around whether computers around the world would malfunction on January 1, 2000, because someone said they weren't programmed to properly read the year's two last digits—00, in the number 2000.

We were warned to brace for an onslaught of insidious viruses riding the wave of Y2K problems. Where had they gone? None appeared.

The hysteria surrounding the year 2000 computer bug was the biggest money making hoax perpetrated in my lifetime. It became an elaborate and perfectly executed scam. I'm in awe of the people who inflated this issue to mythical proportions. Now all that is left to do is listen to all the "experts" congratulate themselves on how they saved us all from certain chaos and the end of life as we know it. But I am certain that now some people realize how seriously, they had been duped. The planes did not fall out of the skies, elevators did not drop to the basements, governments did not collapse (I wish some had). The year 2000 arrived with a yawn.

Millennium hysteria—once the Y2K circus opened its tent, the travelling IT freaks dazzled management into doing anything they asked and pay any price they demanded.

This demonstrated the essence of capitalism and entrepreneurship: find a fear and exploit it to get as much money out of it as possible until it runs dry; then find something else. The Y2K hysteria was a multibillion-dollar worldwide scam.

No ordinary, technology illiterate person like me could stand up and debate any of the Y2K medicine men in public—they had everything going for them. With only a few words, they could easily exploit the fear of the unknown, the fear of computers, and especially the fear of big numbers. One of them opened his speech one day with this doom and gloom line: "Every time bomb has a clock. This time bomb is a clock!" Everyone in the audience saw visions of the coming of the Apocalypse. The doom and gloom advocates were like newly hatched mosquitoes; they only had a short amount of time to suck blood before they die.

What actually dumbfounded me was that, for whatever reasons, many people were looking forward to major chaos and catastrophe (not to themselves, of course). Some actually need to experience temporary chaos in order for wonderful things to happen to them immediately afterward. Then the new event is that much more appreciated.

The year 2000 problem had three advantages that helped to make it a perfect racket. First, it had a basis in reality. Second, it was supposed to be a software problem—something lay people could not easily understand. Third, its association with the turn of the millennium played into superstition and fantasy creations.

The year 2000 scare was a hoax. The computer world did not crash, the planet was not paralyzed, as forecasted by the con men, and chaos did not reign—at least not any more than we were used to experiencing. The clock had turned over on January 1, 2000, with no major disruptions, and cable news chatterers quickly concluded that we'd been fooled. Y2K and the nasty prognostications that came along with it now looked like the sort of problem people invent when the economy's booming and there's nothing else to worry about.

How big a deal was Y2K? In the run-up to the new century, the United States alone, spent about $100 billion dollars combatting the non-existent bug—around $9 billion by the federal government, and the rest, by utility companies, banks, airlines, telecommunication firms, and just about any other corporate entity with more than a few computers. The rest of the world was no slouch either; estimates for global Y2K related expenditures ranged from $300 to $500 billion.

Just about everyone who'd been worried about Y2K before January 1st, slouched away in shame afterward, less interested in assessing what went wrong than in distancing themselves from a perceived boondoggle.

A Period of Adjustment and Retirement Anxiety

The first eight weeks of my retirement "vacation time" was great; however, that light and happy phase of euphoria quickly dissipated. Emily kept working at Laurentian Hospital and she was to continue doing so for another four years until she retired after a thirty-eight-year nursing career.

So I would drive her to work in the morning, come back home and put away the morning breakfast dishes; pace around the house; go outside and do some yard work; go to the running club; come home and get ready to go and pick her up.

I missed the old work atmosphere terribly; I was going insane with boredom and I became depressed. Retirement made me appreciate how much your work environment defines who you are—particularly for men. All of a sudden I had become a nobody; no one needed me anymore, no one brought me their problems to resolve; I felt useless; I missed the planning, the managing of projects, the deadlines and the getting things done; in short order, I became depressed and irritable.

I realized that at age 55, I had retired too early; I should have retired at 60, although I know of a lot of people who, like me, took early retirement and never looked back; they enjoyed every single minute of retirement from the very first day—Emily for example, never missed the hospital—I envied those folks—they were well-adjusted individuals.

I am not the most gregarious person by any stretch of the imagination, but I had to get back in contact with the hustle and bustle of the workplace; I had to get back in contact with people—so, to my wife's dismay, I sought a part-time job.

Part Time at Canadian Tire

As the Human Resource manager perused my career resume attached to my application form, she kept on lifting her eyes from the papers and threw quick glances in my direction, then finally she said, "You just retired barely two months ago. Why are you here?" I looked at her like a timid little puppy who's been caught soiling the carpet, and replied in a lifeless voice, "I'm bored out of my mind." She smiled and said reassuringly, "I see people like you in my office all the time."

She rose from her desk, shook my hand and said, "Come on Monday morning for orientation; you'll need black safety shoes and black pants—we supply the blue Canadian Tire shirt and the red tie that goes with it."

And that is how my short-lived career as the "Door Greeter" at the New Sudbury Canadian Tire store began.

Emily was not impressed. She was downright angry; her immediate comments to me were, "What will our friends think of this? Are you that hard up for money?" And, "You are taking a job away from a poor person, or a poor student who really needs the part-time work." More than angry—she was embarrassed.

My introduction to private enterprise employment was a bit unsettling. I was not to park close to the store; that area was for customers—at city hall, I had underground paid-for parking privileges right next to the elevator entrance; our taxpaying customers parked by the arena, come rain, snow or sleet—here, I was told to park my car at the farthest corner of the parking lot. And when the time came for my fifteen minutes allotted coffee break period, I proceeded to the staff lunchroom; propping up my tired legs on a chair opposite and chatting away with the people there, supervisory types, one of which was the store owner. We had a great discussion and I enjoyed myself, but when I got back to my orientation and safety session lecture, the HR manager who'd hired me and was running the session, took me aside and quietly said, with an embarrassed smile on her face, "Ray, we have two lunch rooms—one for regular, hourly paid staff employees, and one for salaried supervisory staff. Yours is the one on the main floor, not that one located upstairs with the glass overview of the entire store area."

Obviously, mine was not to be the lunchroom with "a view". Someone that I had been having a good and lively discussion with, with my feet propped up on a chair, had taken exception with my liberties and my bold intrusion.

Now the fall of the year is very special to me; it's my grouse hunting and salmon fishing time. Even though I was part-time (and I had specified, no more than twenty hours per week), most of my part-time hours were on weekends. Students wanted to party on weekends, not put in time at work. So the dilemma—where was I going to find time to hunt and fish?

The decision to quit my new found career came fairly early and not long after I had started my job.

The worst place to be assigned to work at Canadian Tire if you are newly retired; are shy and embarrassed about being seen working at a part-time job; (and have a status-conscious wife), is to be assigned—as all new hires were—as the front door "greeter".

People who had been present at my retirement party would walk into the store and give me a hesitant, half delayed wave of the hand as they passed me by; then I would see them bend over and talk to their spouses who would then look back to have a good look at me. One day, Richard Rivard, the Area Manager for the northeastern provincial office of the Ministry of Community and Social Services walked in, (and I wanted to go and hide down the closest aisle); he walked fifteen feet past me and stopped suddenly in his tracks, turned around and came back to talk to me—to make me feel good, I thought.

I really liked Richard, he was a tall, strongly built man, handsome, totally without any affectation, open and very friendly. He shook my hand warmly and said, "It's amazing how many retired friends I see here all the time—and they all tell me the same thing—it's too damned quiet at home!" I could've hugged him—he did make me feel good.

Three weeks after my chance meeting with Richard I had quit my job at Canadian Tire.

Going to work in the middle of the day; coming home in the dark after nine p.m.; the undemocratic set up with the two tier class-based lunchrooms; and probably the key motivators—the interference with my hunting and fishing, made the decision easy.

I try The Home Depot

But this affair with part-time work was not yet out of my system. I thought I'd move one step up in the world of the employer's hierarchy, and maybe reconcile Emily to the whole madness. I began part-time work at Home Depot—with the same ultimate outcome.

By Christmas I had unfastened the orange apron around my waist for the last time—no more embarrassing early morning store Associates' "Pep Rallies"; no more hurly-burly DIY guys asking me where the eight inch lag screws were located (of which location I had no clue); no more little old ladies asking me to cut duplicate keys for them, and bringing the cut keys back later in the afternoon to tell me that they did not work on the door lock mechanism; no more tough guy from Markstay angrily asking me for a refund on a set of car tires when Home Depot did not sell car tires—I told him he must have been drunk when he bought them down the street at Costco—and then I had need to call store security.

Finally, in Synch with Retirement

By the summer of 2000, I was getting adjusted to retirement and I finally started to enjoy my new life. The workaholic in me started to pacify and enjoy the world around him. Among other things; I had my school trustee work and I sat on different boards; furthermore, I had always been an avid reader and I now took advantage of the library at the university.

The University Library: My Informal Studies

Being an alumnus of Laurentian University, I had reading privileges at the university library and I could also take out books and bring them home. I became a frequent user of my university library and I enjoyed my "informal studies".

I read on a broad cross-section of subjects and I read all there was available to read on Buddhism and the Buddhist way of life—the most difficult religion to practice for a layman. A family man would be hard put to renounce the world and materialism and yet keep his marriage intact—and a true Buddhist does not engage in sexual activities. But there is a Buddhist stage of existence where a layperson can practice a modified way of Buddhist living.

Undoubtedly one of the greatest teacher in history, the Buddha has been an immeasurable influence on the thought and life of the human race. He taught that the best—and the worst—that can happen to us lies within our own power, that our suffering stems from desire, and that the only way to remove this suffering, is to deny the existence of a self and of an ego, and from there purify the heart and follow the way of truth.

> When the Buddha said:
> "We are what we think.
> All that we are arises with our thought.
> With our thought, we make the world."

He meant that we are in charge of our destiny. And with those simple words, he revealed the practical and timeless quality of the most important aspect of Buddhist scripture.

When the Enlightened one speaks, he speaks to you in purity; for his words to touch your Buddha nature, they must be received in purity, and herein lies a huge problem: the mind of modern man is not in synch with the Buddha world. For modern man, the Buddha world may as well be hidden somewhere in the far recesses of the cosmos. The Buddha's words come out of divine simplicity; to liberate you they must be heard in simplicity. The words come from the soul to feed that in you which thirsts; the Buddha's words are words of wisdom, not knowledge, they must be heard by the soul, not the intellect. For that which feeds only the intellect entraps, while that which feeds the soul liberates. And it is the soul that thirsts for truth. The intellect thirsts only to satiate its fascination.

Buddhism has a beautiful view on the way lives should be lived—and if lived in "the way", one is well on the path to liberation leading on to the path of "no return".

In theory, it would seem that the achievement of human happiness is very simple: simply follow the Buddhist scriptures on the knowledge of the "Four Noble Truths", and "The Eightfold Path Leading to Liberation"; however, unless you are a monk, clothed in the yellow robe and living alone somewhere in the mountains of Tibet, it is a way of life well-nigh impossible for a western person to follow.

I tried many times. I could never get past the first hour.

However, one aspect of Buddhism that every layman can practice is the state of mindfulness, in every facet of one's life, and the wilful rejection of the positions of extremes.

Paul Passes Away

After a short battle with cancer, Emily's brother Paul died on August 27, 2000, at the age of 61. What started out ten months before as a bothersome back pain, which Paul attributed to having strained his lower back muscles when he helped a friend move to a new house, got progressively worse as the months went by. By the spring of 2000, he was diagnosed with bone cancer and he died three months later.

It was a sudden and unexpected event, but Emily and Paul spent many hours of those last months in reconciling differences and rekindling the love between sister and brother.

Christopher Gets Married

On a happier note, we celebrated the marriage of our son to Shelley. Christopher and Shelley had known each other for a few years and we liked his choice of the kind of person he had decided upon to marry. Shelley Gainer was a Sudbury born and raised girl, she was intelligent, pretty and talented in her professional field as a graphic artist.

They bought a house in midtown Toronto, on Annette Street, and we helped them with the down payment and household appliances in the same fashion we had helped Christine and Troy.

Help Taken for Granted

The year after the purchase I'd been retired for a couple of years and I had time on my hands, so I went down to Toronto with the pickup truck; went to Home Depot close to their house and bought bathroom renovation supplies.

The upstairs bathroom in the old brown brick townhouse needed a complete facelift. I took out the old sink and toilet and tore away the flooring and had the old rustic four legged bathtub re-glazed. I poured cement on the floor to level the surface and I laid down a new ceramic flooring; then I realigned the resurfaced bathtub and installed the new sink and toilet.

I did everything alone while they were at work; at my complete cost, and by the time I had taken all the construction debris to the landfill site, I had spent an entire week working at their house.

Unfortunately, there was only one bathroom in the old house and I felt quite clearly that neither Shelley, nor Christopher, were happy with the inconveniences I was creating, with the water shut off at times; with the noise and the dust raised about the house; as a matter of fact they were arguing with each other. It was not a happy place.

The renovations were a success. However, when I boarded the pickup and headed toward Sudbury I had not yet so much as received a simple "thank you" from either of them.

The End of a Marriage

But one does not know the dynamics in a household unless one lives within it. On the surface, with the exception of the time of the renovation work, Chris and Shelley seemed happy enough for the first four years of their married lives. Then Emily and I started to see the dark clouds of their marital discontents looming on the horizon. Our son was becoming increasingly unhappy.

And we figured that things were not well at all when Chris and Shelley started to visit both sets of parents in Sudbury, and Chris would sleep at our house, and Shelley would sleep at her parents'.

On the eighth year of their marriage, they separated and it was quickly followed by a divorce. There were no children born to the marriage, which simplified the dissolution, but Emily and I who loved them both were saddened and disappointed by the turn of events.

A marriage fails when the love that was in it originally has grown cold and has been replaced by false pride; hurt; anger and recrimination. When laughter, mutually cherished memories, caresses and loving compromises are gone from a marriage, it's time to stop the flagellations; it's time to shake hands, and go your separate ways—life is too short.

CHAPTER 38

A River Cruise and a Visit to Slovakia

Emily and I decided that it was time to take an overseas vacation. It would be a twenty-day tour; we booked a River Cruise down the Danube. We would stay in Prague for three days and visit this charming city, and then travel to Nuremberg to pick up the cruise ship berthed there. We would then sail down the Danube through amazing countryside right up to Budapest, where we planned to rent a car and head north to Kosice, Slovakia, visiting with Emily's relatives while using her cousin, Joe's niece, Marja, as our daily guide.

We contacted her cousins in Slovakia ahead of time so that they were aware of our arrival schedule, and this time—there were no "babushkas", nor anything whatsoever for sale. The Czech and Slovak republics were free from the socialist system; it had been a few years since they had thrown away the bonds of communism, and they now enjoyed a free and open democratic form of government.

I fell in love with Prague all over again—a city for history romantics—for old world charm, it ranks right there alongside Venice and Istanbul. Paris and Rome have gone modern, whereas Prague, Istanbul, Budapest, and Bratislava have remained in a place where time has stood still.

Cruising down the river presented us with many advantages; we sailed through the very heart of the countries we voyaged in; we saw the people at work in the fields and vineyards; we saw them bathing by the shoreline; we sailed at the foot of medieval castles; and we docked ashore every night so that we could disembark and take in the local sights and savour the local atmosphere (where I got introduced to the "wheat" beer I got to love)—things you cannot easily do on an ocean cruise.

The Rented car and the Adventures Therefrom

When we had completed our sightseeing of Budapest, we headed to the airport to pick up our small Japanese made, automatic drive Corolla. And then the adventures began.

When I sat behind the steering wheel I quickly discovered that we could not go anywhere with that car—it was a "standard" transmission shift automobile. We went back inside the terminal and explained the error to the clerk at the car rental desk. They maintained that there were no errors; I then pulled out my car rental confirmation papers where it clearly stated that our car was to be an "automatic", and the cost for that kind of car had been paid for in advance through our travel agency—however, they persisted and maintained that there had been no mistakes—and all of a sudden their fluent use of English disappeared; they found communicating with us very difficult; whereas only fifteen minutes previously we had had no such difficulty.

I then told them I wanted a refund of my money, and that I would go to another car rental outfit farther down in the terminal. We were told a refund was impossible—I told them this was bull crap, I said, "Whoever can receive money, can give the money back." And then I said to the young lady, "I want to speak to your superior, I want to speak to your boss." It seemed to us that we had stepped back in time and that we were dealing with socialist-style bureaucrats.

She disappeared and we were made to wait a surprisingly short time; she came back to the desk, gave us a new set of keys and said that the "automatic" car was waiting for us outside.

I was intrigued as to the kind of scam they were trying to pull off—were they going to skim-off and pocket the difference between the cost of the standard shift and the automatic? We didn't spend much time on that line of speculation, we had our car and we prepared to leave the airport.

Before leaving I asked our clerk for highway exit directions upon leaving the airport perimeter—all I wanted was a northerly heading—the Slovak border was four hours away to the north. Without cracking a smile she gave me a quick set of directions, emphasizing to turn left at the first intersection.

When I got to the intersection in question, I turned left as instructed, and we got thoroughly lost—I was heading back into the city of Budapest—we did not appreciate her Hungarian sense of humour.

Asking for Directions and Enjoying the Confusion

Those were the days prior to the availability of vehicular GPS devices. We were travelling by the good old fashioned multi-folded paper road maps. Once we got ourselves turned around and headed north we had but few occasions of loss of direction.

But it seemed to me that whenever we had to stop and ask directions to connect to a certain highway, we happened upon a bunch of gypsies who were more interested in us, our clothes, and our money than in the giving of directions. They thought we were a curiosity, some kind of travelling show sent their way to excite them out of the boredom of their daily lives. Even when I showed them the map and pointed to where we wanted to go, they seemed oblivious to our dilemma. They would flash a broad toothless smile and tell us, as best they could, to wait right there—they would send away for someone—usually a much younger, somewhat educated and somewhat English-abled person—to better communicate with us. Sometimes this worked and also, sometimes it did not.

A week later, on our way back to the airport to return the car, we got lost again, and when I stopped by a group of gypsies to ask for directions to the airport—again showing the map and pointing to the airport symbol—an international language—no one in the group had a clue where it was supposed to be. When I finally got back on the right track, the airport had been but a few miles away from them; surely they must have heard the planes coming and going over their heads!

But, we had a great time; it was a genuine adventure and it was fun. And we finally made it to the Slovak border, where two sleepy-looking young men in uniform were more interested in the fact that our car was an "automatic" than what our business in Slovakia was all about. And again, it helped that Emily could converse with them in Slovak. We had no problems. They smiled a lot and were indeed very helpful. Emily beside me said, "They just love Canadians." And I looked at them through my open window, took our stamped passports back and said loud enough that they could hear—but probably could not understand—"Yeah, at this very moment their mothers are probably parading around the village sporting your mom's colourful babushkas".

Modern Slovakia

Slovakia had modernized since our last visit there—seemed that everyone on the streets carried their precious "mobile"—the ubiquitous cell phone. The younger generation was well educated and spoke fluent English—many of them worked for American or western European firms. However, the older generation, those on pensions, particularly, pined for the old Soviet-style socialist regime of cradle-to-grave state supported lifestyles. We found a country in transition.

However, one thing that had not changed was the famous Slovak love of family and their great hospitality—their great desire to please strangers. This great desire to please probably stemmed from centuries of having had to please foreign overlords occupying their lands.

I was amazed at how computer literate and technologically savvy the young people were. They were up to date on the latest devices. Once, when we visited a cousin who owned a restaurant, his seventeen-year-old son, Michal, brought us to his room and he said to me, "You don't have to tell me how big your swimming pool is in Sudbury—let me show you—it will show up as a big blue rectangle." I told him that we did not have a swimming pool on Haig Street, but he just smiled at us—to him, everyone in North America owned a swimming pool, in which they jumped in after parking their big cars on their huge driveways.

So, after "Google-Mapping' Sudbury, and inputting my street and house number, it was with some disappointment in his voice that he told his father over dinner that, it was strange, but we, indeed, did not have a swimming pool behind our house, but instead we had an ugly hydro sub-station!

This young man, Michal Bily, now lives in Padua, Italy, running his own company; the head of a successful line of men's underwear.

Brother Louis comes for a Visit

Louis came to Sudbury for a family visit. On his way east from Thunderbay, he stopped in Elliot Lake to have a short visit with our brothers, Pete and Charley and our sister Louise. Pete had bought a house in Elliot Lake, a place he'd retired to. My sister Louise still lived there with her husband Russell and their daughter, Lisa; and Charley was still working at the last opened uranium mine in the town. He lived in an upstairs rooming house with some light housekeeping privileges.

According to Louis; it was in the mid-afternoon of a hot day in July when he and Pete walked up to Charley's rooms. No one answered the door in response to their constant knocking, but the landlady came over to them and after some introductions, and their show of concern over the wellbeing of their brother, she unlocked the door for them.

The place was stifling hot when they crossed over the small kitchen floor, to throw a window open. Then they made their way to the bedroom, entered and turned on the light switch. They found Charley sitting in the middle of the bed with his legs hanging over the side; his face coated in a thick glistening sweat, staring blankly at the opposite wall.

Without looking at them, he blurted out, "What do you want?" Louis, the family elder was at a loss to make out what was going on. He asked him if he was in need of medical assistance; receiving no response he then asked if he'd go out for a walk with them. Still not getting any response, they went in the kitchen and stared into an empty fridge and empty cupboards.

Louis told him to get dressed and the three of them would go out shopping for groceries. At the suggestion that they would pay for something for him, or that someone would do something for him, he started to scream and ordered them out of his rooms; he yelled down the stairs that, "He was not a charity case and that he had more money than both of them put together,"—which proved to be correct—and furthermore, he shouted, "when he'd need anyone's help, he'd ask for it."

And Charley did have a lot of money. He still worked, was without a car and lived like a hermit and he banked all his cheques. He took two meals a day at the mall and he walked all over the town, and a lot of walking he did—we were told later by Pete and Louise that he could be seen anywhere, even in the bush trails out of town—summer and winter—with that same short, dark brown cotton and polyester windbreaker he'd had since his Sudbury days, cigarette hanging down his lower lip.

A few days later Louis was at our house relating this weird episode. He kept shaking his head, and tears were forming in his eyes. "And he's a man," Louis had said, "who's refused to see any of his grandchildren right from the cradle, from the day they were born; a man who could use his money to do a lot of good; but instead, he decides to live like a man who's been damned."

I went up to Thunderbay, three months after this event. I took the bus, I was on my way to purchase his pickup truck and take it back with me. He had two vehicles and he was getting rid of the half-ton. The drive was at a beautiful time of the year, the leaves were putting on a colourful display; the autumn air was bright and crisp.

Ray A. Vincent

Louis and our Older Siblings

Louis was not well, he suffered from COPD, and now in early November, he went around with nasal lines and prongs and a portable oxygen pack trailing along with him wherever he went.

As the elder statesman of the family, he never really took on and asserted himself in that role. He was a lot like our father was—he sat by and observed as things took their own course—he was never an intervener or an innovator. I wish he had been more aggressive and that at times, he would have shown more anger. He could have said something about Rose and Rosario's marriage; and, being childless, he could have financially helped our parents when they were in most need of help. He could have shown more care and concern for our parents and the younger half of the family. Instead, he chose to be silent and invisible. I guess it was not in his nature; he chose the easy path and looked the other way. He was not a coward; but it was difficult dealing with Louis, you never knew where Louis stood—like our father, he never took a position unless forced to by events.

Louis, Pete, Charley and Colette could have rallied the family at a time when it really needed it, and ignited warm feelings of love within it. They could have encouraged and initiated family get-togethers and the bonding of siblings and cousins; they could have fostered and kindled the sparks of love and kindness within a now expanding clan given the sprouting of grandchildren. Sadly, rather than promoting the growing family group they insulated themselves out of fear of rejection, and out of small-minded selfishness; their disinterest showed a deep lack of insight. They were overwhelmed by their own weakness. They denied what mattered most—involvement with family.

They found no time for their younger siblings. And the knowledge that we did not matter to them hurt me. We had nothing to give them, but ourselves. And I felt that we were seen as a filial burden that, if out of sight, then out of mind.

The legacy of love from our mother and father was slowly being perverted. Their all-encompassing love that should have enwrapped us all as in a warm cocoon, was being stifled by the selfish cold-heartedness of older siblings. The family, once the focal point of our life; our very means of finding a reason to keep on going on, was being reduced to meaninglessness.

To Our Children: Some Words of Advice

At about that time, when both our children had graduated from university and were beginning their careers, one in education in a management position, and the other in private enterprise, and when both were living in southern Ontario; I wrote the following letter and sent them each a copy; it read:

"Dear Christine and Christopher:

-Do not change—you got where you are because of who you are.

-Be good and loyal to your staff—you will need them on your side in difficult times.

-At all times state your opinions clearly, but, at the end of the day, do cheerfully whatever direction the board or the Director has decided upon, even though you are not totally convinced.

-Don't get involved in "cliques" or "factions", they are usually made up of self-serving losers.

-It is more satisfying and you see a lot more of what's ahead, by leading, than by following.

-Know who your masters are, the board (politicians), the Director, your superintendents; and, know who their masters are.

-Be clear and concise in your directions to staff. Never be ambiguous.

-Acknowledge and reward staff achievements, but never show favouritism.

-Study your colleagues—copy their virtues and their strengths—avoid their weaknesses.

-Don't be set back by failures—learn from them.

-Success is 20% talent, 80% hard work.

-Work hard. Be honest. Always show up on time.

-Most importantly: leave "work problems" at work; leave "home problems" at home.

-Set standards; lead by example; do as you say—staff is watching you.

-In all things be professional—but never forget; a balanced approach and a good sense of humour will accomplish easily, where professionalism alone will labour."

And I sent it. Neither ever acknowledged receiving it. And if they did, I wondered later if they ever bothered reading it. I figured my children never thought I had anything important to say to them. I was exactly like them at their age—I knew everything; only later did I come to realize how smart my parents had really been.

My Best Friend joins me in Retirement

On June 20, 2004, after a thirty-six year career in nursing, Emily put on her uniform for the last time. She got up one early morning in May, brought out the calendar to the breakfast table, and without fanfare, she made her announcement. She circled the date with her pen and that was it. I was happy for her and I was happy for us; finally, after five years of juggling timetables to allow for vacation time together, now work commitments would not be an issue.

Emily took to the state of retirement like the proverbial duck to water—no post- retirement anxiety periods, no adjustment period for her—she worked her last shift and she never looked back thereafter. I was amazed; she never missed the hectic pace of the Recovery Room; she behaved in her first month of retirement as if she'd been retired for years.

I should not have been surprised; I'd always known what a well-adjusted individual she was. She had done her thing, now it was time to move on to something else.

THE CHRONICLES OF A JOURNEY

Another European Vacation

In celebration of her career and her retirement, we booked a four-week Mediterranean cruise which would start in Venice, sail down the Adriatic to Dubrovnik then on to Rome, Marseille and with stops in Spain, Portugal, Paris, Dover and Canterbury and then to Amsterdam from which we flew back to Toronto.

The highlight of my trip was Venice—an enchanted place. It would be difficult to find a more unique and romantic city on the globe. From the airport, we water-taxied to the Hotel Concordia—our home to be for the next three days. We had booked the hotel from its internet website advertisement. We had wanted accommodations close to St. Mark Square and this hotel was advertised as such—and it was expensive—but Emily could not handle a lot of walking so we paid the fare—hoping we would find the place and the promises as to its location, as advertised.

We got to the Concordia through the back door which faced a water canal. This gave us no idea of its location in relation to St. Mark's. The water taxi tied up to the pier; disembarked our luggage and left us in the hands of hotel staff. It was an old building, but the interior had been completely refurbished in a very elegant and modern fashion. After registration we proceeded to our room—a large and well-appointed room. Emily and I were tired from the long trans-Atlantic flight; so Emily opted to lie down and rest her legs, but I was so excited with nervous energy that I could not lie down and lay still; and as I usually do in this kind of physical stress, not being able to go for a relaxing run, I went out for a walk. I told my wife that I would reconnoitre where the Hotel Concordia was located in relation to St. Mark's.

St. Mark's is an iconic square and gathering place dating back to the 12th century. St. Mark's is Venetian history and Venetian history is the history of the Western world's contact with Asia and the Far East; the early globalization movements of trade and commerce.

I was away on my mission for a space of time not exceeding thirty minutes. My reentry into our room woke up Emily; she stood up in bed, threw a concerned look at me and said, "You've got tears in your eyes! What happened out there?"

Then I told her I just saw the most amazing sight I had ever witnessed in my whole life—St. Mark's.

On exiting the Concordia through its main front doors, I had made an immediate left turn down Calle Larga, a narrow stone cobbled street and after a fifty-yard walk, I was struck speechless by the full force of the beauty of St. Mark's square.

First of all, I had not expected to come upon St. Mark's so quickly, and I could not in my wildest dreams have been able to conjure up such a magical scene, or what presented itself before me.

The late afternoon sun was sifting through the tower of the Basilica on my left, and bathed the vast stone-paved expanse of the square and the whole of the west façade and its great arcades and marble decorations; beams of sun scanned the Romanesque carvings around the central doorway and hit the four gigantic bronze horses which preside over the whole square. And as I moved through the throng of tourists I came upon the dramatic view of the Piazzetta—open to the sea and bordered on the right by the Palazzo Ducal, and on the left by the arcade of Sansavario, backed by the Campanelle on one side and the projecting porch entrance of St. Mark's Basilica on the other.

By the time I had taken in "The Tower" and the "Clock Tower", I was weak-kneed and teary-eyed and I was making my way back to the hotel to report on my visions.

We could not have chosen a better hotel—price be damned—the Hotel Concordia was in the heart of Venice and within a few minutes' walk to the square. We spent the next three days exploring this beautiful living museum of a city; and although we enjoyed the balance of our trip, everything seemed a little anti climatic after our experiences with Venice.

CHAPTER 39

Louis Dies: The Sad Aftermath

Seven months after my visit with Louis in Thunder Bay, he died on April 17, 2005, of the complications stemming from Chronic Obstructive Pulmonary Disease—the second of my brothers to go down with a mining-environment related health issue.

Louis never had any children born to his wife Florence. He had married Florence when she was twenty-five. Florence was a good looking Ojibway Indian girl from the Batchawana Bay reserve in western Ontario. She was intelligent, tall and carried a happy disposition; Louis and Florence were a good match. Louis was thirty at the time of their marriage. Florence had passed away at the age of fifty-two after suffering a series of debilitating strokes.

At the age of sixty-one Louis took up a common-law relationship with Marie, his favourite local restaurant waitress. Marie had been previously married, but at the time she was alone and without dependents; her two grown children were out of the house and married. Marie and Louis got along well; she was simple-minded, but a reasonable cook, and though not a great conversationalist, she was good enough for Louis—except for our sister Colette, who hated her; she thought her slovenly and could not tolerate her in her house when they visited Sudbury—she thought Louis could have done a lot better. But, like our father, he never expected, nor, demanded much out of life. They both lived seemingly happy in his small stucco and vinyl clad house with the wood frame garage at the back.

Following Florence's death, Louis had had a Will made, with Colette, our sister, as sole executor. Now, even though Louis had lived with Marie for almost sixteen years, he had kept his financial affairs separate from her in every aspect. His bank accounts, his small investments, even his house, were all in his sole ownership—none in joint possession with Marie.

Upon getting word of Louis' death, Colette summoned Pete to go up to Thunderbay forthwith and find the safe deposit box key (which she knew Louis had); since in that bank safe deposit box she told him, he was sure to locate our brother's will and last testament. Pete did as he was asked; found the safe deposit box key hidden underneath the kitchen sink amongst some pots and pans; and when he had secured the Will, he came back to Sudbury and put it into the hands of the executor.

Colette made all the necessary funeral arrangements which were to take place in Thunderbay, and also made further arrangements with the Sudbury Cooperative funeral home to hold a memorial funeral service in Sudbury, in memory and in honour of Louis' life—that memorial service was to be held in the latter part of May.

Shortly after the early grass of spring had started to grow on Louis' grave and before the Sudbury memorial service had been held, enquiries were making their way to me from my sisters; the enquiries centering on my knowledge or lack of knowledge as to the content and dispositions of our brother's Will—which of course, I had no knowledge about. But I said I would call Colette and find out what I could—it seemed a straightforward enough thing to do—after all, we were all family.

The Executor is Not Amused

When I called Colette that night from the privacy of my basement den, there was a dead pause on the line, after I entered on the object of my call—the lull before the storm—then her full fury came pouring over my head. She was furious; she was livid and she threw all sorts of invectives on my wife and my sisters and I was left speechless at my end.

She impugn my motives; she said I was accusing her of having used deceit and pressure to influence Louis' decisions; she accused Emily of meddling in our family affairs (she thought Emily had asked me to place the call); and she went on to say that out of the goodness of her heart, she was going to let Marie stay in the little house and turn the ownership over to her; and she continued that, as far as I and the rest of our siblings were concerned, she would give us all a copy of Louis' will at the memorial service set for May. And with that, she slapped the phone down in my ears.

The memorial service came, and the atmosphere was uncomfortable and strained to say the least. There were two camps; the Lalondes in one; and my other sisters and myself in the other. Pete and Monique stayed neutral and friendly to all. Charley, as expected, did not attend.

Colette, her husband, and their family said not a word to me, in greetings or otherwise. At the conclusion of the service, my sisters and I along with other relatives and friends gathered in the Fellowship room for a coffee and small talk.

We Get Served with a Copy of the Will

Colette burst into the room with an armload of large brown envelopes; she went from table to table where I or my sisters were seated and, as promised, we were all hand delivered our individual copy of the Will.

She did not gently hand over the envelopes: she threw them with force and with vengeance, and they gave out a loud slapping sound as they hit the hardwood surface of each table top. And then she left the room as abruptly as she had barged in—in a whirlwind of anger and hate. I looked at my sisters across the floor, shrugged my shoulders and smiled.

Much later that evening, I opened my envelope. In it were the following: an assortment of photos that came directly from Colette's own album collections in which were my children, and Emily and I (Colette and Roger were Christopher's godparents); and other assortments of pictures taken at various times, in various family settings.

Ray A. Vincent

The Will

And then the Will: in it Colette was sole executor and sole beneficiary of Louis' estate; and, as a slap in the face to his younger siblings; in the event of Colette predeceasing the testator, then the executorship would flow to our brother-law Roger, and so would the complete inheritance of the estate.

In effect, Roger Lalonde, who had no blood ties to Louis would get all of Louis' estate.

The will of a silly and thoughtless man; or, the will of a man influenced to so will. I could never figure it out.

But what hurt me most in all this sordid affair, was the unequivocal notice given to me, and to my sisters, that Colette was severing ties with us. The return of her pictures was a clear slamming of the door shut in my face.

I could not have cared less about Louis' money—and this sentiment also goes for my sisters. Our brother was a grown man who could well do whatever he wished to do.

I cared a lot more about my sister Colette's feelings—her lack of love for me.

An Old Friend Dies

I received a call in late June from Jeannine Lapalme; the wife of my good friend Smitty, from City of Sudbury Welfare department days on Durham Street. Smitty had passed away and she asked me if I would be a pallbearer—I told her I would consider it an honour and I gladly accepted. Smitty and Jeannine had been at my retirement party. I was starting to bury old friends.

The funeral was held at St. Jean de Brebeuf church in the Flour Mill, and I met many old colleagues there, amongst which were Simone and Paul.

In talking with Smitty's son, a Sudbury practicing psychologist at the time, he told me he was contemplating writing a history of the Sudbury Lapalmes and particularly about his father; I told him to call me, I had a lot of "stuff" on his dad he'd probably never heard about before. He has not called me yet. Young men and women have more important things to do in their busy lives.

Brother Charley Dies Alone

We were three days into our annual fishing get together on Lac Simard when the call came. We had come off the lake in late afternoon and there was a message from the lodge operator lying on the cabin kitchen table; it said that I was to go to the office, there was an urgent call received from my sister Louise and I was to call her as soon as possible.

When I reached Louise she informed me that Charley was dying. By the time we got home, he was already dead—another one taken away by the mining industry, on August 24, 2006, at age 71.

Charley left an estranged wife, two grown-up children, and four grandchildren. From the first day of his separation with his wife, he had completely cut off all communications with his family; his daughter was a teenager and his son was a young man at that time; of the grandchildren who came later, he totally denied their existence; he never felt the pleasure of holding one in his arms or, so much as set his eyes upon any of them—a man with a huge emotional aberration; an emotional misfit.

The funeral was held in Elliot Lake, with his son and daughter in attendance. At the reception, the words were whispered that Colette was also the executor of the Will and she would be the sole beneficiary of whatever estate my brother Charley had left behind. And indeed the rumours proved perfectly true—and not a penny was directed to the surviving children, nor anything left to the grandchildren.

His daughter retained a lawyer and challenged the last will and testament of her father before the courts—the outcome of that litigation is unknown to me.

More Sombre News

On that day of the reception, Monique asked that we go for a walk around the grounds outside; she had something to tell me. And then she told me of her plans to end her marriage with her husband, Dr. Joe Cybulski. There wasn't much happiness flowing around that day.

Pete: The Last of my Brothers Passes Away

In the past four to five years, it seemed like we were attending one funeral after another; Emily's brother John passed away in June of 2007 after a long battle with cancer; and our brother Pete died in May of 2008, at the age of 77—sadly the last of my brothers, and he too fell victim to the deleterious effects of the mining work environment.

However, in Pete's case, there were extenuating circumstances, and I felt that he was somewhat party to his own demise. Pete had sold his small house in Elliot Lake and he had moved into an apartment in Spragge, off of highway 17 west. Sometime in late March, he contracted a severe form of the flu virus which he decided in his wisdom, not to have looked after at the local walk-in clinic, or the Elliot Lake hospital, only twenty minutes away. He would fight this "bad cold" on his own and see himself back to health.

Prior to this flu Pete's lungs were already much compromised—they were in poor condition. He suffered from an occupational lung disease called pulmonary fibrosis; the tissues in his lungs had become thick and stiff and scarred over time so that when his bad flu turned into pneumonia, he was well on the road of no return—the death knell had been struck.

When Emily and I were called by Louise, we rushed to the Elliot Lake hospital—his landlady had found him unconscious on a hallway floor, and she had brought him to the hospital.

He was on a respirator when we walked in and we were told by the doctor that his lungs were filling with fluids, and there wasn't much the small local hospital could do for him. He was airlifted to the Sudbury General Hospital, but the internist told the family that there was no way to bring him back—and he died within ten days, on May 17, 2008.

"Auntie Collector" and a Sad Bedside Incident

And Colette was the sole executor of his Will and the only beneficiary. And from that moment forward, our son-in-law, Troy, started calling his auntie Colette—"Auntie Collector."

A sad incident had occurred one day at Pete's hospital bedside. This will clearly illustrate the acrimony that had arisen between Colette, her daughter Lise, and the rest of the Vincent clan.

I visited at the hospital early one morning, at around 9:30 a.m. No other family members were present; I was alone with Pete. He was in the same condition as he had been in on the previous evening—on a respirator and unconscious. I asked the nurse if he could hear and comprehend conversations going on around him, and she said, no; she doubted if he could. I made myself comfortable in my chair, and pulled out my paperback novel.

Shortly after 10:30 a.m., Lise and her husband, Dan Charbonneau, showed up. I kept steadfast at my reading and it became quite clear to me that Lise did not appreciate my presence in the room.

At length, not able to contain herself any longer, "Uncle Ray," she said, "we would like to be by ourselves. Would you mind leaving the room while we're here?"

I replied immediately, "Yes, I do mind. And I mind a lot. I'm his brother; much closer to him than you in kinship. I exercise my right to be here and the freedom to remain where I am."

She did not blink an eyelash: she went out and came back with the duty nurse in tow. And, there in front of the nurse, she reached into her purse with great deliberation, and pulled out a document and showed it to her to read; then looking at me she said, "And I, Ray," she continued, dropping the "uncle" honorific, "exercise my legal right to remove you from this room. This is Pete's Power of Attorney," and she waved the papers, "this allows me to speak on his behalf—and we both say, that we want you out of this room, now." She concluded, with a smirk of a smile on her face.

And that is how I got kicked out of my dying brother's sick room, by a mean and vicious niece.

There was another classic demonstration of family dissonance, open for all to see this time, in the small chapel at Jackson and Barnard's: prior to the start of the service, the family had to be seated. As is normal, the family of the deceased were all to be seated together, to the left of the lectern. To the dismay of Geoffrey Lougheed, this did not happen. We seated ourselves in accordance with obvious family factions—and this was totally unplanned—the Lalondes, at the front, left; and the remainder of the family, at the front, right. Friends and other relatives, at the back, left and right.

I take no issue with my older brothers' decisions in regards to their estates; after all, it was theirs to do with as they wished. They made their decisions out of their own free wills. It is more a reflection of the kinds of persons they were than a negative comment on the recipient of their largesse.

What Goes Around, Comes Around: A Lesson in Retributive Justice

But, maybe divine providence looked at it in another whole new light. Beware the hand of retribution, it works by stealth and offers no explanations.

Shortly after these developments, Colette and Roger were faced with trials and tribulations of their own, coming from very close quarters indeed.

The Bag Lady Drives a Dodge Minivan

Late one evening in early fall, we received a phone call from Michelle and she asked if she could drop in to see us. It was well past midnight, but she was my niece, so I said, "Yes, of course, come on over."

Michelle was Colette's eldest daughter, forty-five years old and homeless. She and her husband had separated some years back, and he had custody of their two girls. Michelle was a pretty young woman and one of my favourite niece. She had light brown hair that had been golden blond when she was but a toddler; she had a few freckles on her upper cheeks; an engaging snub nose; and a soft, gentle voice.

My mother used to babysit Michelle when her family lived on Ash Street and I was a high school student. Sheridan Tech was not far from Ash Street, and I would have many of my lunches with mom and Michelle propped up on her high chair, all the while laughing at the funny faces I'd make.

The doorbell rang; she came in and sat down to a hot cup of coffee, and Michelle, Emily and I talked till the wee hours of the morning. It was easy to tell that she mentally distraught; she talked fast and without pause—about everything; her physical fights with her mother; her marital breakup; the brother-in-law she hated—about everything that caused upsets in her life. In a strange way, the one constant topic of conversation that she kept on returning to, was the household furniture she had put in storage in Ottawa.

She talked about her two girls left behind; and she kept on continuously coming back full circle to issues already discussed; how badly she'd been treated by her brother-in-law Dan; and the horrible physical fights she'd had with her mother.

She was an emotional mess.

I could not believe my eyes when I examined her van early the next morning. I'd gone out while she was still fast asleep: it was, from floorboards to rooftop, packed tight with green and black plastic garbage bags full of clothes and personal belongings, and interspersed in between were pots and pans, and such like. She was a high-end bag lady; not the kind pushing a shopping cart around but driving a Dodge minivan.

We found out from her later that she'd been living out of her van for the past year, and was a frequent user of the local soup kitchens.

She was still on good terms with her father—she would contact him and they would meet at Tim Hortons' or on a park bench at Ramsey Lake—and they had an arrangement where he would deposit funds in her bank account on a regular basis, which she would draw on to live. I suggested she apply for social services, she qualified for welfare payments, but she said they were too intrusive, they asked too many personal questions—obviously, she'd been in their offices before.

She lived with us on and off for a few weeks: she'd use us to clean up and shower and wash and dry her clothes. She used the same services at my sister Carmen, in Hanmer. She would pop in; disappear for a while and show up again unannounced. She did the same at Carmen's.

She came in one day ecstatic; she was starting a job in the photo-lab department of a big food chain store in Chelmsford. She dropped in ten days later—she'd quit her job—and never bothered to collect her pay cheque. When I mentioned it was money owed to her, she seemed indifferent.

There was a front page news story in The Star a few weeks after this contact with Michelle. The story went on to say something to this effect: A pretty, soft- spoken young woman driving a van full of clothing, was involved in stopping, and harassing unsuspecting people walking the sidewalks around MacKenzie Street; wanting to talk to them and offering unsolicited advice and counselling on various personal topics. Those interviewed went to great lengths to emphasize that the "good Samaritan" was gentle, soft-spoken and harmless—she was simply importunate and bothersome.

The Van Will Not Start

I got a call late one evening on a cold November night, "Uncle Ray," she said, "I wonder if you could help me, my van won't start." I had very good, heavy gauge booster cables in my trunk, "No problem," I said, "where are you?" she said she was at her usual overnight parking spot, in the large public parking area at the corner of York and Paris Street opposite the Bell Park Amphitheatre.

When I got there I applied the booster cables immediately and told her to crank the engine, which she did—but to no avail—the engine would not turn.

By the sound of the engine, it did not take me long to figure out the problem; there was nothing wrong with the battery—she was out of gas, the tank completely dry.

She said she could not understand how she could be out of gas since she had a quarter tank when she parked. The past few cold nights she'd been turning the engine on and off throughout the night to keep from freezing. I put my CAA membership to good use and we got her started; I gave her $40 to put more gas in the tank. I told her to come over for the night, but we were not to see her again. I was told later on that she was back in Ottawa.

A Marital Separation

New emotional upsets followed us shortly after. Christopher and Shelley agreed to a separation. They both had good jobs, and they were childless—but the fact did not make the news any less upsetting for myself and Emily. There are a few things you can control in life, but there are more things that you cannot, and your children's lives are one of those that you cannot.

Blessed with a Good friend

I have been blessed with good friends in my life, but, none as good and as loyal as my dear friend, Bill Thompson.

I met Bill in 1987, at the Sudbury Masters Running Club. Bill worked for the provincial Ministry of Health. His office was on the eighth floor of the East Tower, in the same complex of buildings where I was located at city hall; we had worked at opposite ends of the square until 1995, when my office eventually relocated to the East Tower—and so we became neighbours at work; and by that time we had well-nigh become brothers in running.

Bill Thompson was not only a good runner; he was a great one. Bill was a good long distance runner, but he was even better in the middle distances—from eight hundred metres to five thousand metres. For many years, Bill held the national record for the mile in the Masters Runners category. And that record held for a long time.

We were alike in many ways and we became inseparable friends—we were so much together that some began to question our sexual orientation. But it was just one of those things that happen between two persons, now and then. We had an amazing affinity to appreciate so many things in common.

We were both from working class families; we had both graduated from Laurentian University; we had both made our way in life, independent of paternal directions; and like me, Bill was not a native Sudburian: he originated from the small town of Palmerston and the farming counties of Southwestern Ontario; we were both very independent minded and politically and socially conservative; both of us had had fathers who were itinerant workers and who had gone through many cycles of on and off employment periods; both of us had married women from an ethnic background; we were both avid runners; we were both estranged from a sibling—Bill from a younger brother and myself from a sister; we both loved travelling, and a good scotch—and not necessarily in that order. There were not many subjects that we disagreed on, and on those that we did, we had an unspoken understanding to withdraw from or stay away from them; and like an old couple who understand each other well, we preferred a compromise to an open disagreement.

Hence the reason for the strong bond still enduring in our thirty plus years of true friendship. I am now over the age of seventy-one and Bill and I still see each other at least twice a week, every week of the year. Bill is a proud and stubborn Scotsman—qualities that have endeared him to me. The Scotsman's prayer—"Lord, grant that I may always be right, for Thou knowest I will never change my mind."—would have found a home with Bill.

The three loves of his life were: his wife Sandra; his running; and their little white dog, Mandy. Bill and Sandra did not have children, but they were always surrounded by a loving extended family of friends. We spent many happy times in socializing with Sandy and Bill. Sandra was not a tall, nor a big woman, but what Sandy lacked in stature she sure made up with her fiery Italian temper—she was no pushover. She was fun to be with and loved to play cards, and she had great dinner parties. She was a very good cook.

I never saw Bill and Sandra argue with each other. Bill always obliged and deferred to his wife; certainly in domestic affairs, he acquiesced readily. Sandy wanted something, Sandy got it; Sandy wanted rooms painted annually, she got it; Sandy wanted to add to her pink cornflower glass collection; Bill bought it.

One day Sandra started to complain of an annoying back pain. After an initial course of treatment proved ineffective, further tests were done and the diagnosis brought down the terrible news—Sandy was very ill indeed.

On April 8, 2010, Bill lost his best friend and loving mate to the ravages of cancer.

I was asked to read the eulogy at Sandy's funeral service. I was pleased to be asked and honoured to do so.

Medical Issues

On one of our weekly walks, many years after Sandy had passed away, I noticed a marked change in Bill's cadence and way of walking. He had complained of dizziness in the past, but these would come and go. But the change to his walking gait was constant, and so was the habit he now had of keeping his left arm close to his rib cage and not pumping that arm up and down as is normal on a brisk walk. And he would drag his left foot against the cement sidewalk.

I stopped him in the middle of one of our walks one day and asked him point blank, "Bill," I asked, "have you had a mini-stroke?" He said no, he had not, and he dismissed my show of concern. Proud men do not easily acknowledge health problems—for us, it's a sign of frailty and personal weakness. But I would not let go that easily.

I pressed the issue and told him, "Next time you see your family doctor, ask to be referred to a neurologist; it may be nothing, but it's better to be tested and find out what's going on." Bill may be stubborn but he's a good listener. He told me the next time we met that he had an appointment with Dr. Mathews, a neurologist. I said, "Great, and when you go, I'm going with you." He didn't object.

The scene in the doctor's office was a bit comical: there was Bill the patient, and me, sitting beside him, as (it must have looked like) the concerned wife. I was pleased to have gone with him because, Bill, purposely or not, left out big gaps in the description of his symptoms. I filled in the blanks.

She had him undergo a few physical tests, and seated behind her desk, she told him; "Mr. Thompson," she said, "you have the onset of Parkinson's disease. There are no cures, it's a progressive disease, but we can give you medication and an exercise regimen that will manage the symptoms to a certain degree."

Both have done wonders for Bill. The vigorous walking has proved of great benefit. His foot-dragging has stopped and he has a near normal swing of his left arm as we walk.

Although Bill was my best and closest male friend, Emily by far was my best all- round friend and my intimate confidante.

CHAPTER 40

My Best friend in Serious Difficulties

My best friend was going through a difficult period in her life; a period of many happenings that neither she nor I, could understand. At age sixty-four, Emily's health was deteriorating quickly and before our very eyes—and no one could figure it out—no one could figure out what was happening to her; not Emily, or her family physician.

Within a matter of twenty-four months, she went from an active, happy person; to a person labouring under bouts of extreme fatigue, and depressive moods. The daily deterioration in her state of physical and mental health had reached such a degree, that there were days when she actually wished that she were not around to bother anyone anymore. She told me this, and she also told her doctor.

Once it began, the downward spiral in her general health condition, progressed very quickly. Emily had, like many women of her generation, been battling a body weight problem for many years running. And she was losing the battle. But I could not believe that that was the underlying cause of her deteriorating health. There had to be something else much more severe—but many visits to the doctor proved fruitless.

Extreme fatigue and Falling Asleep Everywhere

She began staying up nights to a very late hour—reading book after book—and then she would sleep late into the morning. And she began falling asleep at any time of the day—and at some embarrassing times—at church; while attending public lectures; at the dinner table while entertaining friends; in the car, while I drove from our house on Haig Street, to Costco on the Kingsway; while on the toilet in the middle of the night; before we had reached the edge of the city, on our way out of town; in the living room, again, while entertaining friends; and, of course, while watching television.

She came home very upset one day. After 35 years with an unblemished nursing record, she'd been reprimanded by the nurse in charge—someone had complained that she'd been seen asleep sometimes during her coffee breaks. She did not dispute the reports, but, she said, "I was on my break." You sleep at home, she was told—not at your place of work.

Behaviour Changes

These were drastic behaviour changes, and they were compounded by other medical issues. Emily had never had what would be considered a normal menopausal period in her middle years—her body had never experienced a menopause. And now, at this period of extreme fatigue and constant tiredness, she began having some heavy, periodic episodes of vaginal bleeding—and those would come on without any forewarnings.

She was now constantly short of breath; from the front door of our house to the passenger door of the car sitting in the carport, some twenty feet away, was now a difficult undertaking for Emily; she needed at least one rest stop before being able to reach the car. When we got to a mall to do some shopping, she had to ask for the store supplied wheelchair or the little-motorized shopping scooter. She had to opt out of attending some social events since she had not the stamina and endurance to join the functions.

Falling to the Floor and the Complications

And she began falling in the house, in different places and at different times; off of the bathroom toilet at 2:30 a.m.; off the edge of the bed after sitting there to rest and falling asleep in that position; onto the floor in the kitchen while working at the sink.

And these falls were complicated by two issues: her body weight and generalized weakness, and, the gynecological bleeding problem. Once fallen to the floor, she could not get up—and sometimes, there was blood all over the place, onto the carpeting and the ceramic floors.

I usually managed to get her to her feet, but one day when she fell on the kitchen floor, I could not do so. Our dining room had a staircase leading to the downstairs family room, so I rolled her on to a blanket while she lay on the kitchen floor, and I physically dragged the blanket in very small, graduated moves, to the edge of the stairway where we pivoted her legs over the stairs and using the railing for support, we got her vertical and on her feet again.

And when those falls were accompanied by heavy bleeding (usually in the wee hours of the morning), I spent the late nights and the early mornings cleaning up with the special little carpet cleaning machine we had bought for the purpose: great for removing blood stains and blood clots from the carpets—I made good use of my Bissell "Little Green" portable carpet cleaner. And it was very effective.

By the late fall of 2010, Emily's condition and quality of life had reached a crisis. Numerous visits to the family physician and a variety of medical tests produced no positive changes.

Hallucinations

And then bizarre behaviours occurred which made me wonder about her state of mental health. One day she asked me at what time we were leaving the next morning to visit her brother in Oakville; and when I told her we had made no such plans, she apologized for the mistake, thinking we had talked about it. On another occasion, she was in the kitchen and I was reading the newspaper in the living room when she stopped putting dishes in the dishwasher, and she asked, "Ray, when you were in New York City, did you go visit the Museum of Fine Arts?"

I put the paper down and waited a moment, thinking she would correct herself; but sensing she was waiting for my response, I asked her to repeat what she had just said; and she replied, "Oh, nothing," and she changed the subject.

I have never been to New York City in my entire life.

We Never Saw It Coming

We never saw it coming. It was like an insidious fog, malady laden, rolling in quietly, unannounced. It came slowly; it came gradually, but it kept on rolling in, inexorably, and with severe consequences.

I had told our children that their mother was not well; and the first thing they asked was, what was wrong with her? And to my utter frustration, I could not tell them what was wrong with her, except that she was weak; short of breath; confused, disoriented, and fell asleep all over the place—and that even her doctor had not yet determined what had brought about such precipitous changes to her health.

A Battery of Tests

In mid-December, she went for more tests at the medical laboratory on Larch Street. When I picked her up, she looked awful—her lips were blue—I called her doctor when we got home and he advised that I take her to the hospital's emergency department immediately. But Emily demurred, she objected to all the fuss; she said she felt better, and indeed the normal colour had returned to her lips and fingernails.

An appointment for an echocardiogram was booked for December 17th, and I drove her to the clinic at the south end of town, and I waited for her in the waiting room. Shortly after the commencement of the testing procedure, the technician abruptly interrupted the entire exercise and told Emily that she was to present herself immediately to her family doctor's office.

She would not answer any direct questions, but she said that she would call the doctor and inform him of her concerns—in the meantime, we were to go to the doctor's office promptly.

Emily's doctor is also in the south end of town so that within five minutes we were there—and he took her in right away.

Pulmonary Arterial Hypertension: With cause Unknown

He said the findings indicated severe "pulmonary arterial hypertension"—left untreated, patients with severe pulmonary arterial hypertension had a survival rate of 2-3 years; but the cause remained unknown, so he scheduled an appointment for another test—a pulmonary function test—for December 22nd. The location for that test would be on-site at Laurentian Hospital since that was the only place where the test was available.

The Crisis

On that fateful day—like all good self-respecting woman—Emily decided to take a shower before going to the hospital for her tests. The main floor bathroom had a conventional combination bathtub and shower stall; and since Emily had not the strength to lift her leg over the two foot rim of the bathtub, it had become necessary for her to make use of the basement bathroom—which was a two-piece, toilet and shower facility; with the shower stall having a very low floor ledge

She went downstairs on her own, as usual; however, after a few minutes, I heard her calling for me.

By this time she had become so weak and debilitated in her physical condition, that when she tried to lift her foot over the ten-inch ledge to gain entry into the shower stall—she could not do it. I had to pull up her legs, one at a time and assist in getting her settled in the shower.

And then the other problem came up—she could not manage to properly shower herself. This we did as a duo.

With difficulty, but in the same manner in that which she had gotten in, I got her out and toweled her dry. We then walked to the foot of the stairwell and a major challenge stared at us in the face—how to get her upstairs to get dressed.

It took quite a while, but we did it; one step at a time, hanging onto and pulling at the railing; and then resting a moment until she found strength and her breath again; and then another step, followed by a rest period; and so on, until we had made it to the main floor landing. An activity that would take a normal, healthy adult, ten seconds to perform, took us fifteen minutes.

A drive to an otherwise normal medical appointment, which had started on a calm, sunny day, but under very abnormal preparatory circumstances, was to turn into a major traumatic event.

The Crash

The appointment for the Pulmonary Function Test, to be done at the hospital facility, had been scheduled for eleven a.m. By the time I turned left at the lights, going down Paris Street and onto Ramsey Lake Road, her lips were turning blue again. When I reached the main entrance doors of the hospital, Emily looked my way and said, "Get help, I can't move."

And that is when, and where Emily coded. She could not have picked a better location to crash—at the very doors of a hospital. The Lord does work in wondrous ways!

I ran to the security desk in the hospital lobby, and told them, "My wife is in the car outside, she's too weak to get out and she's changing colour."

Within seconds the cardiac-pulmonary arrest "Code Team" came out of nowhere, crash-cart and wheelchair rumbling down the hallway and out through the front doors and on toward the car parked at the entrance—the driver-side door still wide open.

Emily was extricated out of the car, put in the wheelchair and rushed to the Emergency Room, where she was intubated, connected to a respirator and put on life support. And I stood by, speechless and overwhelmed—an absolutely useless observer.

At mid-afternoon, they transferred her to the Intensive Care Unit, where she was to remain for sixteen days.

We could not communicate since she was unconscious and intubated, and when I felt that the medical care necessary had been mobilized and that there wasn't much I could do—then I started to think of other people—I picked up my cell phone and called our children; my sisters and Emily's relatives, and apprized them all of the situation.

The Doctor who makes House Calls—by Telephone

On Emily's third day in ICU; early on Saturday morning, as I was finishing breakfast and making plans to visit at the hospital; I received a telephone call. The caller introduced himself as Dr. Oliphant, a specialist in respirology medicine—a Pulmonologist. He said he'd been called for consultation by the medical staff at ICU, in regards to Emily—they'd asked him to see her and provide his opinion. He had seen her; read her charts, but before providing an opinion he wanted some information from me on specific symptomatic aspects of her illness; things that I may have been in a position to observe.

My first reaction to the phone call was one of great relief: that is, finally, someone was paying attention to her as yet undiagnosed medical problems. It is unusual for a physician to call, on an early weekend morning, and put questions about a patient to that patient's loved one.

The Good Physician

I put Dr. Lawrie Oliphant on the same pedestal next to Dr. Fitzpatrick, the pediatric surgeon at McMaster University Hospital in Hamilton. Both great men in their professional fields, and great human beings. Dr. Fitzpatrick saved the life of baby Noah, and Dr. Oliphant saved Emily's.

A Diagnosis:
Severe Obstructive Sleep Apnea

His first question opened up the floodgates: "Ever noticed anything unusual about your wife's sleep patterns?" he had asked.

Then I told him everything: that she did not have restful sleeps; that she was up often during the night; that she'd come back to bed and have periods of breathing cessation, complete stoppages of breathing for up to 45-50 and plus seconds; where I had to poke her with my right elbow to get her breathing to kick-in again; the extreme daytime fatigues and sleepiness; the falling on the floors for no explainable reasons; and so on.

He listened patiently at the other end, and he asked how long this had been going on, and I told him that I had started to notice certain things in the past 18 months, but that she'd probably been ill before I had started to notice. He enquired further; he asked, "Ever noticed any mood or behavioural changes?"

And then I told him about the strange comments she had made recently about visits to Oakville and New York City, both of which were chimerical.

I will never forget what he said; his voice came clear and calm over the phone, "Hypoxia-induced hallucinations," he said, "Mr. Vincent," he continued, "it is my opinion that your wife suffers from severe obstructive sleep apnea syndromes. Over time, sleep apnea depletes the body tissues of vital oxygen, and saturates the blood with carbon dioxide."

He went on to say that once Emily was out of the hospital, she would be booked to attend the Sleep Clinic to establish a definitive diagnosis of sleep apnea, and if so, the severity of the case.

I was overjoyed at the call. For the past twenty months, no medical person had ever mentioned the words "sleep apnea", or the apneic associated physiological problems that come along with it—it probably seemed too simple a cause; they had to go after more exotic instigators.

Sleep Apnea

Suffering from sleep apnea for a year is probably no big deal; however, the cumulative effect of decades of not having adequate oxygenated blood, and the increasing saturation of carbon dioxide, can lead to a morbid event. Respiratory acidosis caused by severe apneic events brought about the acute respiratory failure, which in turn, brought on Emily's elevated pulmonary arterial blood pressure, and triggered a host of other interrelated physical and mental pathologies. When you do not breathe properly, your lungs cannot efficiently remove carbon dioxide from the blood, and when this gas exchange is compromised, respiratory failure occurs; and then, all of Emily's symptoms; all her demons, would happily come to the fore and show their faces.

Now we had a diagnosis and an explanation of the linked medical expressions coming out of the main causal source. And if the problem was sleep apnea; Dr. Oliphant had a treatment plan.

Dickens Described the Symptoms in 1836

Although the relationship between breathing and sleep has only recently been discovered by medical science, excellent literary descriptions of what we know to be the sleep apnea syndrome were made long ago. The most important literary contributions in this area are by my favourite author: Charles Dickens. His description of Joe, "the fat boy" in the novel, "The Pickwick Papers"—Joe's falling asleep everywhere, snoring at the dinner table, asleep standing up as a livery lad—is an example of his brilliant skills of observation and character description. Dickens, like many doctors today, observed the behaviour, but could not ascribe its nefarious implications in bodily diseases. It was not until about 140 years after "Pickwick Papers" was published, that the medical community understood what he was describing.

Extubation and the Possible "Outcomes"

After she'd been six days on the respirator, Dr. Oliphant called me at home again; and again, early in the morning. He wanted to let me know that they intended to extubate and remove Emily from the respirator the very next morning, and he wanted to let me know about the possible outcomes.

I said, "What do you mean by 'possible outcomes'?" and then he proceeded to explain, in a straightforward manner that, "There are three possibilities once we remove the tube: she picks up breathing on her own and everything's fine; or, we remove the tube and she cannot breathe on her own without a tracheotomy; and the last possibility—remote but possible—is that she cannot breathe on her own, with or without the tracheotomy." And I didn't have to be explained what the consequence of the last "possibility" would entail.

Ever the planner, ever the person who worries to see that all eventualities are accounted for; I started to think about what Dr. Oliphant had just said after we ended our telephone conversation.

I had never been a Boy Scout, but the motto of "Be Prepared", fitted me perfectly. That afternoon, I went and consulted with my funeral director friend, Roger Delongchamp of the Cooperative Funeral Home.

A bit of explanation may be necessary here: with our children out of town, I was alone to sort out and deal with all of the possible scenarios; what if she could not be resuscitated? Would it not be better to know, from a practical point of view, what a funeral entailed? And furthermore, I was only going to see Roger for information; to talk—no arrangements, or selections were being finalized.

A month after Emily was discharged home, I told her (somewhat sheepishly) of my visit with Roger. At first, she thought I was joking, but when she realized that I was not joking, she understood more fully how serious her condition had been. For years following this event, whenever the children were in the house; my visit to the Cooperative Funeral Home was always an interesting and lively topic of conversation.

The morning arrived and Emily was extubated. I had been outside of the ICU, pacing in the waiting room, awaiting the phone call telling me that I could go in to see her. When the call came in; I walked in and saw her alert and breathing well on her own. She was tired, without an idea as to date and time, and although weak, she was able to carry on a limited conversation.

She was on her way to a full recovery; however, she was to remain in ICU for sixteen days prior to a transfer to a regular room on the Respirology Care Unit. She had to remain in ICU until such a time as her CO_2 blood levels stabilized to normal levels, and furthermore; the emergency intubation procedure, sixteen days earlier, had irritated tissues in the airway, which led to infection and pneumonia, the treatment of which had to be started and the bacterial infection brought under control prior to any moves out of ICU.

At night, she slept with a full nose and mouth mask attached to an air venting machine, which she was to make use of for the rest of her life—a Continuous Positive Airway Pressure machine, or, a CPAP machine—an air venting and pressure device which prevents the occurrence of breathing cessation during sleep.

Still High on Carbon Dioxide

An event occurred a few days after extubation, which brought home to me how still highly saturated Emily's blood was with carbon dioxide.

When I walked into her room shortly after suppertime, I was taken aback by the look on her face. It was the look of someone high strung with fear and anxiety; there was panic in her voice, like that of someone who had, or was about to be subjected to something very painful and stressful. She was looking at me with a fixed gaze, eyes wide open with fear, and with trembling lips, she shouted; "Ray, tell them to keep her away from me! I don't want that nurse to ever come in my room again. There's something very wrong here—that woman's evil," she continued, in a lowered voice.

At that point, I strongly suspected that something indeed had happened, between Emily and one of the female nursing staff. The admonitions from the patient seemed so credible. When I went to the nursing station and talked to the staff, a doctor looked at her latest blood gases numbers, and he said that her CO_2 levels were still off the charts—hence Emily's delusional comments—he assured me that nothing untoward had happened in her interactions with the nursing staff.

By the time of her transfer to the South Tower, 6th floor, Respirology Unit—everything was fine with Emily in terms of her CO_2 blood levels; and her normal friendly, gregarious and chatty self, had returned. However, she was still weak and had need of the use of a wheelchair, and then a walker for a while.

My Best Friend Is Back

She was discharged home on January 24th, 2011, having spent over one month in the hospital, more than half of which was in Intensive Care.

Emily came home to a slightly modified main floor bathroom. While she was still in the hospital, I had the washroom bathtub taken out and a floor level, walk-in shower stall installed in its place. She would no longer require my assistance to step into the showers. And she also came home with something that was to develop into a lifelong companion, something she'd have constantly by her side while asleep—at home; away from home visiting family, or, travelling overseas; and at the fishing camp: everywhere she would need to lay down and sleep—her CPAP machine—the first machine on loan until she underwent her sleep assessment at the Sleep Clinic, after which time she would own her personal device.

Straight talk from Dr. Oliphant

Her sleep assessment confirmed a severe obstructive sleep apnea problem. When she saw Dr. Oliphant in his office at the end of February, he did not couch, his words in niceties—he painted a clear, if sombre picture—she needed the CPAP machine and, a significant weight loss or she would be dead before Christmas. The room was quiet momentarily. Then, wanting to lighten up the mood, I reminded Dr. Oliphant that he had now taken on a big responsibility: according to Confucian philosophy, once you save someone's life, you become forever responsible for that person.

He gave us his shy smile, shrugged his shoulders and turned to Emily again. Later on in the conversation, he went so far as to suggest a Bariatric surgical procedure for Emily—at an Ottawa hospital—to promote the weight loss. Emily said she would rather try the weight loss on her own first.

The Weight Loss

Which she did, and joined a professional program—with sensational results—she lost weight to a degree, where she became almost unrecognizable. That and the CPAP machine went a long way toward bringing her sleep apnea under control. Her blood carbon dioxide and oxygen levels, all returned to normal values. And most importantly, with the return of good health, her quality of life and her joy of living returned accordingly.

The Hospital wants Money and They Produce a Forgery to Get It!

The bureaucracy will never fail to astound me; in mid-April, we received an invoice from the Finance Department of the hospital, demanding a payment of $1,020, forthwith, to cover the cost of semi-private accommodations on the 6th floor, Respirology Unit.

I called the manager of the department, Mrs. Jackie Leroux, and asked for explanations. I told her of Emily's health issues at the time and that it was not our choice or decision, for her to go to the 6th floor—it was the medical staff's decision; one which we had no control over. And furthermore, I told her we had no choice in types of accommodations: there were no ward beds in the Unit—they were all semi-private beds!

She listened quietly, and then she said, "Mr. Vincent, I have a signed form in front of me, in which you agreed to pay the daily difference between a ward and semi-private room accommodation."

I honestly could not recall having signed any documents while Emily was in hospital—but I could have—I could have had a form thrust upon me to sign. And if a form was presented to me, and I had signed it, what I had signed was not explained to me and; furthermore, the signature would have been taken under duress, when I was mentally distraught—an activity far removed from an informed consent.

I did not say that to her. I only reiterated the fact that there were only semi-private beds in the Unit, and that we were not offered any other options.

But, before hanging up the phone, my fastidiousness for detail surfaced; and I asked her, "Could I have a copy of the form I signed, please?" she said that was no problem; and when I asked if I could pick it up in person, she said it would be available to me later that day.

I picked up the sealed envelope and drove directly back home. I tore the envelope open and looked at the "Responsibility for Payment" form: a photocopy, duly signed by a "Ray Vincent", on December 22, 2010. It took me a few seconds, then I let out a derisive laugh, and Emily came over and looked over my shoulder at what was so funny. And she started to laugh, and exclaimed, "My God! That is not your signature!"

The form had my name, but the signature was a bold forgery. It was not even close to what my signature looks like, and—it was witnessed by someone with the initials, "PC".

I have retained a copy of this "Responsibility for Payment" form in my files at home—and all pursuant communications with the hospital on this matter. Indeed, I make them "public" documents, for anyone interested in verifying the veracity of this account.

Someone at the hospital—a staff person—had perpetrated a criminal act in order to CTA (cover their asses).

A Letter to the CEO: A demand for an Apology

I did not call Mrs. Leroux back. Instead, I drafted a letter to Dr. Denis Roy, President and Chief Executive Officer at the Sudbury Regional Hospital. The letter explained the situation and included a copy of the hospital document with the forged signature. The letter did not threaten anyone; I simply demanded to receive a written letter of apology from him, as President and CEO of the hospital, in regards to the forgery and his staff's behaviour.

I also requested a cancellation of the $1020 bill.

An Apology Received

Within five days I had a full page apology from Dr. Roy (which I have in my files). The first lines of the letter read:

Dear Mr. Vincent,

"On behalf of the Hopital regional de Sudbury Regional Hospital (HRSRH), I would like to offer you my sincere apology in regards to the mishandling of the "Preferred Accommodation Agreement..."

And the letter goes on to three additional full paragraphs.

The next day we received a letter from Mrs. Jackie Leroux, Manager of Business Operations, informing me that the hospital had adjusted the balance owing to zero (and I also have that letter in my files).

I have already mentioned that I've retained all correspondence and original copies of written transactions on this incident, and as far as I'm concerned—they are public documents for anyone to see.

Ray A. Vincent

A Milestone

A milestone for both, Emily and I this year—we both turned 65—and the federal government rewards us with the return of some of our tax money: the start of old age security payments.

The Luckiest Woman in Sudbury

And in March, the month of her birth year, Emily underwent a complete hysterectomy—no more vaginal haemorrhage—I could finally retire my trusty "Little Green" Bissell carpet cleaner.

Emily had a surprise awaiting her when she went for her post-op visit at her gynaecologist, Dr. Huneault. When she had sat down in front of him, he looked up from the biopsy laboratory report in front of him, and he said to her, "You should go out and buy a lottery ticket. You're the luckiest woman in Sudbury right now. Your biopsy report shows the early formation of uterine cancer cells. We took out the uterus, cancer cells and all, in the nip of time."

Emily was on a roll. She had beat sleep apnea; she was losing a lot of weight, and now she had narrowly escaped a cancerous growth in her uterus. She was happier and more physically active than she'd been for years: we had not gone for long walks since her mid-forties, and now we went out for walks at every opportunity.

We go through life taking a lot for granted; seldom thankful for the small, but important things we already possess. We all know that it is not the longevity, of life that counts—living long for many, means that they have more time to be silly in—it is what you do with the time allotted you; it is what you do that is meaningful to others that really counts. The quality of one's life is important because it allows you to do good and meaningful things to the people around you.

Sickness raises a barrier between you and humankind; it pushes you to the sidelines of life; it segregates you; it draws you away. Many go through life not realizing that the moment is only good if that goodness transmits to others around you. The elusive search for happiness outside of one's self—in things; in status; and in bouts of short-lived euphoria—is like running after a seductive phantom—it always slips away from your grasp, at the time when you think you finally have a firm hold of it.

CHAPTER 41

Still Looking for something to Turn Up

And sadly, Andy had fallen on hard times. In July, we received an email from him; he was 71 years of age at the time, and the content of the text showed how depressed, he'd been when he wrote it; how down and out he was financially.

He'd been living apart from Inge for a while now and things were not going well for him. His "supplement" on his monthly Old Age security cheque had been eliminated because he had taken on a small part-time job the year previous. He was facing difficult times. He'd been selling off valuable personal property for the past few months. Andy was a proud man; this must have been terribly upsetting for him.

His plan was to start a course in September, to become a Mortgage Loans Broker. He had not the money for the tuition and he was asking Emily and me for a loan of $3,000, which he would secure with the collateral of his valuable gold and diamond studded ring, which he'd purchased in Italy in 1986 for the sum of $4,500. And he would repay us the loan within a year, at which time I would return the ring.

We agreed, and in August we lent him the money; furthermore, when we met with him we offered to take him in as a boarder—we had an empty house; he could use the upstairs loft as his living quarters—he said he'd think about it

Twelve months went by, and then twenty-four, and we never got our money back—neither did we return the ring. We met him often after the day of the loan, and we never broached the subject—

and neither did he. Nor did he get back to us on our offer to take him in.

Did he take the Mortgage Broker Course? Maybe not.

Did he gamble away the $3000 in Niagara Falls? I hope not.

But the fact that we never saw the money returned to us did not matter to me, nor did it matter to Emily. We loved Andy before the request, and we still loved him after. Andy had a good soul and he was a warm and kind human being. I know that if we'd been in opposite situations, Andy would have lent me any amount of money I would have asked of him, plus the shirt off of his back—and gladly.

More visits to the Funeral homes

You know you have reached a certain age when a lot of your dear friends and acquaintances are being announced with a disconcerting regularity in the local newspapers' obituary pages.

My dear friend and mentor, Paul Schaak, passed away on December 1, 2011, at the age of 92. Emily and I attended the funeral. Paul was a truly good man. His children ought to be proud of him. He taught me a lot just by watching him. He taught me that one does not have to be formally educated (my uncle Alfred), in order to possess true intelligence. And he taught me that honesty and integrity trump wheeling and dealing any day of the week.

Emily Doing Well

By the spring of the ensuing year, Emily was doing very well, she was still losing weight consistently and with the assistance of the CPAP machine, she was getting good, restful sleeps. One small health issue remained for her to take care of—by the end of the year she had cataracts removed from both eyes, and her vision improved significantly.

Ray A. Vincent

Christine and Troy are moving to Sudbury

And we were to have guests move in with us. Christine called us, enquiring about the possibility of her and Troy temporarily moving in with us, while Troy took a Miner and Driller's course in Sudbury. At that time there was a great amount of media fanfare and industry optimism in the northern Ontario mining community about the possible mining job opportunities to be opened up by the "Ring of Fire" Chromite deposits. This was a massive planned Chromite mining and smelting development project, in the mineral-rich James Bay Lowlands of northern Ontario. There would be a great demand for a trained and skilled workforce.

Troy did not have sound, marketable job skills, and he had difficulty in securing good-paying, full-time employment where they were living—in the farming county of Wyoming, in southwestern Ontario. Christine had a "housebound" portable job, which she could move with her, wherever they lived.

This seemed like a good forward move for them: good for their financial future and also good for Noah's educational prospects. So without hesitation, we agreed. They were to move in with us on Haig Street in early August, in time for Noah to register for his grade eight elementary school classes scheduled to begin in September.

At about the same time that Christine called us in late spring, I received another phone call from entirely different quarters.

An old Friend back on the Scene: the Return of Roger Chamberland

My dear old friend from Flour Mill days called me one day. I had not seen, nor heard from Roger Chamberland, for the past forty-five years—and here he was at my doorstep; with less hair on his head; a bit more corpulent; wearing the same thick glasses; and with the same tell-tale cocking of the head to get better focus because of his bad eye; he had the same short clipped speech delivery, and the same shy, childish smile on his face.

We picked up our relationship as if we had just left each other yesterday. And he became a daily fixture in the house; his health did not strike me as sterling, he still smoked heavily and he was constantly out of breath. He could not tolerate a walk around the block without numerous pauses to rest and catch his breath. When pressed about his health, he said he was being treated for some medical issue, but he was evasive and tight-lipped, so I dropped the subject of his health altogether.

Emily and Roger hit it off famously well from the first minute they'd been introduced. The old, proven and true psychology syllogism, that if A likes B, and B likes C, then, there is a great probability that A will also like C, held quite well in this case. But there was more to Emily liking Roger, than the fact that Roger and I were friends. Emily had heard a lot about Roger from me; about our friendship on Queen Street and the experiences we had shared together; and even more than that, was the plain fact that Roger was a very gentle, easily loveable person. Emily was a good judge of character; she knew, innately, the fraud from the genuine article—and Roger was no affected impostor—he was the real deal.

Furthermore, Emily and Roger shared two habits in common: they loved to play the machines at the "Sudbury Slots"; and they loved to pull jokes at my expense. But the significant common bonding element between the two was that both suffered from sleep apnea, and both were on the CPAP machine.

Roger and his Adventures with Sleep Apnea

One day after dinner, as the three of us were having a drink, and relaxing on the back patio, the subject of sleep apnea came up, and I related to Roger some of Emily's harrowing experiences with the disease.

"Well," he said, "let me tell you my little story about sleep apnea."

This is what happened to Roger one night when he fell victim to an apnea induced hallucinatory episode. Roger did not know at the time that he suffered from severe obstructive sleep apnea. His carbon dioxide blood levels must have been extremely high.

He rearranged himself comfortably in his chair; like someone about to go on a long journey, and he proceeded thus:

This happened on a cold January night, many years prior to our hearing of it. Roger was living with his girlfriend, at her house in Garson. As the evening was getting late, she had gone upstairs to sleep, and as Roger was not a sound sleeper, he decided to lay on the living room couch and watch television. He had taken his shoes off, but he'd kept his socks on; removed his sweater and T-shirt, but kept his pants on, and he slipped under a heavy blanket and settled himself to a late night of TV watching. And before long, he was snoring away and passing in and out of sleep.

In the early hours of the morning, he heard terrible loud banging noises coming from the side entrance door. The frantic banging grew louder, and it became intermixed with warnings and shouts threatening to take his life if they got their hands on him. He screamed to his girlfriend upstairs to call the police; but hearing no response from her, and by this time the side door was cracking to the breaking point; he scrambled to the front door; opened it, and ran across the snow-covered front yard in his stockinged feet and bare chest, for the safety of the house on the opposite side. He stomped through a snow bank and made his way up the neighbour's stairs and banged on their door.

The terrified lady who answered the door knew Roger and his girlfriend from across the street. It so happened that her husband was working the night shift, and she found herself very reluctant to open the door wider than a few inches. Roger pleaded to be let in, lest he be molested by the mobsters at his house, wanting to do him harm—and could she please call the police immediately.

She relented, and let him come inside the cold front porch and sit on a chair, while she placed a call to the police station. By this time she was sure that she was dealing with a psychotic, high on some drug overdose.

The police arrived and were met with a teeth-chattering-unable-to-speak, psycho; and they took Roger straight to the hospital to get him detoxified.

He related that the longer he remained in the waiting room with his shoeless feet, and with a blanket thrown over his shoulders, he slowly began to get his bearings and regain his wits about him. When he finally got into the hands of medical staff—staff who had already received a picture of the events leading to hospitalization from the police, and the story from the neighbour—they determined that Roger had suffered a series of auditory delusions, mixed with hallucinatory reactions.

His girlfriend had picked him up early in the morning. She had not heard any screams—his, or anyone else's; she had taken the side door an hour earlier that morning and had found it locked and in perfect condition—no attempt had been made to force an entry—and there were no traces of footsteps to the side, or back of the house to indicate a "mob" milling about there.

Roger went to the sleep clinic shortly after this adventure, and he was diagnosed with severe obstructive sleep apnea and put on the CPAP machine.

He had stopped his true story momentarily, to light a cigarette; and then he continued. "So," Roger said, winking at Emily, "you and I know what it's like to live a while in the twilight zone," and then he said, smiling, "Ray can only imagine it."

Roger had reconnected with me in late spring and I never questioned the motive—good friends do not second guess each other—they let their friendship speak for itself. However, three days before Christmas, while seated at our favourite coffee shop on Lorne Street he came clean.

"Ray," he said, in his normal delivery, with the same shade of a smile on his thin lips, "I'm told that I'm not going to be here in six months. I'm dying of cancer."

I must admit I was shocked. He did not look in great health, but he did not look like a man about to die either. He told me that he had taken the last six months and spent them in reaching out and contacting all his old Flour Mill friends, of which some, like me, he hadn't seen in many years.

We went to Sudbury Downs and the "Slots" in Chelmsford as often as we could—some days, when he was short of funds, we would give him gambling money. One day, he came over and handed me a present. He had taken his father's old 8 millimetre "Home Movies"—those that had me and him in them; as 15 and 16-year-olds, playing yard hockey or just hanging around the house; and he had them converted into VHS format. I watched the clips with him and I had tears in my eyes. How happy, and young, we were then!

He spent the last two months of his life at his daughter's in Ottawa. I called him one day and said, "Roger, get your ass back here, your lucky machine is just about ready to pay out." He laughed, and his last words before we hung up was, "Ray, I doubt I'll ever see Sudbury again. I'm pulling my last pull at the "one-armed bandit."

We sent him a big basket of fruit that same afternoon. He called to thank us when he received it. Roger died the week after that.

The Stress of Sharing your House, and your Privacy

The unwritten agreement, when Christine and Troy moved in with us, was that they would remain on Haig Street for approximately a year, to allow Troy time to complete his "Common Core" course and then he would secure employment, and they would move to their own house or apartment. Well, now it was getting close to a year; Troy had completed his program and he was working, and no one was making a move. Emily was getting stressed and frustrated: she wanted her house back. She started to mind being crowded for such a long period of time; and so did I.

To add complications and stress to the new family structure was the fact that when the Van Belles' relocated to Sudbury—increasing the composition of the household from two, to five overnight—was that Emily and I had not accounted for the inconveniences of living, not only with three additional human beings but also with a dog—a big, black constantly-shedding-hair dog—Begheera, the black Labrador. And, as dog lovers well know, and as Christine would remind us, "He was part of the family."—well, her family.

When we had agreed to open up our house to them, we had completely forgotten about this additional family member—the black Lab. He was an intelligent, well-behaved dog. But he shed hair all over the house—big, black cork-screw shaped, coarse hair—when he shook his coat, it was like water coming off a sprinkler head. People used to living with dogs and pets around them probably would not have noticed the hair as much as I did. I am meticulous to a fault on cleanliness in the house, and here we had dog hair all over the carpets; dog hair on the ceramic floors and particularly in the corners; dog hair under the tables; dog hair on my clothes and stuck to my socks; and how it got there I don't know, but we even had dog hair on the kitchen counters.

I made it a rule that Troy and I would vacuum the entire house every other day; we would each take a turn, and that helped somehow in keeping the problem under some control. And I put in another rule: our house on Haig was pretty well carpeted throughout. So, some way had to be found to keep the black Lab's paws clean—hence, the towelling rule. To my horror, the dog tracked mud and dirt all over the house with its dirty paws when he came back in, tail a-wagging. So we set up dog-towels at the two doors entranceways, with injunctions that; whoever was to let the dog back in, had to wipe its paws clean.

Living with a dog in the household, became "the" problem. It became the biggest irritant in our relationships with Christine and her family.

Christine and Troy make a Purchase

Christine and Troy had sold their house in Wyoming, and they began house shopping in the Sudbury region. They were not happy with what was being offered on the local housing market; a house with the quality they had been able to afford in the small farming community of Wyoming, in southwestern Ontario was out of their price range in Sudbury; and there were a lot of inferior houses in that same price range—the Sudbury housing market was high at that time.

They were finding it difficult to make the desired move. So we held a family meeting. Emily and I had been looking at a Condominium development on Algonquin Road, at the south end of the city. We liked the "Garden Homes" housing plans and the general layout of the complex. So we made Christine and Troy an offer: purchase our house on Haig Street, and we would move to the condominiums.

And so it came about, that after almost fifty years of marriage, we moved to our third domicile. Roger, who was still living at the time, would look at us and laugh when he heard of the transaction with Troy and Christine: he'd cocked his head and said, "Your daughter came in town and kicked you out of your house."

He was not far off the mark.

But we saw it as a positive event for both, our daughter and ourselves. Christine and Troy got a good house at a fair price, and we downsized to a new bungalow that we very much enjoyed, and where we made many new friends.

Christopher Remarries and we take Tania Target Shooting

Three weeks before the move to our new house, we had to attend a wedding in Brampton. Our son Christopher was getting married again.

Chris was marrying a lovely young lady. She was a high school teacher working for the same Catholic school board as Christopher's. We had already been introduced to Tania the year before; she was full of energy, pretty and intelligent. And Tania would speak her mind when she had to; she had opinions and she could make them known—a character trait I've always enjoyed in a woman. Tania had been to the Moffet fishing camp the previous summer, and she had even taken a side trip with Chris and Emily, and visited Belleterre. Tania was not the type who intimidated easily: we had put her to a little northern Ontario test. On a late August day of the previous year, we had introduced her to our grouse hunting trails, behind Lake Agnew.

Chris and I had set up several shooting targets, and we gave her the 410 gauge, and she fired the shotgun without flinching—and hit the target. Then we raised it up a notch and had her fire the 20 gauge, with the same results. Then I handed her the 12 gauge—but with some gentlemanly advance caution as to the strong recoil to be expected—she levelled the gun at the glass bottle fifty feet away, pulled the trigger and blew it away to pieces, without wincing as the force of the recoil pushed her upper body backward. She was all smiles when she passed the shotgun back to me.

We liked Tania's mom, Antonella; and her grandmother, "Nona"; and her uncle Fidele, from the first moment we met them. They were all good, sensitive and unaffected, down to earth people.

Tania Brasil had an Italian heritage from her mother and Portuguese blood on her father's side. Tania's father had passed away some years ago and her mom had not remarried. Tania was an only child, and her uncle Fidele, Antonella's brother, had a quasi-surrogate fatherhood role toward Tania.

Fidele reminded me in many ways, of Emily's brother, Andy. Both were extroverts, big men, loud and in your face. And both were wheelers-and-dealers in their own different ways.

At the engagement party—a party that was as extravagant and as sumptuous as most people's wedding receptions—I found myself alone with Fidele at one point. And he led the conversation and I found that where he took me in our talk was very puzzling indeed. We were alone in a quiet corner and he said; out of nowhere, "You know, Antonella doesn't have much money—she has a five-hundred thousand dollar life insurance policy—her house and a bit of savings; that's about all." I was dumbfounded and speechless—I could not follow the logic of his comments. I found his comments, at this particular time and on this particular special occasion, downright offensive; and when upset, emotions can get the better of me.

So, I looked at him, sipping on his expensive cognac, and I said, "Let me make this perfectly clear, Fidele; my son is not about to marry your niece for her money; he's marrying her for who she is and because he's in love with her."

In a weird way, this seemed to me so much like another Auntie Balint objecting to Emily marrying Ray, kind of scene. Not in the same context, but it had similarities.

He apologized profusely for the misunderstanding, saying that was not what he had meant; and he apologized to me throughout the evening, every time our paths crossed that afternoon.

On our drive home to Sudbury, I said not a word of the conversation to Emily. But, as I looked down on the highway in front of me, I kept on playing it in my mind, over and over again. If that was not what he implied; then what did he really mean by the bizarre comments. If my first suspicion was incorrect, was he suggesting that Antonella could not afford to put on the wedding, and indirectly asking me to contribute?

The Groom has a Technical Problem

The wedding date was set for July 19, 2013. We drove down the day before. Round about noon, somewhere on the 400 highway, as we were approaching Barrie, my car phone rang. It was our son.

"Dad," he said, "we have a small technical problem. I've lost my best man." I almost burst out laughing because Christopher does not have a good sense of humour, and therefore, I knew that this was real—he was not joking.

"What do you mean," Emily and I shouted in unison.

Now it was Christopher who was laughing; he managed to say between chuckles, "Well, I called his cell phone to see when he'd be leaving Sudbury, but I got no answer. So, I called his house and got his wife who said that Mike had disappeared—no one seems to know where he's gone to. He's been gone for three days—he could be in hospital—I'm totally confused."

This whole conversation seemed to be have been lifted out of some TV sitcom script.

"That's weird," I said, (I was at a loss for words that could say anything that would be more appropriate), then I inquired, "Who's your backup?"

"Well dad," he said—and the way he said that I knew what would follow. "Would you step in in his place if necessary?"

"No problem Chris," I replied, "I'll be your best man."

"Thanks, dad," he said, and we hung up.

Life has no end of fun curves to throw your way. I attended my son's wedding as the father of the groom—and the groom's best man. And I walked down the aisle of the church twice—with my son, to deposit him with the priest at the front of the church; and later walking down with the maid-of-honour to join the bridal party. The church audience unaware of the absconded best man must have thought that this was how we did things in Sudbury.

The church ceremony was well attended, and it was both, a solemn, and yet a very happy event. In an ineffable way, you felt the stirrings of a joy-filled church. And the reception was memorable; for the food; the music; and the happiness and love shared by everyone.

I was happy to have my dear friend Bill Thompson present and at my side, and so were my sisters there; with the exception of Colette—she had not been invited.

We start Packing for the Move

Upon our return home, we started packing for the big move to our new house on Algonquin Road. We had made arrangements with the developer to get a key, and we, therefore, gained entry into the house, three weeks prior to the closing date of August 13th. So that by the closing date, most of our small personal items had been moved; what remained were the larger (and heavier) furniture items, which a professional mover would handle.

And we had to coordinate our moving out, with Christine and Troy's moving in; when they had sold their house in Wyoming, they had put all of their furnishings in storage; and as we were to move out of Haig Street on August 13, they were to be moving in with their truckload of furniture and other personal effects the very next afternoon. We had left Christine our fridge, stove, microwave oven and all window dressings.

The heartbreaking moment came for me when I was forced to downsize my library. I had a thousand book personal library collection in my den downstairs, and I could not bring all of my books with me to our new place—we had not the room. I gave some away; I sent many boxes to Value Village; some ended up in neighbours' garage sales, and still others I threw away in my municipal Green Box, as recyclable. I kept about five hundred books of my main collection with me.

We worked throughout the day at the old house packing boxes, and we worked in the late evenings at the new house, unpacking and putting things where we thought they belonged. By the time the movers came to pick up the furniture and the heavy items, we were exhausted.

I think Christine was surprised at how well disciplined and organized we'd been. She did not think that our new place would be all set in place for weeks, if not months—we were all settled in, with everything in their proper locations (including all pictures hanging on the walls), within a week of having moved in.

And I got involved with the condominium board of directors immediately. Before our first year of residency was done, I sat as a director on the board, and became its president in 2016.

CHAPTER 42

I take Leave of my Second Mother

My first, and most beloved boss with the city of Sudbury welfare office, Simone Patterson, died in that year of our move to Algonquin Road. She passed away on October 21, at the age of 93. Another one of my dear friends saying goodbye and moving on.

Many people will walk in and out of your life, but only true friends will leave footprints in your heart. And Simone left hers in mine.

I was very grateful for my wife's foresight, and pressing me with requests that we visit Simone at the Vale Hospice, in the few months prior to her death. We had heard in early summer that Simone was not doing well and that she'd been admitted to the hospice—and people admitted to a hospice do not usually come out—it provides a dignified end of life stage.

We went to visit my friend (and second mother) on three occasions—the last one, a week before her death. Her mind was strong and sharp as ever, although her voice and lips quivered from the effects of Parkinson's; and she still demonstrated an amazing memory for names and events. She related stories and mentioned the names of staff who had worked with us at the welfare office; naming peoples full names—names I had forgotten a long time ago. And she'd grab my hand as soon as we entered her room, and she would not let go of it until it was time for us to take our leave. And while she talked about those early days, her eyes would light up and a big smile would bathe her face.

Our last visit and our last goodbye coincided with the close of summer; the turning of the leaves; and the dying of the garden blooms; the approach of the winter season.

And I thank Emily for having been demanding and forcefully importunate: she had made it a point that I should "grab the moment", and that I should go and visit Simone.

Another proof of the soundness of her philosophy of attending to "the important". Do not put the important off, otherwise; the opportunity may never present itself again. I was to witness the veracity of this approach to life, again and again. Emily knew all about this intuitively.

A Phone Call from Tammy: An Unfortunate Accident

And then the clock struck the fateful hour for another of my good friend and fishing buddy; and one very close to Emily's heart: Andy died July 5, 2014, at the age of 74.

We were on the highway, heading to the Toronto airport when we got the call from Tammy. We were to board a flight out of Canada the next afternoon, for a planned tour of Greece, the Greek Islands and a cruise up to Turkey and Istanbul.

Tammy's voice was heavy with concern. She said that her dad had had a fall, and he'd broken some ribs which had damaged some internal organs; and he was now in ICU at an Oakville hospital, in serious, but non-life threatening condition. We said we would go and see him before checking into our hotel, on the airport strip.

The Patient

When we saw him later that afternoon, he was in reasonable shape and good humour. He joked with Christopher and Tania, and he was his normal gregarious self. His legs and his abdomen were swollen with fluids, but we were told that the swelling had to do with the contusions to the spleen and that the swelling would go down in a few days. Surgeons would repair the spleen laparoscopically the next morning and swelling reduction should follow. The patient was in good spirits and we saw no reason not to go ahead with our trip.

And this is how the accident happened: very much like my brother Pete; if more caution had been exercised, Andy would not have been in a hospital intensive care unit that day.

The Accident

To save money he had moved to a new address the previous month—somewhere in Burlington. The morning of the accident, he'd gone back to his old place in Oakville to pick up any residual mail that may have accumulated there. As he was leaving the building clutching some letters in one hand, he stopped on the concrete porch landing and extended himself on the edge of the concrete deck in order to reach a lilac tree in full bloom. As he snapped some bloom laden branch with his free hand; the railing he was leaning against, gave way, and he lost his balance, falling headlong down the porch with his chest hitting the concrete steps.

Andy was a big, heavy man—he fractured some ribs and the broken ribs punctured his spleen.

After getting himself up, he managed to make it to his car and he proceeded to drive himself to a hospital emergency room. But, in a short while, the pain would not let him drive any further. Andy did not own a cell phone—again, a matter of economy—so, he parked his car on the shoulder of a very busy freeway, painfully stepped out of his car and hailed passing motorists whizzing by. A young man stopped to offer assistance, and at the sight of Andy's condition he wanted to call an ambulance, but Andy would not let him; instead, he used the young man's cell phone and he called Tammy.

Tammy found him where he'd parked the car on the shoulder of the road. His condition had worsened and she rushed him to the hospital.

Ray A. Vincent

A Return to the Hospital to find a Patient in Critical Condition

Our visit to Greece and Turkey was a very enjoyable one, but Andy was on Emily's mind, even though we had left his bedside without obvious cause to worry. When we landed back in Toronto sixteen days later, we made our way to the hospital immediately.

He was not the same man we had left some two and a half weeks previously. He was on a respirator, unconscious and fighting for his life. The family was distraught. The repair of the damaged spleen had not been successful. His abdomen was grossly distended, and his legs; from the thighs to the toes, were frightful to behold; swollen to a huge size with fluids.

It was difficult to get any explanation as to what had gone wrong; why had his condition reached this stage? And it was difficult to get any sense as to what was being planned, medically speaking, in terms of immediate treatment. Why had they not simply removed the damaged spleen? Emily asked. People live productive lives without a spleen. The doctors were not easily accessible. It looked to me like they purposely stayed away, while the family was in and about the room.

Something had gone awfully wrong—and no one of the medical staff wanted to take responsibility—or, do the decent thing: offer an explanation.

The three adult children surrounding the bedside presented a sad and pitiful picture indeed—faces that had been smiling and laughing two weeks before, were now silent, bewildered and confused. And they were alone—Andy's estranged wife was with them at the latter stage of his hospitalization.

The Termination of a Life

We returned to Sudbury the next day, but within four days we got a call from Tammy. They'd had a family meeting with the medical staff, and made the decision: if there were no changes in his condition in the next forty-eight hours, they were going to give their consent to terminate life support procedures.

We, therefore, returned to Oakville to offer our last goodbyes to a dear friend.

We were all assembled in the small room, the three children, and Emily and me. With five minutes, or so, before disconnection; one by one, starting with the eldest of the kids, we went to Andy, held his hand and said our last words to him. When it came to J.P.'s turn to approach, he took his dad's hand into his, and putting his lips close to his father's ear, he whispered something that had personal meaning between father and son only.

Emily followed, and I was last. I took his hand firmly and said loud enough for everyone in the room to hear, "Andy, when you're on that big lake up there, fishing; don't catch them all, leave a few big ones for me when I join you."

And a most amazing thing happened—it was so unexpected, it was eerie—his lips broke into an unmistakable gentle smile—and everyone in the room was witness to it.

Anyone who says that intubated and unconscious patients are in a coma, and therefore unaware of what's going on around them, better think twice on the subject.

The nursing staff promptly came in, and as they commenced disconnecting the life support lines, Wendy, the middle child, (a professional opera singer), began to sing—a powerful "Amazing Grace"—and everyone started to cry.

A Baby Is Born

And oh, how the pendulum swings to the unstoppable rhythms of life: from death to life. Our second grandchild; baby Severn was born on July 31, 2014—Christopher and Tania's first child.

Ray A. Vincent

I Meet an Old friend— News of a Planned Reunion

While on our annual fishing trip to Lac Simard, I had the great joy of coming across my old Belleterre friend, Ronald Savard, at a local restaurant. I introduced him to Emily and we went over the cherished memories of childhood, and the simple life and the happiness-filled days of fifty-five years past. Ronald told us that the town of Belleterre would be celebrating its 75th anniversary as an incorporated town, sometime in July of 2017, and a big town party was being planned. We exchange phone numbers and I asked him to keep me posted. This was a party my sisters and I would not want to miss.

The Amish businessman with a Life at 50 Percent

It was at this particular fishing expedition that I got another lesson in the vagaries of life and the different kinds of people you can come across—and all of them, carrying their own stories.

The headwaters of the Ottawa River have their beginning source ten miles north of Lac Simard, and the outflow of the river empties into the lake and proceeds in a southwesterly direction toward Lake Temiscaming, and thence southeasterly to the Mattawa River and becomes the Ottawa River again farther south; and on to the St. Lawrence and ultimately, the Atlantic Ocean.

Coming from the north, the river flows with a significant current into the lake, and when a strong south wind hits the river mouth, the furling effect on the outflowing water creates very high and unpredictable waves, making that part of the lake, difficult and dangerous to navigate.

That day, I had come off the lake early due to the high winds, and later in the evening, over a crackling campfire, a young American man and his father related the adventure they had just lived through, round about mid-afternoon—at the time that I was making my way to the safety of the lodge.

A large, middle-aged man was in a small sixteen-foot aluminum boat powered by a 20 horsepower outboard motor. He was alone in the boat and without a life jacket on. He was attempting to come out of the river against the fierce headwind, and cross over onto the big lake.

From the vantage point of a protected bay inside the river, my two storytellers had a good look at what was about to happen. Having no ballast in the bow, and with a big man at the stern, the small craft was riding on its stern with the bow raised off the water at a 45-degree angle. When he came onto the waves, the bow raised further upward and the strong winds did the rest: the boat flipped completely, end over end, and he disappeared under. But luckily, he popped-up from under the boat and hung on to the gunwales for dear life.

Pat and Matt, the father and son team, had a heavy and stable Boston Whaler fishing boat powered by a 160 horsepower motor. They rushed to the rescue. The man in distress was a huge man and he hung on to his upturned boat, and even though at times he would disappear under the water when the boat came crashing up through the water, so would he—still hanging on.

Always adjusting to the heavy seas, Pat navigated his craft within twenty feet of the victim, and he yelled to him to pick up the rope that Matt was about to cast in his direction; but to their amazement, the drowning man brushed them off—he shook his head; consumed by fear and panic, he would not let go of the capsized boat.

Through the howling wind, Pat yelled at the top of his voice, "Take the fucking rope, or you're a dead man." And Matt cast out the heavy rope, which by an act of God hit the man across the forearms. He grabbed it and held on. They maneuvered him to the stern of their boat and hauled him in.

He was an American and this was his first trip to Lac Simard. Turns out he was an Amish minister, and a well-to-do businessman at that, who owned many stores across the state of Pennsylvania, specializing in vintage wood crafted furniture.

He thanked his saviours gratefully, and after he had recovered somewhat of his composure, and while they were still making their way to the lodge, he said to Pat and his son, "My stores are open to both of you, at any time and on any day. All you have to do is call me; anything you wish to take with you is 50 percent off!"

I burst out laughing—and so did my story-tellers—they had come to the punchline and I had understood it—the man had set a price tag on his life; and it was going cheap at 50 percent off of a wood dining room set—or, whatever.

The Bionic Woman

In the spring of 2015, Emily made another visit to the hospital; this time to repair an umbilical hernia. The surgery went well and without complications. She would have to make another hospital visit in the next year or so to undergo a total right knee replacement procedure—she had undergone so many medical interventions since 2010 that I started to call her, "The Bionic Woman." But on the practical side, all the interventions proved successful and improved her quality of life.

Friends

Over the years, we had developed a close and warm friendship with Gil and Marlyn Salo. Gil and I became fast friends; we had much in common—a similar situation as that which I shared with my friend Bill Thompson. Gil and I came from very large working-class families. And he was a Finn—and I loved Finlanders. He loved the outdoors, was opinionated and conservative in social attitudes—which suited me just fine.

Marlyn was a pretty blond, tall and slender woman—but very frail. She was a "Fielding"; her father, Cecil, had been a very successful Sudbury businessman. I was always amazed at the reaction of people when the name "Sudbury Fieldings" was ever mentioned—

their opinions were that the "Fieldings" were awash in money: but that opinion is misleading and prejudiced—whatever money the "Sudbury Fieldings" may have; they have worked hard for, and earned after putting up with many risks and sacrifices.

We had met Gil and Marlyn in 2004, at the Sudbury Bridge Club, and we struck a friendship which has lasted through to this day.

Following Emily's hernia repair, we planned a River Cruise with the Salos'—a Rhine river cruise. I had been told to be careful: some couples went out on a trip as friends and came back without wanting to speak to each other, ever again. But we discovered that we were real and true friends indeed. We had a wonderful time together.

We had made an informal agreement: we were to be on our own in the morning and at the lunch breaks, but we would always have dinner together; we would play bridge thereafter, socialize and end the evening in amity. And it worked well. We came back home happy and stronger friends.

Seventy Years

February 2016 came and went, and I had quietly stepped into my seventieth birthday, still enjoying life and otherwise healthy.

If I was to write a letter to my children about the landscape ahead of them: about the wisdom, if any, that's stuck to me like the barnacles on the hull of an old ship, it would run like this:

"Dear Christine and Christopher:

-Grab the moment—there are not many of them. Let your heart be your guide.

-As far as possible, without surrender, be on good terms with all persons.

-Married life is a joint account. Shy away from separate bank accounts—that practice is not conducive to teamwork.

-The old adage that there are only two certainties in life, death, and taxes—is not quite accurate. There is a third: aging. The world may be meant for the young, but it is the old who are now increasingly populating it. Therefore, plan for it.

-Old people get sad and depressed just like the young do.

-Physical activity need not end at 65—Fauja Singh ran the Toronto Marathon at the age of 100.

-Take good care of your heart: by the time you die, your heart will have chalked up roughly three billion beats.

-Elder abuse is a fact.

-Your brain will be slower, but experience will make up the deficit.

-As you get older, you will handle social conflicts more effectively.

-Happiness it turns out, is a U-shaped curve: we are happy in youth; unhappy in middle-life; and by the time we are seventy, we are happier than we were at eighteen.

-Your sex life doesn't go away; in fact, it may get better.

-Life is a journey with a single path and you travel it only once; therefore, look for opportunities along the way and harvest them in due season. And lastly,

-Be yourself. Be cheerful. Strive to be happy."

That is the kind of letter I could have written to them as I turned 70 years of age. But, I did not do so. They had not read a similar letter of mine, sent twenty years previously. I entertained little hope that they would read this one.

A Baby Girl!

Another happy moment in our life, and certainly in Christopher's and Tania's—the birth of Sloane, our very first granddaughter—Emily was ecstatic: finally a little baby girl to buy pretty dresses for!

Searching for Peter Oleksiuk

We made plans to go to Brampton and visit with Christopher and Tania during the school March Break period. The Belleterre town reunion, slated for July was on my mind a lot. And I set out searching for Peter Oleksiuk—his last known address was Toronto and since we were to be in Brampton, just north of Toronto, I was hoping to make contact with him and plan a get-together in Belleterre—even in Mud Lake.

I searched the Internet but found no one by that name in the Toronto area. However, there was one Peter Oleksiuk living somewhere, in a small town by the name of Morinville, in Alberta. I called the phone number listed and I got no answer to my call, but I left a message on the answering machine: stating my name—the French as well as the English pronunciation—and I said that I was in search of a Peter Oleksiuk hailing from Mud Lake and that if he was the person in question; could he get back to me.

After a week had gone by without a return call, I put an end to the hope and we made preparations to go to Brampton.

The Voice of my Childhood Friend

Upon our return to Sudbury four days later, the blinking red light on my answering machine was on. And there was only one message.

"Hello, Real," the voice said, pronouncing in the French fashion, "This is Peter Oleksiuk, your Mud Lake friend. Give me a call when you get my message."

I was overtaken with joy and excitement. I left the luggage where I had dropped them and I called him immediately.

We were like two teenagers talking excitedly about some adventure we had just recently gone through. We covered as much historical ground as we could. He had moved out of Toronto after retirement, and he and his wife Louise had relocated to Morinville, Alberta, to be closer to their children. His voice had not lost any of its deep, Oleksiuk-Ukrainian baritone. It was deep and husky like his brothers had been. We talked about our families, past and present, and about a host of other old memories. We talked animatedly like we would have talked to each other when we were boys. And we talked with feeling and love.

However, Peter was not well. He'd just spent two weeks in hospital and he had just gotten home, but a few days ago. He was scheduled to return to hospital in May, to have a malignant tumour removed; he was undergoing treatment for cancer.

I mentioned the Belleterre reunion coming up on July 21st, and asked if he would be able to make it. He said he would be there if he could; it would depend on the outcome of his surgery and how he would feel, given the treatment regimen he was to undergo.

But he said his sister Olga would be at the reunion, and she would look forward to seeing me, and he gave me her phone number. I promised to pray for him and that I would call him after his surgery, and I wished him well and we ended our conversation.

In my excitement, it seemed to me that we had talked for about twenty-five minutes.

However, when the telephone bill came in later in the month, it showed that Peter and I had talked to each other for one hour and fifty-five minutes!

The Babysitters

Tania was coming off her maternity leave, and she had to return to the classroom in the third week of May, and Christopher would be tied up with work at his school until the end of June; therefore Emily and I volunteered to babysit for six weeks—a three-year-old and a one-year-old! Some of our friends thought that we had gone insane, and I must admit that it was exhausting work; however, we enjoyed every minute that we spent, close and intimate with our adorable grandchildren.

CHAPTER 43

A Tearful Conversation: Peter Remembers

On May 29, I called Peter from Brampton. He had just recently been discharged from hospital. He'd had his surgery to remove the tumours and he was on heavy painkillers. He was weak and the surgical area had developed an infection. He said he could barely walk; he certainly would not make it to the reunion.

And he proceeded to talk to me of a haunting and recurring dream—and he started to cry over the phone. The dream that kept on coming back every night since he'd come back home, was about the day the police cruiser had come to Mud Lake to pick up his unsuspecting and mentally debilitated mother.

He said through his sobs, "You remember Ray? You and I were playing cards by the window, and we saw that car coming—we thought it was going to Hamelin's—but no, the dogs were coming after my poor, helpless mother. Remember? How we ran after the car when they were leaving, throwing rocks at it?" he said all this haltingly, in between heavy sobs.

And I did remember full well, and I told him so. And we said goodbye, with promises to get back to each other.

A Return to Belleterre, the Friends, and the Memories

I, Carmen and Louise, and our spouses were on our way to the reunion; we would split the cost of the van rental three ways. I had rented a large van and booked three rooms at the motel in Latulipe, 18 miles away from Belleterre since there was not one room to be had in Belleterre. Early on the morning of July 21st, we headed east and out of Sudbury.

Great weather attended the three days of celebrations. We drove into Belleterre at about 2:30 p.m. The town, at its peak population point in the mid-fifties, was home to an excess of two-thousand people—now, it counted less than two-hundred and fifty. And for the three days of the 75th-anniversary reunion, guests and visitors probably tripled the local population—and we were everywhere; meeting each other in the old familiar streets and laneways; sharing exclamations of joy and going over past memories.

It was an emotion-filled three days. Upon arrival on Friday, we went to Hein's and registered for the Saturday evening reunion banquet. Then, my sisters and I walked the streets and the laneways. At times I was speechless; we pointed at houses that had sheltered friends and relatives; we pulled events and names out of the recesses of our memories, and the recovered memories gave birth to other memories; we walked to the old school, and the church still standing guard beside it; I tried to open the church doors, in order to go into the basement and rediscover my story-books—but they kept the church doors under lock and key nowadays.

We walked to the lake and sank our toes into the sandy beaches—and I could hear, coming out of the past, the admonitions of our mother: not to go in for a swim while "our stomachs were full"…

Not much had changed as far as the town's physical appearance was concerned. Sure, the people were different and some houses had undergone facelifts, but, the four Avenues with their laneways and the four intersecting streets were there. None had been added. And the houses were still located where they had once stood, in the mornings of our childhood.

A Walk through our Old House

And my sisters and I visited the two houses on First Avenue that we had once called home. The first one, besides what had been a bank; that had the holding cells in the cellar at the time—where I had scared Louise and Monique—was still there; refurbished and rehabilitated. The present owner came out and invited us all in for a walk-through—a very nostalgic experience. We took pictures, inside and outside. And we visited our second house, across from Paquin's; and then we went for supper at Paquin's restaurant—still of the same name; at the same location; and still owned and operated by a Paquin family member.

A Visit with Olga

Later in the afternoon, I made enquiries about Olga Oleksiuk. She had a summer home in Belleterre, and after driving along the shoreline of the lake, we found her. She was at home with her daughters and her son—her family had come in for the reunion.

I had knocked at the cottage door and asked one of her daughters if there was a beautiful Ukrainian woman in the house; and she came out of the living room, walking with strong, steady steps. She came straight to me with a beaming face and hugged and kissed me. We talked about our families, who was living and who was dead. We talked about Peter, and she enquired if Colette was with us.

We kissed goodbye. We would meet each other again the next day at the banquet.

The Banquet: Meeting old Friends and Joe Lariviere's Daughter

The next day was another day spent in meeting old friends and in reveling in sentimental nostalgia. At the old curling club, Emily came to me and pointed toward a table occupied by two native, aboriginal ladies; and she said that I may know them. I made my way to them, and to my great joy, I met Cecile Lariviere and her daughter; Cecile was the daughter of Belleterre's first policeman, and game warden—Joe Lariviere. Joe, the policeman without the gun holster. We had a lot of humorous anecdotes to share—but I did not tell her about finding her sister Marie and her boyfriend making love in the beach change-cubicles.

The banquet was a veritable walk through childhood memories. A tearful walk. I met many old friends there. The bodies were not so recognizable—but the voices and the mannerisms were. Old, dear friends of my childhood: Ernel Paquin; Donald Hein; Raymond and Fernand Thibault; Donald and Jean Phillips; Ronald Savard: Carmelle Audet; Marcel Denomme (my cousin); Laurent Paul; and the Rocheleau twins. Many were not there that I would have very much wished to meet.

Those who Remember Talk about my Mother

Early in the evening, before the meal was to be served, the Rocheleau twins (83 years old) made their way to our table. They wanted to talk about my mother, and of the fond memories, they had of her—particularly, the nightly Friday circle of kids on the floor, around a hot stove, and my mom's oral narration of stories, which endeared all the neighbourhood children to her. And they mentioned the sleepless nights they would go through, after her scary rendition of "Barbe Bleu"—"Blue Beard". The twins had separate beds, but that night they had slept together.

A Return to a Place called Mud Lake

Before leaving for our return journey to Sudbury, I took Emily's "tablet" and walked alone, along the little bush trail; all that was remaining of the road leading to Mud Lake.

I took the car a couple of miles out of town, where the trail began, and I walked for a half hour until I reached the edge of the lake. Of the houses, log cabins and the ramshackle habitations that once dotted the lakeside, and the hill beyond, nothing remained.

Not even the remnants of a foundation. However, there were the odd clearings which stood witness to a house having once stood there.

I moved about and kept the video rolling—this was to be sent to Peter in Morinville. This was my present to him. He may not have been able to be at the reunion, but this would be closer to his heart.

The sky was a pale blue, dotted here and there with light patches of clouds. The lake was peaceful and so were the woods around me. Where life and a vibrant little community had been, all was now quiet and any signs of human activity covered up.

In the shadows of my memory, I could hear the happy voices of children screaming and jumping in the water; and I could hear Peter, calling after me, to hurry and join in.

Authors Biography

Ray A. Vincent attended Laurentian University and graduated with a Bachelor of Arts degree in Psychology, and Certification in Social Work. He went on to work with the City of Sudbury's Welfare Department, initially as a caseworker and later moving on to supervisory and managing positions. He spent 35 years in the "helping profession" until his retirement in 1999.

Ray was born in Canada, in a log cabin, in the mining backwoods of Northwestern Quebec. Growing up in poverty and in a large family of twelve, brought the young man face to face with what was significant and with what was trivial in life.

He knew that in his family, once you walked in the house, you were taken in, welcomed, and covered in the warmth of love and personal attention that only good parents can have for you. "That's all they had to give us," he said, "but there was a lot of it, and it was unbounded, unconditional and selfless."

His mother was a great storyteller and he inherited from her a great love of books which fed a voracious appetite for reading.

The family moved to Sudbury, Ontario, when Ray was coming into his teenage years. The cultural transition of moving from a small town, French Canadian environment, to English speaking Canada proved difficult and challenging but it opened many venues to opportunities and personal growth. He was blessed with an acute visual memory. The colorful events of childhood and professional activities have taken Ray across a rich and varied landscape of experiences—some of which make for compelling stories.

Ray married his sweetheart, Emily, fifty years ago. They live in Sudbury, Ontario.

www.ingramcontent.com/pod-product-compliance
Lightning Source LLC
Chambersburg PA
CBHW031747220426
43662CB00007B/311